To Ben + Nan,
who know what a civil society
is. With admiration,
Bell

October, 1989
Washington

TOWARD
A MORE
CIVIL SOCIETY?

TOWARD
A MORE
CIVIL SOCIETY?

The USSR Under
Mikhail Sergeevich Gorbachev

An Assessment by the
American Committee
on U.S.-Soviet Relations

Edited by

William Green Miller

1817

Harper & Row, Publishers, New York
BALLINGER DIVISION

*Grand Rapids, Philadelphia, St. Louis, San Francisco
London, Singapore, Sydney, Tokyo*

International Standard Book Number: 0-88730-220-3

Library of Congress Catalog Card Number: 89-17589

Printed in the United States of America

Library of Congress Cataloging-in-Publication Data

Toward a more civil society? : the USSR under Mikhail Sergeevich
  Gorbachev : an assessment by the American Committee on U.S.-Soviet
  relations / edited by William Green Miller.
      p. cm.
    ISBN 0-88730-220-3
    1. Soviet Union–Politics and government–1985- 2. Perestroika.
  3. Glasnost. I. Miller, William Green. II. American Committee on
  U.S.-Soviet Relations.
  DK288.T68   1989
  947.085′4–dc20   89-17589
                                                               CIP

CONTENTS

Introduction

General Secretary Gorbachev has taken the Soviet Union in a radical new direction that offers the possibilities for a long-term stable peaceful relationship between the two superpowers. The central issue is whether the reforms of *perestroika, glasnost,* and *demokratizatsiia* will move the Soviet Union firmly in the direction of a more civil society.

Chapter 1: The Dynamics of Change in Contemporary Soviet Society

Soviet society over the past fifty years has undergone fundamental changes that have altered the structure of society and the attitudes of its citizens. This chapter examines Gorbachev's social policy and how it aims to meet the demands of a transformed Soviet society and to redefine the parameters of the socialist "welfare state." The chapter also analyzes the unintended social consequences of Gorbachev's reform efforts, such as raising popular expectations to levels of hope that are unlikely to be fully met and arousing social group conflicts.

Chapter 2: Political Reform in Gorbachev's Russia

This chapter focuses on four aspects of the political process now underway in the Soviet Union: (1) the context from which the political reform program emerged—the effort by the regime to restore the credibility of political authority; (2) the imbedded aspects of the existing political system that constrain Gorbachev's ability to change the system; (3) the relationship between the means used by the leaders to consolidate power and the evolution of the leadership's policy agenda; and (4) the prospects for successful political reform.

Chapter 3: Cultural Reform in the Soviet Union

This chapter examines the political and cultural debates over the role of *glasnost* in the Soviet Union under Gorbachev. It provides an overview of the current cultural scene, including the release of previously suppressed works, the advent of a youth culture, and the emergence of experimental art and theater. There is also a discussion of the place of culture and the unique role of the artistic intelligentsia in Soviet society.

Chapter 4: The Dilemma of Economic Reform in the Soviet Union

By the time Mikhail Gorbachev assumed the post of General Secretary of the Soviet Union in 1985, the Soviet economy was stagnated; growth rates had declined steadily since the mid-1970s and the country's level of technological development lagged far behind the West, threatening to endanger the USSR's position as a great military power. This chapter analyzes Gorbachev's two responses: first, his pursuit of intensive growth policies stressing modernization of capital and labor discipline; and second, his introduction of an unprecedented set of systemic reforms, including greater decentralization of decisionmaking and more emphasis on the use of market forces to guide economic activity. Although the success of Gorbachev's program is still in doubt, his bold efforts will have lasting effects on the Soviet political and economic system.

Chapter 5: The Gorbachev Leadership's Redirection of Soviet Foreign Policy

Moscow has placed a new emphasis on economic concerns in its foreign policy, and now appears to favor a more cautious security policy in the Third World. Internal economic requirements have contributed in a substantial way to the current changes in Soviet foreign policy. Soviet international economic and security policies are being shaped in an effort to offset the economic power of the United States and to establish friendly ties with powers in all regions of the world over the long term.

Chapter 6: Soviet National Security Policy under Gorbachev

Soviet national security policy has begun to change radically under General Secretary Gorbachev. In recent years, the outline of a new international security paradigm has emerged within the Soviet national security apparatus.

This paradigm is based on new principles of security based on what have been called "sufficiency" and "defensive defense," and has developed over three stages: the recognition of crisis, the development of concepts in response to crisis, and the translation of these concepts into policy.

Chapter 7: Conclusions

The views of senior members of the American Committee on U.S.-Soviet Relations presented in this book reflect very different kinds of experience, vocation, and perspective. In all cases the conclusions presented are based on long and direct involvement with policy making or policy analysis concerning the USSR.

Appendices

Appendix I, "Selected Sources for Research on the Soviet Union," is intended to serve as an introduction to important Soviet sources in the social sciences, particularly those that help to illuminate the changes taking place under Gorbachev.

Appendix II consists of organizational charts of the Soviet government and Communist Party.

INTRODUCTION

William Green Miller

There are new faces in the Kremlin. Profound changes have already been made by the new men who rule the USSR under the leadership of General Secretary Mikhail Sergeevich Gorbachev. They have taken the Soviet Union in a radically new direction that offers for the first time in the seventy years of the Soviet state the possibilities for a stable, long-term, peaceful relationship between the United States and the Union of Soviet Socialist Republics.

REAGAN AND GORBACHEV HAVE LED THE WAY TO A MORE STABLE PEACEFUL RELATIONSHIP

It would not have seemed possible just a few years ago, but during the Summit meeting in Moscow at the beginning of June 1988, Ronald Reagan declared that he no longer considered the Soviet Union to be an "evil empire." When questioned by reporters about his change of view, Reagan explained, "The merit, of course, lies chiefly with Gorbachev as the leader. All this is taking place thanks to the change in the country. I read his book *Perestroika*, and found a great deal in it that I agree with."

Reagan's views carried great force, not simply because they were a president's words; they had unusual significance because they were the new attitudes of a man who throughout his adult life had been deeply suspicious of Soviet motives, and was on record as opposing any agreements with the

USSR because he believed that the Soviets could not be trusted. Despite his long standing enmity, Reagan's leadership in negotiating and concluding the INF Treaty dramatically marks the beginning of the end of the Cold War after more than forty years of hostility, hatred and suspicion. For hundreds of millions of people from several generations throughout the world, the consequences of the Cold War have been tragic and costly. A dangerous and wasteful military and political confrontation between the East and West in Europe and elsewhere all over the globe has squandered precious resources and cramped the spirit of human freedom and the promise of greater productive and creative endeavor.

After so many decades of armed hatred and suspicion, there is finally, a leadership in both superpowers which shares a common view that overwhelming military dominance is unattainable by either nation, and they have both concluded that military might, in itself, provides no lasting advantages or durable answers to fundamental political differences or economic needs. There is finally a leadership in both countries that is willing to meet face to face, to see the other country first hand, and discuss across the negotiating table the reality of the U.S.-USSR competition. When Ronald Reagan, the most conservative president in the post World War II period, after a lifetime of political opposition to any and all agreements with the Soviet Union, engaged in four summit meetings and concluded a major nuclear arms reduction agreement eliminating all of a class of nuclear weapons, and stated that he was willing, in principle, to conclude a treaty reducing strategic nuclear weapons by 50 percent, even the most cautious and skeptical of analysts of the U.S.-Soviet relationship knew significant changes were taking place in Moscow and Washington.

As President Reagan and now President Bush both recognized, Gorbachev represents a new force in Soviet politics. He is the leader of a new dominant governing elite bent on radical reform. The declared purpose of the reform is to restructure the entire Soviet system to integrate the changes that have taken place in Soviet society. The Gorbachev leadership recognizes fully that the demands of the Soviet people for greater freedoms must be embraced by the political system and that the desires for benefits from the economy must be met if the Soviet Union is to survive and flourish.

It is the premise of this overall assessment by the American Committee on U.S.-Soviet Relations that the new men in the Kremlin have brought new ideas and possibilities into play. It is the purpose of this book to bring to the attention of concerned Americans and others in the West the substance and implications of those new ideas.

NEW IDEAS, NEW DIRECTIONS AND AN END TO THE COLD WAR

As the Cold War comes to an end, these new ideas which powerfully suggest new dynamic directions that will affect peace in the world and the possibilities for economic improvement and development deserve close analysis. While almost without exception Gorbachev is regarded by states-men throughout the world as a leader of great ability and intelligence, there are some analysts who believe his influence will be overpowered by the weight of an essentially unchangeable, unworkable economic and political system. There are others who foresee evolutionary change in the direction of a more civil society with greater freedoms within the goals of a socialist society laid down by Lenin and those who overturned the monarchy seventy years ago. And there is yet another group that believes Gorbachev is repre-sentative of a substantial new elite that has a vision of a new social contract that is far more encompassing than that held by previous leaders because of a growing recognition that changes in social and historical circumstances have created new necessities and opportunities.

In light of these divergent views, Gorbachev's new ideas deserve close and careful analysis to see if there is a new reality emerging, or whether it is just an old pattern in new cloth. A fresh look at what is happening in the Soviet Union is very much needed, and this book is intended to meet that need. The assessment and conclusions contained in this volume are based on careful reading of the new documentary material that is pouring out of the USSR and on the basis of firsthand experience — considerable direct contact with the new Soviet leaders and observations from extensive travel within the USSR by senior members of the American Committee on U.S.-Soviet Relations.

A CLOSED SOCIETY HAS BEGUN TO OPEN UP

It has always been difficult to travel to the Soviet Union, more difficult to travel outside of the main cities, and even harder to meet with anything more than a tiny part of the spectrum of Soviet leaders or with ordinary citizens to discuss and observe fully what was happening in the country. Churchill's often-quoted remark made in a speech to Parliament in 1939 that Russia "is a riddle wrapped in a mystery inside an enigma" was fully appropriate. Foreigners were permitted to meet only with a few "safe," fully controlled groups. In the hostile atmosphere that such a closed regime creates, detailed knowledge was very hard to obtain. There were glimpses of the reality and occasional flashes of insight, as well as gross distortions, from émigré scholars, diplomats, journalists, businessmen, travellers, and from intelligence sources. Until the past few years, it was very difficult to obtain fully expressed information and explanations about what was happening in the Politburo, the Kremlin, the military, the institutes, the intellectual life, the arts, on the farms or in the factories, or even ordinary, everyday life. There was an official view shaped by doctrine and propaganda found in *Pravda* or *Izvestiia* and other party organs. Underground opinions—most of them from dissidents—were found in *samizdat* literature and tracts that were smuggled out to the West. Important details about what was happening came from defectors, the impressions of journalists, from businessmen, scientists, and tourists who travelled to the USSR on occasion, and the analyses of experienced diplomats helped to fill in a basic outline. Kremlinology, the art of reading between the lines of official statements and noting the significance of nuances in official statements and behavior, the piecing together of fragments like detectives assembling clues, and even hunches, intuitions, and guesses assumed great importance. Open, straightforward data, discussions, and analyses were hard to come by and, if available, distorted, and all too often suppressed if written. The picture of the Soviet Union from the outside was very dim and unclear at best. All that has begun to change in the past several years.

There is now a flood of information—much of it accurate. Indeed, there is a deluge of writing, conferences between large numbers of official and private groups on an increasingly broad range of activity, subject matter, and vocations, and an even greater number of smaller meetings and reports and analyses. While it is still difficult, it is now possible to travel much more widely throughout the Soviet Union. Whereas in the past there was only a meager, meandering trickle of reliable information, now there are torrents.

In dealing with a tightly closed society, as the Soviet Union was until the emergence of Gorbachev, past behavior rather than future possibilities is inevitably a governing factor in planning or conducting international relations. Therefore, past behavior measured by history, anthropology, and previous patterns of military and political action is taken as the main basis for anticipating future action. In this respect, the memories of Stalin, Beria, and Brezhnev, all for different reasons, have cast a deep shadow on the present.

The deeply etched awareness of the secrecy, intrigue, internal repression, and harsh military aggression, and most importantly, the absence of open discussion and free give and take of previous decades, makes the worst of the past a constant, uncomfortable reminder of a possible present and future.

SOME CONTACTS WERE MAINTAINED EVEN DURING THE COLD WAR

Even during the most hostile periods of the Cold War, there have always been some channels of communication between the United States and the Soviet Union. Businessmen, journalists, and diplomats have managed to carry on their work with assigned counterparts no matter how strained official relations became. Over the years, the United States was extremely fortunate to have had men of extraordinary ability to serve in the Soviet Union as diplomats, such as George F. Kennan, Averell Harriman, Charles E. Bohlen, and Llewellyn Thompson. The Foreign Service of the United States has continued to produce an able corps of officers who know the language and have served in Moscow for three or four assignments over a career. Diplomats as well as journalists have been constrained, however, by the nature of formal relations that have been generally poor, with very few exceptions, until the emergence of Gorbachev.

Scientists from both nations continued to meet, discussed scientific matters, and worked closely together even in periods of official hostility. Fortunately, the Academy of Sciences of the USSR and its American counterpart organizations have provided the means for Russian and American scientists to meet on professional matters, and have also served as an intellectual link between the two countries on the subject of arms control and other means of lessening tensions between the two superpowers. For several decades, conferences sponsored by groups such as Pugwash, the Dartmouth Conference, and the American Committee on U.S.-Soviet Relations have brought together experts on nuclear weapons, and specialists on a broad range of troubling regional issues. Many of these experts are former high officials or distinguished scholars from both the United States and the USSR. They have explored new concepts and possibilities when it was difficult or impossible for officials to discuss such matters. These informal channels have been an important way of bridging the gap created by official enmity.

THE DANGERS OF FALSE PERCEPTIONS
AND UNCERTAIN COMMUNICATIONS

Unwarranted or exaggerated concerns by the United States or the Soviet Union based on limited or false information or incorrect assumptions about the other's intentions in areas of vital national importance can have dangerous consequences. When inherent conflicts of national interests are exacerbated inadvertently, relatively minor actions can lead to unexpectedly hostile counteractions and risks of escalation.

This is not an abstract issue. There have been a number of occasions that have been documented when one of the superpowers was at a high state of tension based on its own assessments of the other that were largely or completely erroneous, and the other was totally unaware or incredulous. Four cases illustrate well the dangerous situations that can develop as a result. In two instances the mistaken assessments were theirs; in the other two, ours.

Berlin, 1961. When Nikita Khrushchev spoke to the Soviet Communist Party Congress in mid-October of 1961, he dropped his year-end deadline threat of signing a separate USSR peace treaty with Germany. Since it was this threat that had precipitated the Berlin crisis initially, heightened by the start of construction of the Wall two months earlier, Western governments widely assumed that the crisis was over. Shortly after the Party Congress speech, however, senior Soviet officials later revealed, the Soviet government received intelligence from German sources it considered reliable that U.S. forces had been directed to break down the barrier dividing the city in an attempt to incite an East German uprising.

The attack would come in Nikita Khrushchev's words, with "bulldozers . . . followed by tanks and wave after wave of jeeps with infantrymen." Khrushchev issued orders to bring Russian tanks into Berlin with minimal notice and to have them ready to open fire on the American forces if the United States took the anticipated actions. In fact, of course, the Western powers had accepted the Wall as a *fait accompli*, although President Kennedy had sent troop and tank reinforcements to Berlin and named General Lucius Clay as his special representative there as part of a show of the flag and to help allay German concerns. While the details of the Soviet intelligence report are unknown, several factors may have become known to the Soviets and caused their alarm. Clay favored knocking down the Wall and had not taken pains to hide his views in unofficial or official contacts, although he never received administration encouragement, or approval. Unbeknownst to Washington, Clay planned for the Army to set up walls in a West Berlin forest and practice knocking them down.

On 27 October, after U.S. tanks had been sent to Checkpoint Charlie to underscore concerns about new East German procedures requiring American civilian officials to show the papers to East German guards on entering the eastern sector, the U.S. forces were surprised to be confronted by Soviet tanks, whose presence in the city had just been discovered. U.S. tanks, some equipped with bulldozer blades, were brought into positions less than a hundred yards from the Russians, who brought up more tanks. Although a pullback occurred without incident after a sixteen-hour confrontation, a minor accident might have escalated quickly. The U.S. tank commander, Lieutenant Colonel Tom Tyree said at a later date, "My major concern . . . was to make sure something unexpected did not happen such as a nervous soldier accidentally discharging his weapon . . . (or) some tanker stepping accidentally on the accelerator leading to a runaway tank." Some senior Soviet officials consider the tank confrontation as the most dangerous moment in the postwar period, because, unlike more distant events, it involved an area of paramount security interest to them.

Cuba, 1962. During the 1962 Cuban missile crisis, Khrushchev later explained that he was concerned about the precedent of locating "devastating" U.S. Jupiter missiles "in Turkey literally right next to us." He then proposed removal by the United States of its offensive missiles in return for withdrawal of Soviet offensive missiles in Cuba. However, President Kennedy and his advisers viewed this as an unacceptable effort by Khrushchev to alter the status quo on NATO's eastern flank by the surreptitious Soviet move in Cuba. The president remarked to his small "Ex Com" group of advisers at the time that "if we suddenly began to put a major number of MRBMs in Turkey . . . that would be goddam dangerous." When reminded that the United States had already done so, he said, "Yes, but that was five years ago." Kennedy had indicated in 1961 that he wanted the liquid-fueled, "antiquated and useless" Jupiters withdrawn, but action had been delayed because of Turkish sensitivities. Two most critical days went by before the Soviets undertook to withdraw their missiles from Cuba. These days were spent trying to work out in private arrangements for the subsequent withdrawal of U.S. missiles from Turkey. Soviet concerns about the Jupiters may have been real. But neither Kennedy nor any of his advisers knew or recalled at the time that the agreement with Turkey to deploy the missiles had not been reached until October 1959, that deployment had not even begun until 1961, and that control over the first Jupiter site was not turned over to the Turks, ironically, until the same day as the president's Cuba quarantine speech.

Cuba, 1979. In the second half of 1978, after a period of diminished U.S. monitoring of Cuba, reports began to be received of unusual Soviet troop actions on the island. Although nothing new of significance was observed, more reports continued to arrive and in the spring of 1979 stepped-up coverage and review of the situation was ordered by the White House. The increased yield of photographs and reports after a slack period led some analysts and some other officials to conclude that there was a new Soviet "combat" brigade in Cuba conducting field exercises not connected with the established Soviet role in training Cuban troops. Reports to this effect reached the Congress and the public during the summer. When the Soviets were asked if they had brought in new troops, they charged that we had deliberately manufactured the whole affair. Their somewhat belated general disclaimers of any change in force levels or status were not deemed credible at the time. Later U.S. analysis of all available data led to the conclusion that the Soviet troop unit had been in place since 1962 and had been identified as a brigade a few years later, and that the only apparent new element not monitored before was field training without visible Cuban training involvement, a fact compatible with a wide variety of interpretations. Public statements about the "unacceptability" of the situation made by executive and legislative branch officials before an informed accurate analysis could be made later proved to be inaccurate and were seriously damaging to Senate approval of SALT II.

War Alert, 1981–83. From Oleg Gordievskii, KGB chief in England who defected in the spring of 1985, British and American officials learned that the KGB in England, and presumably the KGB stations in the United States and other countries as well, received instructions from Moscow in early 1981 indicating that the United States was going to attack the Soviet Union at an unspecified date and placing the KGB under standing orders to observe any unusual government activities, such as VIP travel, et cetera. Those orders remained in effect until well into 1983, and the KGB dutifully reported such matters as a Greater London Council blood donation drive as a possible preparatory move. Gordievskii, who was viewed as a credible source by debriefers, had indicated that KGB field agents believed that the directive was unduly alarmist, but he noted that such a major diversion of manpower and resources must have solid, high-level backing in Moscow. The United States was unaware of these misplaced Soviet concerns which could have been aggravated dangerously by inadvertent actions on our part as well as by the harsh rhetoric of the period.

Each of these cases poses difficult, unresolved questions. Was there an available process that could have enabled the Kennedy administration to be aware of Soviet fears about our intentions in Berlin? Why didn't Khrushchev indicate Soviet security concerns about the new deployments of Jupiter missiles in Turkey in his first message to Kennedy? If the Soviets had been more specific in their denial that there were any new forces in Cuba in 1979, would we have believed them? What occasioned the false 1981 to 1983 KGB intelligence alert? Was it the same concern former Politburo member Grigorii Romanov was referring to in a Kremlin speech on Nov. 4, 1983, in describing the international situation as "thoroughly white hot?" Or was it that same concern that Gorbachev was referring to in his address to the 27th Party Congress, when he stated that "never, perhaps, in the postwar decades has the situation in the world been so explosive—and hence, more difficult and unfavorable—as in the first half of the eighties."

What would have happened if the government that made the mistaken assessment had been willing to indicate its concerns to the other at the time?

All that seems certain is that unwarranted concerns existed on one side which were unknown or seemed incredible to the other, and that no timely or adequate efforts were made to dispel the tensions before events were allowed to run their course. We were all lucky.[1]

THE FUTURE AGENDA FOR U.S.-SOVIET RELATIONS AND THE INFLUENCE OF THE NEW THINKING

To be prepared to meet, in some sensible way, unexpected crisis is one problem, but what are the international issues that can be forecast, that can reasonably be expected to affect the U.S.-Soviet relationship in the next few years? If Gorbachev continues to press for further deep reductions in strategic arms and conventional forces as seems likely, the nature of the Warsaw Pact-NATO confrontation could be considerably changed if agreements are, in fact, reached. If anything like fifty percent cuts of strategic arms and a reduction of the conventional forces of both alliances to a lower level at parity is agreed to, then the competition between East and West will be on economic and political grounds rather than military. The dynamic is presently in the hands of Gorbachev. Gorbachev's ability to control the foreign policy agenda was clearly shown by the General Secretary in his speech at the United Nations in New York on December 7, 1988 in which he revealed the decision of the USSR to reduce its conventional forces by half a million men. The challenge for the United States and the West is how to meet that dynamic, dominating policy effort. Thus far, the response from the West has been reactive rather than anticipatory. Clearly, an overall concept of how these possible drastic changes in military doctrine and force levels away from a significant offensive posture to a defensive force will affect the security and well-being of all parties is an understanding that is desperately needed. What is of significance is that the Gorbachev leadership has consistently sought to discuss with the United States and the West the reasoning behind their new thinking and the consequent change in policy, and has said they want to create together a new framework and possibilities for the future relationship.

The so-called new political thinking has been given thorough philosophical, ideological, and policy expression by Gorbachev in his major speeches to the Party Congress and the Central Committee, and his view is explained fully in his book, *Perestroika*. The new political thinking is a departure from the class conflict-based ideological framework of the past. It is evident from a recent policy debate, carried on in the absence of Gorbachev, between Eduard Shevardnadze and Aleksandr Iakovlev on the side of the new thinkers and Egor Ligachev who holds to a more orthodox class conflict approach that Gorbachev's vision continues to be contested. A speech given in August 1988 by Iakovlev describes well the new political thinking that has been put forward as the basis for the Soviet Union's new foreign policy.

Averting the nuclear threat, disarmament for the sake of peace, confidence, and cooperation, for the sake of mankind's security and survival—that is the key task of today. But if we think in historical terms, it is only the first, the most necessary precondition for people to be able to embark on the just, democratic, and rational resolution of their other problems. To feed the hungry. To conserve nature on the planet, without which we cannot live. To handle sensibly the earth's far from infinite resources.

Common human interests—that is not an abstract concept arrived at through speculation in the isolation of a thinker's study. In our time, when the whole planet has apparently shrunk to an unprecedentedly small size, when the fate and history of mankind could be broken off by the pressing of a button, when any event becomes known to five billion people in a few hours, common human interests have acquired flesh and blood.

And they really are the interests of all mankind. That means they are ours too, because we are a part of mankind and one of the most important factors in his social progress. They are interests that unite mankind, and that means that they are capable of overcoming the forces of disunity, opposition, confrontation, and war that have already held back the development of civilization by centuries. This is a case of opposites converging: The interests of one person merge with the interests of all people, a philosophical, abstract, general historical concept merges with purely practical, worldly, real, day-to-day realities.[2]

The policy makers of both the United States and the USSR have to understand changed circumstances and fit many new pieces together, of which lower levels of strategic nuclear forces and conventional forces are only a part. The Middle East, for example, is seen as the area of greatest volatility by the Gorbachev planners as well as policy makers in the West. With the end of the Iran-Iraq war, the nature of post-Khomeini Iran is very much a question mark. Iran and the Gulf is frequently referred to as an area that needs the most careful attention. The Palestinian uprising, King Hussein's move to drop any Jordanian claim for the West Bank and Yasir Arafat's acceptance of a two-state solution, have raised the stakes in the Arab-Israeli conflict even higher and made a complicated situation even more complex.

In the light of these regional instabilities, UN peacekeeping is now a real possibility, given the changed attitude within the USSR about the usefulness of the United Nations. Efforts now being made with the support of Gorbachev to settle the Angola-Namibia-South African wars appear close to solution. Cambodia and Vietnam are in the process of a possible settlement and there are the first signs of some new understanding between the two Koreas. There is no question that the USSR has given a high priority to its relations with Pacific nations to increase trade, obtain economic help and to create a new overall political and economic relationship. Major agreements to control environmental pollution such as the greenhouse effect, the ozone hole, toxic waste disposal, and preserving the forests, fisheries, and water sources are already under discussion.

This list of initiatives by the Soviet Union is in itself an agenda that the United States must grapple with. But there are other vital issues that have to be addressed. Emigration and human rights issues remain although there has clearly been progress under Gorbachev in both areas of concern. The future trade relationship between the United States and the Soviet Union will require consideration of whether the USSR should become a full participating member of the world economy. Should it become a member of the International Monetary Fund and a signatory to the General Agreement on Tariffs and Trade? Will it be possible to make the ruble a convertible currency? Should the USSR be accorded Most Favored Nation status and given favorable terms of credit and other financial benefits? And should the sanctions of the past such as the Jackson-Vanik Amendment designed to punish a hostile USSR be relaxed in the light of significant changes in domestic and international behavior?

The extent to which the United States can shape, modify, or contend with the policy dynamism underway largely depends on the overall view of the world that the Bush administration formulates. The success of a new policy intended to deal with the new challenges and opportunities that have emerged as a result of the Gorbachev reforms will, of course, depend in large measure on the ability of President Bush to understand and deal with the vigorous new leaders of the Soviet Union.

AMERICAN AND SOVIET EXPERTS CAN HELP FORM THE NEW U.S.-SOVIET RELATIONSHIP

Fortunately, both President Bush and Gorbachev will have considerable expert help available. Expertise in the USSR about the United States has deepened and grown over the past two decades. In addition to the diplomats who have served in Washington, such as Ambassador Anatolii Dobrynin, Iulii Vorontsov, Aleksandr Bessmertnykh, or Politburo member Aleksandr Iakovlev who served as Ambassador to Canada, there are many other able diplomats with deep experience in American affairs who have risen to the top of the Soviet leadership. A very large and capable group of Americanists such as Sergei Plekhanov, Vitalii Zhurkin, Sergei Rogov, Andrei Kokoshin, Vladimir Pechatnov, and Genrykh Trofimenko have been trained at the Institute for the Study of the USA and Canada under the direction of Georgii Arbatov. Other institutes such as IMEMO (The Institute for World Economy and International Affairs) under its Director, Evgenii Primakov, Deputy Director Oleg Bykov, and Alexei Arbatov also have a large number of analysts that work on all aspects of American life. The KGB and the military also cover the United States from their particular national security perspectives. Given the major emphasis and importance assigned to the "American problem" for several decades, it is not surprising, therefore, that a substantial group of Americanists are among the chief advisors to General Secretary Gorbachev.

On the American side, the Department of State, the Central Intelligence Agency and the Defense Department, as well as Sovietologists in a number of think tanks and graduate universities, have made great efforts to know and try to understand the USSR—just as their Soviet equivalents have done in trying to understand the workings of United States policy. Yet, it is evident that the Soviets have made a far greater investment and more consistent effort to keep informed about the United States than has been made by the United States to know about the Soviet Union. Despite misrepresentations, misjudgments and failures of communication, and perhaps also because of these failures, the growing informed awareness on the part of a substantial number of well-trained experts on the U.S.-Soviet relationship has helped bring about the present openness between the two nations.

NEW OPENNESS IN THE SOVIET UNION UNDER GORBACHEV

This openness was evident in the extensive press and television coverage given to the May–June Summit between President Reagan and General Secretary Gorbachev. The more open attitude between the United States and the USSR has had an impact on both domestic and international politics and opinions as was shown in the recently concluded 19th Party Conference held from June to July 1988 before an astonished Soviet and world audience. The USSR is now more open to direct observation, scrutiny and analysis than at any previous time since 1917 and the first few years of the new revolutionary government. The 19th Party Conference revealed more of the inner workings of the government, a new level of open discussion and decisionmaking, absorbed more self-criticism, and demonstrated a greater range of debate than had been thought possible. Because of this emphasis on institutional openness, the Gorbachev rhetoric of change describing an intention to restructure the whole of Soviet society in a more beneficial, humane, civil, and peaceful direction is being taken seriously and is not being dismissed out of hand as propaganda without substance.

Accurate on-the-spot press and television coverage and more richly detailed histories are an inevitable consequence of public openness. The truth of Stalin's rule has begun to emerge for wide public discussion. In this respect, the ghost of Stalin—the constant, monumental reminder of a brutal past—ironically provides a legitimate contrast, a benchmark, and a substantial basis for the judgement that the "evil empire," Ronald Reagan's shorthand characterization of the Soviet Union, may, in fact, refer to "a different period, a different time."

A NEW SENSE OF HISTORY UNDER GORBACHEV

By championing the publication of objective history, Gorbachev has encouraged a fuller exposure of the harsh realities, brutalities, and mistakes of Stalin and the corruption and stagnation of Brezhnev. As a leader committed to reform and radical structural changes, Gorbachev sees history as a necessary factual benchmark and point of departure. Gorbachev has made the case to his own people that rigorous objective history, the systematic and careful analyses of the successes and failures, the achievements as well as the brutalities of past leaders and regimes have to be made in order to chart a more reasoned path within the socialist system toward a better life. Gorbachev's report to the nation, in 1987, on the occasion of the seventieth anniversary of the October Revolution, included his own historical analysis of the course his country has followed. The emphasis given by Gorbachev in his history of the Soviet Union stressed the necessity for a full understanding of the realities of the past as a basis for present and future action.

Beyond the insistence that history requires a fully documented record of past events, particularly written records, a belief is prevalent in Moscow, Leningrad, and elsewhere that, because fully documented history was not to be found, reliable history requires a kind of certification or legitimatization given by those who have directly experienced the period in question and who are respected for their intellectual courage and integrity. The USSR is only seventy years old. A significant number of people who have been witness to the entire history of the Soviet state including the events leading up to the revolution are still alive. Among this older group is Academician Dmitrii Likhachev of Leningrad, a revered historian who suffered for his independent views and forthright integrity under Stalin. He is presently Chairman of the Cultural Foundation and an advisor to Gorbachev and his wife, Raisa. The great discrepancy between official histories and the direct experience of many still living distinguished Russians may have helped bring about the present opening up of the records to public awareness.

There is also a strong sense of contending generational experience. Most of those who fought in the Great Patriotic War against the Nazis under Stalin's leadership, and who so proudly display their medals of honor, see Stalin in a very different light than their comrades and contemporaries, the "children of the 20th Congress," as the Khrushchev reform group called itself. Khrushchev, in his secret report to the party leadership in 1956 and his supporters, the children of the 20th Congress, first expressed the horrors of forced collectivization, the purges of the 1930s, and the *gulags* of Stalin's regime. The generation that came into positions of power and privilege during the long tenure of Brezhnev tends to see the whole 1965–1981 period not as a period of stagnation as the Gorbachev group terms it, but rather as a time of relative stability, law and order, and accomplishment. The generation now entering political awareness did not fight in the Great Patriotic War, nor did it experience the worst of the Cold War, and unlike its grandparents was able to receive a good education in an urban environment in relatively secure and stable circumstances. For all these reasons, the present generation is the first able to face the full realities of its nation's history in all of its complexity of success, failure, glories and horrors. Because the older generations were unable or chose not to convey their full awareness of what had occurred to the younger generations, the revelations about the past, particularly the Stalin period, have come as a shock.

Two recent films about the Stalin period that have wide impact in Moscow and elsewhere in the USSR are entitled *Repentance* and *The Cold Summer of 1953*. *Repentance*, which takes place in Georgia is a thinly veiled satiric, sometimes comic portrait of Stalin. The second film, *The Cold Summer of 1953*, made in Karelia and in the form of a gripping plot pitting one brave man against seven desperate killers, is a powerful thriller that explicitly and symbolically links Beria with criminality, while virtue and courage are bestowed on the political prisoners he and Stalin put in gulags. By these films, the horrors of arbitrary repression and brutality so much a part of the Stalin period are powerfully evoked. Another film, *Is It Easy To Be Young?*, among other contemporary issues, takes up the theme of the choices, difficulties, pitfalls, and opportunities that face the young just entering adult life. The film documents the duties of the youth and their escapes from obligations, new music, the drug culture, Afghanistan, the illusions of parents, the State, and the illusions of the youth themselves. The cinematic confrontation with present reality contained in the film is emblematic of the contemporary questioning mood that observers from the West who have gone to the Soviet Union have noted as so prevalent. These films are beginning to be shown in the United States.

While the press and television are the most evident means of arousing political interest, the issues of reform are also found embedded in popular entertainment. For example, the circus is used to convey political messages.

The contemporary political mood is found in the ballads of Vysotskii and Rozenbaum, in rock music groups like Black Coffee, Aquarium, and Time Machine, and even in the chatter and props of the clown acts, especially in the theme of the grand finale, in which the performers and clowns salute peace and *perestroika*. There are, also not surprisingly, political comments in the dialogues written for the popular puppet shows. The Taganka Theater, famed for its experimental daring, recently made its own declaration of freedom. The Taganka, one of the great avant-garde theaters of the world, had chafed in recent years under the enforced orthodoxy of State control. The noted director of the theater, Liubimov, was forced out and into exile and continued his work in the West. A good example of his dramatizations, which were censored by the Brezhnev regime, is his adaptation of Dostoevsky's *Crime and Punishment*, which was favorably received by critics and audiences in London and elsewhere. It was given accolades by those who saw it powerfully presented under Liubimov's own direction at the Arena Theater in Washington. Nonetheless, the memory of the Taganka's greatness is cherished by the Moscow intelligentsia. Liubimov's exile was commemorated by his former company and by his successor, director, and friend Nikolai Goubenko through the image and reality of an empty director's chair placed in the director's office of the Taganka. Suddenly this past spring, Liubimov was permitted to return for a visit. The Taganka Theater marked his return, not surprisingly, with a dramatic gesture. The empty chair in his office had not been sat in since his exile. When he returned to his beloved theater, Liubimov was placed in his old chair to the applause of his old company of actors, and his close friend and successor, Nikolai Goubenko. In July 1988, Liubimov was offered the Director's post at the Taganka once again, and Goubenko offered to step down for his friend.

Pravda and *Izvestiia*, the Party newspapers which had in the past a well-deserved reputation for their boring style and an unrelieved touting of the official line now are read for their vigorous reporting and commentary. Regional newspapers throughout the country have followed the lead of the Moscow papers and fully report the controversy and debate that surrounds the reform movement underway. A good example of newly enlarged freedom for the press is the exposure of differences within the Politburo between Gorbachev, Eltsin, and Ligachev over the pace of reform which took place in the editorial pages of several major newspapers during five or six weeks in the spring of 1988. The press became not only the forum for the respective views of the contending Politburo members, but also a kind of barometer of rising and falling degrees of power.

Popular publications like *Ogonek*, *Novyi Mir*, and *Literaturnaia gazeta* are also full of debate and controversy, and now publish for wide distribution works like Boris Pasternak's *Dr. Zhivago* and the poetry of Anna Akhmatova that had been long suppressed and available only in the West or circulated in the USSR by underground means.

Correspondents from the West have far more access to the government and to all segments of Soviet society. There are about forty correspondents in the press corps from the United States and they are, by their own accounts, stretched to keep abreast of the changes underway. Press conferences on a broad range of issues with both the foreign and domestic press are held on a frequent basis. For example, in June 1988 I attended a typical press conference which addressed the progress of arms control. The press conference took place at the well-appointed Ministry of Foreign Affairs Press Center. The spokesman, Gennadi Gerasimov, read a brief statement on INF and START. His remarks were followed by those of General Chervov, representing the military, followed by Deputy Minister of Foreign Affairs Petrovskii, who reviewed the actual negotiations. Roald Sagdeyev, Director of the Institute for Space Research, discussed technical issues. The panel then received questions for an hour from the press. These sessions are often very lively and occasionally contentious. The days of the occasional official handouts and no give and take between the press corps and officials have receded into memory.

GORBACHEV SEEKS THE SUPPORT OF THE INTELLIGENTSIA

Gorbachev, thus far, has sought the active support and has used the ideas of the intellectuals. He appears to share the views of many of the intellectuals who have been highly critical of the failure of the government structure to meet the needs of the country. Gorbachev has openly solicited their views and ideas for change and has told the intelligentsia that he needs them to spread the message of the necessity for change to all parts of the society, particularly the masses. A good case illustrating how Gorbachev has reached out to gain the support of the intelligentsia concerns his direct intervention in the case of the great physicist and human rights activist, and symbol of freedom and integrity, Andrei Sakharov, who had been exiled to Gorkii for his dissident views. In February 1987, Gorbachev called him by telephone to say that he was free to return to Moscow. Upon his return to Moscow, Sakharov immediately participated, undiminished, in his characteristic outspoken way, at an international forum that brought many of the world's most distinguished scientists, authors, artists and political leaders together to discuss the grave problems facing mankind. In January 1988, I was present at a meeting of the newly established International Foundation for the Survival and Development of Humanity held in the Kremlin at the initiative of the General Secretary. Gorbachev asked for the help of intellectuals throughout the world to give politicians the means to solve the major problems that face mankind: how to reduce the dangers of nuclear war, destruction of the environment, the ravages of poverty, disease and underdevelopment. During a discussion of the new foundation's purposes and future work with distinguished scientists, former governmental leaders, and executives from the United States, the USSR, and throughout the world, one of the International Foundation's founding board members, Academician Dmitrii Likhachev, told Gorbachev that great nations must not only work for the survival of mankind, but should also strive to improve and develop the quality of life of humanity. Likhachev said, "It is not enough to survive biologically, but as humans." He added that the USSR had in the past unjust leaders, men without integrity, and that without just leadership by men of integrity little could be accomplished. Gorbachev answered that he fully understood Academician Likhachev's concerns and that he was in full agreement. At that point, Academician Andrei Sakharov spoke up and said that he was aware by his own experience that there was injustice in the legal system of the Soviet Union and he knew that there were many people now in prisons unjustly. Gorbachev answered and said to Sakharov that he understood, and that as a lawyer he recognized that the law lagged behind the reality of society, but was confident that legal reform under *perestroika* would remedy these failings in the law. At this point Sakharov stood up and handed over several hundred files of people whom he said were in prison unjustly. Sakharov asked Gorbachev to look into these cases. General Secretary Gorbachev said that he would. Almost all have been released and the few remaining are under review.

What is remarkable about this dramatic encounter is not just that this was the first time the two had met each other, but rather the directness, the mutual respect and intelligence, and forthright candor with which the two discussed fundamental issues before their country and all nations. This willingness to listen and presumably learn from outspoken, even dissident views on the part of Gorbachev has helped bring the support of the intelligentsia to his reforms. Further evidence that Sakharov's views on human rights, arms control, and the future of Soviet society are taken seriously by Gorbachev

was given when Sakharov was permitted to travel to Washington to participate as a board member of the new International Foundation and to chair
a meeting of its human rights committee.

REFORM AND THE DANGER OF UNREALIZED EXPECTATIONS

There is a danger that the noble rhetoric and the far-reaching reforms hoped
for will not be sufficiently matched by meaningful, timely, visible progress.
The pace of actual changes has been, thus far, very slow and the legal
structure and bureaucratic means being used for implementing change are
still very uncertain. Furthermore, the rhetorical and intellectual ferment that
is evident in Moscow and Leningrad has not yet reached the same levels in
the smaller cities and towns throughout the vastness of the Soviet Union.
There is some opposition and considerable skepticism. There are very different generational reactions to the changes taking place. These differences
are reflected in the great variety to be found in the new open politics, new
music, painting, the films, some television programs, the theater, new fash-
ions in clothing, experiments in hair styles, and even in the kinds of food
eaten. Most bureaucrats, workers, and farmers are waiting to see if the
stirring words will produce results that will benefit them. Despite radical
agricultural reforms, such as the legalization of family farms, more food
is not yet in the stores and consumer goods remain in short supply. The
anti-alcohol campaign is highly unpopular and there is little to buy with
hard-earned money. Unrest in some of the Baltic States and in Armenia,
Azerbaijan, and Georgia has shaken the confidence of some in the ability of
the Gorbachev leadership to maintain law and order. But, despite all these
problems, without question there has been an opening up of the system
to free discussion and expression, inluding criticism and complaints about
the failure of the government to provide promised benefits and services.
To say that expectations have been aroused is an understatement. The new
freedoms and the expectations of a freer, more materially prosperous life
have created many unexpected reactions. These freedoms and expectations
and all of these problems were aired in the turbulent, charged debate of
the spring of 1989 that took place in the Congress of People's Deputies.
There is a fear that the system of order will break down into dangerous divisions. But as Raold Z. Sagdeev, academician, prominent physicist
and newly elected Deputy from the Academy of Sciences said, "As the

Bible says, in the beginning was chaos, but better such chaos than the kind of order we had before."[3]

THE NEW THINKING: *GLASNOST, PERESTROIKA* AND *DEMOKRATIZATSIIA*

The "new thinking," an overarching slogan identifying the Gorbachev reform program, is linked with three other slogans, all with highly elastic meaning that have become familiar to the West, namely: *glasnost*—openness, *perestroika*—restructuring, and *demokratizatsiia*—democratization. They are all terms that have very different meanings for different people. Two main strands can be discerned in the "new thinking." The first is a decided sense of limitation and constraint that has arisen out of global concern and an apocalyptic awareness that irresponsible actions by any great power could unleash catastrophic nuclear war; that the earth's environment is in danger of severe degradation; that the problems of poverty, disease, and underdevelopment could unleash uncontrollable, disastrous wars, plagues, and unrest.

The second strand in the new thinking concerns Gorbachev's vision of what his government should try to achieve. These goals are a result of rigorous analysis of the social development of the USSR, particulary since 1930, that have been made over the past decade by sociologists like Tatiana Zaslavskaia in her report made in Novosibirsk in 1983; by philosophers and ideologists like Georgii Shaknazarov, Vadim Medvedev, Ivan Frolov, Vadim Zagladin, Fedor Burlatskii, and B. T. Gregorian. The utopian socialist vision of Lenin has not been lessened, but it has been given new definition and direction by the principal figures in the Gorbachev group who have shaped the new thinking.

Perhaps more than any other single intellectual construct that underlays the new thinking, Tatiana Zaslavskaia's Novosibirsk critique identifies the fundamental nature of the crisis facing the new leaders as well as giving a rationale for radical systemic change. Zaslavskaia's Novosibirsk report takes as its first point of reference the social structure of the USSR in the 1930s when Stalin imposed collectivization of the farms, severely limited all freedoms, and pressed the nation into an all-out, almost wartime effort to transform a backward society into a modern state. Stalin's concept of the needed social system, Zaslavskaia writes, made people as "cogs" in the mechanism of the national economy and [they] behaved themselves just as obediently (and passively) as machines and materials.[4]

In 1983, when the report was written, Zaslavskaia observed that the "structure of the national economy long ago crossed the threshold of complexity when it was still possible to regulate it from one single centre." The most crucial point made by Zaslavskaia in her powerfully argued analysis is her summary description of the transformed socialist workers for whom, she says, the State exists to serve:

> The level of education, culture, general information, and awareness of his social position and rights, has grown incomparably. The main body of skilled workers, on whom above all the effectiveness of the production process depends, nowadays has a rather wide political and economic horizon, is able to evaluate critically the leader's economic and political activities, accurately recognizes its own interests and can defend them if necessary. The spectrum of needs and interests of workers is today more abundant and broader than that of workers in the 1930s; moreover, in addition to economic, it includes social and spiritual needs. It testifies to the substantial increase in the level of the workers' personal development.[4]

THE NEW THINKING HAS OPPONENTS

The new thinking has its opponents and critics. In July 1988, Politburo member and Minister of Foreign Affairs, Eduard Shevardnadze, who is a close ally of Gorbachev,[4] held an important conference on international affairs which considered among other issues how to deal with universal human problems such as the possibility of catastrophic nuclear war, the destruction of the world's environment, and the ravages of poverty, disease, and underdevelopment. According to the Gorbachev new thinkers, such issues, by their global nature, transcend class interests and cannot be explained by the conflict between the capitalist and socialist economic systems. As Gorbachev said in his political report to the 27th Party Congress on February 26, 1986:

> In a word, the modern world has become too small and fragile for wars and the politics of force. It will be impossible to save and preserve it, if we do not break—decisively and irrevocably—with the manner of thoughts and actions which were built on the acceptability and permissibility of wars and natural conflicts.[5]

Egor Ligachev has taken exception to this view, believing as his predecessors Brezhnev and Chernenko that:

> we proceed from the class character of international relations. . . . Therefore, active participation in the solution of universal human problems in no way means any artificial deceleration of social and national liberation struggle.[7]

On the first of October 1988, Gorbachev was elected President, following a sudden convening of the Central Committee which made major shifts in the membership of the Politburo and the composition of the Central Committee leadership. Gorbachev decisively moved to strengthen his base of support in the face of consistent opposition to his reforms. This election marks the beginning of an aggressive phase for active "*perestroika* and the renewal of our society" said Gorbachev. In the course of a short but important speech accepting the post of President, Gorbachev referred to foreign affairs as he views it in the overall pattern of policy:

> Our course in foreign affairs is clear. It is aimed at eliminating the danger of nuclear catastrophe, at normalizing international relations, setting up equitable and mutually advantageous ties between the world's countries and people, at broad cooperation in the most varied areas, at insuring the right of every people to a free choice for its future.[8]

This is but one area of policy in which there are differences between Gorbachev and Ligachev on the fundamental concepts governing the reforms underway. While Ligachev fully supports the need for restructuring and retooling the economy, he does not seem to embrace fully the Zaslavskaia view that the Soviet worker has been sufficiently transformed to play an increasing role in the shaping of his own life without the overriding paternalistic direction of the Party leadership. He and others in the Politburo and the Central Committee are wary of ideological change and fearful that opening up the system as some of their colleagues advocate will weaken rather than strengthen the State. Because of a freer flow of information, individuals and groups within the Soviet Union are now able to express their hopes and desires and expectations—and they are doing so. It is now evident that the national perception of the proper balance between the rights of the individual and the needs of the State is slowly shifting in the direction of privacy and individual freedoms with the "insurance of legality," but not without a struggle, as the continuing debate between Gorbachev and Ligachev demonstrates.[9]

TOWARD A MORE CIVIL SOCIETY

Gorbachev studied the law as a student at Moscow University. As a lawyer and as political leader of his country, he understands well the necessity for the government and the laws by which it is empowered, defined, and limited, to reflect, as he told Andrei Sakharov at the meeting with the International Foundation for the Survival and Development of Humanity in January 1988, "the reality of society." As a result of observations like these made by Gorbachev and by the emphasis he has placed upon open processes of discussion, decisionmaking and the choice of leaders and representatives as clearly evident in the recent 27th Party Conference, the 19th Party Conference and successive Central Committee Plenums held over the past two years, and the elections to the new legislative body held in the Spring of 1989, there is a growing belief that he understands and largely shares Zaslavskaia's analysis, and that he intends to move the USSR, through his reform program of *perestroika, glasnost*, and *demokratizatsiia* firmly in the direction of a more civil society. This is the expressed hope of many in the Soviet Union, and it is the crucial issue leaders in the United States and the West must carefully follow and respond to if the promise of a stable, long-term, peaceful relationship is to have a lasting reality.

Notes

1. William G. Miller and Benjamin H. Read, "Strengthening the U.S.-Soviet Communications Process to Reduce the Risks of Misunderstanding and Conflict: A Report by the National Academy of Public Administration," Washington, D.C., 1987, pp. 12–13. The four cases cited here are adapted from this report.
2. Egor Ligachev, Foreign Broadcast Information Service: Daily Report, *Soviet Union* (FBIS-SOV), 17 August 1988, p. 30.
3. As quoted in *The New York Times,* 4 June 1989. P.E3.
4. Tatiana Zaslavskaia, "The Novosibirsk Report," *Survey,* vol. 28 no. 1 (Spring 1984): p. 90.
5. Ibid., p. 91. A vitally important book, *Inogo Ne Dano* (No Other Way Is Given), Iurii Afanaseev, ed. (Moscow: Progress 1988), written by the reform group now called the *perestroiki,* has a lead chapter by Zaslavskaia. The book, which also includes a chapter by Andrei Sakharov, was published in time for the 19th Party Conference in July. It is a widely discussed book, but has disappeared from the

bookstores. In her chapter Zaslavskaia has brought up to date her views on what is required for significant reform.

6. Mikhail S. Gorbachev, Political Report to the 27th Party Congress, 26 February 1986, p. 7.

7. FBIS-SOV, 5 August 1988, p. 33.

8. *The New York Times,* 2 October 1988, p. 14.

9. The idea of "civil society" within the Soviet Union expressed here owes much to the discussions I have had with S. Frederick Starr over the past two years.

1 THE DYNAMICS OF CHANGE IN CONTEMPORARY SOVIET SOCIETY

Gerald M. Easter and Anne M. Gruber

Since 1985, the Soviet Union has been in the throes of political and social change of revolutionary proportions. A new political leadership, intent on bringing about a regeneration of the sclerotic Soviet system, is in the forefront of this revolution whose primary cause was not political, but social. Toward the end of the 1970s, the Soviet Union fell into a decline marked by the deterioration of health and living standards, a number of social ills resulting from industrialization such as urban overcrowding and alcoholism, and a sharp decrease in the productivity of the workforce. Moreover, by the 1980s, a sizable "middle class" had emerged in Soviet society. Because of its education and professional skills, the middle class was regarded by the new political leadership as the key to efforts to reinvigorate the listless Soviet economy. *Perestroika*, Gorbachev's comprehensive program of reform, provided the middle class with an opportunity to help shape the development of Soviet society as it prepares for a new century. Not surprisingly, the interests of the middle class dominate the numerous discussions on various aspects of reform now taking place in the Soviet Union.

The new leadership's efforts to alter fundamentally social policies, which have been in place for decades, first required the identification of the causes underlying the country's economic and social crises. Why were Soviet youth so much more apathetic about the Soviet system than their parents? What aspects of the social structure contributed to stagnation in

1

labor productivity? These queries were answered by analyzing how Soviet society had evolved since the 1930s and how the government had failed to adapt to these changes. Recognizing the failure of his predecessors to address effectively social problems and their implications for the economy, Gorbachev—relying on the recommendations of a group of Soviet social scientists—has modified official attitudes toward social policy. At the center of this new approach is a reformulation of the concept of "social justice." This new sense of social justice has guided Gorbachev's efforts to reform the Soviet Union's welfare state, to raise material living standards, to promote greater individual responsibility, and to reorganize the educational system to prepare students for life in a technologically advanced society. But these efforts have already produced adverse unintended consequences, such as the intensifying of inter-ethnic conflict. One of Gorbachev's biggest challenges if he can shake the country out of its current economic stagnation will be to create new, more flexible structures for Soviet society that will accomodate rather than resist the unanticipated consequences that inexorably accompany social development.

The Dynamics of Social Change in Contemporary Soviet Society

"The fundamental premise of a revolution," according to Leon Trotsky, "is that the existing social structure has become incapable of solving the urgent problems of the development of the nation." By the time Mikhail Gorbachev assumed the position of General Secretary in March 1985, Soviet society had begun to resemble the situation described by Trotsky. Gorbachev himself stated on numerous occasions that the Soviet Union had fallen into a state of "pre-crisis." The new General Secretary recognized that the existing structures for political and socioeconomic life no longer served the needs and desires of the Soviet population. It was as if a gap between the regime and the public had developed, the potential consequences of which seriously threatened the long-term stability of the Soviet system of rule.

Structural Changes

In 1985, the Soviet Union began a reexamination of the fundamental tenets that have long governed the relationship between the state and society.

This reexamination was initiated by the new political leadership, as part of an effort to put together a comprehensive program of reform for Soviet society. The reform program included a reevaluation of the existing social structure of the Soviet Union, since it is at this basic level that the more visible economic and political problems are rooted. There was a recognition by the new political leadership that the Soviet population was no longer in sync with society's functional processes. For several decades, social changes were occurring at a slow but steady rate. By the 1980s, new social groups had emerged that could not be integrated into the existing routines of economic, political, and social life. An impasse had developed between the political and economic structures created to make society work and the population for whom this structure was created.

The emergence of this impasse marked the end of a cycle of change which had begun a half century earlier. It is an example of a historical pattern of social change seen before in Russian-Soviet society, when comprehensive state-directed, socioeconomic reform led to unintended changes in the social structure. The dynamics of this pattern of social change are as follows: (1) The political leadership attempts radical reform of the existing socioeconomic structures of society in order to modernize the country's economy and to strengthen its military in relation to stronger Western states; (2) The successes achieved by these reform efforts lead to a gradual process of social change, in which new social groups emerge out of the economic activities created by the radical reform; and (3) As these new groups become established, forming identities of their own, conflicts arise because the original reforms did not anticipate corresponding modifications in the structure of political authority, economic reward, and social status which would accomodate these new groups. These conflicts, when left unresolved, eventually create a revolutionary situation in society, characterized by repeated economic failure and a loss of regime legitimacy.

To illustrate this pattern, during the decade of the Great Reforms in the nineteenth century, Russia's autocratic state made concerted efforts to move away from an agrarian economy, based on serfdom, towards a more modern, industrial economy. From a social perspective, the long-term results of these policies led to the emergence of new groups: an urban proletariat, an urban counter-intelligentsia and, in the countryside, a declassed peasantry. By the turn of the century, these new groups had become the main source of tension and instability in Russian society. The inability of imperial Russia's leadership to meet the challenges of its changing population resulted in two decades of social struggle. From 1905 to 1917, Russia endured one attempt at radical sociopolitical reform from above, which was aborted in a wave of conservative reaction, and two revolutions from below, the second of which destroyed the social and political institutions of the Old Regime.

An analagous process of social change began again in the 1930s, the decade of Stalin's "Revolution From Above." Stalin's program of radical reform included an ambitious state-directed drive to restructure fundamentally the Soviet economy for the purpose of rapid-paced industrialization, focusing in particular on the development of a productive and technological base that would support military-related industries. The reforms of the 1930s successfully transformed the Soviet Union into an advancing industrial society. But at the same time, it began a new cycle of social change arising from the demands of the rapidly industrializing economy. New occupational groups emerged: technically skilled workers for the new industries; scientists and engineers; and economic managers. These occupational groups formed the core of the Soviet Union's new and growing middle class, demographically distinguishable by their education, occupational skills, and place of residence. Although these groups emerged as a direct consequence of the State's socioeconomic reforms of the 1930s, this new class did not fit in well with the socioeconomic and sociopolitical institutions created at the same time.

The rapid industrialization of the Soviet Union led to a process of accelerated urbanization, as waves of displaced peasants migrated to the cities in search of a better life. In 1939, the majority of the population still resided in the countryside, with only 32.5 percent of the population living in the city. By the late 1960s, however, the Soviet Union was no longer a predominantly agrarian society as 56 percent of the Soviet population was living in the cities. In 1987, the figure for urban residence had grown to 66 percent, with only 34 percent of the population remaining in the countryside.[1] Today twenty-three Soviet cities have more than a million residents.[2] In the last decade, the greatest movement has occurred from middle-sized to larger urban cities. It has become increasingly difficult, however, to move to the largest cities, Moscow, Leningrad, and Kiev, as the government has taken active measures to stabilize the populations by restricting migration.

As the Soviet population moved to the cities, educational opportunities multiplied. The Soviet Union at the beginning of the 1930s was predominantly a peasant country and much of the population was illiterate. Only 10.8 percent of the population over ten years of age had secondary or higher education. The overwhelming majority of peasants and workers, most of whom had just recently left the villages, had only an elementary education. By 1987, official Soviet statistics cite more than 70 percent of the Soviet population over ten years of age have had at least some secondary or higher education. Of this total, nearly 12 percent have completed higher education, nearly 17 percent have a specialized secondary education, and almost 40 percent have completed secondary education.[3] In addition to increases in education, there has been an enormous rise in the amount of information through various media channels. Nearly every Soviet citizen now has access to newspapers, journals, radio and television. By 1986, 93 percent of the population had access to Soviet television, which covered nearly 86 percent of the Soviet Union's territory. This is an enormous leap from 1960, when only 5 percent of the population had access to television.[4] Today there are over 8500 newspapers published for a population which official sources claim has now reached almost total literacy.[5]

The increasing complexity and expansion of the Soviet economy over the past several decades, along with increasing urbanization and education levels, led to the decline of blue collar, semiskilled workers in the labor force. In 1939 only 16.5 percent of the labor force was engaged in mental work; by 1987 this figure had expanded to over 26 percent.[6] In modern urban centers, roughly 40 percent of the population belongs to this social group.[7] As the small urban professional segment of the population increased, the political system fashioned by Stalin to rule a rural, uneducated, and technologically backward society remained for the most part unchanged. The failure of the system of governance to adapt to the changing social character of the country is the main cause of the increased dissatisfaction of the Soviet people over the past two decades with their political and economic systems.

Attitudinal Changes

Along with the structural changes in Soviet society, there is increasing evidence that attitudinal changes have aroused the concerns of the political leadership. These attitudinal changes have occurred mainly in the Soviet Union's growing middle class, whose frustration and dissatisfaction were increasingly evident during the second half of Brezhnev's rule. This emerging middle class includes, to a large degree, the second and third generations

of Soviet industrialization, whose historical experiences were vastly different from those of their forebears. The social and economic conditions under
which they were raised bore little resemblance to that of their ancestors who
lived in the first three decades of Soviet rule.

Those of the second generation of Soviet industrialization were born
during the thirties and forties. This generation was too young to have
participated in the political struggles of the 1930s and the hard-fought battles
of World War II, while its memories of poverty in the cities or famines in
the countryside during the early thirties are faint at best. This group came of
age in the 1950s and the early 1960s. By this time, the standards of living
had risen considerably from pre-war levels. Despite uneven development,
the Soviet economy was still growing and provided ample opportunity for
upward mobility. This generation, living in the relatively liberal atmosphere
engendered by the reforms of Nikita Khrushchev, distanced itself from the
suspicion and repression of the late Stalin years. The optimism of this
group in its formative years, however, soon changed to pessimism under
the stultifying social conservativism and the dismal economic performance
of Brezhnev's last decade.

The third generation of Soviet industrialization, those born in the fifties
and sixties, are the young adults of the present Soviet Union. This group is
even further removed from the direct experience of World War II and the
early years of industrialization. For young adults, these events are blurred
with other remote events like the Civil War and the Revolution. The third
generation takes for granted such benefits of contemporary Soviet society as
the comprehensive social-welfare system, guarantees of education, employment, and security from foreign invasion. The politically formative years
of this group were the late Brezhnev period, a time when Soviet society
was dominated by an aged and sickly political leadership, a suffocating
and corrupt bureaucracy, and a failing economy. In addition, they were
denied outlets for the popular expression of their own ideas by the regime's
ultraconservative cultural policies, which censored all art and literature that
hinted of nonconformity. For this third generation, withdrawal into apathy
or engaging in counter-cultural activities became common outlets.

The frustrated ambitions of the second generation of Soviet industrialization and the cynical passivity of the third generation resulted in significant
negative attitudinal changes toward the regime. Empirical evidence of these
attitudinal changes can be documented by comparing the results of two
extensive surveys of Soviet émigrés. The first, the Harvard Project, carried

out in the 1950s, interviewed soldier émigrés who chose not to return to the Soviet Union after World War II. The second, the Soviet Interview Project, was conducted in the early eighties and analyzed the wave of émigrés who had left the Soviet Union in the 1970s.

According to the Harvard Project data compiled in the 1950s, sympathetic attitudes toward the Soviet system tended to vary inversely with age. Younger respondents generally expressed a positive attitude towards the existing political and economic institutions in Soviet society. When younger members expressed disaffection with the established order, it was usually the result of a personal run-in with authority, and not because of a generally negative impression of the system.[8] Older respondents, especially those who could recall pre-revolutionary Russia, were much more likely to express hostility or alienation from the regime.[9] In the 1980s survey data, by contrast, levels of dissatisfaction with regime performance and with standards of living were much greater among the younger respondents. The youngest respondents surveyed were more likely than older groups to engage in "nonconformist" political behavior. Furthermore, the findings indicate that in terms of material well-being, contemporary Soviet youth are more inclined to compare themselves with their counterparts in other European countries and are less impressed than their parents with the achievements of the Soviet economy during industrialization.[10]

A similar erosion in support for the regime occurred among those with higher education. Thirty years ago the better-educated members of Soviet society were much more likely to support the established political and economic order. In the 1950s sample, the intelligentsia (71 percent of whom had at least begun college education) consistently appeared as the social group least hostile to the regime. If hostility was expressed by the better educated members in the sample, it tended to be directed toward specific political leaders and not at the system as a whole.[11] The results of the 1980s survey reveal that an inverse relationship has developed between education and both economic satisfaction and political support: the higher the level of education, the more likely one expressed a negative attitude towards the Soviet system.[12] Not surprisingly, as more and more information became accessible to Soviet citizens, especially from nonofficial sources, the better educated strata in society became disillusioned with official propaganda and rhetoric. By contrast, the 1950s survey data showed that the higher one's level of education, the more accepting one was of information disseminated by the regime.[13]

The 1980s survey reveals attitudinal changes in other social categories important to the regime. For example, attitudinal changes were discernable in the views of urban and rural respondents. The 1950s data showed that the collective farm peasantry was the most hostile group in Soviet society at that time. At present, even though it remains desirable to live in one of the Soviet Union's larger cities, respondents who hailed from Moscow or Leningrad tended to be the most critical when discussing the quality of their lives.[14] In addition, there has been a noticeable change in attitude along ethnic lines. Whereas the 1950s survey indicated little interethnic hostility, the 1980s survey showed that Russians have become more dissatisfied with their place in the system in comparison with non-Russian nationality groups.[15] As economic growth has slowed and job advancement has become more difficult, there has been a concurrent increase of resentment on the part of Russians toward Central Asians, Baltic peoples, and other nationality groups, whom they feel enjoy higher living standards at their expense.

The pattern of attitudinal change revealed by this comparison is a manifestation of the larger process of structural change. The categories which reflect the greatest change—age, education, place of residence—are the same categories which define the Soviet Union's growing middle class. This middle class largely consists of people from the second and third generations of Soviet industrialization, who tend to be better educated and reside in major urban centers. The survey results indicate that this strategically important group harbors attitudes of frustration with and alienation from the Soviet system.

Consequences

The structural and attitudinal transformations that emerged over several decades have become the root cause of the problems that presently plague Soviet society. Many of the occupational subgroups of the middle class provide the knowledge and expertise necessary for developing the kinds of information and technology systems that have become necessary for advancing industrial productivity in the 1980s. But as the surveys indicate, the middle class places the most demands for satisfaction of material needs on the Soviet economy. Their willingness to contribute to the economy is, at present, tempered by their dissatisfaction with current living standards. On a political level, the middle class displays indifference to, rather than support for, the regime. The widespread political disaffection among society's well educated and youth has created a potentially destabilizing environment for the regime.

The new Soviet leadership which came to power in the spring of 1985 has demonstrated an awareness of this situation. It has recognized the changes that have taken place in society, and the need for popular support if the restructuring process is to succeed. Mikhail Gorbachev has been direct in his assessment of these negative structural and attitudinal trends in Soviet society. He expressed this concern in describing the imperatives of his program for the radical restructuring of the Soviet Union:

> Perestroika is an urgent necessity arising from the profound processes of development in our socialist society. This society is ripe for change. It has long been yearning for it. Any delay in beginning perestroika could have led to an exacerbated internal situation in the near future, which, to put it bluntly, would have been fraught with serious social, economic and political crises.[16]

The leadership has developed a package of social reforms aimed at gaining the support of the Soviet middle class. Much attention, for example, has been focused on improving the quality of life in the urban areas; including the provision of quality housing and health care, the development of a reliable service sector and the creation of a more efficient distribution system for consumer goods and food products. There also have been efforts to address the aspirations of Soviet youth by opening up more opportunities to them, by giving legitimacy and approval to many of their cultural pursuits. The new leadership already has made great strides in overcoming the disaffection of the better educated in Soviet society. The leadership has been successful in removing the backlog of grievances accumulated by the intelligentsia against the Brezhnev regime, such as the political repression of some of its outspoken members and the imposition of a constrained and sterile intellectual environment.

THE NEW APPROACH TO SOCIAL POLICY

The social agenda is being used by the present leadership as an instrument to overcome both the continuing stagnation of the economy and the increasing isolation of the regime from important segments of society. The issue of social reform has provided substantially more than political rhetoric promising a better life; indeed, it has generated a broadly based public debate over the need for an entirely new approach toward social relationships in Soviet society.

Conceptual Foundations of the New Approach

Public discussion on social reform has provided a national forum for the ideas of a group of Soviet academics who until recently were considered an "out" group within official intellectual circles. This group, which includes such leading social scientists as Tatiana Zaslavskaia, Abel Aganbegian, and Oleg Bogomolov, has studied socioeconomic trends in the Soviet Union since the late sixties. Although they were aware of the deterioration in social and economic well-being as early as the mid-seventies, they were routinely denied the opportunity to present their findings, as well as their implications, or to conduct further investigations into what were forbidden areas of research.[17] Once Mikhail Gorbachev declared that his regime was committed to a thorough and realistic examination of the underlying social causes of the country's economic problems, the members of this "out" group rose very quickly to prominence as the leading advocates for social reform. Their views now appear regularly in the mass media and collectively they have become known as the *perestroiki*, because of their active role in the reform discussions.

These scholars have offered a thorough critique of some of the most basic elements of the regime's social policy, calling into question patterns that have dictated the norms of behavior between state and society for several decades. Significantly, the Soviet Union's system for social welfare provisions, which has long been celebrated as one of the state's greatest achievements, as well as the system for reward and advancement, are now believed to be elements that have contributed to the faltering state of the economy.

Until recently, the regime's social policies were grounded in a conceptual view of Soviet society that included two classes, worker and collective farm peasantry, and one stratum, the intelligentsia. This view of the class structure has been a fundamental ideological tenet of the regime since the second half of the 1930s. In this scheme, Soviet society was said to be moving toward social unity as class conflict gradually lessened. Analysis based on these large, amorphous social categories, however, revealed very little about the dynamic forces within society that were creating new social groups and greater diversity, rather than homogeneity. One of the chief contributions of these social scientists has been to redefine the analytical framework used to examine Soviet society. Their new conceptual scheme provides a more sophisticated view of society, taking into account the differences in lifestyle and interests within classes as well as between them. Accordingly, the past approach to social policy, which was generally nondiscriminating and collectivist, has been challenged by a new approach that is far more sensitive to intragroup and even individual interests.

A critical element of the new approach is the concept of "social justice" as the principal criterion for evaluating social policy. In an article in *Kommunist*, the Party's leading theoretical journal, Tatiana Zaslavskaia defined "social justice" as both a means and an end for Soviet society. In her view social justice ultimately requires that the system insure "political, social and economic equality among social groups, that is, ensuring the equal social value of their status while retaining a number of differences in specific manifestations."[18] In the meantime, however, social justice requires a much closer link between an individual's productivity and compensation in the workplace. Zaslavskaia argued that "our society includes people who are ready to work quite intensively, but not under general conditions, but somewhat 'individually,' such as on the basis of family contracts, cultivation on their private plots, participation in seasonal construction brigades or in other types of piece rate work."[19] Proponents of this particular definition of social justice, which emphasizes inequality of economic reward, stress its ideological correspondence with Marx's well-known characterization of economic life under socialism: "from each according to ability, to each according to work."

The concept of social justice, as defined by Zaslavskaia and other proreform academics, encapsulates a vision of Soviet society that combines inequality of reward with equality of opportunity. Wages would be directly linked with personal productivity under the assumption that incentives designed to appeal to individuals will produce greater motivation. In this approach, inequality of reward is considered a positive social norm since an individual's contribution ultimately benefits the whole. Ideally, social reform would also ensure equality of opportunity for upward mobility. Equality of opportunity in this case means that the structure of socioeconomic life must provide each individual with the chance to gain skills and to develop talents. This equality must also extend to the workplace so that those who display greater initiative and work productively are given the opportunity for greater compensation and career advancement. This conception of social justice requires a fundamental restructuring of the prevailing system of reward and advancement, which at present is geared more towards a leveling equality.

To realize this new vision of Soviet society, it is necessary to establish and adhere to objective criteria for the evaluation of an individual's work performance. Subjective criteria, it is argued, have become too influential in determining reward and advancement to the detriment of the overall social and economic well-being of Soviet society. The widespread application of subjective criteria is the result of the efforts of the country's bureaucratic-administrative elite to protect its own socially advantaged position. The reform debate has generated a number of new proposals concerning the distribution of material rewards and social welfare benefits as well as access to society's channels of upward mobility. Addressing the specific issue of career advancement within state and economic organizations, for example, M. I. Piskotin, the editor of the journal *Sovetskoe gosudarstvo i pravo*, offered an insightful illustration of the general themes raised in these arguments:

> [The] placement of people based in various positions or their promotion to higher posts not on the basis of their objective qualities and merits but also on the basis of the 'patronage' of influential people, has, unfortunately become a common occurrence in our country . . . [this practice] reduces the qualitative level of management cadres, expecially executive cadres, since it means the promotion not of the ablest but of those with the powerful support . . . we should devise methods making it possible to restrict the discretion of officials, which now plays a considerable role in the resolution of cadres problems.[20]

Piskotin goes on to recommend the creation of a merit-based point system to determine promotions and job placement even to the highest executive positions in state and economic bureaucracies. Such a point system, in principle, would provide a more objective standard for reward and advancement.

The proposed reform of the system of reward and advancement reflects the aspirations of the emerging group of well-educated, middle class professionals. Director of the Institute of Sociological Research, Vilen Ivanov, has stated that "the reforms offer considerable opportunities to the skilled managers, specialists, and highly skilled workers—the sort of people who will be needed to run future high-technology operations."[21] Middle class professionals are already better rewarded in general than blue collar workers and collective farm peasants; however, this is not so in comparison with the country's bureaucratic-administrative elite. A social reform carried out along these lines could potentially provide middle class professionals with a means for wresting control over society's social privileges from the bureaucratic-administrative elite. The Soviet economy has entered a new stage of development in which the application of scientific and technical knowledge has greater value than administrative fiat as a means of obtaining economic results. The new approach to determining reward and advancement evident in contemporary social reform debates represents a claim by a rising social group, middle class professionals, against the vested interests of a declining one, the bureaucratic-administrative elite. This clash between social groups is an example of the process of "the circulation of elites," to use Pareto's phrase, that all societies are prone to when the material-technological prerequisites of socioeconomic life are transformed and, subsequently, change hands.

Influence on Social Policy Formation

From its debut in the 1960s, the discipline of sociology in the Soviet Union suffered from both underdevelopment as an academic subject and underutilization as a policy science. What is most significant about Soviet social scientists, such as Zaslavskaia, is the ready manner in which their views and opinions have been incorporated into mainstream discussions on social reform. The findings of these sociologists have opportunely filled a void for the political leadership in its effort to devise and legitimate a new strategy for reinvigorating the Soviet economy. There is a recognition in the leadership that information and analysis about socioeconomic trends provide a formidable tool for shaping policies designed to stimulate greater individual productivity. Social scientists thus have come to play a greater role in the process of social policymaking. The enhanced influence of social scientists is evident from the creation of new policy-related institutes as well as the adoption of many of their views by the members of the political leadership, in particular Mikhail Gorbachev.

A number of steps have been taken to strengthen the connection between sociological research and the policymaking process. Most significant has been the creation of sociological research institutes in Moscow, where there is greater accessibility to both political officials who are involved with social policy issues as well as to the mass media which is capable of disseminating information and views to a wide domestic audience. Some of the most outspoken members from the proreform group of social scientists have been appointed to direct the operations of these new institutes, including Tatiana Zaslavskaia at the All-Union Center for the Study of Public Opinion on Social and Economic Questions and Vilen Ivanov at the Sociological Research Institute.

These new research facilities have been assigned two principal tasks: first, to investigate and analyze the relationship between social factors and workers' behavior; second, to develop a reliable system for sampling public opinion.[22] Concerning the first task, social scientists were able to provide the political leadership with a general assessment of motivations and behavior in the workplace drawing from various past research endeavors. In *The Novosibirsk Report*, for example, Tatiana Zaslavskaia elaborated on a number of social influences on economic productivity levels, including demographic factors, such as age, health, and region; education levels; occupational status; and the structure of incentive systems.[23] The development of a system for reliable public opinion sampling has moved at a much slower pace, because of a lack of computer facilities and the long official aversion to such practices. Nonetheless, the Soviet press is beginning to publish on a regular basis the results of public opinion surveys conducted by the new research institutes which address peoples' attitudes toward various aspects of *perestroika*. This feedback information is especially important for the leadership as they grapple with such issues as price and wage reforms. In an article in *Pravda* publicizing the work of the new research institute, Zaslavskaia spoke of the advantages for political officials of having public opinion data available: "Reliable two-way contacts with the population are necessary for the normal functioning of the state, the national economy, and the consumer services sphere, and the correct solution of many topical questions of political and social life."[24]

In July 1988, the credibility of social scientists was further enhanced by the issuance of a Central Committee resolution that confirmed sociology's new status as a policy science. The resolution explicitly linked the work of sociologists with the regime's efforts to carry out fundamental economic and political changes in Soviet society:

> [T]he pursuit of radical economic reform and an active social policy, the com-
> prehensive democratization of society, and the renewal of its spiritual and moral
> sphere require the intensification of the role of Marxist-Leninist sociology in the

provision of scientific support for restructuring, the solution of the key theoretical and practical problems of socialism, and the molding of socio-political thinking among the broad working masses. This makes qualitatively new demands on the development of sociology as a science and on the results of sociological research in the practical management of social processes.[25]

This resolution outlined a comprehensive plan to strengthen the profession of sociology by raising the standards of research in the field, developing a network of research and training facilities throughout the country as well as upgrading existing programs, and removing the obstacles which at present hinder the study of contemporary social issues.[26] The resolution marks an important first step toward institutionalizing the relationship between social scientists and policymakers by laying out the groundwork for a wide network of supporting research facilities.

The development of this network would not have been possible without General Secretary Gorbachev's personal endorsement of many of the positions espoused by the proreform social scientists. To begin, Gorbachev's view of Soviet society demonstrates an awareness of a complex pattern of mutually incompatible group interests, in contrast to past Soviet leaders' idealistic view of a society in which only "nonantagonistic" group interests existed. Gorbachev's remarks at the 27th Party Congress clearly expressed this view:

[A]nalyzing problems involved in the interrelationship of classes and social groups is of vital importance for a Marxist-Leninist party. The unity of socialist society by no means implies a leveling of public life. Socialism encourages diversity of people's interests, requirements and abilities, and vigorously supports the initiative of public organizations to express this diversity.[27]

At the January plenum in 1987, Gorbachev spoke about "social justice" in the same vein as the proreform social scientists:

Injustice had prevailed for decades drawing a pessimism from members of society, and has led to much of the alienation citizens feel from the State . . . The violation of the organic relationship between the measure of work and the measure of consumption, not only disfigures the attitude to work, holding back the growth of productivity, but leads to the distortion of the principle of socialist justice.[28]

Further, at the February plenum in 1988, Gorbachev delivered an address that provided an ideological foundation for many particular aspects of his *perestroika* reform agenda. He used this occasion to reaffirm that "the correct, consistent application of the socialist principle 'from each according to his ability, to each according to his work'" must be incorporated into society's system for the allocation of socioeconomic rewards.[29]

Not everyone in the Soviet Union accepts the desirability of redefining the offical understanding of social justice. Opponents of Gorbachev's policies assert that by permitting greater social inequality and relying more on market forces, the reformers are betraying socialism. "In my region," a collective farm worker recently complained to *Pravda*, "capitalism is being reborn . . . Some families now earn more than the whole of our brigade of metalworkers. If this continues, nothing will remain of socialism. If this is *perestroika* and democratization, I oppose it categorically."[30] A conservative economist, Mikhail Antonov, has accused some of Gorbachev's advisors—including Zaslavskaia and Leonid Abalkin—of "economism," a term coined by Lenin to attack opponents within the socialist movement who he considered vulgar Marxists, too bourgeois in their thinking.[31] In Antonov's view, the theories espoused by these reform economists willfully ignore the socialist ethic of equality, instead treating human beings as mere "labor resources." The program of market socialism, according to another ardent critic, will lead the Soviet Union to economic chaos as well as "intellectual and moral degradation."[32]

REFORM OF THE SOCIAL POLICY AGENDA

"Today," Gorbachev declared, "social policy is being advanced to the forefront."[33] According to the General Secretary, an "active social policy" is an integral component of *perestroika*. In contrast to past reform attempts in the Soviet Union, the present leadership views social reform as crucial for economic and political change. The leadership's immediate interest in social reform is instrumental: to overcome the continuing listlessness of the economy and to reverse the growing alienation of society from the regime. Since 1985, the social reforms that have appeared can be divided into four basic categories: (1) redefinition of the system of social welfare and income differentiation; (2) improvement of the quality of daily life in Soviet society; (3) promotion of norms of responsible social behavior; and (4) development of the necessary skills for an advancing industrial society.

Redefining the System of Social Welfare

The Soviet Union boasts one of the most comprehensive systems of social welfare coverage in the world today. Unlike most of the country's socioeconomic structure, the existing system of social welfare is not a vestige of the Stalin years; rather it evolved incrementally during the reigns of Stalin and Khrushchev, becoming fully developed under Brezhnev. The Soviet social welfare system includes three major provisions: first, direct compensation to those temporarily absent from their jobs as well as those permanently retired from the workforce; second, a generous and extensive subsidy program for many basic living necessities, including food and housing; third, an array of social guarantees for all citizens, including healthcare, education, and employment. In the 1980s, however, in the midst of a decline in economic productivity, the system of social welfare has become less an object of admiration for the political leadership and more a costly burden and obstacle to raising workers' productivity.

The leadership has been forced to reevaluate its economic commitment to the social welfare system. The Soviet press, in a break with former practices, has begun to speak critically about the enormous costs of maintaining the welfare state. *Izvestiia*, for example, reported that in the first half of 1987 alone over seventy-seven billion rubles were invested in social consumption funds, affecting education, healthcare, social security, social insurance, and housing subsidies.[34] This problem is in part the result of demographic changes in the Soviet workforce. As the population ages, there has been a marked increase in the number of citizens receiving pensions, disability and social security payments. By 1986, over 57 million people, almost one-fifth of the total population, were dependent on State pensions.[35] Soviet officials believe they must now reexamine the workability of the pension system as the number of retirees each year continues to outpace the number of new recruits coming into the workforce.[36]

Furthermore, certain aspects of the social welfare system indirectly hinder the Soviet Union's overall economic performance. The right to work, for example, has created the phenomenon of hidden unemployment throughout the economy, since many factories and collective farms are forced to retain more workers than are actually necessary. Consequently, in individual enterprises, the efforts of economic managers to improve efficiency and profitability are impeded by oversized staffs and, in general, the economy suffers from a gross underutilization of its available manpower. Another example of the social welfare system's negative effect on the economy is in its impact on workers' attitudes toward productivity. The social welfare system has tended to decrease initiative since so many socially valued services, such as housing and healthcare, are provided by the state and distributed on an administrative basis. The Soviet worker thus sees no direct linkage between personal productivity and the attainment of a better life.

To date, much of the discussion about social reform has focused on the need to redefine the parameters of responsibility of the Soviet welfare state. According to this view, the present reach of the system of social welfare services and benefits would have to be scaled back considerably. State expenditures for social welfare would be consolidated with the aim of establishing basic, but qualitative, levels of coverage for all of society. Socially valued services beyond these minimum guaranteed levels still would be available to Soviet citizens, but they would no longer be obtainable through the existing social welfare administrative process. Rather the more valued services would be distributed through market mechanisms. The purchasing power of individuals, in turn, would vary according to their personal productivity in the workplace. In this way, the reformers theorize, the Soviet welfare state would uphold its commitments to society, while at the same time become less of a burden on the economy.

These changes in the social welfare system, the leadership hopes, will instill greater initiative in the workforce. At the 18th Trade Union Congress, in February 1987, Gorbachev declared that "labor, and labor alone, should be the measure of a man's worth, his social prestige and material well-being."[37] Soviet officials have begun to work out a program of interconnected policy reforms which would bring Gorbachev's ideal into reality. In the first place, this program requires the scaling back of the State's enormous subsidy programs and the development of a network of paid social services beyond the basic level provided by the State. As described by one of the reform economists, Abel Aganbegian: "All citizens are equal in regard to guaranteed social benefits. But should anyone wish to get something over and above the social norm, he must pay 'full ruble' for it. This is the just socioeconomic approach."[38]

Accordingly, this program also calls for a comprehensive reform of the wage system that would both significantly increase the real wages received by workers and introduce greater income differentiation throughout the workforce.[39] The subject of wage reform and, in particular, its connection to worker productivity, was discussed at the 27th Party Congress: "It is necessary in order that the State's policies in the area of wages guarantee a strict dependence of wages to the quantity and quality of labor."[40] It is necessary to raise the real capital income of workers as the extent of state subsidized goods and services are scaled back and the number of paid services increases. The head of the Department of Wages in the State Committee for Labor and Social Affairs, Vladimir Shcherbakov, speaking about wage reform in late 1986, remarked that basic pay rates were expected to increase by 20 to 25 percent on average; although higher skill occupations would profit substantially more than lower skill ones.[41] In an interview in the Italian Communist Party's newspaper, *L'Unita*, Gorbachev defended the abandonment of wage leveling in favor of differentiation:

> Socialism cannot ensure living conditions and consumption that is identical for everyone. That will happen under communism. Under socialism the criterion for the distribution of social benefits is different "from each according to one's abilities, to each according to one's labor."[42]

Finally, this program entails the reexamination of the Soviet State's commitment to full employment. The Soviet economy's continuing low levels of labor productivity led to a revised employment policy that will be more responsive to job efficiency, instead of job security. Soviet economists have estimated that between ten to twenty million jobs will be eliminated before the turn of the century as existing enterprises and administrative agencies are streamlined.[43] Although many of these workers will either retire from the workforce or move into other jobs in the still developing service sector, it is likely that there will be at least transitional periods of unemployment. In anticipation of this, the notion of the right to work has been redefined so that it can no longer be considered an unconditional state guarantee. In the discussions on labor reform, new concepts have been introduced, such as "rational full employment" and "efficient employment," which directly link the right to work to economic productivity. An article appearing in *Kommunist* in late 1986, for example, offered the following qualification of the right to work:

> The principles of socialism are not principles of charity that automatically guarantee everyone a job regardless of his ability to work. A person should have to enter into an economic struggle every day to hold on to a job that is suited to his abilities.[44]

In January 1988, *Pravda* published a resolution on employment. Clarifying the leadership's position on the right to work, the resolution confirmed that labor policies must be governed henceforth by the notion of "efficient employment." Furthermore, a policy was outlined to ease the personal and systemic burdens caused by mass layoffs. The main features of this policy were the authorization of state-provided short-term unemployment compensation and the creation of a nationwide network of job placement centers to deal with the process of relocation and retraining displaced workers.[45]

Improving the Quality of Life

While Gorbachev's new approach to social policy emphasizes the need for each member of society to contribute productively, it also recognizes that the leadership must offer its constituents more in return for their work. To improve the quality of life in the Soviet Union the leadership has initiated several reforms intended to raise material living standards and improve the quality of healthcare.

The twin problems of providing better food and housing continue to plague the Soviet economy and generate pervasive social discontent. Despite substantial investments, agricultural production has not improved since the early 1970s. Although wages have risen steadily, there continue to be persistent shortages of goods, long queues, and periodic rationing for basic foodstuffs such as meat and butter. Some consumer commodities, such as shoes and children's clothing, are frequently in shortage, while those that are available are of poor quality. The persistence of these supply problems, admits A. P. Biriukova, the government's main spokeswoman on consumer affairs, inevitably affects the public's confidence in restructuring:

> The problems on whose solution [affects] the people's mood and vigor, and therefore their support for the party's political line, . . . are concentrated primarily in the social sphere . . . One of the most urgent of these problems is saturating the market with consumer goods and services.[46]

The consumer sphere of the economy is in a poor state according to Soviet planning officials. There are shortcomings in every sector: material, scientific, and technical, poor quality of raw materials, as well as the low status accorded to managers and workers in consumer and service industries. At the February plenum in 1988, Gorbachev stated that:

> The situation in the consumer market remains strained, and the population's effective demand is not being satisfied. Last year industry produced consumer goods worth 3.6 billion rubles less than envisaged in the plan.[47]

In August 1988, a resolution was adopted that stressed the need for providing a diverse supply of consumer goods. Coupled with increased investment, the reformers believe that greater reliance on market forces will alleviate the shortcomings in the consumer goods sector. To achieve this goal, an effort is underway to eliminate government subsidies for food production, introduce a thorough price reform, and permit private enterprise to play a larger role in satisfying the demand for consumer goods and services. Although these policies, if successful, will improve living standards in the long term, the leadership has been careful to assure the population that they will not suffer in the short term from inflation. At the 19th Party Conference, Gorbachev promised that "finances currently paid out by the State in the form of subsidies will be given to the population in full in the form of compensation."[48] Hence, higher food prices must be accompanied by a rise in wages, pensions, and student stipends. While recognizing the importance of meeting the material demands of the population, Soviet officials have thus far failed to increase the variety and quantity of consumer goods.

Another acute social problem for the Soviet leadership is its inability to provide an adequate and sufficient supply of housing to the Soviet population. A number of factors have contributed to the poor state of the housing sector, including shoddy construction, corruption in the allocation system, and an inefficient system of residential rent. As with the food problem, the Soviet leadership has indicated that the provision of adequte housing is an absolute necessity to give the labor force greater incentive to work harder and to support the reform program.

The inadequacy of the housing supply is illustrated by the fact that the number of new families that come into being each year is larger than the number of apartments constructed; in 1986, there were over 2.7 million new families, but only 2.1 million new apartments were built.[49] To remedy this, Gorbachev has pledged to provide every Soviet family with a separate apartment by the year 2000. Reaching this goal will require massive increases in construction; officials have estimated as much as 36 million apartments, or approximately 2.4 billion square meters of housing must be built.[50] In addition to increasing state investment in construction, Gorbachev intends to allow greater latitude for individuals and cooperatives to build housing. The plans also call for the lifting of other restrictions that have hindered the housing sector, including limitations on personal credit, building codes limiting the size of buildings, private ownership of housing, and reduction of state subsidies that serve to keep rents at roughly 3 percent of family budgets. The state is not considering a renunciation of the guarantee of a mini-

mum housing standard for all Soviet citizens, but in the future higher quality, larger, or better located accommodations will be priced at higher levels.

The priority Gorbachev puts on the improvement in Soviet health has
been visible since the onset of his tenure as General Secretary. At the 27th
Party Congress Gorbachev stated:

> For every person, and indeed for society, there is nothing more valuable than
> health. The maintenance and strengthening of people's health is a matter of pri-
> mary importance . . . It is necessary as quickly as possible to satisfy the demands
> of the population throughout the nation for high quality medical treatment, pre-
> ventive healthcare and pharmaceuticals.[51]

As a result of stagnation in the administration of health services and
diminishing allocation of resources to the Soviet health sector during the
past fifteen years, the state of healthcare in the Soviet Union today stands
at a primitive level. Poor organization in the administration of healthcare,
a deterioration in medical equipment and buildings, widespread corruption,
a failure to emphasize preventive medical care, and a deterioration in the
training and education of medical personnel are all contributing factors to
the overall poor quality of Soviet health services. It has been reported that
of the 4000 district hospitals in the USSR, 1000 of them do not have a
sewage system, 2500 do not have running hot water, and 700 are without
either hot or cold running water.[52] The Minister of Health has reported
that due to poor training, one-quarter of the doctors entering the field are
only marginally qualified to practice.[53] As a consequence, Soviet health
standards rank poorly compared with other industrialized countries. Life
expectancy has barely improved in the past two decades and is now about
sixty-nine years.[54] Infant mortality has actually increased from 22.9 deaths
per thousand in 1971 to 25.4 per thousand in 1986 according to official
statistics.[55] One health official is on record saying that in some regions
of the Soviet Union infant mortality rates are comparable to the levels in
Paraguay and Thailand,[56] or about forty-two deaths per thousand.

To reverse the deterioration of Soviet healthcare, the leadership hopes
to restore prestige and competence to the medical profession, emphasize
preventive healthcare, and grant more autonomy to medical institutions.
The stress on competence was demonstrated by the appointment of the
distinguished cardiologist and Nobel Laureate Evgenii Chazov as Minister
of Health in early 1987. In July of 1988, Chazov announced that capital
investment in the healthcare field was to be increased from nine billion
rubles per year to twenty-five billion.[57] Also in 1988, a new commission
was established to monitor incompetence and criminal negligence in the

medical profession, with the authority to close medical institutions with inefficient training facilities. Resolutions adopted by the Central Committee in August 1987 and June 1988 call for pay increases for medical personnel and stress the need for medical personnel to focus on the quality of care they give, and not the quantity of patients they see. Improving the quality of education and training of medical personnel by incorporating recent achievements in medical science and research into the daily care of the public has also been stressed by the new appointees at the Ministry of Health. In August 1987, the Central Committee and the Council of Ministers adopted a resolution that promised annual medical examinations for the entire Soviet population by 1995.[58]

Soviet officials have addressed the issue of cost efficiency in healthcare. Following the process underway in other parts of the economy, hospitals and clinics are now expected to operate on the basis of *khozrachet*, or financial cost-accounting. In the future, the budgets of medical establishments will be based on the size of the population they serve. Clinics and hospitals will also be required to pay for additional care necessitated by mistakes such as faulty diagnoses. The new system "will make it possible to organize the treatment process in such a way that the patient's state of health and the effectiveness of his treatment will have a direct bearing on the material well-being of the doctor and the medical establishment as a whole.[59] Experiments are also being conducted to test the effectiveness of paid medical services; such services at present represent less than 5 percent of the total, but plans call for this figure to increase as medical centers become financially autonomous.[60] The first fee-charging hospital, specializing in surgery, opened in Moscow in 1987.[61] Despite the stress on introducing more market mechanisms into the healthcare system, officials maintain that the socialist guarantee of free healthcare is not being threatened:

> Free Medical Service is one of the greatest gains of socialism, and the principle of free treatment is emphasized and runs right through the entire decision. Of course, certain sections of fee-charged medical services are to be expanded, if our self-financing institutions are to be expanded, but they amount to a small percentage of the total volume of provisions of medical assistance in the country.[62]

Raising the Norms of Personal Responsibility

Another element of the leadership's social reform program is the campaign to encourage responsible social behavior. Official attitudes towards alcohol and drug use reflect the leadership's desire for a better disciplined and sober population. Almost immediately upon taking power, Gorbachev initiated an anti-alcohol drive, relying on drastic measures to reduce liquor consumption. Starting in May 1985, the state cut back production of vodka, cognac, and fruit wine,[63] and wine production was to be phased out entirely by 1988. The number of liquor store outlets and sales hours were reduced. The legal drinking age was raised to twenty-one years. As a further deterrent to buyers, prices rose 15 to 20 percent in 1985 and 20 to 25 percent a year later.[64] Meanwhile, the authorities instituted stricter penalties for drinking on the job and in public as well as for illegal production or trade of alcohol. Despite these measures, a shadow alcohol industry developed to supply the Soviet population with *samogon*, homemade liquor. Evidence suggests that illicit distilling increased by as much as 40 percent[65] and is believed to have caused the widespread sugar shortages that have necessitated rationing throughout the country. While the production of *samogon* has always been illegal, penalties for engaging in this activity have become more severe; monetary fines, for example, were raised from 100 to 200 rubles. In 1987, 3.6 million liters of home brew were confiscated, along with 167,000 home stills.

Without corresponding improvements in other aspects of the quality of life, such as consumer goods, the public has come to view the anti-alcohol campaign as yet another sacrifice imposed arbitrarily from above with no discernable benefits. In some respects the policy has backfired because problem drinkers have turned to *samogon*, or other sometimes lethal concoctions, while social drinkers must endure frustrating queues or turn to the black market. Although the campaign was credited with reducing the death rate, it has not improved labor productivity or enhanced respect for law and order. In September 1988, government officials tacitly admitted that the anti-alcohol campaign had failed when they agreed to increase state alcohol production and lengthen liquor store hours. A few weeks later a *Sovetskaia Rossiia* article attacked the anti-alcohol program by describing the futile efforts of one factory to combat alcoholism; it noted that the campaign had not reduced on-the-job drinking and that *samogon*—some of it produced at the factory—was widely available.[66]

The Soviet government's response to the growing problem of illicit narcotics has in some respects been even less enlightened than the anti-alcohol effort. Drug abusers, primarily hashish and opium addicts, are supposed to register with the police; however, since drug use is a criminal offense and registrants are subject to mandatory rehabilitation, only 52,000 of the Soviet Union's addicts have registered. This policy reflects the government's ambivalence about whether drug abuse should be considered principally as a medical or criminal problem. There is a severe shortage of facilities for drug treatment; at last count there were only 31 hospitals and 410 clinics equipped to treat drug addiction in the Soviet Union.[67] To restrict the production of narcotics, the Soviets have tried to discourage cultivation of poppies and the harvesting of hemp, which grows wild throughout much of Kazakhstan. The police have also made large scale arrests in an attempt to break up the distribution networks established by organized crime.[68]

Some Soviet officials are beginning to acknowledge the importance of high-quality treatment programs in the struggle against drug abuse. Before the existence of the drug problem was acknowledged, in 1986, there were no trained specialists to treat drug abusers, yet by mid-1987, even officials of the militia, the Soviet Union's civilian police force, were stressing the important role of quality, anonymous treatment for addicts in the struggle against narcotic abuse.[69]

Developing Skills For An Advancing Industrial Society

The Soviet leadership has indicated that the reform of the Soviet educational system constitutes one of the highest priorities in the restructuring of society. This commitment is illustrated by the Central Committee plenum held in February 1988 devoted exclusively to educational reform. The leadership recognized that a key element contributing to the long-term success of *perestroika* will be the leadership's ability to correct the major failings that have developed in the educational system over the last two decades. In his address to the February plenum, General Secretary Gorbachev stated that, "the future of socialism depends, without exaggeration, on the teaching and instruction of the new man."[70] Higher productivity and techno-logical advancement of the economy are closely linked to the reform of the educational system. The increased complexity of Soviet industry and technology has created a high demand for an educated and highly skilled labor force. Accordingly, the retraining of workers already in the workforce and the training of new workers is of fundamental importance if workers are to take advantage of the latest technological changes and improvements. At the plenum, Ligachev asserted that "without major changes in the public education system, without the whole of society turning toward the urgent problems in this area, we cannot achieve a rapid pace of creative work, cannot start climbing steeply uphill."[71]

The troubled state of education in the USSR can be attributed to the low priority given by the government and the inadequate budget devoted to education during the last two decades. In 1970, 11 percent of the national budget was allocated to education, and by 1986 this figure had diminished to 8 percent. School buildings are inadequate in many regions of the country. It is estimated that 21 percent of all schools in the Soviet Union do not have central heating, while 30 percent lack running water, and 40 percent have no indoor toilets.[72]

The February 1988 education plenum also affirmed the need for providing secondary education to all citizens in the Soviet Union. The resolutions approved at the plenum called for the development of a system that would allow for a process of continuing education and retraining that would enable all citizens to stay informed about the latest technologies. To achieve this will require greater cooperation between educational institutions and enterprises. The plenum affirmed that educational institutions must gain more independence both financially and administratively and that there should be more public involvement in education through new advisory councils including students, labor collectives, social organizations, teachers, and parents. In this spirit, the plenum also called on educational institutions to elect their leaders democratically. There was in addition a call for improvement in training of teaching cadres and to raise the prestige of the teaching profession through salary increases and a media campaign.

The head of the National Education Committee, Gennadii Iagodin, has stated that the restructuring of education will take 12 to 15 years. The first priority on the agenda is the modernization and rationalization of educational institutions engaged in training specialists for industry and new technology. This program of special training will be financed by funds from industries. The educational institutions will finance part of the activity themselves, by soliciting orders from enterprises for the education and training of specialists and the carrying out of scientific experiments. The leadership's emphasis on institutional accountability, teacher competence and skills training for a high-tech economy is consistent with goals in other areas of social and economic reform.

In addition to redefining the mission of secondary and higher education to meet the technical needs of society, the Soviets are also laying the groundwork for a system of job retraining centers and placement bureaus to assist workers moving from smokestack industries to employment demanding higher technical skills. These proposals are outlined in the resolution on employment approved by the Central Committee and the Council of Ministers in January 1988.[73]

UNINTENDED SOCIAL CONSEQUENCES OF *PERESTROIKA*

Gorbachev has equated the process of *perestroika* with a revolution, initiated from above, and arousing active participation from below. The most significant policies to emerge from *perestroika*—radical economic reform, *glasnost*, and democratization—involve a devolution of decision-making responsibilities and an enhanced role for popular input in the management of Soviet society. Central political authorities, of course, never intended that these policies would undermine their own control over the direction and scope of the reform program. Gorbachev himself has stated that "*perestroika* is not a spontaneous, but a governed process."[74] The magnitude of this program as well as the nature of the reforms themselves make it almost inevitable that central guidance over the process of change will weaken at some point. There is already evidence that *perestroika* has resulted in unintended consequences that serve to complicate and frustrate the regime's reform efforts. Two of the most serious unintended social consequences of Gorbachev's *perestroika* include the increasing assertiveness of various social and ethnic groups and in the raising of popular expectations throughout society.

As an industrial, multinational society, the Soviet Union contains a wide cross-section of social groups and subgroupings, defined by economic, professional, cultural, and regional criteria. Throughout most of Soviet history, the regime has used both organizational and coercive means to prevent such groups from pursuing their own interests and activities independently. *Perestroika* has ushered in, at least temporarily, a period of loosened central control and a public debate on what the prerogatives of central authority in Soviet society should be. In this atmosphere, a surge of spontaneous activity has emerged from various social groups. Some of these groups want to establish a greater degree of autonomy and self identity within Soviet society. Two social groups, in particular, the non-Russian nationality groups and the informal voluntary clubs, have taken full advantage of *perestroika* in this regard and, consequently, have created a new set of unanticipated problems for the leadership.

Non-Russian nationality groups pose perhaps the most serious threat to the reform process now underway in the Soviet Union. For the leadership, the devolution of decision-making powers on important economic and political matters entails the risk that local non-Russian authorities will act in the interest of their own ethnic enclaves and disregard centrally planned goals. Gorbachev addressed this concern during a visit to Yugoslavia in early 1988: "We are developing the initiative of the republics, but we have to maintain a regulating role at the center to safeguard against mistakes."[75] It is therefore surprising that after three and one-half years the Soviet Union's new leadership team has yet to put forth a coherent nationalities policy; instead, official statements on the nationalities issue are a mixture of idealism, persuasion, and threats. The remarks of General Secretary Gorbachev are typical in this respect, reflecting both vagueness and anxiety: "National feelings of people should be respected, and cannot be ignored. But speculating on them amounts to political irresponsibility, if not a crime. It is a tradition of our Party to combat any manifestations of nationalist narrow-mindedness and chauvinism."[76] In a break with the practices of Brezhnev's rule, central political authorities have assumed a much stronger interventionist role in the political affairs of the non-Russian regions, carrying out a series of purges of ethnic political machines and imposing solutions on ethnic-related conflicts. This approach constitutes a preemptive effort by the leadership to assure that the non-Russian regions of the country demonstrate sufficient accountability to the center during the implementation of the various aspects of *perestroika*.

Despite stern warnings, non-Russian nationality groups have used the opportunity created by *perestroika* to secure greater autonomy over their own affairs and to redress past grievances against central political authority. Many of these efforts have focused on obtaining official sanction for the public expression of elements from their own native cultures, including: the greater use of native languages in schools and official discourse; the rehabilitation of ethnic authors and literary works; and the restoration of suppressed historical figures and episodes. In economic affairs, several ethnic republics have sought to rid themselves of their obligations to the nationwide, five-year economic plans. Uzbekistan, for example, has tried to relinquish its "internationalist duty" to provide cotton to the rest of the Soviet Union so that Uzbek peasants can plant more profitable food crops.[77] In both Lithuania and Estonia, national interest groups have advocated turning their regions into "economically sovereign republics."[78] Ethnic republics also have demanded the revision of central economic plans out of a growing concern for the ecological damages that have been inflicted upon native lands and resources.

The political challenges of the non-Russian nationalities have created the most serious problems for central authorities. Under Gorbachev, the regime has assumed a generally more tolerant attitude toward popular demonstrations and displays of civil disobedience. The reluctance of authorities to employ force has permitted an outlet for ethnic groups to vent their frustrations toward the centralized, Russian-dominated Soviet system. Displays of ethnic dissatisfaction have ranged from the relatively mild public protests from small ethnic groups, such as Crimean Tatars and Jewish dissidents, to the peaceful mass demonstrations that have occurred in all three Baltic republics, to Estonia's Constitutional challenge to the authority of Moscow in regional affairs, to the incidents of violent protest, including the outbreak of riots in Kazakhstan, in reaction to Moscow's purge of the republic's ethnic leaders, and the prolonged and bloodied conflict between Armenians and Azerbaijanis.

The mass demonstrations and ethnic violence that have rocked the Soviet Transcaucasus have become a critical test for Gorbachev's reform program. Azerbaijani control of the Nagorno-Karabakh region of the Transcaucasus, which has a majority of Armenian residents, has long been a source of resentment for Soviet Armenians. In February of 1988, this simmering resentment of Armenians finally erupted. Following the Politburo's formal rejection of the local Soviets' call for reunification with the Armenian republic, a series of mass protests began in the Armenian capital city of Erevan, involving street demonstrations, estimated in the hundreds of thousands, industrial strikes, and school boycotts. Similar scenes were played out on a smaller scale in other Armenian cities and in the disputed region of Nagorno-Karabakh. These demonstrations provoked outbursts of ethnic violence in both republics, including riots in the Azerbaijani city of Sumgait in which over twenty-five Armenians were killed.[79] The central leadership undertook a series of measures over the following weeks in an effort to placate hostilities and restore order to the region: a package of substantial economic grants was put together for Nagorno-Karabakh;[80] a number of local political officials were replaced, including the first secretaries of both republic party organizations; Soviet armed troops were moved into the area as a show of force; and several of the most prominent figures in the Armenian demonstrations were arrested.[81] Nonetheless, in May, the sentencing of a young

Azerbaijani accused of murder in the Sumgait riots to fifteen years in prison sparked a new wave of mass demonstrations in both republics and a general strike in Stepanakert, the capital city of the Nagorno-Karabakh region, that paralyzed the city for over a month.

The leadership's worst fears of losing control of the reform process were realized with the events in the Transcaucasus. At a special session of the Supreme Soviet convened in July of 1988 to discuss the Nagorno-Karabakh crisis, Gorbachev addressed this issue:

> *Perestroika* requires democratization and *glasnost*, but we can see in this case how under the banner of democratization shameless pressure is being applied by irresponsible people on work collectives and on the populations of republics and how bodies of power, including the USSR Supreme Soviet Presidium, are coming under pressure as well . . . Just look at the forms of pressure they are using: nonstop mass demonstrations, rallies, and, finally, strikes. In other words, we can see that democratic rights and the new conditions opened up and created by perestroika are being exploited for antidemocratic purposes.[82]

Although this meeting of the Supreme Soviet promised a compromise solution to the Nagorno-Karabakh crisis, the proceedings offered no indication that a more clearly defined nationalities policy would be forthcoming.

In addition to the non-Russian nationality groups, the leadership has been forced to contend with another unanticipated social phenomenon—the informal groups. The spontaneous emergence of these informal associations and clubs is one of the most remarkable developments of the reform process in Soviet society. For State officials, *perestroika* has created an atmosphere of uncertainty and a hesitancy to take action against many formerly banned social activities. It is this uneasy tolerance, above all else, which has made the proliferation of informal groups possible. In the evolution of State-societal relations in the Soviet Union, the emergence of the independent informal groups represents a historic challenge: an attempt on the part of societal elements to reclaim the right of association away from the Soviet State. The final outcome of this challenge has enormous implications for the fate of *perestroika* itself as these informal groups have the potential to provide the social basis of support for reform policies that would curb the responsibilities of the state and enhance those of civil society.

From the sixties through the early eighties, a small number of unsanctioned informal associations appeared in Soviet society; the activities of such groups, however, were limited by the intimidating tactics of police officials.

Since General Secretary Gorbachev introduced his reform agenda for the Soviet Union, there has been a phenomenal growth in the number of informal groups. As of March 1987, *Pravda* estimated that the number of newly created informal associations had reached the thousands.[83] Informal groups have been created around a variety of interests; most of the groups fall into one of seven categories: ecology and environmental conservation; history and preservation of cultural monuments; professional associations; leisure activities; nationality issues; youth clubs; and, sociopolitical concerns. There is as yet no comprehensive study of membership compositions of the informal groups; nonetheless, the available fragmentary information suggests some common traits. The members are generally young, usually in their twenties, professionally trained, and residents of urban areas. Aside from the non-Russian nationalities, the largest memberships belong to the ecological and conservation groups. Leningrad's Episentr, an umbrella association for a number of environmental groups, claims a membership that runs into the thousands. The most numerous groups are the youth clubs, although they report the smallest individual memberships. One poll conducted by Soviet sociologists showed that in Moscow more than 70 percent of the youth clubs have less than twenty regular members.[84] The informal associations exist across the Soviet Union from Siberia to the Baltics, but they are concentrated in the largest cities, particularly Leningrad and Moscow.

The Soviet press has covered both sides of the debate about the proper role and place of informal associations in Soviet society. Those who are encouraged by the emergence of the informal groups and favor limited State control argue that they are a necessary and natural result of the reform policies of the leadership. One of the most prominent defenders of the informal groups is Boris Rakitskii, vice president of the Soviet Sociological Association. He has described the phenomenon of the informal groups as "the first sign of the awakening of [Soviet] society."[85] In an article appearing in *Moscow News*, Rakitskii stated that "The expansion and deepening of democracy is directly connected to the expansion and deepening of unofficial sociopolitical movements, which are a form of activating the masses."[86] A leading spokesman for the environmental group Delta, P. Kozhevnikov, argued that his association was providing an important service to the Soviet public and helping to keep *glasnost* alive: "People have a right to know what kind of water they are drinking, and what kind of air they are breathing. Down with secret departmental projects, which threaten the health, perhaps the lives, of millions of people."[87]

Most of the attacks on the informal groups have come from the representatives of several political bureaucracies: the Communist Youth League (the Komsomol); the provincial and local Party organizations; and the two police organizations, the militia and the KGB. Criticism of informal groups is most often aimed at discrediting their leaders and alleging that these groups are being used as a platform for "anti-State" activities. An article in *Komsomolskaia Pravda*, for example, referred to the organizers of youth clubs as "imposters" and "social imitators," who are seeking "to lead young people into clannishness and away from large-scale and socially important deeds."[88] An official from the Leningrad provincial Party organization, N. Larionov, who has become an authoritative spokesman for the opponents of the informal groups, warned that "politickers are attaching themselves to a movement . . . people who are natural leaders, but failed leaders, people with ruined lives, people who are malicious and hostile."[89] In Leningrad, where the informal groups are probably the most active, party officials are wary about where this phenomenon is likely to lead; this fear was clearly expressed at a plenary session of the provincial Party organization: "Have we let this process get out of control? Are we not conniving at the spread of harmful views?"[90] In a major address delivered in the autumn of 1987, then KGB head Viktor Chebrikov suggested that "foreign subversive centers" were attempting to influence the members of informal groups into "antisocial positions and onto the path of hostile activity." Chebrikov went on to assert that "we have examples of extremist elements penetrating the leadership of certain independent associations," who wish "to perpetrate actions objectively aimed against our society's interests."[91]

The concerns of Soviet officialdom about the informal groups are not groundless. As the State's domination over civil society is gradually relaxed, previously suppressed or muted interests and demands find new vehicles for expression, which, subsequently, can become politicized. For the leadership, the danger exists that the transition period may embolden social movements that threaten to undermine the authority of the State. Some of the new informal groups have an expressly political agenda, calling for radical changes in the Soviet political system that are well beyond the leadership's vision of political reform. The Leningrad informal group *Perestroika*, for example, has consistently pressed for political and legal reforms and the introduction of "real socialism." Similary, the Moscow group, *Spassenie*, has demanded that the regime respect Soviet society's right of "freedom of assembly."[92] The most serious challenge, however, has come from two groups, claiming to be alternative political parties. The first such association, the Estonian National Independent Party, appeared in January 1988, but was quickly suppressed by the authorities and its leaders were exiled to the West.[93] The second self-proclaimed opposition party, the Democratic-Union, also has incurred the wrath of Soviet officialdom. The Democratic-Union was formed in early May 1988 in Moscow, comprised of over one hundred representatives of various informal groups from across the Soviet Union. Before this founding conference could complete its work, however, police authorities broke up the proceedings, arrested some of the participants, and sent the rest back to their hometowns. The leaders of the Democratic-Union have issued a political platform that includes: the abolition of the one-party system; freedom of the press; independence for trade unions; private ownership in the economy; the elimination of obligatory military service; and, the removal of Soviet armed forces from Eastern Europe, the Baltic states, and the Western Ukraine.[94]

In the absence of a clearly defined policy on the informal groups, official responses to their activities have combined restraint, watchfulness, and harassment. The description of a member of a Leningrad informal group would seem apt: "the fate of the movement depends entirely on the goodwill of the authorities, it seems to me that one principle is acceptable: Do nothing damaging."[95] The leadership has formed a commission for the task of creating a draft law, which would establish recognizable codes of behavior for both informal groups and State officials. The commission, which operated under the auspices of the Ministry of Justice, completed a draft at the end of 1987, but this draft has never circulated publicly in the Soviet Union. This particular draft has been sharply criticized for its numerous restrictions on the informal groups, such as granting governmental ministries the authority to intervene in their affairs.[96] A much different view of this law, stressing the limits on the State's activities instead of the informal groups, was expressed in the Theses for the 19th Party Conference:

> There is a need to formulate right now a legal basis for the operation of social organizations, voluntary societies and independent associations. The political criterion to go by is that any social activity should be recognized as long as it stays within the Constitution and does not jeopardize the progress of our Soviet socialist society.[97]

Through the summer of 1988, divisions within the leadership continued to hold up the issuance of a draft law on the informal groups that would provide a clearer indication of the limits of the State's tolerance of Soviet society's "right of association."

Another unintended social consequence of *perestroika*, which ultimately may harm the progress of reform, is the rise of popular expectations. The social reforms so crucial to *perestroika* have promised Soviet citizens a higher standard of living, more suitable living accommodations and a just system of reward and advancement; however, the ability of the Soviet economy to achieve these goals anytime in the near future is most unlikely. *Perestroika* and *glasnost* have focused much attention on the neglect that the social sphere has long experienced. General Secretary Gorbachev has emphasized reinvigoration of the social sphere as a necessary precondition for the success of the reform movement. The costs for these social programs are substantial and will require a considerable reallocation of state funds. Given the leadership's priority for modernization of the productive base of the economy, it is likely that well-intentioned social programs, such as housing construction and upgrading the healthcare system, will remain underfinanced. The preliminary reports on the results of the current five-year plan indicate that many social programs will fall well short of their original targets.[98]

If *perestroika* does not live up to the claims it has made about raising the quality of life for Soviet citizens, then popular attitudes toward the reform movement are likely to grow more negative and cynical. There is already some evidence from Soviet sociologists studying public opinion and the reform movement that such dissatisfaction is on the increase. A comparison of the results of two surveys involving 11,000 industrial workers and collective farmers, one conducted in 1986 and the other in 1987, showed a marked increase in the number of respondents who felt that *perestroika* was neither leading to any improvement in their own lives, nor forcing official organizations to work more efficiently. The conclusions drawn by Zh. Toshchenko, a professor in the Central Committee's Social Science Academy and a vice president of the Soviet Sociological Association, identified this growing pessimism as an adverse reaction to the unrealized expectations of Soviet citizens:

> [P]eople judge real change in the life of society by the changes which take place in their own lives and which concern them directly . . . An absence of these changes is fraught with the danger that faith in perestroika will be undermined . . . [and] a second braking mechanism may come into play: Unconfirmed expectations of radical change will develop into greater skepticism and public apathy.[99]

So much of the success of the reform movement depends on *perestroika's* ability to motivate Soviet citizens to assume greater responsibility and more positive attitudes toward their own roles in society, and especially in the workforce. If the rhetoric of *perestroika*, however, continues to outpace its accomplishments, then *perestroika* will become an increasingly meaningless concept in people's lives.

Notes

1. *Narodnoe khoziaistvo SSSR za 70 let* (Moscow: Financy i Statiska, 1987), p. 373.
2. *Demograficheskii entsiklopedicheskii slovar* (Moscow: Sovetskaia Entsklopedia, 1985), pp. 430–37.
3. *Narodnoe khoziaistvo*, p. 523.
4. Ellen Mickiewicz, "Making the Media Work: Soviet Society and Communications," in Maurice Friedberg and Heyward Isham, eds., *Soviet Society Under Gorbachev* (New York: M. E. Sharpe, 1987), p. 132.
5. *Narodnoe khoziaistvo*, p. 574.
6. Ibid., p. 11.
7. Moshe Lewin, *The Gorbachev Phenomenon* (Berkeley: University of California Press, 1988), pp. 51–52.
8. Alex Inkeles and Raymond Bauer, *The Soviet Citizen: Daily Life in a Totalitarian Society* (Cambridge, MA: Harvard University Press, 1959), pp. 254, 274, 275.
9. Ibid., pp. 260, 273–280.
10. James R. Millar, ed., *Work and Daily Life in the USSR: A Survey of Former Soviet Citizens* (Cambridge, UK: Cambridge University Press, 1987), pp. 52–53, 95.
11. Inkeles and Bauer, pp. 138, 235, 252, 260.
12. Millar, pp. 117–118.
13. Millar, p. 131; Inkeles and Bauer, pp. 179–180.
14. Millar, pp. 42, 130; Inkeles and Bauer, pp. 117, 171.
15. Miller, p. 327; Inkeles and Bauer, p. 266.
16. Mikhail S. Gorbachev, *Perestroika: New Thinking for Our Country and the World* (New York: Harper & Row, 1987), p. 17.
17. O. I. Shkaratan, *Problemy sotsial'noe struktury radichego klassa SSSR* (Moscow: "Mysl," 1976); and S. A. Kugel, *Novoe izuchenii Sotsial'noi Struktury Obshchestra* (Leningrad: Obshestvo "Znanie" RSFSR, 1968). (These represent two examples of the early efforts of Soviet social scientists to present a more sophisticated view of Soviet society.)

36   GERALD M. EASTER AND ANNE M. GRUBER

18. Tatiana Zaslavskaia, "Sotsial'naia spravedlivost i chelovecheskii faktor ekonomicheskogo razvitiia," *Kommunist* no. 13 (September 1986): p. 66.
19. Ibid.
20. M. I. Piskotin, "The Soviet Executive," as translated in *Soviet Government and Law* vol. 26 no. 3 (Winter 1987–1988): p. 44.
21. As quoted in *The Christian Science Monitor*, 3 December 1987, pp. 18–19.
22. *Trud*, 29 March 1988.
23. Tatiana Zaslavskaia, "The Novisibirsk Report," *Survey* vol. 28 no. 1 (Spring 1984): pp. 92–94.
24. *Pravda*, 18 March 1988.
25. Ibid., 12 June 1988.
26. Ibid.
27. Mikhail S. Gorbachev, *Selected Speeches and Articles* (Moscow: Progress, 1987), p. 401.
28. *Pravda*, 28 January 1987.
29. Ibid., 19 February 1988.
30. Ibid., 24 September 1988.
31. Mikhail Antonov, "Idt-l svoim putem," *Molodaia Gvardiia* no. 1 (January 1988): p. 198. See also *Sovetskaia Rossiia*, 7 August 1988.
32. Aleksandr Truhkin, "Sem raz otmeri," *Molodaia Gvardiia* no. 1 (January 1988): p. 221.
33. Gorbachev, *Perestroika*, p. 103.
34. *Izvestiia*, 10 October 1988.
35. "Sotsial'no-demograficheskii portret strani sovetov," *Ekonomicheskaia gazeta*, no. 46, November 1987: p. 18.
36. *Pravda*, 12 September 1986.
37. Ibid., 26 February 1987.
38. *Moskovskie Novosti*, no. 35, 6–13 September 1987, p. 5.
39. *Trud*, 22 November 1987.
40. Gorbachev, *Selected Speeches*, p. 396.
41. Foreign Broadcast Information Service: Daily Report, *Soviet Union* (FBIS-Sov), 1 December 1986, pp. R1, R2.
42. Reprinted in *Pravda*, 20 May 1987.
43. *Sovetskaia kultura*, 4 January 1986; and *Izvestiia*, 21 January 1988.
44. S. Shatalin, "Sotsial'noe razvitie i ekonomicheskii rost," *Kommunist*, no. 14 (September 1986): p. 63.
45. *Pravda*, 19 January 1988.
46. FBIS-Sov, 22 July 1988, p. 53.
47. *Pravda*, 19 February 1988.
48. Ibid., 29 June 1988.
49. *Narodnoe khoziaistvo*, p. 510; and, *Ekonomicheskaia gazeta*, no. 46, November 1987, pp. 18–19.

50. *Izvestiia*, 27 May 1988.
51. Gorbachev, *Selected Speeches*, pp. 399, 400.
52. B. Bolotin, "A More Complete Picture," *Moscow News* no. 11, 20–27 March 1988, p. 9.
53. *Trud*, 24 March 1987.
54. *Narodnoe khoziaistvo*, p. 409.
55. Ibid., pp. 404–409.
56. *Sovetskaia Rossiia*, 23 October 1987.
57. *Izvestiia*, 7 July 1988.
58. *Pravda*, 15 August 1987.
59. *Izvestiia*, 6 January 1988.
60. Radio Free Europe/Radio Liberty (RFE/RL), *Radio Liberty Research Bulletin*, 367/87.
61. *Moskovskie Novosti*, no. 35, 6–13 September 1987, p. 14.
62. FBIS-Sov, 25 November 1987, pp. 48, 49.
63. Vladimir Treml, "Gorbachev's Anti-Drinking Campaign," RFE/RL, *Supplement*, 2/87, pp. 10–11.
64. Ibid., p. 9.
65. Ibid., p. 15.
66. FBIS-Sov, 28 September 1988, p. 59.
67. *Trud*, 3 August 1988.
68. Sergei Voronityn, "The First Year of the Campaign Against Drug Addiction in the USSR," RFE/RL, 70/87, pp. 2–3.
69. *Izvestiia*, 13 May 1987.
70. *Pravda*, 19 February 1988.
71. Ibid., 18 February 1988.
72. Felicity Barringe, "Soviet Schools Sharply Faulted by Top Officials," *The New York Times*, 18 February 1988, p. A1.
73. *Pravda*, 19 January 1988.
74. Gorbachev, *Perestroika*, p. 56.
75. *The Washington Post*, 16 March 1988, p. A18.
76. Gorbachev, *Perestroika*, p. 121.
77. A. Minkin, "Zaraza Ubiistvennaia," *Ogonek*, no. 13 (March 1988): pp. 26–27, and *Izvestiia*, 22 April 1988.
78. See, for example, FBIS-Sov, 13 July 1988, p. 65.
79. E. Fuller, "New Demonstrations in Armenia and Azerbaijan Exemplify Polarization of Views over Nagorno-Karabakh," RFE/RL, 220/88, p. 1.
80. *Izvestiia*, 25 March 1988.
81. V. Tolz, "The USSR This Week," RFE/RL, 139/88, pp. 1–2.
82. *Pravda*, 20 July 1988.
83. Ibid., 30 March 1987.
84. *Izvestiia*, 17 May 1988.

85. *Sotsialisticheskaia industriia*, 21 June 1988.
86. *Moskovskie Novosti*, no. 19, 8 May 1988, p. 10.
87. *Sotsialisticheskaia industriia*, 21 June 1988.
88. FBIS-Sov, 31 January 1988.
89. *Sotsialisticheskaia industriia*, 21 June 1988.
90. Ibid.
91. *Pravda*, 11 September 1987.
92. FBIS-Sov, 24 May 1988, pp. 62, 63.
93. Vela Tolz, "Creation of the Democratic Union," RFE/RL, 189/88, p. 5.
94. Ibid., pp. 2–3.
95. FBIS-Sov, 7 July 1988, p. 78.
96. *Izvestiia*, 17 May 1988.
97. *Pravda*, 27 May 1988.
98. See, for example, the speech by Leonid Abalkin at the 19th Party Conference, in FBIS, 30 June 1988, pp. 4–7.
99. *Sotsialisticheskaia industriia*, 9 February 1988.

2 POLITICAL REFORM IN GORBACHEV'S RUSSIA

Gerald M. Easter

The rise of Mikhail Sergeevich Gorbachev to the highest political post in the USSR has excited much interest in the outside world to the plight of the Soviet regime as it enters its eighth decade. The Soviet Union is seen to be at a crossroads, with its future course still to be determined. In the West, in particular, there has been widespread attention to Gorbachev as an individual, to his innovations to Soviet domestic life, and to his ideas about war and peace. For many, who have long held the view of the Soviet Union as the chief nemesis to Western security, this moment in history appears to provide new and unexpected opportunities for improved Soviet-Western relations. The internal changes taking place under Gorbachev, however, have raised many themes that are familiar to Soviet and Russian society in the twentieth century: the search for a solid social base for political authority; the effort to realize new methods of economic modernization, to avert the consequences from falling too far behind the West; and, the dilemma of the reforming autocrat, whose tenuous mandate for change must overcome the seemingly pervasive forces of conservatism, cynicism, and apathy. The crossroad at which Gorbachev now stands offers a point of departure from the politically inert and economically stagnant final phase of Brezhnev's rule. Still, Brezhnev's long respite followed a half century of tumultuous change and extraordinary devastation. Gorbachev's attempt to rekindle and enlist the dynamic elements in Soviet society for a long-term, evolutionary program of change has not been welcomed by all. The General Secretary's statements and policies already have aroused dramatic confrontations. The prospects for the success of Gorbachev's program of domestic political reform are best understood in the context of long-range goals, the structural setting for reform, and the actual process of carrying out change.

LONG-RANGE GOALS

Since the April plenum in 1985, when Gorbachev confirmed his commitment for reform, the policy agendas of Soviet officials have become crowded with new initiatives. Western observers overtaken by the pace of events should not despair, since most Soviet administrators have found themselves in a similar position. The reform movement now underway is far-reaching, encompassing all major policy areas of Soviet society. The domestic front in particular has been the scene of some of the better known policy innovations: *glasnost, demokratizatsiia*, and *perestroika*. The proposed domestic political changes are connected with the reform efforts in other policy areas. Reform of the country's internal political processes, in fact, was driven by two other leadership concerns: the failing productivity of the Soviet economy and the impending decline of Soviet Great Power status in the international arena.

The Soviet Union entered the 1980s haunted by the specter of economic stagnation. The reinvigoration of the economy lies at the core of much of the reform activity now occurring throughout Soviet society. The plans, hopes, and ambitions of the present leadership as the Soviet Union heads toward the twenty-first century are linked to a reversal of the declining output levels that have persisted across the different sectors of the economy in the 1980s. A quarter century ago, Nikita Khrushchev boasted that socialism would be outproducing capitalism in just two decades; instead, the Soviet economy has lost its former dynamism as the methods and machinery of its earlier successful days have grown obsolete. This decline raises an issue for the regime with serious long-term consequences: What is the fate of socialism as a system of economic and political organization if it cannot match the productive strength of capitalism? Gorbachev himself has spoken in such terms: "[W]e shall achieve a substantial acceleration of socioeconomic progress. There is simply no other way . . . The country's historic destiny, the position of socialism in the world today in large measure depends on how we shall act next."[1] The present reform movement is also driven by the fear that the Soviet Union was in jeopardy of losing its Great Power status, achieved at high cost under Brezhnev, having never fully realized the expectations of an enhanced global role. In the 1980s, conservative and defense-minded governments came to power in the West, threatening to raise the ante on Soviet defense expenditures with the introduction of more technologically sophisticated weapon systems. This threat was compounded by the impaired state of the Soviet economy. The present leadership, including Gorbachev, has no desire to preside over the waning of Soviet Great Power status. In one of the earliest statements made by the General Secretary, he asserted:

> The attainment of military-strategic balance with the states of the aggressive NATO bloc is a historic achievement of the fraternal countries of socialism. This parity must be preserved by all means for the sake of peace. . . As before, we shall spare no efforts in providing the Soviet Armed Forces with everything necessary for the defense of our country and its allies.[2]

Although the initial impulse for reform was stimulated by economic and military concerns, it was not long before questions of internal political change found their way into the reform discussions. The issue of domestic political reform soon developed a dynamic of its own under the sponsorship of some members of the leadership who were cognizant of still another long-term negative trend in Soviet society: the decline in the credibility of political authority. This decline of credibility could be found in each of the forms through which political authority is manifested in any society: representative, institutional, and symbolic. The representatives of political authority—the vast body of political, administrative, and law-enforcement officials—evoked the most negative of popular images. Having grown accustomed to an environment with little or no effective checks upon their behavior, Soviet officials increasingly displayed arrogance and abused their powers and privileges. By using their public offices as personal fiefdoms, political officials became identified with an ethos of self-service and self-aggrandizement. The loss of confidence in and respect for those in power extended to the institutions of political authority. The proceedings at Party committee and Soviet meetings, for example, were customarily dominated by their executive boards, who elicited "rubber stamp" endorsements for policies worked out in advance. The electoral and the legal systems as well have long been manipulated by political officials. Although the Soviet Constitution and the Party Statutes provide for a number of democratic institutions, in practice they have been void of any significant popular participation. Finally, many of the symbols of political authority propagated by the regime have lost their emotive effect in contemporary Soviet society. The efforts of Brezhnev and Chernenko to fabricate their own leadership cults, by exploiting the same techniques used by their predecessors—renaming towns and factories in their honor, widely displaying public portraits of themselves, and exaggerating their intellectual prowess and heroic feats—were met with indifference, if not disdain, by a majority of the Soviet public. The official texts on Party history, where the regime tried to sustain its own heroic folklore, and the pervasive image of Lenin as a symbol of infallible guidance, have increasingly aroused public disbelief and skepticism.

The decline in the credibility of political authority did not in itself pose a direct threat to the stability of the regime; it was not channeled into active displays of popular discontent. Rather, most Soviet citizens expressed their loss of faith in the system through passive cynicism. These deep-seated negative attitudes of passive cynicism have led to a profound difference between the behavior of ordinary Soviet citizens in their public, or official, capacity, and their private behavior. Soviet citizens have come to disbelieve officially released information, and are disillusioned by the failure of the economic system to bring them the benefits they believed they have earned. Soviet citizens developed their own, private outlets for expression and participation. For example, the official media's distaste for contemporary popular culture did not prevent the emergence of unsanctioned cult figures, such as the singer-poets Vladimir Vysotskii and Bulat Okudzhava. Perhaps it is in the Soviet citizen's role as an economic actor that the greatest discrepancies between public and private behavior is shown. Although outlawed, black market trading for goods and services has become a necessary and accepted way of life for countless Soviet citizens. This illegal activity is able to thrive because of the proliferation of informal circles of cooperation among family, friends, co-workers, and even supervisors.

This contrast between "official" and "private" behaviors has given the contemporary Soviet political leadership much cause for concern, particularly the consequences of widespread apathy in the workplace. The behavioral norms of the Soviet worker are frequently cited by Soviet leaders as an obstacle to reversing the decline in economic productivity.[3] Of further concern is the possibility that this passive cynicism could at some point erupt into popular demonstrations against the regime. Such a scenario is not improbable when the economic reforms contemplated by the leadership, including price increases for basic food products, the reduction of social welfare subsidies, and transitional periods of unemployment, are taken into account. A similar combination of factors led to the dramatic confrontations in Poland between workers and the regime from 1980 to 1981. Gorbachev himself summarized the domestic situation of Soviet society in the mid-eighties as "verging on crisis."[4]

The different policies that have been incorporated into the domestic political agenda under Gorbachev have a common long-term goal: to reverse negative popular attitudes toward political authority and, subsequently, to affect changes in the behavioral norms of Soviet citizens. To accomplish this goal, the domestic political agenda has been crafted to break down the barriers that separate public and private behavior. In effect, this means that the general indifference exhibited by many people in their official capacities must be replaced by a genuine willingness to cooperate and participate. A number of the resolutions and decrees on domestic reform have been aimed at reorienting Soviet officialdom to recognize and respect privately rooted interests, tastes, and desires. Under Gorbachev, the regime has demonstrated openmindedness and restraint, where once there was disapproval and repression. For example, *glasnost* has brought into the open many cultural themes about contemporary Soviet society as well as its Stalinist past that have long been officially denied public expression.[5] The legalization of a number of hitherto black market services represents another example of a more sensitive approach to private needs.[6] The regime additionally has demonstrated a new tolerance toward religious worship, especially for the Russian Orthodox Christians.[7] Such measures contribute to a lessening of the interventionary power of the Soviet State over the private activities of its citizens. Gorbachev has been at the forefront of this effort to curb the State's authority over civil society. Such actions are an essential part of his plan to unleash the "human factor" in Soviet society: if political authority is used to protect, and not trample, private interests, then people will be encouraged to work within the system.

The political reform agenda that has emerged since Gorbachev assumed the post of General Secretary is an ambitious attempt to realign political authority in Soviet society with the public's interests. Policies have already been enacted which are intended to restore a sense of responsibility and discipline among the representatives of political authority. One of Gorbachev's first measures was the resumption of Iurii Andropov's campaign against official corruption with a renewed enthusiasm for law and order. The Soviet press has been replete with stories about officials who have been reprimanded or removed from office for their abuses of the public's trust, most notably the show trial involving Brezhnev's son-in-law, Iurii Churbanov, and several corrupt Uzbek officials.[8] Gorbachev also has acted to redress lost credibility from the regime's symbols of political authority. Large portraits of Party leaders are no longer displayed in public and the speeches at Party meetings no longer include obligatory flattery of the General Secretary. Gorbachev has commissioned the writing of a new Party history, which promises to be a more realistic interpretation of the regime's past.[9] The most significant political reforms, however, involve changes at the institutional level. The General Secretary has initiated a number of measures that would radically alter the basic functioning of Soviet political institutions, such as: multicandidate elections for political leadership positions; a system for the regular turnover of political office holders through fixed terms and mandatory retirements; the conversion of the Supreme Soviet into a full-time, genuine legislative body; and, the enhancement of the system of justice by establishing greater judicial independence from political authorities and providing stronger legal protection for civil rights. Taken as a whole, these many reforms represent an ambitious effort to restore the credibility of political authority by making its institutions more accountable and accessible to the Soviet public.

The program for political reform initially emerged for defensive reasons. Within the leadership there was a realization that the negative economic and social trends of the late seventies and early eighties could no longer be ignored. A loose consensus formed in the leadership favoring limited political reforms in order to forestall a potential crisis, such as Poland experienced from 1980 to 1981.[10] Here one is reminded of the justification put forth for the radical reforms of Tsar Aleksandr II more than one hundred years earlier: "If we do not carry out this change from above, then we surely will be toppled from below." But in the hands of Mikhail Gorbachev, the process of political reform has developed a dynamic of its own, moving beyond its original defensive intent towards a more fundamental transformation of Soviet political life. His public statements reflect an awareness that deep political changes are necessary if the other elements of his reform program are to succeed. At the 27th Party Congress, for example, Gorbachev remarked: "[T]he acceleration of society's development is inconceivable and impossible without the further development of all aspects and manifestations of socialist democracy."[11]

To what extent will the Soviet political system actually change if Gorbachev's program for political reform is implemented successfully? By Western standards, the regime would still be characterized as authoritarian, featuring the continuing dominance of the Communist Party. Nonetheless, significant changes are possible while remaining within the broad framework of a single-party state. To date, the political reform agenda has been aimed at providing the Soviet public with an enhanced role in the political process. The most important efforts in this regard are those reforms that would increase popular influence upon the selection of leaders, heighten public accountability of political officials, create channels for the articulation of various social interests, and establish forums for the expression of public opinion tolerant of a diversity of views. If over the long term these policies become institutionalized as part of the working political process, then the authoritarian structure of Soviet political life will be eased considerably.

Western media have focused much attention on Gorbachev and his reform efforts, but these events are only part of a larger historical process occurring throughout the socialist world. For many socialist countries, the 1980s has become a period of reform and reevaluation of the basic operational premises of their systems of economic and political organization. In the West, these events are sometimes construed as a rejection of socialism, which is depicted as a kind of aberrant experiment gone bad.[12] As a historical phenomenon, however, socialism cannot be written off so easily. For those socialist regimes that came to power as a result of the interplay of indigenous forces, such as the Soviet Union, China, Yugoslavia, and Vietnam, their early achievements should neither be disregarded nor minimized. In these countries, underground socialist parties were a part of larger national revitalization movements, which arose out of civil war, foreign intervention, and economic backwardness; which restored national unity, internal order, and military strength; and which built the foundations for an industrial economy. In the drive to accomplish their goals, these socialist regimes resorted to extreme forms of centralization and authoritarianism as well as the extensive use of coercion, all of which became institutionally embedded in the newly created systems.

By the 1980s, several developments had made the highly authoritarian and centralized structure of the "socialist system" anachronistic: the threat of foreign invasion had receded; the world economy had entered a new stage of development, requiring greater innovation, diversification, and the more efficient use of resources; and new socio-occupational groups had emerged demanding higher standards of living. The process of reform now underway in the socialist countries does not represent a fundamental break from the principles of socialism, but rather a break from the institutional legacy of this early phase of socialism in power. The reform program in the Soviet Union, for example, has been presented as a redemptive movement, trying to recapture the humane and progressive ideals that socialism was once associated with. Soviet leaders have described *perestroika* as "going back to the basics of Marxism," "deepening socialist democracy," "restoring Lenin's concept of socialism," and "proceeding toward better socialism."[13] In the brief history of socialism in power (the Soviet Union is the only existing socialist regime that predates World War II), the 1980s marks an important benchmark and possibly the beginning of a fundamental redefinition of the roles of the state and society in the socialist countries.

STRUCTURAL SETTING

Mikhail Gorbachev's personal qualities have impressed many Western observers. In contrast to the Kremlin's Old Guard, who dominated the top leadership in the late seventies and early eighties, Gorbachev projects the image of an energetic, sophisticated and flexible leader. His political shrewdness and public-relations skills appear to make him the consummate politician. In the Soviet political system, the personal qualities of a General Secretary are an important contributing factor to his overall authority, but the political strength of the General Secretary is not wholly determined by personal factors. The leader's authority is limited by systemic constraints. Strong pressures are exerted on the General Secretary to remain within the limits of these institutionally defined norms. Two structural elements of the contemporary Soviet political system, in particular, have tempered the radical edge of domestic reform: first, the extensive bureaucratization of political and economic processes in Soviet society, and, second, the oligarchic structure of Soviet leadership politics. General Secretary Gorbachev has already encountered considerable resistance from the bureaucracy and the oligarchy to his own personal authority and to his program of reform.

The trend toward the bureaucratization of a wide range of societal processes in the Soviet Union began shortly after the regime first came to power. In the 1920s, a number of political processes, including recruitment of leaders and decisionmaking, came under the control of the expanding Party apparatus. Various opposition groups at that time proposed limits to the increasing bureaucratization of the party and of political life generally, but they were in the end defeated by Stalin. During the 1930s, the Soviet Union experienced still further bureaucratization as a centralized State apparatus expanded its control over the functional areas of society. In the economy, for example, bureaucratization was stimulated by the ambitious plans for industrialization and agricultural collectivization. It was left to Party and State bureaucrats to put this new economic system into place and to assure its continuing operation. At the same time, bureaucratization spread through the cultural and social realms of society. Although Stalin has long passed from the scene, the vast bureaucratization that flourished during his reign remains an imbedded feature of Soviet society. Furthermore, the elite members of these bureaucracies have long provided the main base of social and political support for the regime.

Gorbachev's public attacks on the bureaucracy have become a staple feature of *perestroika*. In particular, he has stressed that the "command-administrative methods" of Party and State officials have led to the poor functional state of Soviet society and are the main reason for widespread negative popular attitudes toward the government. Gorbachev's early response, however, to chide party and state bureaucrats to work harder, attacks the symptom and not the cause. The "bureaucracy problem" in the Soviet Union is not bureaucrats per se, but, rather, the excessive degree of bureaucratization in the functional processes in society. Excessive bureaucratization has hampered the performance of many intelligent and energetic officials. Although the General Secretary's rhetoric expresses a strong desire to devolve many functional responsibilities away from the bureaucracy, in practice he has moved toward this end with the utmost caution.

Past Soviet reform experiments have more often aimed at improving the performance of the bureaucracy, rather than challenging the system of bureaucratic control itself. In his first two years in office, Gorbachev stayed within traditional approaches to reform, focusing his efforts on making existing bureaucratic organs operate more efficiently and exhorting bureaucratic officials to be more responsive to the public's needs. In the Soviet economy, where administrative control mechanisms have long been preferred for such functions as pricing and supply, Gorbachev had spoken of a need to utilize market mechanisms to a greater extent. But the specific economic reforms that emerged did not diminish the use of bureaucratic controls. For example, in order to improve the quality of Soviet manufactured goods, a new bureaucracy was created, the State Quality Control Agency, rather than allowing the standards of quality to be determined by the product's destined consumer market. Other economic reforms that seek to utilize market mechanisms, such as the effort to place industrial enterprises on a self-management principle or the legalization of certain personal services for extra income, still leave much control in the hands of political administrative officials.[14] Attempts to reduce bureaucracy in the political realm proved even more difficult to carry out, as Party and State officials strongly opposed all forms of popular intrusion into their internal affairs. In the spring of 1987, for example, multicandidate elections were conducted in selected local organizations as a limited experiment using a popular check on local political officials; however, Party and State bureaucrats retained the right to choose the candidates.[15] These first experiments did not seriously alter the bureaucracy's control over the leadership selection process.

The alternative to reforms that work within the system are those which require the devolution of control for particular socio-political and socio-economic functions away from the Party and State bureaucracies. But this approach is uncertain for both political and practical reasons. To begin, there is the inevitable resistance from those bureaucratic officials whose positions of authority, economic livelihood, and social status would be undercut by such a reform. Besides providing the basis of social support for the regime, the elite strata of Soviet officialdom are also entrusted with considerable functional responsibilities. Despite their many shortcomings, the Party and State bureaucracies have consistently provided the Soviet public with at least minimal levels of social and economic services. Reforms that would sharply curtail their responsibilities offer no guarantees that the quality of life in Soviet society will improve. Furthermore, lessened bureaucratic control could result in a potentially destabilizing situation for the regime: the withdrawal of the mainstay of its social support combined with the widespread disruption of vital social and economic services. Such a scenario would be all the more unsettling because the dismantled centralized network of administrative control would impede the regime's ability to preempt spontaneous mass demonstrations.

Despite the inherent risks, beginning in 1987, Gorbachev has demonstrated a commitment to move beyond the traditional approaches to reform and to push his program in the direction of de-bureaucratization. A good example is a proposed agricultural reform that would shift control of production decisions away from agricultural administrators. In discussing this proposal, the General Secretary remarked:

I read a letter in *Sovetskaia Rossiia* from a group of Gorkii oblast collective farm chairmen. They complained that the collective farms were obliged to maintain the entire structure of higher management through their own incomes, and to deduct for its upkeep 15 percent of net profit and 10 percent of the amortization sum. What good is this? *Who needs this apparatus?*[16]

Gorbachev, however, is not unaware of the potential dilemmas of de-bureaucratization. At the same time that he started promoting reforms aimed at dismantling parts of the system of bureaucratic control, he also renewed the call for order and discipline in society and instructed newspaper editors and media chiefs to refrain from publicizing information that might stir up popular resentment.[17] The ongoing ethnic conflict between Armenians and Azerbaijani in Nagorno-Karabakh is a constant reminder to the leadership of the vulnerability of the Soviet State in the face of widespread social disorder.

The second component of the contemporary political system, constraining Gorbachev's authority, is the oligarchic structure of Soviet leadership politics. Whereas the extensive bureaucratization of society is a carryover from Stalin, collective rule was instituted by his successors as a precaution against the reemergence of a tyrannical ruler. At the 20th Party Congress, in 1956, Nikita Khrushchev delivered a speech, exposing many "excesses" of Stalin's rule, thereby undermining the likelihood of another personal dictatorship. The reestablishment of an oligarchy is perhaps the most enduring systemic change in Soviet politics of the past thirty-five years. In Soviet parlance, the oligarchy is referred to as "collective leadership." The importance of "collective leadership" as an operational concept for Soviet leadership politics is underscored by its incorporation in the Party Program, which contains the major ideological tenets of Party rule.[18] Indeed, it was Khrushchev's own attempt to override the constraints of oligarchic rule, in violation of the principal of "collective leadership," that prompted his removal from high office by his Politburo colleagues.

The bloodless coup which removed Khrushchev from the Kremlin in October 1964 was an unprecedented act in Soviet history and a triumph for oligarchic rule. Over the next two decades, the oligarchy became a basic feature of Soviet leadership politics. Furthermore, the internal patterns of operation within the oligarchy were defined more clearly than at any time in the Soviet past. Brezhnev used the collegial institutions of the leadership to open up access channels for bureaucratic representatives from the most important functional areas of Soviet society. Thus, within the

Politburo, positions carrying full voting privileges were accorded to the military, the police, the provincial Party bureaucracy, the State bureaucracy, industrial, and agricultural interests, as well as foreign affairs. The oligarchy as it evolved under Brezhnev became a repository of institutionally based interests, representing the elite strata of the major bureaucracies. Brezhnev's role in this arrangement was less that of an absolute ruler and more that of a power broker.

This leadership arrangement was the product of both political and practical considerations. Of immediate political concern to the bureaucratic elite was the possible return of a personal dictatorship. Khrushchev had raised this fear with his constant assaults on the bureaucracy and his efforts to disregard the voting process on the Politburo. For the bureaucratic elite, dictatorship and insecurity went hand-in-hand. In Brezhnev's Politburo, the allocation of authority, based on a formalized balance of institutional representation, protected against the rise of a dictator. In addition, the incorporation of leading bureaucratic representatives into the oligarchy served the practical side of policymaking. By the mid-sixties and early seventies, the major policy issues confronting the leadership had grown more complex; for example, arms control had become an essential component of military and foreign policies and the efforts to apply the results of scientific-technological research to the economy. The leadership under Brezhnev attempted to take into account the views of functional specialists, not just political generalists, in the policymaking process. The routinization of input from the different bureaucratic chiefs was intended as a means of preventing the enactment of groundless and ill-fated economic and military policies, as had been the case at various times during both Stalin's and Khrushchev's reigns.

The structure of leadership politics as it evolved under Brezhnev survived his death and the subsequent interregnum period of Andropov and Chernenko. When Mikhail Gorbachev assumed the reins of leadership in March 1985, he too was confronted with this preestablished internal division of authority. Despite a commanding leadership style far more assertive and activist than his predecessors, Gorbachev's ability to gain control over the policymaking agenda in the Politburo is constrained by this arrangement. On major policy and political questions, Gorbachev cannot override this arrangement and impose his own personal solutions; instead, he must put together a working consensus for his initiatives. He has been successful in replacing the former status quo consensus on the Politburo with a more dynamic, proreform consensus. Nonetheless, limits are still in force as to the extent to which Gorbachev alone can determine the pace and scope of the reform program. Although Gorbachev might at times find this an obstacle in the way of achieving his policy goals, one can be certain that his leadership colleagues are both supportive and protective of this arrangement. At the 27th Party Congress, Egor Ligachev addressed this issue: "It is important to emphasize that in all cases, whether it concerns domestic or foreign policy, the burning questions of the day or strategic tasks, the Politburo and the Secretariat act collegially, in a manner of high exactingness and frank exchange of opinions."[19]

POWER AND POLICY IN THE REFORM PROCESS

Gorbachev's vision of change for Soviet society entails an interconnected reworking of existing political, economic and social norms of behavior. The comprehensiveness of Gorbachev's vision of reform means, in all likelihood, that Soviet society will undergo an incremental process of state-engendered change for a number of years, in which there will be frequent setbacks as well as successes for the reform program. The reforms now underway in the Soviet Union can be illuminated by two major elements of the reform process: the consolidation of power and the evolution of the policy agenda for political reform.

Consolidation of Power

In a period of just over sixty years, the Soviet Union has witnessed six leadership successions, three of them in the 1980s. During this time, the process of succession has undergone some fundamental changes. The deaths of Vladimir Lenin in 1924 and Iosif Stalin in 1953 led to transition periods characterized by intense factional strife within the political leadership. Western observers of the Soviet political system described this transitional phase as the "succession crisis," in which a leadership void was said to exist until a new dictator emerged.[20] These earliest Soviet successions were marked by intraleadership power struggles for control of the policy agenda. Without a predetermined consensus on the direction of policy, the contenders for power were left to their own devices to build a working coalition for support of their policy positions in the Politburo, the system's top decisionmaking organ, as well as a broader base of support in the Central Committee, the larger and more amenable body of leading central and provincial officials. The eventual victors in these early succession struggles, Iosif Stalin and Nikita Khrushchev, were both chief executives of the Communist Party bureaucracy, a position with great organizational powers, including the responsibility to oversee personnel placements to both the Politburo and the Central Committee. They adeptly manipulated their control over the *nomenklatura*—the system's recruitment and promotion mechanism—to enhance their own personal authority and to develop a base of support for their own policy platforms. The signal marking both Stalin's and Khrushchev's triumph in their respective succession struggles was the issuance of their policy positions in the form of officially sanctioned and binding resolutions that were soon followed by the removal of their principal rivals from responsible leadership posts.

After Khrushchev was forcibly removed from office in 1964 and Brezhnev became General Secretary, the succession process changed, although the connection between patronage, policy and power in this process has remained crucial. The earlier succession struggles of Stalin and Khrushchev, characterized by a leadership void and an overt factional strife, evolved into a more subtle and controlled process, referred to as the "consolidation of power." In this process, it is recognized beforehand that the individual who holds the post of General Secretary of the Party will also serve as the top executive of the ruling Politburo. When the seat of General Secretary is vacated, the remaining members of the ruling oligarchy meet in closed session and choose a new leader, who is then presented to the rest of the Party. The political system, thus, does not experience a prolonged leadership crisis as was the case in the past. The authority of a new General Secretary, however, is limited by prevailing policy views of his fellow Politburo members as well as the division of labor within the leadership. From the moment he is chosen as leader, a General Secretary must work to consolidate power by enhancing his own personal influence among his leadership peers and to define the direction of the leadership's policy agenda.

The consolidation of power process in the Soviet Union requires several years, and in some respects can never be considered complete. It took Brezhnev, for example, a little over five years to emerge as the dominant figure on the Politburo. During the consolidation of power process, a General Secretary acts in several ways to bolster his personal authority. First, a General Secretary must try to establish his own policy platform within the leadership.

Second, a General Secretary must manipulate the process of personnel selection, by promoting those who demonstrate both personal loyalty and similar policy inclinations. This includes the selection of provincial first secretaries, who comprise the largest bloc in the Central Committee, and the appointments to the top political organs in Moscow, especially the voting memberships on the Politburo. Third, a General Secretary can distinguish himself from the rest of the leadership by showcasing his authority in public forums. This might entail delivering the keynote address at major political conferences and anniversary celebrations, as well as participating with other world leaders at international summits.

The process of consolidating power is by no means a smooth one for a new General Secretary; in particular, two additional factors affect the process. Short-term policy results can bolster or diminish a General Secretary's status among his Politburo colleagues; this depends, of course, on whether the results of a policy, personally endorsed by the General Secretary, have brought success or failure. The consolidation of power is also affected by unanticipated, intervening events, which can suddenly provide an opportunity to swing leadership opinion to a particular policy view. A General Secretary has only limited control over short-term policy results and virtually no control over intervening events, and, therefore, it must be stressed that they can work against him, just as easily as for him.

Overall, Gorbachev has demonstrated considerable political skills in consolidating his power. Since becoming General Secretary, Gorbachev has made an impressive showing, in terms of defining the direction of the leadership's policy agenda, promoting new people to high level political offices and publicly setting himself apart from his leadership colleagues. Gorbachev inherited an advantageous situation in the spring of 1985 for consolidating power. First, Gorbachev did not need to stake out his own reform consensus within the leadership, but rather tap into an already existing one, forged by Andropov in 1982 to 1983. The Politburo's selection of Andropov, the former KGB chief, as General Secretary reflected the growing sentiment in the central leadership and among the country's political and professional elites for a departure from Brezhnev's policies of complacency. Because of his unexpected early death, the drive for change was temporarily stalled, but the constituencies in favor of change remained intact and waiting in the wings. In fact, Chernenko's brief stay in power, marked by the image of this frail leader's efforts to turn back Andropov's policy course, only served to strengthen the proreform consensus for Gorbachev. As his reform proposals have become more radical, Gorbachev has tried to sustain support by keeping attention focused on the "crisis" in society and the urgent need to confront it. At the June

1987 plenum, for example, he argued: "History has not left us much time. Socialism's potential, its practical usefulness for people. . . will be judged precisely on the progress of *perestroika* and its results."[21]

After being named General Secretary in March 1985, Gorbachev moved swiftly to remove potential rivals from political office. Both Grigorii Romanov and Viktor Grishin, two veteran Politburo members and likely opponents to a reform program, were ousted from the top leadership by the year's end. Following the 27th Party Congress in February 1986, five new appointments were made to the Secretariat, including: Grigorii Razumovskii, who had established a reputation as an anticorruption advocate during his tenure in a provincial Party post, to handle the important task of personnel placement for the Party bureaucracy; and, Aleksandr Iakovlev, who had earned the wrath of the Brezhnev Politburo for his criticisms of Russian chauvinism and exiled to a diplomatic post in Canada, was assigned to handle matters related to propaganda and ideology. By the spring of 1987, it appeared that Gorbachev had secured a majority on the Politburo, when three Party Secretaries, Iakovlev, Nikolai Sliunkov and Viktor Nikonov, were promoted to voting status.[22] A policy conflict developed at the same time over the pace and scope of *perestroika*, however, which deprived the General Secretary of a consistently reliable Politburo consensus.

The stalemate which arose in the leadership over policy issues also affected Gorbachev's ability to force additional personnel changes in the top leadership bodies. At the July plenum in 1988, the leadership's differences over political reform and agricultural policy were finally decided, in principle at least, in favor of Gorbachev. Emboldened by this tenuous policy victory, Gorbachev acted in late September to enhance his power within the leadership. He took over the post of President of the Supreme Soviet from Andrei Gromyko, who was honorably retired. Although the presidency has been a largely ceremonial position, Gorbachev's planned reform of the Supreme Soviet would give this position enormous powers to influence domestic affairs.[23] Gorbachev also moved to undercut the position of the Politburo's conservative bloc. Mikhail Solomentsev, the head of the Party Control Commission, was relieved of his duties and removed from the leadership. Other members of the conservative bloc, Egor Ligachev, Viktor Chebrikov and Vitalii Vorotnikov, while retaining full membership status in the Politburo, were effectively cut off from their organizational bases and given new portfolios.[24] Meanwhile, Vadim Medvedev was promoted to voting status on the Politburo and given overall responsibility for ideology. Medvedev's first major address in his new role emphasized the themes that have become closely identified with the reformers' camp.[25] In addition, two surviving members of the Old Guard, Petr Demichev and Vladimir Dolgikh, were replaced as candidate Politburo members by three Gorbachev-era appointees, Aleksandr Biriukova, Anatolii Lukianov and Aleksandr Vlasov. Gorbachev's September power play appeared to have successfully overcome the institutionally based leadership structure inherited from Brezhnev, which directly linked the oligarchy with the major political bureaucracies. As of the fall of 1988, the military and the KGB had been deprived of formal representation at the voting level in the Politburo. Furthermore, the provincial Party apparat had been reduced to just one Politburo representative with voting privileges, the Ukraine's Volodymir Shcherbitskii.

Beyond the central Party organs, Gorbachev benefited from the fact that the Soviet political elite had grown old, thus creating ample opportunity for personnel changes through forced retirement, infirmity, or death. Over 40 percent of the Central Committee membership elected at the 26th Party Congress, the last of the Brezhnev era, were removed at the 27th Party Congress in February 1986. Between March 1985 and August 1987, sixty-eight new appointments were made to the Council of Ministers, representing a turnover of more than 60 percent. Also by mid-1987, more than half of the first secretaries in the provincial Party organizations had been replaced.[26] Although Gorbachev spoke enthusiastically about continuing the "renewal of leading cadres" through the first half of 1987, the momentum for this program was stalled at that time. Gorbachev's effort to use the 19th Party Conference to carry out further changes in the membership of the Central Committee was thwarted by conservatives in the leadership.[27] Following the July and September plenums in 1988, the process of personnel change in the provincial organizations was revived with a renewed momentum. And, in the spring of 1989, Gorbachev was able to force over one hundred Central Committee members to retire.

In considering the different means Gorbachev has used to build his authority and prestige in the leadership, public relations is clearly an area in which he has excelled. His public style contrasts sharply with the staid public presentations of the political leaders that Soviet audiences had grown accustomed to since the 1970s. Gorbachev's flair for public forums, including his animated delivery of speeches and his ability to develop a rapport with his audience, would make any Western politician envious. Gorbachev has been anything but neglectful toward the customary showcases available to a General Secretary, such as delivering the keynote addresses at major political and professional conferences. Furthermore, Gorbachev has used foreign summits, especially with Western leaders, to reinforce the image as "his own man" on questions related to Soviet national security and foreign policy. Gorbachev has shown much enthusiasm, however, for going beyond these traditional public forums. His frequent television addresses provide the General Secretary with an ideal medium for getting his views across to the Soviet public. In this format, Gorbachev is viewed as a single voice of authority, seated alone at a desk, without the familiar staged backdrop of fellow Politburo members. In addition, Gorbachev has benefited from impromptu gatherings of factory or collective farm workers, which, not surprisingly, are accorded much fanfare in the national media. These impromptu meetings serve as public relations events in which the General Secretary delivers his message of reform in an informal, personal setting and then engages the group in discussions about their own grievances and suggestions for improving the existing situation.

Concerning the two factors over which a General Secretary has little control, short-term policy results and intervening events, Gorbachev's efforts to consolidate power have been affected both positively and negatively. The restoration of Andropov's discipline and anticorruption campaigns produced short-term increases in the availability of some consumer goods and food products, as hidden stocks suddenly reappeared on store shelves. The agricultural output figures announced toward the end of 1986, one year after Gorbachev's reorganization of the agricultural administration, surpassed the annual figures for the previous five-year period.[28] But Gorbachev has suffered costly short-term policy setbacks as well. In the summer of 1988, popular skepticism and discontent appeared to be on the rise because *perestroika* had yet to improve material living standards; as a result, Gorbachev was put on the defensive at the Party Conference in June and again in a well-publicized exchange with workers at a Siberian factory in September.[29]

An unanticipated event, which Gorbachev seized as an opportunity to consolidate his power, was the bizarre odyssey of the young West German pilot, Matthias Rust, who flew his small plane across the Soviet Union's western border, past Soviet air defenses, before finally touching down outside the Kremlin walls in Moscow. Gorbachev swiftly sacked several top military officials, including the Minister of Defense, Sergei Sokolov. Gorbachev replaced Sokolov, a holdover from Chernenko's Politburo, with an outsider to the military establishment's own chosen elite in Moscow, Dmitrii Iazov, the commander of the Far East forces.[30] Another unanticipated event which worked to the advantage of the General Secretary was the publication of the Andreeva letter in *Sovetskaia Rossiia* in March 1988. The antireformist views expressed in this letter apparently crossed the line of acceptable polemics and provoked a strong counterattack by the proreform forces and set in motion an intensive anti-Stalin campaign throughout the spring and summer of 1988.[31]

In October of 1987, Boris Eltsin delivered an unexpected speech to a Central Committee plenum, breaking the leadership's normally observed public decorum, in which he gave an unabashedly critical assessment of the progress of reform and implicated by name several Politburo officials to account for this situation. The incident had several negative consequences for Gorbachev: first, Eltsin's subsequent dismissal from candidate membership in the Politburo deprived the General Secretary of a proreform voice in the leadership; second, and more importantly, Eltsin's outburst became the pretext for a confrontation between Gorbachev and the more conservative Politburo members over the priorities of the reform program, which resulted in the modification of his reform agenda.[32] A more serious unanticipated event was the eruption of ethnic violence between Armenians and Azerbaijani in the Soviet Transcaucasus. The inability of central political authorities to restore order to the region has bolstered the conservatives' argument that the devolution of authority away from the Party and State bureaucracies during this period of economic transition will create the preconditions for social disorder.

Evolution of the Policy Agenda

Gorbachev's domestic political agenda has evolved in a few short years from a narrowly defined campaign for imposing model ethical standards on Party and governmental organizations into a comprehensive, abstract program for reshaping political life in the Soviet Union. Gorbachev has labeled this program *perestroika*, which is most commonly translated as "restructuring." For Gorbachev, *perestroika* means much more than a political reform; it is a program encompassing economic and social change as well as foreign policy. And, although it entails structural reform, it has as its end a transformation of peoples' attitudes across Soviet society. Gorbachev did not espouse this vision of radical reform when he first assumed the position of General Secretary in March 1985. Although it was clear he would seek a reform agenda, the goals he targeted were far more limited and the tone of his rhetoric more conciliatory than has been the case since the beginning of 1987. From 1985 through the autumn of 1988, the domestic political reform agenda has passed through three distinguishable phases.

April 1985–January 1987.   In the spring of 1985, the overriding concern of the Soviet political elite could be summed up with the single question: what had gone wrong? The early seventies had held such promise for the Soviet Union: abroad, the Soviet military was recognized to be on an equal footing with the world's most powerful country, the United States, while anti-Western sentiments dominated the post-colonial regimes of the Third World; at home, Brezhnev's economic programs had led to increases of industrial productivity as well as higher standards of living for most Soviet citizens. But a decade later, the Soviet Union was a country increasingly on the defensive in the international arena and in decline internally. Chernenko's brief and uninspiring tenure did little to reverse this situation, confirming to many that "politics as usual" had ceased to be an acceptable alternative for the country's political leadership. It was in this atmosphere that the youngest and ablest member of the Politburo was selected by his peers to become General Secretary.

Mikhail Gorbachev's appointment as General Secretary is indicative that a consensus for change existed in the Soviet Union's political leadership. Andrei Gromyko, in his nominating speech at the March plenum in 1985, emphasized Gorbachev's abilities as a problem solver:

> You know it often happens that problems—both internal and external—are very difficult to consider if you are guided by the law of "black and white." There may be intermediate colors, intermediate links, and intermediate decisions. And Mikhail Sergeevich is always able to come up with decisions that correspond with the Party line.[33]

Gorbachev himself confirms that members of the leadership regularly discussed the need for reform in the years prior to his coming power. "[T]his analysis," Gorbachev revealed, "began a long time before the April Plenary Meeting and that therefore its conclusions were well thought out. It was not something out of the blue."[34]

The prochange consensus in the Politburo was united in its desire to reverse two negative trends of the late-Brezhnev period that continued to plague Soviet society in 1985: the deterioration of the ethical standards of leading Party and governmental officials and the overall decline in economic productivity. No member of this group, including Gorbachev, offered any concrete plan at the time to reverse these negative trends; instead, the early emphasis was on restoring order and discipline in both the bureaucracy and in the workplace. Within a month, three additional appointments were made to the ranks of voting membership on the Politburo, each of whom appeared well-suited for the task at hand. Joining Gorbachev were Egor Ligachev, who had established a reputation for his anticorruption campaigns as a provincial Party official in Tomsk; Viktor Chebrikov, who was Andropov's successor as chairman of the KGB; and, Nikolai Ryzhkov, who had gained much experience from various high-level economic posts in the Party and State bureaucracies.[35] The April plenum of 1985 marked the end of the holding phase that Soviet politics had fallen into following Brezhnev's death. These four individuals made up the new leadership team that would lead the country toward the twenty-first century. The new team was reminiscent of the Brezhnev-Kosygin-Suslov triumvirate, which emerged after Khrushchev's ouster in the mid-sixties. And not unlike their forebears, the new leadership team eventually came apart in disputes over the prerogatives of power and policymaking.

Gorbachev did not attempt to force a distinctive mark upon the policy agenda in the first months following the succession. His address to the April plenum in 1985 indicated that the new leadership, for a while anyway, would take a deliberate and cautious approach to reform. "In the ten months left before the opening of the Congress," Gorbachev declared, "we are to make an all-round analysis and a realistic assessment of what had been done since the 26th Party Congress and to determine the prospects for further development and the tasks of domestic and foreign policy."[36] Although no specific proposals were initiated, Gorbachev's April speech hinted at the extensiveness that future changes would require: "But life and its dynamism dictate the need for further changes and transformations, for bringing about a qualitatively new state of society, in the broadest sense of the word."[37]

Throughout the second half of 1985, the new leadership was preoccupied with economic and foreign policy questions. The domestic political agenda at this time featured the campaign to restore order and discipline to the country's laborforce and to its political-administrative organs. Gorbachev elaborated on this policy in an article appearing in *Pravda* less than a month after the April plenum: "Our people are becoming more intolerant of abuses, breaches of the law, bureaucratism, drunkenness, extravagence, wastefulness, and other negative phenomena."[38] This campaign was aimed at the eradication of the flagrant abuses of power that had become part of the bureaucracy's functional routine during the second half of Brezhnev's rule, especially in the provinces. The most corrupt and neglectful officials were removed from office and, in some instances, tried for criminal offenses.

The order and discipline campaign served several purposes for the new leadership. First, it reasserted central authority throughout the provinces, where party and governmental organizations had been allowed to establish their own operational routines with only a minimum of interference from Moscow. From the beginning of his tenure, Gorbachev stressed the need for provincial cadres to become more accountable for their performances and to put an end to their attempts "to hide the true situation in their areas."[39] At the April plenum, it was announced that provincial first secretaries would have to make firsthand reports periodically to the Politburo and the Secretariat.[40] Second, the campaign was used to expedite the process of personnel turn-over of central and middle level officials, which is part of any leadership succession. The official explanations for the removal of Brezhnev stalwarts Viktor Grishin from the Moscow Party Committee and Dinmukhamed Kunaev from the Kazakhstan Party Committee, for example, stressed their benign tolerance of the rampant corruption in their own organizations.[41] Third, by including the bureaucracy within the scope of the campaign for order and discipline, the new leadership sought to restore public confidence in the established system of political authority. Under Brezhnev, Party and governmental leaders commonly operated beyond public scrutiny, creating a situation that nurtured arbitrariness and abuse. Throughout this campaign, the new leadership demonstrated its commitment to promoting political officials who were public-serving instead of self-serving.

Only ten months after the new leadership team had been assembled the 27th Party Congress was convened in Moscow. Although there was serious consideration within the leadership to postpone the Congress, it opened as scheduled in February 1986.[42] As the first major political event of Gorbachev's rule, the convocation date for the Congress was symbolically important for the new General Secretary: first, holding the Congress on time signaled the new leadership's intolerance of the lethargy that had become an operational norm of the Brezhnev gerontocracy; second, the opening date of the Congress, 25 February 1986, marked the thirtieth anniversary of Khrushchev's famed "secret speech," which exposed the violent excesses of Stalin's dictatorship and was a crucial step toward launching his own reform program in the second half of the 1950s.

The 27th Party Congress did not offer any substantial new policies for the domestic political sphere. The campaign for order and discipline was reaffirmed in the speeches of top leaders and in the text of the new Party Program.[43] The agenda set by the Congress for the country's political-administrative elite stressed the need for economic renewal. In the resolutions of the Party Congress, it was stated that "the main sphere of the Party's activity was and remains the economy."[44] The Congress, however, did not neglect the issue of political reform. The ideas that would soon become the basis for reform initiatives, as well as the future debates over these reform proposals, could be discerned from the presentations of various leadership members at the Congress.

In his keynote address, Mikhail Gorbachev provided an outline of the major issues that would eventually appear on the domestic political agenda. He argued that certain features of the Soviet political system were no longer appropriate for the tasks of governing contemporary Soviet society:

> There has been an immeasurable rise in the general level of education and culture of the Soviet people, and an enrichening of their sociopolitical experience. And this means that there has been an enormous growth in the possibility and need for every citizen to participate in the managing of the affairs of State and society. Democracy is the healthy and pure air only in which the socialist public organism can live in full vitality.[45]

Just as he prescribed for the economy, Gorbachev declared that the Soviet political system must also undergo a restructuring (*perestroika*). He suggested a number of institutional and attitudinal changes that would be necessary to carry out this restructuring, including: broadening citizen's rights and strengthening the legal protection of such rights; increasing the role of popular participation at various levels of the political process; establishing more effective checking devices on political-administrative officials; and developing an atmosphere of openness (*glasnost*) and straightforwardness in the work habits of the bureaucracy and in its conduct toward the public.

The proceedings of the Congress also revealed glimpses of the internal debate on political reform that would soon cause a major rift within the leadership. No other full voting Politburo member fully endorsed Gorbachev's outline for political reform. His suggestions to broaden civil rights, to employ popular checks on the bureaucracy, and to increase public accountability through *glasnost* were all but ignored in the reports delivered by fellow Politburo members Ligachev, Chebrikov, Solomentsev, and Shcherbitskii. The other members of the leadership favored programs that fell short of major institutional reform; instead, they focused on making use of internal bureaucratic control devices and improving the educational-ideological training of political officials. By contrast, Boris Eltsin, a nonvoting member of the Politburo, called for "radical changes" in his report to the Congress. Eltsin supported some of the specific proposals put forth by Gorbachev, such as subjecting political authorities to popular checks. The First Secretary of the Moscow Party Committee went one step further than Gorbachev when he suggested that the Party's central apparat should be internally reorganized so that it would no longer interfere with the work of governmental and economic agencies.[46]

Throughout 1986, Mikhail Gorbachev attempted to push his political initiatives onto the leadership's policy agenda. The General Secretary used the opportunity of the June plenum, convened for the purpose of approving the twelfth five-year plan, to remind the Party's Central Committee that political reforms could not be avoided much longer:

> Since the Congress, Soviet people have shown a growing interest in the Party's affairs and in the processes taking place in society. They want to find their place in the countrywide work to realize the ideas advanced at the Congress . . . Speaking frankly, we should reorganize and eliminate the elements of arbitrary administration at all levels—from the primary organizations to the Central Committee . . . in the spirit of the Congress we must enhance criticism.[47]

Gorbachev also delivered his message for political reform in the provincial capitals. In July in Khabarovsk, for example, he argued:

> our Party, government, and economic personnel must learn to work under the conditions of extending democracy, motivating the human factor, and developing the people's initiative. Unfortunately, some of our personnel have resented the people's sharp reaction to the processes taking place in society.[48]

And in September, he met with local officials from Krasnodar and Stavropol, where he stressed that *perestroika* meant political as well as economic change. "It is necessary," he stated, "by all means to expand *glasnost*, all forms of democratism, to strengthen control from below, to find in meetings and in the pages of the press the burning issues, which unsettle Communists, the workers of the region, the departments, and the enterprises."[49]

During this time, initial steps were taken to bring some of the political reforms suggested by Gorbachev at the 27th Party Congress closer to their realization. An authoritative article on the new openness appeared in *Izvestiia* at the end of June, arguing that "we all still have to learn how to live under the conditions of *glasnost*."[50] In August, a Central Committee resolution was issued criticizing the efforts of the Party's main theoretical journal, *Kommunist*, to support *perestroika*. In particular, the resolution informed the journal of "the principaled significance it has to work out the concepts for furthering the democratization of society, based in the deepening of socialist self-management of the people in all its forms, the spread of *glasnost*, and the strengthening of socialist legality."[51] In the autumn of 1986, a resolution was published concerning the effort to raise the standards of legality throughout Soviet society, which stressed both a more vigorous enforcement against bureaucratic abuses and an expansion of civil rights.[52] Gorbachev attempted to convene a Central Committee plenum in the second half of 1986 to present a program for domestic-political reform; his efforts, however, were repeatedly thwarted.[53] As soon became evident, resistance to major political reform existed at the highest levels of Soviet government.

January 1987–October 1987.   A Central Committee plenum was finally convened to discuss the sensitive subject of political reform in January 1987. In the area of domestic politics, this meeting marked a watershed in Gorbachev's tenure as General Secretary. Up to this point, the leadership's policies focused on improving the performance of the bureaucracy through reorganization schemes and chastising officials. Gorbachev used the occasion of the January plenum to push the policy agenda in a new direction—toward political institutional reform. This policy shift reflected Gorbachev's basic understanding of the crisis in Soviet society: the widespread alienation of the public from established political and economic systems. In Gorbachev's view, reforms aimed at eradicating bureaucratic inefficiency were in themselves inadequate as long as Soviet citizens had no desire to perform for the system; instead, for the reforms to succeed, they must demonstrate that the Party, the Soviets, and other official bodies exist to serve the general public. Accordingly, *perestroika* must concern itself with overcoming negative attitudes and bringing people back into the system as the starting point toward creating conditions for the revitalization of the economy and society. "A house can be put in order," the General Secretary observed at the January plenum, "only by a person who feels that he owns the house."[54]

Since January 1987, Gorbachev has vigorously promoted a program of political reform, usually referred to as democratization (*demokratizatsiia*), as an essential component of *perestroika*. At the January plenum Gorbachev declared:

> We need democracy like air. If we fail to understand this and even if we do understand but make no serious and genuine steps to broaden and advance it (democracy) and to draw the country's working people widely into *perestroika*, our policy will be choked and *perestroika* will fade away.[55]

As it has been described in the reform discussions, democratization represents a series of measures that will provide Soviet citizens with a greater sense of participation in the process of working out solutions to the problems directly affecting their lives. These measures include: the routinization of some form of popular control on political-administrative officials; the establishment of public forums for the expression of diverse views and opinions; and the development of the means for regular, though indirect, public participation in the leadership selection and decisionmaking processes.

At the January plenum, two controversial issues—the accountability of leading Party officials and political institutional change—were linked together and moved to the forefront of the reform agenda. In his report, Mikhail Gorbachev, in the most explicit terms, blamed the past negligence of the country's leaders, in Moscow and in the provinces, for the many social and economic problems which had overtaken Soviet society. Furthermore, according to the General Secretary, a number of Party and State organizations were continuing to show complacency in the face of this crisis situation. "[T]he most important demand," Gorbachev argued, "is the high moral standard of our cadres, such human qualities as honesty, incorruptibility and modesty." The time had come to work out the actual policies and plans for implementation of the program of political change that was outlined nearly a year earlier at the 27th Party Congress. Gorbachev emphasized that political reform had become inevitable: "We need to make this decisive turn because we just do not have the choice of another way. We must not retreat and do not have anywhere to retreat to."[56]

The resolutions issued at the plenum's conclusion endorsed the notion that decisionmaking bodies and administrative organs must become more accountable to the Soviet public. "It is essential," the official resolution noted, "to establish an efficient system of control over our leading cadres." In this regard, the plenum initiated the first cautious step toward political institutional reform, beginning with the electoral process. "Refining the Soviet electoral system," the resolution read, "is one of the key avenues of the democratization of social life."[57] The reform was supposed to introduce multicandidate slates and secret ballots into the electoral process, which had long been manipulated by political officials. Experiments with the electoral reform were carried out on a limited basis throughout the spring and early summer of 1987. These elections received much fanfare in the Soviet press and helped to sustain the momentum for political reform. The experiments were confined to local levels, excluding all provincial and national offices. The highest administrative level affected by the reforms was the position of first secretary of the district (*raion*) Party committee. The elections were held not only for political offices, but included the management of economic enterprises as well. Responsible executive bodies still exercised control over the proceedings, however, by reserving the power to select the organizations eligible for the reform and to choose the nominees.[58]

Although electoral reform was the most noteworthy political development in the weeks following the January plenum, important steps were taken toward restoring the credibility of political authority in its representative and symbolic forms as well. The Soviet press kept alive the issue of creating a new work ethic for political leaders through a series of editorials emphasizing their "professional and moral qualities."[59] In early March and again in early April, Central Committee Secretaries Lev Zaikov and Grigorii Razumovskii brought a large group of officials from the local and provincial Party organizations to Moscow to discuss organizational matters and to attend training seminars aimed at "raising the qualifications of leading Party, Soviet, and ideological cadres."[60] In April, at the 20th Komsomol Congress, Gorbachev argued that a rejuvenation of Party history had become necessary. In his address to the Komsomol Congress, Gorbachev declared that the time had come to remove the "blank pages" from the Party's history and provide a more "honest" and "courageous" account of the past.[61] One of the intended functions of Party history, of course, is to provide a political folklore for the regime and serve as a symbol for the regime's authority.

Another Central Committee plenum was convened in June of 1987, at which Gorbachev again went on the offensive against officials whom he claimed were holding up the progress of *perestroika*. The General Secretary criticized the performance of the central ministries, the Party control bureaucracy, and even the military; but his strongest attack was directed toward the Party organizations. Gorbachev insisted that the Party organizations having had two years to acquaint themselves with the leadership's reform program must now prepare for the second stage of *perestroika*, in which there must be real progress toward solving the problems of Soviet society. The resolutions issued at the plenum's conclusion stated that it was "necessary to increase the Party's influence over the direction of *perestroika*; Party organizations are called to be in the vanguard of the realization of the transformation."[62] Party officials, thus, were no longer responsible for the reform movement as a matter of principle, but were responsible for the actual results of the various political, economic and social reforms. As events showed, Party officials proved none too eager to assume this responsibility.

The June plenum marked the high point of the second phase in Gorbachev's bid to control the policy agenda. Political institutional reforms and the removal of Party officials were both sensitive subjects that others in the leadership were not anxious to act on. In his speech at the plenum, Gorbachev alluded to a division in the Politburo over the timetable for the implementation of the reforms. In the months that followed, opposition sentiment to Gorbachev's program of political reform began to appear in the party's most authoritative publications. In August, *Kommunist* printed an unsigned article on the Chinese Communist Party's experiments with political reform, which implicitly drew numerous parallels with Gorbachev and *perestroika*. The lessons to be drawn from the Chinese experience were clearly intended to sound an alarm to Soviet readers: General Secretary Hu Yaobang's redirection of the Chinese reform movement away from socioeconomic change toward political change had two immediate results—a purge of the Chinese Communist Party's leading officials and the rise of mass student demonstrations calling for Western-style democracy. The article also reminded its readers that General Secretary Hu Yaobang, having created this situation, was forced to resign in January 1987.[63] In September, then-KGB chief Viktor Chebrikov, in a major speech commemorating the birthday of the Bolshevik founder of the secret police, Feliks Dzherzhinskii, spoke reservedly about domestic political reform. Chebrikov warned that Western reactionary forces were using the opportunity created by democratization to carry out sub versive acts against the Soviet State, including: "instilling in Soviet people the bourgeois understanding of democracy," "splitting the monolithic unity of party and people," and, "installing political and ideological pluralism."[64]

October 1987–September 1988   By the autumn of 1987, Gorbachev's proposals for political change had aroused deep fears within Soviet officialdom: one concern was that the central authorities were gearing up for a sweeping purge of the country's political elite, which would be announced at the June Party Conference; a second concern was that the more liberal political climate would incite social disorders (the Soviet press reported on a labor strike in a plant on the outskirts of Moscow which lasted for three days).[65] Within the Politburo, Gorbachev's program for political reform divided the leadership team that had been assembled in April of 1985. The general consensus in favor of reform which had united this group two years earlier did not then include measures that might challenge the leading position of the Communist Party or undermine law and order in Soviet society. In October, the more conservative members of the Politburo finally moved against Gorbachev's program of political reform.

The incident that served as the pretext for this policy reversal was Boris Eltsin's impromptu speech at a Central Committee meeting in October 1987. Boris Eltsin, First Secretary of the Moscow Party organization and a candidate member of the Politburo, had by this time emerged as the leadership's most outspoken proponent of political reform. At this meeting, which was called to discuss the contents of Gorbachev's anniversary speech for the October Revolution, Eltsin broke with the norms of leadership politics and publicly divulged the details of an ongoing personal feud between Egor Ligachev and himself over the reform movement. For Gorbachev, Eltsin's outburst forced an unwanted discussion in the Central Committee about his program for political reform. At the end of this debate, Eltsin was removed from the leadership and Gorbachev was forced to retreat on certain aspects of his policy agenda.

In mid-November, *Pravda* published the leadership's official account of the Eltsin episode, which also included the policy platform of the Politburo's conservatives.[66] Their disagreement was not over the necessity of reform, but rather the pace and scope of reform and the extent of the Party bureaucracy's accountability in the process. Although the conservative platform agreed with Gorbachev's position that the first stage of *perestroika* had been completed, it cautioned that concrete results still could not be realistically expected in the immediate future. Accordingly, a period of two or three years was necessary for a fair and accurate evaluation of the results of the second phase of *perestroika*; this directly conflicted with Gorbachev's plan to use the Party Conference in June 1988 to assess the progress of the reforms. In addition, citing the difficulties of pursuing economic, social, and political change simultaneously, the platform restored economic reform as the top priority of *perestroika*. Only when the problems of securing a basic level of material well-being were resolved, it was argued, would it be possible to consider the larger issues of socioeconomic and political reform. Finally, the platform defended the efforts of the Party bureaucracy and advocated the use of internal mechanisms of control, such as retraining programs, to improve its effectiveness.[67] The publication of this policy platform represented the reassertion of the interests of the Soviet Union's powerful political-administrative elite into the reform process.

This same *Pravda* article carried Gorbachev's response to the conservatives' platform. The General Secretary accepted the conservatives' modified pace for the reform movement, but, consistent with his understanding of the problems, strongly opposed their effort to make political reform a secondary priority of *perestroika*. Gorbachev reiterated his commitment to political reform and criticized the opponents of reform:

> Our enemies call us utopians and predict that we will fail. They say so because they fear our *perestroika*. Before the January plenum they declared that this was just another campaign. . . When the January plenum had been held, and the June plenum had been held, they panicked. Now all is being done to sow doubts with the working class, and a lack of faith with the workers, to compromise *perestroika*.[68]

Gorbachev's objections, however, were not enough to prevent a series of official acts during the last weeks of 1987, which attempted to place new restrictions on democratization and *glasnost*.[69]

By the beginning of 1988, there were no signs of either a compromise between the reformists and the conservatives in the Politburo or any clear cut policy victories. These policy differences over the pace and scope of reform had created a stalemate in the leadership. Gorbachev himself likened the situation to the 1920s, a decade in which the political leadership was rife with intense factional struggles for control of the policy agenda. This conflict within the Politburo reflected a much wider public debate over the future of Soviet society. Through the first half of 1988, this debate, which received full coverage in the Soviet press, focused on the Party Conference scheduled for June.

The idea of holding a Party Conference was introduced by Gorbachev at the January plenum in 1987 (formal approval came five months later at the June plenum) as a means of furthering his program for domestic political reform.[70] Gorbachev's revival of the Party Conference was motivated by a need to circumvent the Central Committee, where his program for political reform had received little support. The General Secretary's expectation was that the Party Conference could be used to create a climate of opinion favorable for political reform, to authorize institutional changes and to dislodge conservatives from the Central Committee. "As is well-known," Gorbachev argued:

> Party conferences used to be convened in our Party between congresses. There was a period until 1941 when this practice was a regular practice. Many conferences at crucial stages in history resolved problems which were far beyond being tactical. In a number of instances strategic tasks were advanced, and changes were made to the statutory norms and the composition of the central organs of the Party.[71]

As the date for the Party Conference drew closer, the public debate intensified. The opinions and views aired by the official media produced the most wide-ranging political debate witnessed in the Soviet Union since the 1920s. Authorities interceded only on several occasions against the radical fringe of both the left and the right.[72] Although the proreform forces dominated the propaganda battles that raged in the press, the conservative forces triumphed in a more important area, the selection of the Party Conference's 5000 delegates. From the fragmentary information available, provincial Party officials apparently were in a position to determine the composition of the delegate groups from their regions; they used these discretionary powers to limit the presence of reform advocates and outspoken critics.[73] Meanwhile, the leadership was engaged in a conflict for control over the Conference's agenda and the extent of its authority. Again the hopes of proreform advocates were dashed when on the eve of the Conference a ranking spokesman for the leadership revealed that neither institutional reform nor personnel changes would be forthcoming.[74]

The 19th Party Conference opened on 28 June 1988 and lasted for four days; the proceedings were unlike anything in Soviet history. Numerous speakers engaged in a freewheeling, unrehearsed, and often caustic debate over *perestroika*, most of which was replayed for the entire nation on evening television. This format, on the one hand, turned the Party Conference into a major media event; for the first time politics in the Soviet Union had become a mass spectator sport. On the other hand, the format of the Conference marked an important step toward remaking the Communist Party into an overarching political organization, through which diverse social interests would be represented. "A salient feature of our time," the pre-Conference Theses noted, "is the appearance of a real pluralism of opinions, open comparisons of ideas and interests."[75] Gorbachev urged that the format of the Conference serve as an example for Party organizations throughout the country.[76]

The Party Conference was originally called to begin the process of institutionalizing political reform, but on this score it did not live up to its advanced billing. The proreform group had sought to use the authority of the Conference to give official sanction to a number of items on the domestic political agenda: to reassure that the policy of *glasnost* would not be reversed and to protect historians, writers and journalists from the wrath of political conservatives; to strengthen the notion of a "law-based" State through a more vigorous enforcement of Constitutionally guaranteed civil rights, such as the freedoms of speech, assembly, and the press; to develop popular checks on political leaders and to assure for periodic changes in the leadership through multicandidate elections, fixed terms in office, and mandatory retirement ages; and, to redefine the jurisdiction of the Party bureaucracy and the legislative role of the Soviets in the political system. Although many arguments were heard in favor of these reforms at the Conference, the views of the Party's conservatives were also well represented. In the end, the Party Conference issued a series of resolutions, which were generally supportive of political reform but postponed any attempts for its immediate realization: "The reform of the political system is a major intensive task that *will require* the adoption of responsible Party decisions and major legislative acts, including substantial changes in the Soviet Constitution, the constitutions of the union and autonomous republics, and also the CPSU statutes."[77]

In the weeks following the 19th Party Conference, the Politburo held further discussions on the reforms that had been approved in principle in the Conference resolutions, as well as the practical steps necessary for their realization. In late July, a Central Committee plenum was convened in Moscow at which a number of provincial Party leaders and central ministerial officials debated the next step in Gorbachev's program for political reform. The July plenum moved three issues in particular to the top of the political reform agenda: an electoral reform that would permanently establish multicandidate slates for all elections held in the Party and governmental organizations; an internal restructuring of the Party apparat; and a major reform of the Supreme Soviet and the office of its president. In addition, it was announced that an ad hoc commission would be formed to work out the organizational details of these reforms; the commission was chaired by Gorbachev and included a select group of central and provincial Party officials.[78] Gorbachev intended to use this alternative authoritative body to circumvent the Politburo and the Central Committee in devising an implementation scheme for his political reform program.

The results of the July plenum indicated that Gorbachev's program for political reform had been accepted, at least in principle, by the leadership. Meetings of the Central Committee and the Supreme Soviet were scheduled for the late fall, at which the organizational details for implementation would be announced. Gorbachev, however, did not wait. In late September, in an old-style Kremlin power play, he moved to preempt the opposition to political reform by undercutting the authority of its chief opponents in the leadership and forcing the implementation of the reorganization of the

Party apparat. These moves marked the end of the third stage of the reform process. Dealing from a strengthened position in the leadership, Gorbachev pushed his program for political institutional reform closer to its realization. The internal reorganization of the central Party apparat, for example, consolidated over twenty departments into six overarching commissions and eliminated more than a third of the employees. This reform, which was replicated at the provincial levels, is intended to remove the Party from its excessive involvement in the "tactical" issues of governing—overseeing the performance of the economic ministries and other large public organizations—in order to focus on the "strategic" issues—the development of the Soviet economy and society as a whole.[79] Upon assuming the position of President of the Supreme Soviet at this same time, Gorbachev reiterated his commitment to remake the Soviets into genuine legislative bodies, accountable to the Soviet public: "I see my task in this post," Gorbachev said:

> in doing everything to enhance and raise the authority of the Soviets and make them real agencies for the absolute power of the people. . . The moment has come when one should not wait for further instructions from above, but actively implement everywhere the decisions adopted: at the shopfloor, in the town and countryside. The most important role here belongs to the Soviets as the true bodies of government by the people.[80]

The events of late September and early October in 1988 showed that Gorbachev had forcibly broken the stalemate which had existed for more than a year in the leadership. The opportunity was created for the implementation of political institutional reform; the first targets for which included: the Party bureaucracy, the Supreme Soviet, and the electoral system. By forcing the issue as he did, however, Gorbachev personally assumed responsibility for the results of these reform policies and, thus, may become more vulnerable to a countermove in the event of an unforseen crisis or if popular discontent with *perestroika* increases significantly.

PROSPECTS

Mikhail Gorbachev's attempts to transform some of the most fundamental aspects of the Soviet Union's authoritarian political system, has forced him into playing one of history's most difficult roles—the reforming autocrat. Writing nearly 500 years ago, Nicolo Machiavelli described the inherent dilemma facing the reforming autocrat:

And it should be kept in mind that there is nothing more difficult to carry out nor more dangerous to manage than to introduce a new system of things; for the introducer has as his enemies all those who benefit from the old system, and lukewarm defenders in all those who would benefit from the new system.[81]

Machiavelli's words are indeed relevant for the reform process now underway in the Soviet Union as they touch upon the most crucial element in determining its long-term success—the creation of a reliable social base for these new policies. Gorbachev's reform program threatens to undercut the status of the bureaucratic elite, the group that has enjoyed the most privileged position in Soviet society for over half a century. Unless this reform program can find a new base of social support, Gorbachev and his agenda run the risk of falling victim to a conservative backlash. Historical precedent for such an outcome already exists with the ouster of Nikita Khrushchev, whose reforms sufficiently antagonized the bureaucratic elite, but failed to take hold with an alternative social group.

To date, Gorbachev's reform program has found its strongest base of support in the creative and scientific intelligentsia. Under Gorbachev, the relationship between the regime and the country's intellectuals has improved dramatically from the late Brezhnev period, when the conservative guardians of culture and ideology drove a wedge between the two. This division posed a potential danger for the regime as throughout history the disaffection of the intelligentsia has been a contributing factor in the making of a revolutionary situation. An early priority of the General Secretary was to establish a working alliance with the Soviet Union's intellectual establishment. At a meeting in June 1986, he ordered the Party's central apparat "to adopt a new style of working with the intelligentsia. It is time to stop ordering it about, as this is harmful and inadmissable."[82] Accordingly, an effort has been underway to enlist the support and services of the intelligentsia for the reform drive; in return, the regime has relaxed control over the levers by which political officials have long manipulated intellectual activity in the Soviet Union. As important as this alliance is for Gorbachev's reform efforts, the creative and scientific intellegentsia represents only a narrow stratum in Soviet society; it is necessary to build a broader social base of support to assure the long-term success of this reform program.

Gorbachev's reforms have yet to secure solid support from the two largest social groups in Soviet society: industrial workers and collective farm peasants. Since 1985, the regime has made little progress in building an alliance with industrial workers. Although Gorbachev has suggested the introduction of some form of worker democracy in the factories, such as holding elections for plant director, there has not been any serious attempt to implement these measures. The General Secretary also has encouraged Soviet trade unions to assume a more independent stand in relation to management on social and environmental issues. Overall, however, *perestroika* has not worked to advance the interests of the industrial workforce. While workers are constantly implored to give more of themselves while on the job, there have been no corresponding increases of compensatory rewards; living standards, meanwhile, remain inadequately low. Furthermore, the wage reforms that have been proposed would shift the criteria of reward away from the collective and toward an individual basis. Wage policies that pit individual workers against one another are not likely to be popular with an industrial laborforce.

In his first three years, Gorbachev's reform program failed to develop an agricultural policy, which would enlist the backing of collective farm peasants. Gorbachev first promoted a contract system, which would enable small groups of peasants to have the opportunity to enter into seasonal agreements with collective farm authorities; on fulfulling their contractual obligations to the State, these small groups would be allowed to sell their surpluses in private markets. Few peasants were willing to enter into such agreements, however, in the absence of legal guarantees that the State would not renege on its own contractual obligations. In the summer of 1988, Gorbachev proposed a far more radical agricultural reform—long-term leases. In this reform, actual control over land, livestock, equipment and facilities would be assumed by individual peasant families for a period of up to fifty years. With long-term leasing Gorbachev argued: "People become the real masters of the land and have a vested interest in seeing that the land and other means of production leased by them are used as efficiently as possible and yield the highest return."[83] Long-term leases would in effect strip agricultural administrators of many of their powers and responsibilities; the collective farms would be converted into associations, or holding companies, for the new, small-scale production units. With its emphasis on private incentives and individual autonomy, long-term leasing is a policy, which, if realized, could eventually become the basis for a stable alliance between the regime and the peasantry.

The strongest potential ally for Gorbachev's reform program is the Soviet Union's growing middle class. This social group is, in general, young or middle-aged, urban, and well-educated. The members of this group have the occupational training and experience which are most valued by the regime and seen as crucial for the success of its efforts to revitalize the

Soviet economy, including: production specialists—engineers, technicians, and skilled workers; business specialists—economic managers and financial and marketing analysts; research and development specialists—scientists and policy and social analysts; and the traditional professions—academia, law, and medicine. The Soviet Union's middle class has grown steadily in the post-war period. By the 1980s, the middle class had become a social force that Soviet political leaders could no longer ignore. Although Gorbachev's selection as General Secretary by fellow Politburo members in March 1985 was not motivated by a particular concern for this group, since assuming the office, his reform program has increasingly come to represent the interests of this middle class, usually at the expense of the bureaucratic elite. *Glasnost* and what it has encouraged in the arts, history, and the news media, for example, has been well-received by the once culturally and informationally starved middle class. The proposed wage reforms and the system of reward in society will favor the occupational groups of the middle class to a far greater degree than industrial workers or political administrators. Furthermore, the middle class is most likely to be the beneficiary of sociopolitical reforms that would lead to greater participation in the political process, increased popular control over the powers of political-administrative officials and formal recognition of the right to independent association.

The staying power of a political regime is to a large extent determined by the reliability and strength of its social base. Even the most authoritarian political regimes must confront this issue. Gorbachev's *perestroika* represents a wager on the middle class to provide the Soviet economy with expertise and services, to restore positive growth and to provide the regime with a solid social base of support. In this respect, Gorbachev's role is comparable with Petr Stolypin, a former provincial governor, who as Prime Minister tried to revive a Tsarist regime, shaken by war and revolution, through political institutional reform and the realignment of the regime's social base. Palace intrigue soon cut short Stolypin's life and his reforms were quashed by political conservatives; in less than a decade of these events, Russia's Old Regime was felled by a social revolution. Neither the Tsarist autocracy nor Stalin's totalitarianism could forestall the emergence of social forces that eventually challenged their systems of political order. How well Gorbachev handles this challenge is the most important factor that will determine the fate of his own ambitious plan to change the course of Soviet history. If Gorbachev can build a solid alliance with the middle class and implement the institutional reforms that complement such an alliance, while withstanding the fierce opposition of political conservatives, then the prospects for a fundamentally transformed Soviet polity will be greatly enhanced.

Notes

1. Mikhail S. Gorbachev, *Izbrannye, rechi i stat'i* (Moscow: Politizdat, 1985), p. 10.
2. Ibid., p. 23.
3. *XXVII s'ezd kommunisticheskoi partii sovetskogo soiuza: stenograficheskii otchet* (Moscow: Politizdat, 1986), vol. 2, p. 16. See Nikolai Ryzhkov's remarks, for example.
4. Mikhail S. Gorbachev, *Perestroika: New Thinking for Our Country and the World* (New York: Harper and Row, 1987), p. 24.
5. Nancy P. Condee and Vladimir Padunov, "Reforming Soviet Culture: Retrieving Soviet History," *The Nation* (13 June 1987); pp. 815–820, and idem., "The Frontiers of Soviet Culture: Reaching the Limits?" *The Harriman Institute Forum* vol. 1 no. 5 (May 1988). These give an overview of recent cultural developments.
6. "Individual Labor Activity" in *Pravda*, 21 November 1986.
7. The chairman of the Council of Minister's Council for Religious Affairs, K. Kharchev, published an authoritative article in early 1988, stating that "a person, regardless of his attitude to religion, feels himself to be a master of his fatherland, that everything that is best in him is brought out, and that his thoughts and actions are in full accord with his conscience." *Izvestiia*, 27 January 1988.
8. *Pravda*, 30 August 1988. One of the many editorials villifying Iurii Churbanov.
9. *Pravda*, 17 April 1987. Gorbachev made this announcement at the 20th Komsomol Congress in April 1987.
10. Oleg Bogomolov, "Soglasovanie ekonomicheskikh interesov i politiki pri sotsializme," *Kommunist* no. 10 (July 1985): p. 41. The view that the Soviet Union was on a similar course as Poland was expressed in this article appearing in the Party's leading theoretical journal.
11. *XXVII s'ezd: sten. otchet*, vol. 1, p. 77.
12. Zbigniew Brzczinski, *The Grand Failure: The Birth and Death of Communism in the Twentieth Century* (New York: Scribners, 1989); and, William Pfaff, "The Question Not Asked," *The New Yorker Magazine* (1 August 1988): pp. 60–65.
13. A. N. Iakovlev, *Pravda*, 13 August 1988; E. K. Ligachev, *TASS*, 24 June 1987; A. N. Iakovlev, *Pravda*, 28 November 1987; M. S. Gorbachev, *Perestroika*, p. 37. The quotes are from these, respectively.

14. *Pravda*, 27 June 1987 for the "Basic Provisions" for economic reform announced at the June 1987 plenum, and *Pravda*, 21 November 1986 for the resolution on "Individual Labor Activity."

15. *Partiinaia zhizn* E. Nikitina, "Plenum raikoma izbiraet pervogo sekretaria," no. 5 (March 1987): pp. 32–35. A. Mudrakov, "Tainym golosovaniem izbram pervyi sekreter raikoma," no. 6 (March 1987): pp. 43–46.

16. *Pravda*, 30 July 1988. (emphasis added)

17. Ibid., 25 September 1988.

18. *XXVII s'ezd: sten. otchet*, vol. 1, p. 621.

19. Ibid., p. 233.

20. Merle Fainsod, *How Russia is Ruled* 2nd ed., (Cambridge, MA: Harvard University Press, 1965), pp. 90, 91; and Myron Rush, *Political Succession in the USSR* (New York: Columbia University Press, 1965), ch. 4.

21. M. S. Gorbachev, "O zadachakh partii po korennoi perestroike upravleniia ekonomikoi," *Kommunist* no. 10 (July 1987), p. 6.

22. Thane Gustafson and Dawn Mann, "Gorbachev's First Year: Building Power and Authority," *Problems of Communism* (May–June 1986): vol. 35, pp. 1–19; and, idem., "Gorbachev's New Gamble," *Problems of Communism* (July–August 1987): vol. 36, pp. 1–20.

23. *Pravda*, 30 July 1988. See Gorbachev's description of this reform at the July plenum of 1988.

24. In this reshuffling of leadership posts, Ligachev, who had been speaking out on a wide range of issues, was assigned the specific responsibility for agriculture in the Central Secretariat, indicating that he would no longer act as the leadership's "Second" Secretary; Chebrikov was transferred from the top position in the KGB to the Party's Central Secretariat; and, Vorotnikov was moved from the Chairmanship of the Russian republic's Council of Ministers to the still largely ceremonial post of the Presidency of the Russian republic.

25. *Pravda*, 5 October 1988.

26. Gustafson and Mann, "Gorbachev's New Gamble," pp. 12–18.

27. M. S. Gorbachev, "O zadachakh partii po korennoi perestroike upravleniia ekonomikoi," *Kommunist* no. 10 (July 1987): p. 50. At the June plenum of 1987, Gorbachev argued that the Party Conference should be vested with the authority to remove Central Committee members, but this was not achieved.

28. *Pravda*, 7 November 1986.

29. Foreign Broadcast Information Service: Daily Report, *Soviet Union* (FBIS-Sov), 30 June 1988, pp. 4–7. See the speech by Leonid Abalkin at the 19th Party Conference. FBIS-Sov, 16 September 1988, pp. 30–33 gives the events in Siberia.

30. *Pravda*, 31 May 1988. Commander of the Air Defense Forces, Marshal Koldunov, was also removed.

31. *Sovetskaia Rossiia*, 13 March 1988. The article which launched the anti-Stalin campaign was an editorial in *Pravda*, 5 April 1988.

32. *Pravda*, 13 November 1987.
33. As quoted in Archie Brown, "Gorbachev: New Man in the Kremlin," *Problems of Communism* vol. 34 no. 3 (May– June 1985): p. 9.
34. Gorbachev, *Perestroika*, p. 24.
35. Brown, pp. 21–23. Brief biographies of the new leadership can be found here.
36. Gorbachev, *Izbrannye, rechi i stat'i*, p. 8.
37. Ibid., p. 9.
38. *Pravda*, 18 May 1985.
39. Gorbachev, *Izbrannye, rechi i stat'i*, p. 18.
40. Ibid., p. 19.
41. *XXVII s'ezd: sten. otchet*, vol. 1., p. 103 for a criticism of Grishin's Moscow organization. FBIS-Sov, 26 June 1987, p. 47 for a criticism of Kunaev's Kazakhstan organization.
42. Gorbachev, *Perestroika*, p. 61.
43. *XVII s'ezd: sten otchet.*, vol. 1, p. 237 for Ligachev; Ibid., p. 104 for Gorbachev; Ibid., p. 594 for the Party Program.
44. Ibid., vol. 3, p. 533.
45. Ibid., vol. 1, p. 77.
46. Ibid., p. 142.
47. *Pravda*, 17 June 1986.
48. Mikhail S. Gorbachev, *"Restructuring is Urgent, It Concerns Everyone and Everything"* (Moscow: Novosti Press, 1986), p. 26.
49. *Spravochnik Partiinogo Rabotnika* (Moscow: Politizdat, 1987), vol. 27, p. 608.
50. *Izvestiia*, 29 June 1986.
51. *Spravochnik Partiinogo Rabotnika*, p. 579.
52. Ibid., pp. 644–649.
53. *Pravda*, 26 February 1987. Gorbachev revealed that there was high-level resistance to holding a plenum devoted to political reform in his address to the All-Union Trade Union Congress in February.
54. *Pravda*, 28 January 1987.
55. Ibid.
56. Ibid.
57. Ibid., 29 January 1987.
58. *Partiinaia zhizn* E. Nikitina, "Plenum raikoma izbiraet pervogo sekretario," no. 5 (March, 1987), pp. 32–35. A. Mudrakov, "Tainym golosovaniem izbram pervyi sekretar raikoma," no. 6 (March 1987), pp. 43–46. Descriptions of the multicandidate elections for the post of first secretary of the district Party organization are provided in these articles.
59. *Pravda*, 7 March 1987.
60. *Pravda*, 6 March 1987; *Izvestiia*, 5 April 1987.
61. *Pravda*, 17 April 1987.
62. M. S. Gorbachev, "O zadachakh partii po korennoi perestroike upravleniia ekonomikoi," *Kommunist* no. 10 (July 1987): p. 52.

63. Ibid., no. 12 (August 1987): pp. 106–115.
64. *Pravda*, 11 September 1987.
65. *Moskovskie Novosti*, no. 42, 18 October 1987, pp. 8, 9.
66. *Pravda*, 13 November 1987. This Politburo bloc, which opposed radical political reform, appears to have included Ligachev, Chebrikov, Solomentsev, Shcherbitskii, and Vorotnikov.
67. Ibid.
68. Ibid.
69. *Pravda*, 16 November 1987. An article in *Pravda* stressed that democracy cannot exist without discipline; it stated that "even in the conditions of democratization, 'dictatorship' is still necessary. A dictatorship of the conscience." In early December, police authorities renewed their harassments against dissident groups, including one episode in which 25 people were arrested. See, for example, FBIS-Sov, 9 December 1987, p. 62; and, ibid., 7 December 1987, p. 67.
70. M. S. Gorbachev, "O zadachakh partii po korennoi perestroike upravleniia ekonomikoi," *Kommunist* no. 10 (July 1987): p. 53.
71. *Pravda*, 26 June 1987.
72. *Pravda*, 5 April 1988. In April, for example, *Pravda* published an editorial strongly condemning the views of a reactionary article appearing in *Sovetskaia Rossiia* and reprimanded that newspaper for publicizing an "antirestructuring manifesto." FBIS-Sov, 10 May 1988, p. 41. In June, authorities broke up a meeting of the informal group, Democratic Union, which had convened for the purpose of issuing a radical political program, including the abolition of one-party hegemony and the removal of Soviet armed forces from the Baltic states.
73. Thane Gustafson's comments in "The 19th Conference of the CPSU," *Soviet Economy* vol. 4 no. 2 (April–June 1988): pp. 105–109. See for a thoughtful, though impressionistic, discussion of the delegate selection process.
74. FBIS-Sov, 27 June 1988, p. 42.
75. *Theses of the CPSU Central Committee for the 19th All-Union Party Conference* (Moscow: Novosti Press, 1988), p. 6.
76. FBIS-Sov, 5 July 1988, p. 117.
77. *Pravda*, 5 July 1988. (emphasis added)
78. Ibid., 30 July 1988.
79. Ibid., 1 October 1988.
80. *Izvestiia*, 2 October 1988.
81. Nicolo Machiavelli, *The Prince and the Discourses*, (New York: The Modern Library, 1940) pp. 21, 22.
82. Gorbachev, *Perestroika*, p. 81.
83. *Pravda*, 30 July 1988.

3 CULTURAL REFORM IN THE SOVIET UNION

Gerald M. Easter and Janet E. Mitchell

INTRODUCTION: CULTURE AND POLITICS IN THE SOVIET UNION

In the spring of 1985, Mikhail S. Gorbachev began the formidable task of reforming Soviet society. The problems he inherited were numerous and acute. Along with a failing economy and serious political concerns, cultural life in the USSR had become stagnant; its vitality sapped by nearly two decades of conservative authoritarianism. Interpretations of important historical episodes that differed from official versions were not permitted. Many of the ordinary daily experiences of citizens in the modern Soviet state were considered too controversial or too negative by the regime's ideological censors for public expression. Many of the country's greatest talents were in exile, either internally or abroad. Officially sanctioned cultural works produced for the Soviet public were typically mediocre in quality and sterile in content. From an early date, Mikhail Gorbachev expressed the need for cultural reform. He recognized that official culture without roots in society at large contributed to the already evident popular alienation from the regime and he launched an intensive effort to reinvigorate cultural life in the Soviet Union. Among the many facets of *perestroika*, Gorbachev's comprehensive program to restructure Soviet society, the cultural field has yielded the greatest successes. Gorbachev has attempted to redefine the role of culture in society and the relationship between culture and politics in a fundamentally different way from past Soviet leaders.

Cultural life in the Soviet Union has long been dominated by its political rulers, a situation that developed in the early years of Soviet rule for political, ideological and normative reasons. The paramount concern of Bolshevik party leaders in the period immediately following the October Revolution was political survival. In the midst of a bloody civil war, the Bolshevik leaders resorted to many of the same repressive means of authoritarian rule that had characterized the Tsarist autocracy, including the establishment of a censorship apparatus. During the 1920s, most cultural professions operated with a fair degree of autonomy from political authorities, although "counterrevolutionary" ideas were strictly controlled. With the rise of Iosif Stalin, however, the sciences, the arts, and the mass media were subjected to far greater levels of scrutiny and interference from the regime's censors and ideologues. The words of M. B. Mitin, a radical, pro-regime philosopher in the early thirties, became reality by the decade's end: "There is not and cannot be a philosophy that wants to be considered Marxist-Leninist philosophy while denying the necessity of ideational-political and theoretical leadership on the part of the Communist Party and its leading staff."[1] Stalin's dictatorship forced a deepening encroachment of politics into the realm of intellectuals in Soviet society by intensifying the regime's efforts to root out political nonconformity and intellectual independence and to centralize the process of information exchange in all cultural fields. Since the 1930s, the regime has maintained close control over cultural life. There have been brief periods of relaxation, most notably Khrushchev's cultural "thaw," as well as periods of heightened vigilance, such as the "Zhdanovshchina" at the conclusion of World War II, and the crackdown on dissident activity following the Daniel-Siniavskii trial in 1966.

Ideological factors have also led Soviet political authorities to restrict cultural expression. From a Marxist viewpoint, culture is a manifestation of the economic relationship between society's social classes. Culture expresses dominant themes and artistic styles and reflects the tastes and values of society's ascendant social class. Other deeply rooted and broad-based cultural values such as religion, serve to reinforce a hierarchical status quo among the social classes. The Bolsheviks came to power with a determination to overturn Russia's social hierarchy, and to move the working class into ascendancy. Lenin had argued that the effort to remake society would not succeed, however, unless the political revolution was followed by a cultural revolution, that is, that the general public would develop an understanding of the value of trying to construct socialist forms of organization for society. "[T]here must be a veritable revolution—the entire people must go through a period of cultural development . . . without universal literacy, without a proper degree of efficiency, without training people to acquire the habit of bookreading . . . we shall not achieve our object."[2] Consequently, the Bolsheviks became actively involved in cultural life. They promoted the growth of a new proletarian culture in the arts and education and developed a new belief system for society based on Marx's scientific socialism. Through political manipulation, cultural expression in Soviet society was required to be consistent with the basic principles of Marxism-Leninism, which was not institutionalized as a cultural support for an ascendant proletariat, but rather as an ideology of State power.

Soviet political authorities have long recognized the power of culture as an instrument of socialization. Various cultural media are used to promote the social values and behavioral norms sanctioned by the regime. In literature and films, for example, the chief protagonists typically display exemplary moral character serving as suitable role models for Soviet citizens. The primary theme which political authorities have most encouraged in cultural works is "collectivism." From the 1930s, when political officials assumed greater control over cultural expression, the collective theme has been most prevalent in the creative arts: leading characters in novels, plays, and films typically give up personal comfort and security because of a commitment to higher, collective aims—patriotism, proletarian consciousness, or revolutionary élan. Collectivist values were by no means alien in this society which was still dominated by the peasantry in the 1930s; however, as the processes of industrialization and urbanization unfolded and the State enhanced its control over society, Soviet writers and artists began to confront the issue of "individual" fate and modern Soviet life. But works that dealt with individualist values were discouraged and suppressed by political authorities, who preferred that cultural media disseminate collectivist values.

The political rulers of the Soviet Union have been able to control cultural works in Soviet society by two principal means: a centralized and comprehensive administrative apparatus, and alliances with conservative factions from the cultural intelligentsia. Since the 1930s, a number of State agencies have been created to oversee nearly all aspects of the production and distribution processes of literature and the arts. The officials from these agencies determine such issues as the financing of film projects for movie studios, approving program selections for the performing arts, and choosing the appropriate books for public library shelves. The central element of control in the State's administrative apparatus is a large censorship bureaucracy, commonly known by its Russian acronym, *Glavlit*, which was responsible for reviewing the contents of all journals, newspapers, books, films, and theatrical productions *prior* to their public release. Another important element of administrative control was the State-chartered unions for writers, artists, filmmakers, historians, and the like. Those who desired to work in these professions were forced to join these centrally administered unions, or run the risk of criminal prosecution on the charge of "social parasitism."

The second tactic enabling political authorities to influence the shape of cultural works was the forging of alliances with particular factions in the various cultural fields. In this way, the outcomes of intellectual disputes were forcibly settled by political officials, who intervened on behalf of those who represented points of view that the regime found acceptable. Through the influence of political officials, the members of these chosen factions were placed in positions of authority, such as the top administrative posts in the leading research institutes and academies, the seats on the editorial boards of professional journals and publishing houses, and the executive boards of the various unions for creative workers, where they effectively established the acceptable parameters for important intellectual debates and decided whose work would be promoted and whose would be suppressed. In the 1930s, for example, Aleksandr Fadeev, an early proponent of "realist" literature, and V. P. Stavskii, an author of bland stories about collectivization, were part of a campaign of accusations against fellow Soviet writers, whom, they claimed, were trying to sabotage the regime by not following the Party's prescribed literary form. Both Fadeev and Stavskii were rewarded with secretarial positions on the Executive Board of the Union of Soviet Writers.[3] In Khrushchev's time, the charlatan scientist Trofim Lysenko held several positions of authority in the Academy of Sciences, where he was able to promote bogus theories and research on agrobiology, while authentic scientific inquiry into the biological subfield of genetics was banned.[4] More recently, under Brezhnev, Sergei Trapeznikov, whose historical writings praised collectivization, was placed in charge of the Central Committee department that oversaw the field of Party history. From this post, Trapeznikov played a leading role in suppressing the wave of new inquiry and historical revision that had begun in the early sixties.[5]

Although Soviet political authorities have succeeded in their efforts to influence the cultural production process, they have failed in a more fundamental sense. For any society, the functions of culture are several: relating the stories of a people's existence, present and past; providing an instrument that explains their physical and social environments; establishing standards of beliefs and values as well as norms of behavior; and conferring on individuals a sense of identity with and affinity to a particular group. In the Soviet Union, the regime's "official" culture has been only partially successful in fulfilling these functions. This official culture was manufactured for the general public, but it was a culture which to a large extent did not relate to reality, or acknowledge the needs and desires of that public. Many genuine elements of the popular culture—the hardships of everyday life, tragic episodes from the past, and different themes from religious, youth, and ethnic subcultures—were not allowed to be expressed openly. Attempts to participate in these forbidden zones of popular culture often led to harassment and persecution from police authorities. In addition, the official culture set standards for intellectual work in both the creative arts and sciences, which discouraged innovation in methods and approach as well as the advancement of new theories and interpretations. Soviet writers and artists, for example, have had to work through "socialist realism," a style conveying a realistic and positive depiction of socialist society. And Soviet social scientists have long been hampered in their efforts to explore and understand the inner workings of society because of the officially-sanctioned views concerning social structures and class relationships in the Soviet Union. Finally, the regime's attempt to use culture to develop in society behavioral and attitudinal norms reflecting the values of the regime has not been realized. In fact, the imposition through cultural media of desired social norms and values, which the representatives of political authority themselves blatantly ignored, have had just the opposite effect—popular disaffection with the regime and an unwillingness to work for its goals.

Because official culture failed to achieve widespread acceptance, an underground, or "unofficial" culture developed in Soviet society. This unofficial culture directly addressed the issues that the political-administrative guardians of Soviet culture had attempted to ban from public expression. The unofficial culture was sustained by a small group of intellectuals who refused to adhere to the regime's prescribed norms of intellectual work. Although disagreements with official intellectual and policy positions were commonly expressed in private, the members of this group were distinguished by their efforts to publicize their nonconformist views. The consequences for such behavior were often severe; including: ostracism within one's chosen profession; confinement in a state psychiatric facility; arrest and internment in a prison-labor camp; or, forced exile abroad. The members of this "dissident" intelligentsia were held in high esteem by many Soviet citizens because they spoke to the issues that directly affected their lives and because they followed their own convictions and not the dictates of the "official" line despite the personal risks involved. Aleksandr Solzhenitsyn, for example, suffered repeatedly at the hands of Soviet authorities and was eventually forced to leave the country for his persistent efforts to recount through literature the personal hardships endured by millions of loyal Soviet citizens in Stalin's prison camps. In his autobiography, Solzhenitsyn provided some insight into the motivations of the "dissident" intelligentsia:

> Underground is where you expect to find revolutionaries. But not writers . . . I entered into the inheritance of every modern Russian writer intent on the truth: I must write simply to ensure that it was not all forgotten, that posterity might someday come to know it . . . that it would someday smite the heads I had in my sights, and that those who received its invisible emanations would understand.[6]

Whereas the officially appointed guardians of culture were seen to represent formal-political authority in society, the "dissident" intelligentsia became identified with informal-moral authority.

The reformers who came to power in the Soviet Union in 1985 recognized that the dull and spiritless offerings of official culture produced harmful social effects. The reluctance and inability of the custodians of official culture to address with understanding and sensitivity many of the issues and concerns of contemporary Soviet society led to a situation described by one Soviet specialist as "a crisis of ideology, ethics and motivation."[7] Gorbachev, in particular, has indicated an awareness that the imposition of an official culture on society has contributed to the alienation of the ordinary citizens from the regime. "To achieve a radical change in this area," Gorbachev noted at the 27th Party Congress, "it is important to structure all cultural-educational work so that it fully satisfies the spiritual needs of the people and meets their interests."[8] Cultural reform, consequently, has become a major component of the larger process of domestic change now underway in the Soviet Union. Consistent with this larger process, the long-term aim of cultural reform is to break down the barriers that have long separated official culture from unofficial culture, formal authority from informal authority, and to demonstrate a genuine common cause between the regime and ordinary citizens. The program of cultural reform that has evolved under Gorbachev contains three principal means for moving toward this long-term goal: revising the ideological tenets governing the relationship between the State and society; creating a more accommodating environment for free expression; and legitimating many elements of the popular culture that have long been denied public expression.

Gorbachev has remarked on several occasions that *perestroika* requires a "revolution in the minds and in the ways of thinking" of the Soviet people.[9] This "revolution" would be facilitated by reforms that would open up the different cultural media in society to more innovative and thought-provoking presentations. For cultural reforms to be successful, they must be accompanied by ideological changes. The cultural realm of Soviet society is supervised by the Party's vast ideological and propaganda apparatus, which maintains offices in every Party organization from the center to the localities. The officials in this apparatus receive their instructions from the Party's chief ideologues in Moscow, who define in practical terms the limits of cultural expression based on ideological and political considerations. Under Brezhnev, the ideological frameworks established by Moscow theoreticians grew sclerotic and the work of the ideology and propaganda bureaucracies became a rote exercise in censorship and promotion of official policy lines. Conservative ideologues invoked the doctrinal tenets of Marxism-Leninism to support their actions. But Marxism-Leninism no longer functioned as an ideology of social progress; instead, it had become a State religion which in effect only justified the existing political and socio-economic hierarchy in Soviet society. The reformers who have come to power in the Soviet Union need to redefine the regime's ideological concepts so that the practical work of the ideology and propaganda bureaucracies will encourage rather than oppose the processes of change, especially in the cultural realm.

Additionally, cultural reform is attempting to establish a more accommo-dating environment for free expression, indicating that the regime's position on intellectual freedom is undergoing revision. In the past, the concept of intel-lectual freedom in itself was a rebuke to a government that required censorship and manipulation to inspire loyalty. It was not surprising that defenses and rationalizations were developed to justify repression and censorship in the cul-tural realm. One such rationalization appeared in the newspaper of the writer's union, *Literaturnaia gazeta*, in 1958, at a time when Khrushchev's reforms had sparked a debate over the autonomy of intellectuals:

> The socialist revolution has eliminated the question of freedom for creative work in the sense that it was an issue in exploiting societies. For an artist who truly serves the people in a socialist society, the question "Am I free or not in my

creative work?" simply never arises . . . What sort of reason can anybody have in our socialist conditions to pine for "freedom of creativity?" . . . The reason can only be sought in philistine individualism, a mortal sickness distinguishable from the plague perhaps only in that outbreaks of it still occur. Anybody who feels himself restricted by his part in the common cause should look deep in his own heart: he will probably find a wretched individualist lurking there.[10]

Such posturing was unable to blunt the issue of intellectual freedom. During the Brezhnev years, when the regime retreated from the more liberal cultural policies of Khrushchev, several outspoken intellectuals angered Soviet political authorities because of their repeated calls for the free expression of ideas. Andrei Sakharov, the acclaimed physicist, was one of these dissident intellectuals; in 1968, he wrote:

intellectual freedom is essential to human society—freedom to obtain and distribute information, freedom for open-minded and unfearing debate and freedom from pressure by officialdom and prejudices. Such a trinity of freedom of thought is the only guarantee against an infection of people by means of mass myths, which, in the hands of treacherous hypocrites and demagogues, can be transformed into bloody dictatorship. Freedom of thought is the only guarantee of the feasibility of a scientific democratic approach to politics, economy and culture.[11]

This view of intellectual freedom is similar to that of Gorbachev's and the reformers' in the political leadership. Under their influence, the relationship between political authority and culture in Soviet society is being redefined in such a way that the creative and scientific intelligentsia will have greater autonomy over their work. The responsibilities of the relevant bureaucracies have been scaled back, including the interventionary powers of cultural administrators to censor and to become involved in intellectual disputes. In addition, many of the once officially sanctioned factions in the arts and sciences have lost their monopolistic holds, and now must contend with competing factions for administrative positions and intellectual respect. It must be stressed, however, that these measures are intended to reduce, not eliminate, the influence of political authority in cultural affairs.

Finally, cultural reform seeks to legitimate many elements of Soviet society's popular culture, which were formerly considered taboo by the regime. The various groups that make up Soviet society—ethnic, regional, generational, occupational, educational—have long been denied the opportunity to fully develop their own subcultures. Instead, political authorities tried to fit a supraculture over all society, which was characterized by one set of values, standardized symbols, and uniform interpretations of present and past events. Elements of the various subcultures that conflicted with this supraculture were rooted out by the regime's ideological-administrative officials, and those who continued to pursue these subcultural themes were punished for their actions. By continually excluding subcultural themes, however, a situation developed in which the official supraculture became more distant from the reality of people's lives. The Soviet Union's new reformers recognize this situation. Aleksandr Iakovlev, for example, in an interview in *Moscow News* observed that "the Soviet individual has started experiencing a certain distrust in everything presented to him or her as spiritual food."[12] In an effort to reverse this trend, the present leadership has shown a greater tolerance for formerly banned subcultural themes, with the aim of creating a new relationship between politics and culture in Soviet society, marked by a coexistence between political authority and popular culture.

IDEOLOGICAL REVISION AND GLASNOST: SOVIET POLITICAL CULTURE IN TRANSITION

The reformers in the Soviet Union recognize that their efforts to restructure and reinvigorate the cultural realm might prove temporary, unless accompanied by a fundamental ideological revision and the development of a new political culture. Accordingly, a new theoretical framework is being elaborated under the ideological concept of "socialist pluralism," and an operational framework for the establishment of a more open society is likewise being fashioned, under the rubric of *glasnost*.

Throughout Soviet history, Marxist-Leninist ideology has served mainly a supporting role for policymakers. Even the first generation of Bolsheviks, in particular Lenin, realized that Marxist theory was not always a practical guide for action. The demands of governing often forced the Party's leaders into choosing policies that did not accord with their own professed ideological beliefs. Marx's writings could not be abandoned, however, since the Party derived legitimacy for its dominant political position in society by identifying itself as the vanguard organization of an inevitable socio-historic movement toward a more just social order, which Marx had prophesized. For the Party's leaders, the dictates of power proved less malleable than its ideology. When political leaders attempted major domestic and foreign policy reforms, ideological revision was used as a means of justifying and sanctifying these changes. New conceptual frameworks have been developed throughout Soviet history, which help to define the range of policy options available to political leaders as well as the range of acceptable behavior for ordinary citizens. These conceptual frameworks, in addition, attempt to demonstrate a lineage to Marxist-Leninist theory. The copious writings of Marx and Engels as well as Lenin's fifty-five volumes of collected works have provided Soviet leaders with a diverse store of opinions and pronouncements on the socio-economic and political development of society, which are selectively cited to support major policy changes.

Gorbachev is intent on revising the ideological framework that he inherited from Brezhnev. Brezhnev's domestic agenda, in marked contrast to his predecessor, Nikita Khrushchev, avoided dramatic policy reforms, ambitious mobilization campaigns and frequent personnel shake-ups; instead, this agenda sought to maintain the status quo in Soviet society. Theoretical concepts were employed to complement this conservative domestic agenda; for instance, it was said that the Soviet Union had entered a new historical-ideological stage—"the period of developed socialism and the gradual transition to communism." Under the rubric of developed socialism, a theoretical framework was devised that indicated that major policy reforms were no longer necessary, adhered to the position that a unity of interests existed in society, and reaffirmed the dominance of Party officialdom over the rest of society. "The main feature of this stage," wrote the regime's chief ideologist, Mikhail Suslov:

> is that the USSR has built mankind's first developed socialist society which is functioning successfully . . . Mature socialism presupposes the comprehensive and harmonious development of the economic, sociopolitical and cultural spheres . . . Developed socialism is characterized by mature social relations which are formed by undivided rule of socialist ownership, the abolition of all exploiter elements, and the formation of a politically and ideologically united society . . . The whole course of social development shows that as the tasks and scale of communist construction are extended, so the leading role of the Communist Party, its political, organizational, ideological and theoretical activity grows.[13]

Armed with this conservative ideological thesis, the regime's ideologues and propaganda officials, who oversaw the work of the artistic community, the mass media, and the academic institutions, prevented intellectual controversies or pointed criticisms of the system from reaching the public.

For Mikhail Gorbachev, an extensive ideological revision is necessary in order to undermine the formal base of cultural support for the political and socio-economic systems inherited from Brezhnev. Gorbachev has sought to relax the hold of ideological officials over cultural life and has also encouraged criticism and debate about these systems. In late 1986, *Pravda* strongly criticized the ultraconservatism of Brezhnev's rule, including the regime's underlying ideological principles, "where formalism took root and alienation from reality became the rule."[14] In early 1987, Gorbachev shifted the program of domestic reform in a new, more radical direction, intensifying the need for a new theoretical framework to legitimate these new policy proposals. Then-Party Secretary for ideology, Aleksandr Iakovlev, published an important article in the Party's main theoretical journal, *Kommunist*, in May 1987, stating that "it was necessary . . . to understand theoretically the problems and contradictions of the new society . . . [and] to work out concepts for the future."[15] In February 1988, Gorbachev delivered a major speech on the "ideological aspects of *perestroika*." The General Secretary insisted that his reform program was consistent with the principles of socialism and strongly criticized the former regime's confining ideological framework:

> [W]e are not deviating by a single step from socialism, from Marxism-Leninism, from everything won and created. But we are resolutely renouncing the dogmatic, bureaucratic and voluntarist legacy, because it has nothing in common either with Marxism-Leninism or with true socialism . . . Creative Marxism-Leninism is the unfailingly objective, profoundly scientific analysis of living, developing reality; critical analysis, evading nothing, concealing nothing, fearing no truth . . . Questions of theory cannot and should not be resolved by decrees of any kind. A free competition of minds is needed.[16]

The effort to legitimate new theoretical concepts for *perestroika* was resisted by members from the political and cultural elites, who opposed Gorbachev's proposals for more radical political and economic reforms. Within the Politburo, their views were represented by Egor Ligachev, who throughout 1987 and the first half of 1988 defended many of the Party's existing ideological tenets. Ligachev frequently clashed with the most outspoken reformers in the leadership, particularly Iakovlev, on various points of theory and procedure for Party rule. In September 1988, Gorbachev forcibly broke this stalemate within the Politburo by making a series of high-level personnel changes, including the reassignment of both Ligachev and Iakovlev to nonideological posts, and the promotion of Vadim Medvedev to the role of the Party's chief spokesman for ideological matters. In his first major address in this position, Medvedev confirmed that extensive theoretical revisions, under the guiding concept of "socialist pluralism," were in the process of being worked out to support Gorbachev's reform program.[17]

As a political and ideologial concept, pluralism had been viewed negatively by Soviet officials in the past because of its association with, first, "bourgeois" democracy and, later, with apostate movements, like Dubcek's "Prague Spring." Gorbachev was in office for almost two years before he used the term socialist pluralism in reference to his own reform program. By the second half of 1987, however, the notion that society's best interests were served by the public expression of a plurality of opinions was gaining credence in discussions on reform. In a speech before Soviet journalists, in July 1987, Gorbachev said that "even in the most extreme point of view there is something valuable, something rational, because a person who defends his point of view honestly displays concern for the common cause."[18] Only recently, this statement would have been considered too unorthodox to be spoken by the head of the Soviet State.

By the time the 19th Party Conference convened, in June 1988, socialist pluralism had become the main ideological concept underpinning *perestroika*. Socialist pluralism provided the reformers with a theoretical framework that supported the development of fundamentally new policy approaches to the problems of government and the conduct of societal affairs. On the eve of the Conference, for example, *Izvestiia* endorsed the notion of pluralism, stating that "a multiplicity, a diversity of forms of political, economic and spiritual life is not only not contradictory, but it is a condition for releasing the potential for socialism."[19] In his closing remarks to the Conference, Gorbachev observed that "the life and logic of restructuring are lifting us all and, combined with *glasnost* and the socialist pluralism of opinions, people are opening up and new ideas are appearing."[20] Although the 19th Party Conference was an important benchmark in the process of ideological reform, it was the September 1988 plenum, when the responsibilities for ideological affairs were turned over to Vadim Medvedev, that marked the point at which socialist pluralism was no longer an object of debate, but had become the accepted guiding ideological concept for Soviet politics in the reform process. In his first major address as the Party's chief ideologist, Medvedev strongly criticized the concept of developed socialism, claiming that it represented a "retreat from the methodology of Leninism," and endorsed the new concept of socialist pluralism, which "takes into account the real structure of society and the multitude of interests and aspirations of all social groups and communities of people."[21]

Although socialist pluralism is an abstract concept, it has enormous implications for the actual work performed in the cultural realm of Soviet society. Socialist pluralism signals a new standard of public discourse for Soviet society. Ideally, it entails the establishment and institutionalization of forums for public expression in which a diversity of opinions and viewpoints can be articulated. In these forums, the concerns and interests of the artistic, literary and scientific community as well as ordinary citizens can find expression. Political authorities would relinquish their monopolistic control over the means of mass communication and their imposed standards for intellectual activity. The workings of Soviet officialdom would become less secretive and more accessible to public scrutiny. The Soviet Union would be a more open society in which political authorities no longer tried to impose a monolithic culture, but, instead, learned to coexist with a diversified culture.

The extent to which cultural reform can be carried out in the Soviet Union is conditioned by the progress of political reform. At the 19th Party Conference, Gorbachev stated that "we have done a lot in the spiritual sphere and . . . we will conduct a radical economic reform. But this will get bogged down unless we reform the political system."[22] Although important measures have been taken to move toward a more open society, this transformation could still be reversed unless a new political culture is developed which is capable of accommodating a considerable increase of free expression within society. Gorbachev has openly addressed this dilemma: "Our political culture is still inadequate. Our standard of debate is still inadequate; our ability to respect the point of view of even our friends and comrades—even that is inadequate."[23] Socialist pluralism provides an ideological framework for the development of this new political culture. As a practical means toward achieving this goal, the reformers have relied on the new policy of openness—*glasnost*.

In his first major speech as General Secretary, in April 1985, Gorbachev used the term *glasnost* in a brief reference to the need for a more open relationship between the Soviet State and society. "The preparation for the 27th Party Congress," Gorbachev declared, "must understandably arouse the activeness of the Soviet people. The party committees must concern themselves with this, in order to guarantee openness (*glasnost*), in order to work through all channels of communication with the masses."[24] At the 27th Party Congress, the concept of *glasnost* was formally expanded to encompass the mass media. A resolution issued at the conclusion of the Congress stated:

The Congress notes the growing role of the means of mass information and propaganda in the realization of the economic strategies of the party, its social policies, in the formation of social consciousness, and considers television, radio and the press as profound instruments of *glasnost* and social control.[25]

In the months that followed, *glasnost* was promoted with greater frequency as a principal element of domestic reform. Authoritative articles appeared in the press urging Soviet officialdom and the general public "to learn to live under the conditions of *glasnost*."[26] In meaning, *glasnost* evolved into an umbrella term, encompassing the various policies intended to bring about a more open society.

In this effort to establish a new manner of political discourse in Soviet society, *glasnost* has three specific functions: restoring the credibility of the regime as a source of information; making political officials subject to criticism and public accountability; and, creating forums where public opinion can be voiced and different social interests represented. The regime under Brezhnev had lost its credibility as a reliable source of information about contemporary Soviet society. During this period, Soviet officials exaggerated the levels of economic production and inflated reports about the standard of living. At the same time they prohibited the publication of negative news, such as crime statistics or industrial accidents. This practice extended to the regime's interpretation of world events and even its own history. By the 1970s, the Soviet public had become better educated and in general more discerning of information supplied by the regime's propaganda officials. The result was described by Gorbachev in a speech to Soviet journalists, in July 1987: "When you and I tried to paint everything in rosy colors, the people could see through it all. They lost interest in the press and public activity, and they felt they were being degraded and insulted when they were presented with a fake."[27] This practice has gradually been reduced under the conditions of *glasnost*. Since the Chernobyl disaster, in April 1986, when public acknowledgement was delayed for several days, the Soviet press has been considerably more prompt and candid in its coverage of Soviet society.

Glasnost also is being used as a means for making political officials more accountable to the public. The proceedings of Party and Soviet meetings are reported more fully by the news media. Even the Politburo now issues a brief summary of the issues discussed during its weekly sessions. The Soviet press has been encouraged to develop the techniques of investigative journalists in order to act as a nonbureaucratic checking mechanism on the activities of Party and State officials. As part of *perestroika*, Gorbachev has stressed that political authorities must assume greater responsibility for their actions and subject themselves to public criticism whenever there are serious lapses in their work. At a meeting of media representatives, in February 1987, the General Secretary observed that "criticism is a bitter pill, but illness makes it an essential one."[28] *Glasnost* has provided the Soviet Union's political reformers with a policy, which demonstrates that political authority exists for the benefit of the general public, and not vice-versa. This theme was sounded by Boris Eltsin at the 19th Party Conference: "The Party is for the people, and the people must know all that it does."[29]

Lastly, *glasnost* has helped the transition to a new political culture through the creation of new forums for public expression and the reinvigoration of old ones. Nearly all the means of mass communication in Soviet society now provide some kind of forum in which issues can be debated and public opinion vented. Professional journals and newspapers regularly feature "letters to the editor" columns, where a wide range of opinions about the current reform process are published. Soviet television has also adapted some of its news and talk programs for audience participation, where it is not uncommon to see government officials put on the defensive by direct questioning from the audience. The more open climate in the academic, artistic, literary, and filmmaking communities has given these media the opportunity to express a diversity of views on contemporary Soviet life as well as the Soviet past. Furthermore, there has been an effort to restructure the format of the formal meetings of political and socio-cultural organizations so that open debate is the norm. The 19th Party Conference served as a model of how this end could be pursued: the proceedings were marked by lively exchanges over the most critical issues in the reform process, while the public enjoyed full coverage from the news media. As a form of political discourse and public communication, the Conference successfully provided a national forum in which a plurality of opinions was heard.

It must be stressed, however, that *glasnost* is not without its limits, even for the reformers in the political leadership. Not all subjects, for example, have been accorded the same degree of openness and scrutiny. The reigns of both Stalin and Brezhnev have been denounced in sweeping terms, despite the positive accomplishments of each, but overt criticisms of Lenin still appear only rarely. Although the inner workings of Soviet officialdom have become less secret, political authorities continue to withhold a considerable amount of information about their activities from the general public.

A notable example is the leadership's refusal to publish the text of Boris Eltsin's impromptu speech, delivered at the October 1987 plenum, in which he personally attacked Ligachev as an opponent of reform and, subsequently, led to Eltsin's removal from the Politburo. The editor of *Izvestiia*, I. D. Laptev, who is generally depicted as a reform supporter, has warned that *glasnost* is becoming too negative: "Won't we repeat the error of our predecessors, who presented history as a sequence of unadulterated epoch-making achievements? Won't we rush to the other extreme by presenting history as a sequence of nothing but errors?"[30] And, in a speech to media representatives, in September 1988, Gorbachev chided the press for its coverage of *perestroika*: "It [the press] must resolutely eschew incorrect approaches or the compilation of 'hair-raising' cases. This is what the conservatives and the fair-weather progressives are waiting for! . . . And when people write that working people are disenchanted with restructuring and have no faith in it, they are being irresponsible."[31]

Gorbachev's program of change for the Soviet Union has not been well received at all levels of Soviet society. In particular, ideological revision and the policies of cultural reform have been opposed by conservative representatives from the country's political and cultural elites. The views of this group have received prominent attention in the mass media through the influence of sympathetic editorial boards and program directors. The editor of *Sovetskaia Rossiia*, V. Chikin, for instance, has argued that Gorbachev's radical reforms are heading in the directon of "ideological homelessness."[32] Within the leadership, the conservative position was defended by Egor Ligachev, who for more than two years was one of the Party's leading authorities on ideology, and Viktor Chebrikov, who during this same period served as head of the KGB. They opposed the adoption of the new ideological concepts which legitimated Gorbachev's radical reform agenda and publicly criticized the application of the concept of pluralism to Soviet society. In a speech before Soviet teachers, in August 1987, Ligachev argued that "political and ideological pluralism" would eventually lead to social disorder.[33] In September of the same year, Chebrikov warned that certain groups within the country were trying to cultivate "the bourgeois understanding of democracy, removing the process of increasing the working people's sociopolitical activeness from the party's influence, splitting the monolithic unity of Party and people, and instilling political and ideological pluralism."[34] In addition, the conservatives have disputed the position taken by the reformers, that certain periods of Soviet history, especially that of Stalin's, represented a sharp deviation from Lenin and a disruption in the development of socialism in Soviet society. Ligachev has written that "people abroad, and even people in our own country, try to denigrate the entire path of the building of socialism . . . to present it as an unbroken chain of errors . . . Some authors even go so far as to claim that after Lenin's death the country took a different path."[35] Ligachev's view implies that a comprehensive revision of the regime's guiding ideological precepts is not necessary.

For the conservatives, the policy of *glasnost* must have well-defined limits. *Glasnost* should not be directed toward the development of a new political culture, but, rather, toward the eradication of cynical attitudes and irresponsible behavior throughout Soviet society. This position has been most clearly defined by Egor Ligachev and has been referred to as "constructive *glasnost*." There are three points that distinguish the conservative's constructive *glasnost* from the reformer's *glasnost*. First, under constructive *glasnost*, the normative functions of culture are emphasized. The notion of "art for art's sake," for instance, is simply not recognized; the socialization function of culture supercedes its aesthetic value. Ligachev urged representatives from the television and radio media, for example, to conduct "active propaganda of socialism's indisputable advantages over capitalism."[36] Second, the intellectual and administrative authority of the regime's political-ideological officials must be recognized in the various cultural fields. "We won't diverge," Ligachev wrote in *Sovetskaia kultura*, "from the principles of classicism, realism in art and the communist direction of art and the spiritual sphere."[37] Third, the representatives of the mass media and the creative arts must demonstrate social responsibility and, through their work, emphasize the positive in Soviet society. At the 27th Party Congress, Ligachev assailed the press for its excessive criticisms: "Unfortunately, some newspapers, including the editorial board of *Pravda*, have allowed shortcomings. Criticism should be aimed at the eradication of the obsolete, at the strengthening and development of socialist democracy and social construction."[38]

This struggle between reformers and conservatives over the attempt to redefine the contours of Soviet political culture is especially relevant for the cultural sphere. The extent to which the reformers are successful in establishing a more open environment for political discourse will determine the new boundaries for the work of Soviet journalists and artists. "[W]e are now speaking about a pluralism of views," Iakovlev commented at the 19th

Party Conference, "so that everyone can freely express himself, put forward his proposals, uphold them. The wisdom of democracy, including in the party, should manifest itself in truly sensing these interests, sentiments and uniting them."[39] Socialist pluralism and *glasnost* provide the theoretical and the practical frameworks through which these changes are currently being realized.

EXPANDING THE BOUNDARIES OF FREE EXPRESSION

If the Soviet Union is to make the transition to a more open society as its leaders have claimed, then steps must be taken to redress the institutional structure of Soviet culture. Although socialist pluralism and *glasnost* provide the necessary foundation, the reforms must also reach the levels of cultural production, distribution and administration. The general theoretical and policy principles which encourage greater freedom of expression must be accompanied by a genuine effort to scale back the presence of political authorities in the institutions concerned with cultural activity. It is through such institutional checks that free expression has been stifled for so long. Three institutional impediments, in particular, have become the targets of cultural reformers: the legal framework, which defines the limits allowed for cultural workers; the executive boards of the creative unions and the editorial boards of the various newspapers and journals, which have been monopolized by conservative factions; and the State's own administrative apparatus, which oversees the cultural realm of Soviet society.

Although provisions for free expression have always existed in the Soviet Union's Constitution as well as in the bylaws of the creative unions and publishing houses, these guarantees were never enforced. Political authorities routinely infringed upon these rights whenever it was deemed expedient to silence a nonconformist point of view. Although *glasnost* has led to a climate of greater tolerance on the part of political authorities, fears still exist among the advocates of cultural reform that *glasnost*, like Khrushchev's thaw, will prove to be short-lived. At their urging, an effort is now underway to enact well-defined and enforceable regulations, which will provide genuine legal protection for free expression in Soviet society. The historian Leonid Batkin argued this position in an article appearing in June 1988:

> *glasnost* should lead to the elimination of "*glasnost*." And it should be replaced by freedom of speech. That is, from being a process permitted and encouraged,

directed from above, and welcomed by us, it should turn into the legally guaranteed expression of the diverse opinions of citizens and their organizations in line with, or, perhaps, at variance with, official points of view.[40]

This effort has been countered by conservatives, who represent the vested interests of Soviet officialdom and the sentiments of a portion of the general public who are uncomfortable with the numerous criticisms that *glasnost* has unleashed. Rather than opposing the effort to draft new legislation for *glasnost*, the conservatives have attempted to use the opportunity to establish new limits on free expression and to reaffirm the authority of political-administrative officials over the cultural sphere of society. The process of drafting new regulations and laws for Soviet culture thus has become one of the crucial battlefields in the cultural reform movement.

At the 19th Party Conference, in June 1988, the first result of these efforts, the long-awaited resolution on *glasnost*, was published. The resolution was intended to work into the fabric of Soviet law and society a clear reading of the limits and expectations of cultural reform. Although the resolution was generally supportive of cultural reform, the language was ambiguous and cautious, suggesting the influence of the political conservatives in the leadership. On the pro-reform side, the resolution noted that *glasnost* had yet to reach its limits and that more change was necessary. In addition, the resolution stated that *glasnost* meant a public airing of "a diversity of interests . . . and the socialist pluralism of opinions." "Ultimately," the resolution read, "*glasnost*, criticism and self-criticism serve the interests of the people, reflect the openness of society's political system, and are evidence of its strength, political viability and moral health." Most importantly, the resolution explicitly linked the policy of *glasnost* to the notion of the "right to know." The resolution said that it was "the inalienable right of every citizen to obtain, on any social issue, full and authentic information that does not represent a State or military secret." The resolution concluded that "*glasnost* is the natural atmosphere of the life and progress of a democratic and humane socialism."[41]

On the conservative side, the resolution stressed that *glasnost* could not be used to promote selfish interests identified as "personal ends," "cliquishness," "demagoguery," "ethnic-regional" interests, and "corporate egoisms." These qualifications suggest that free expression will be tolerated only to the extent that the interests of the State do not become the subject of dispute. For the conservatives, the inclusion of this list of qualifications, even if vague, is significant because it affects the overall debate about *pere-*

stroika, which in fact is focused on the redefinition of the legitimate balance between the interest of the State and society in the Soviet Union. The resolution on *glasnost* issued by the Conference was intended to serve as a general guide until a more authoritative and less ambiguous law on *glasnost* was published, but, as of the end of 1988, this law was still being debated.

Throughout 1987 and 1988, the effort to draft a new law concerning freedom of the press also became a point of contention between cultural reformers and conservatives. In his trial in 1967, the dissident Vladimir Bukovskii raised the issue of free expression in a context which has now become acceptable: "We know that freedom of speech and of the press is, in the first place, freedom to criticize. No one has ever been forbidden to praise the government. If these articles about freedom of speech and of the press have been put into the Constitution, then the Government must have the patience to listen to criticism."[42] The difficulty of defining the proper role for the press in Soviet society can be discerned from the remarks of Viktor Afanasev, the editor-in-chief of *Pravda*, who at the 19th Party Conference described the press as both the "socialist opposition" and the "mirror of party work . . . [and] party organizations."[43] In the more open atmosphere of *glasnost*, the Soviet press has developed dual, but contradictory, functions: serving as a propaganda instrument for official organs and acting as a watchdog over these same political organs. Although the press has been used for propaganda since the earliest days of the Soviet regime, it has not had much experience watching over government activities. Since 1985, however, Gorbachev has encouraged the press to act as a check on the activities of Soviet officialdom. Not surprisingly, the political and cultural conservatives in Soviet society have reacted strongly to this new idea. Iurii Bondarev, for example, a Deputy Chairman of the Board of the RSFSR Writers Union, has called for a retreat from the current wave of "nihilistic" journalism that "cannot teach morality to others" and that "molds public opinion by stunning readers and viewers with sensationalist noise and abuse, and juggling with and distorting historical facts."[44] Egor Ligachev has addressed this issue on a number of occasions; at the 19th Party Conference, for example, he warned that "some newspaper editors . . . clearly took the respect and trust shown them by the Central Committee to mean an opportunity to do as they wish, to evade Party control, and to use newspapers for settling personal scores."[45] The reformers, who favor the notion of a more independent press, have argued for a law defining press freedoms. Georgii Baklanov, the editor of *Znamia*, the monthly journal of the USSR Writers Union, made such a plea at the 19th Party Conference: "there must be a law on the press. The press cannot subsist on a whim: Today it is for *glasnost*, and tomorrow it may be against it . . . . What kind of socialism will there be without *glasnost*? The socialism of the voiceless."[46]

M. A. Fedotov, a senior lecturer at the All-Union Juridical Institute, provided an insightful discussion on the formulation of a law on the press and information in an article, published in 1987, in the official journal of the Ministry of Justice, *Sovetskoe gosudarstvo i pravo (Soviet State and Law)*. Fedotov urged that the law should apply to all forms of mass media with the capacity to disseminate information on a wide basis and that the new law must provide a legal basis for a new relationship between the press and political authorities, which would increase the autonomy of publishers and editors. He argued that the new law must clarify the meaning of "free expression" and the "formulation of opinions" in order to eliminate the gray areas between what at present is sanctioned by law and the actual practices of publishers and editors. Further, Fedotov made several suggestions for making the process of obtaining information easier for members of the mass media and the creation of a formal process by which public officials were forced to justify in writing why some information was denied to the press. Fedotov concluded that the new law on the press and information must provide both "a powerful new impetus to the participation of the press in *perestroika*" and "a uniform legal mechanism governing the relations between the local Soviet and Party and the Soviet press organs."[47]

Through 1988, authorities had yet to promulgate a new law on freedom of the press while reformers and conservatives continued to debate its content. To date, the evidence suggests that conservatives have had the most influence on the process. In a roundtable discussion of this new law, covered by *Moscow News*, Iurii Baturin, of the Ministry of Justice's Institute on State and Law, revealed that a draft law on press freedoms had already been composed, but was witheld from public circulation and discussion. According to Baturin, this particular draft was "heavily censored" by political authorities, who opposed taking steps to give Soviet journalists greater independence. He said, for example, that the provision requiring formal written explanations, for information denied to journalists had been deleted from the draft version.[48]

Another area of conflict between the cultural reformers and the conservatives is the selection process for positions on the executive boards of the various creative trade unions and the editorial boards of the major newspapers and professional journals. Because of the centralized structure of the cultural professions, members of these boards are able to exert enormous influence over whose work will be recognized and supported. With the consent of political authorities, these board positions have been monopolized for a number of years by conservatives, whose actions more often reflected political, rather than artistic and intellectual, considerations. Iurii Afanasev, the head of the State Historical-Archives Institute and one of the leading spokesmen for reform in the history profession, has assailed the "administrators" of history, who carried out "a campaign to stop scientific quests in historical science at the beginning of the 1970s."[49] The political reformers in the leadership have tried to lend assistance to the effort to dislodge the conservatives from positions of authority in the different cultural professions. Aleksandr Iakovlev, in particular, has frequently criticized the monopolistic holds of these conservative factions. In a speech to the country's leading social scientists, gathered at Moscow State University in November 1987, Iakovlev argued that "monopolization and cliquishness" had led to an "unhealthy atmosphere" in the social sciences, leaving the field badly underdeveloped both for scholarly pursuits and as an aid to policymakers.[50] The effort to break the hold of the conservatives thus far has produced mixed results; some creative unions and publications are now undergoing a virtual renaissance through the vitality and intellectual interests of new directors, while other executive and editorial boards remain bastions of conservatism.

Most of the leading literary journals have recently had a turnover in editors, many of whom are changing the contents and directions of their respective journals or newspapers. Since August of 1986 the journal *Novyi Mir*, the leading monthly of the USSR Writer's Union, has been run by Sergei Zalygin, a respected author in his own right. Zalygin is continuing in the progressive tradition of Aleksandr Tvardovskii, *Novyi Mir*'s editor in the 1960s, by publishing many formerly banned and controversial works. Another monthly of the USSR Writers' Union, *Znamia*, is headed by Georgii Baklanov, who has significantly rebuilt the journal's reputation. *Znamia* has provided some of the most daring tests of the new openness to date, publishing Mikhail Bulgakov's *The Heart of a Dog*, a satirical look at Lenin's time in power, and Evegenii Zamiatin's dysutopian novel, *We*, the forerunner of Orwell's *1984* and Huxley's *Brave New World*. The appointments of Vitalii Korotich as chief editor of *Ogonek* and Egor Jakovlev as chief editor of *Moskovskie Novosti* were among the most important editorial changes, as these two publications have been at the forefront of cultural reform.

Another means of controlling culture in the Soviet Union are the various artistic unions. Only union members can publish widely or are allowed to produce artistic works for public presentation. Many members of the artistic world who were considered potentially disruptive were denied membership to the artistic unions or had their memberships revoked. However, in a series of elections held since just before Gorbachev took power, a dramatic turnover in the leadership of the artistic unions has taken place. Currently, the majority of the artistic unions (in fact, all but the Congress of Composers), have eased the creative constraints imposed during the late Brezhnev era by electing new union leaders to replace the bureaucrats who previously directed the organizations. The people now in control of these unions are, on the whole, respected active members of their profession and supporters of perestroika.

In May 1986, for example, the 5th Congress of the Cinematographers Union voted out the entrenched leadership of the last two decades and placed Elem Klimov at its head. Klimov is a noted filmmaker with a history of producing works that test the limits of political tolerance, such as his film *Come and See*. Under Klimov, a Disputes Commission was formed that has released formerly banned films, such as *Repentance* and *Commissar*, with many more releases expected in the future. The replacement of Georgii Markov by Viktor Karpov at the 8th Congress of the Writers Union in July of 1986 was another example of the restructuring of the leadership of the artistic unions. At this Congress, a number of other changes were called for, including a demand for reorganization of the publishing industry, establishing a process for the review of editorial decisions, and creating a Pasternak commission.[51] The theater world was also shaken when the VTO (All-Russion Theatrical Society) was disbanded and, under the leadership of Oleg Efremov, was replaced by the First Congress of the RSFSR Theater Workers Union.

The final institutional impediment to free expression is the regime's extensive administrative apparatus, which closely supervises all aspects of culture. The proponents of cultural reform in the leadership recognize that to be successful they must relax the powerful bureaucratic controls that have prevented many popular themes from being expressed. Aleksandr Iakovlev, for example, has warned that although people can be forced into silence, "you cannot prohibit them from thinking. And the silence is always explosive." Accordingly, Iakovlev has argued that the rejuvenation of Soviet culture requires "throwing off to a significant extent the burden of pedantic over-regulation that consumed a great deal of time and energy."[52] There is an attempt now underway to place greater distance between the administration of culture and creative processes.

As part of this effort, there has been an almost complete turnover in the top leadership positions of the various cultural bureaucracies. In the Party bureaucracy, for example, in addition to Vadim Medvedev's appointment as the new chief ideologist, leadership changes have been made in the Central Secretariat's departments for propaganda, ideology, and culture. The new head of the Culture Department, Iurii Voronov, is especially noteworthy, since he made his reputation mainly as a poet, and not as a politician. Within the government offices that monitor and are responsible for culture, there also have been important leadership changes. In September of 1986, the Minister of Culture, Petr Demichev, was replaced by Vasilii Zakharov. Zakharov has been outspoken in his support of greater independence for artistic unions, the elimination of "bans" on certain topics, and a reduction of the interventionary powers of the cultural bureaucracies.[53] Also replaced were the chairmen of *Goskino* (State Committee for Cinematography), *Goskomizdat* (State Committee for Publishing Houses, Printing Plants, and the Book Trade), *Gostelradio* (State Committee for Radio and Television), and *Glavlit* (Main Administration for Safeguarding State Secrets in the Press), the official censor, which was responsible for editing all works and making final determinations about what was and was not permissible.

The Soviet bureaucracy is now coming under attack for perpetuating a "cult of secrecy" in society. These attacks in particular have called for a reexamination of the censorship process. In an interview with *L'Humanité*, the French Communist Party newspaper, Gorbachev addressed this issue:

> [censorship] exists in our country . . . Its purpose is to prevent the publication of State and military secrets, the propagandization of war violence, affronts to personal dignity, and pornography in the press. The screening, editing, abridgement, etc. of works for publication is the business of the mass media and the book publishers themselves, of their editorial boards and editorial councils.[54]

The fate of the State's vast censorship bureaucracy has become one of the most important issues affecting cultural reform. In a break with past practices, the new head of *Glavlit*, V. A. Boldyrev, granted an interview with an *Izvestiia* correspondent, in which he discussed the problems of finding a compatible fit between *glasnost* and censorship. Boldyrev acknowledged that in the past Soviet censors helped to foster an air of secrecy around the activities of Soviet officials in order to conceal shortcomings and failings. He argued that it was necessary to move away from the excessive secrecy of the past and towards a more open, "information society." Boldyrev stressed that *Glavlit* was contributing to this process. For example, he claimed that the number of topics which could not be discussed in public has been reduced by almost a third, and that over 7500 previously banned book titles have been returned to public library catalogues. Boldyrev summed up *Glavlit's* new policy with the following: "Whatever is not forbidden is allowed." The list of forbidden topics supplied by Boldyrev, however, contained several ambiguous categories, such as "using the press for the purpose of undermining the socialist system" and "the publication of material not compatible with the requirements of social morality."[55]

Boldyrev also took a firm stand in favor of continuing the practice of "prior censorship," which in the past entailed the prescreening and editing of almost everything that goes to press. Boldyrev emphasized that prior censorship performs a valuable "preventive" function for Soviet culture. "We have drawn a clear conclusion," he stated, "prior control is a more effective and less 'painful' method of safeguarding State secrets in the press." For cultural reformers, however, prior censorship remains a significant obstacle to the establishment of a genuinely open society. As M. K. Ivanov has argued, it now "seems timely and practicable to free the press and other information carriers from preliminary censorship."[56] And Mikhail Fedotov has said that "the essentially bureaucratic, preliminary censorship looks like a monument to the style of administrative command."[57] The political reformers in the leadership have yet to support the elimination of prior censorship. In fact, in November of 1988, Vadim Medvedev forced the editorial staff of the literary journal *Novyi Mir* to recall and revise over a million copies of its magazine when its cover advertised the imminent publication of Aleksandr Solzhenitsyn's *Gulag Archipelago*, thereby reaffirming the official ban on his writings.[58]

While the institutional and administrative agencies that control publication are now somewhat less instrusive, there is still strong State involvement in determining what will be published. Control of printed materials is maintained in the Soviet Union through a variety of means. The publishing industry is, of course, owned by the State. Only State publishing houses in the Soviet Union have access to printing presses and paper supplies on a large scale. Book publication is controlled by the State Commission for

Publishing, Printing and Book Trade, as well as the publishing houses of organizations like the Party, the Academy of Sciences and the Ministry of Defense. Large-scale independent publishing has in the past been impossible. Newspapers are also monitored, since they are usually the official organs of either political or administrative organizations. For example, national newspapers like *Pravda* and *Izvestiia* are officially the papers of the Party's Central Committee and the government's Supreme Soviet, respectively. Other papers represent individual ministries or public institutions. In each case, the editorial boards determine what makes its way into print.

If true cultural independence is going to exist in the Soviet Union, there must be an acceptance of nonofficial cultural expression. The establishment of independent publishing houses and co-operative theaters and newspapers would be an obvious indication that the State is allowing a greater degree of cultural freedom. Since an integral element of Gorbachev's economic reforms is the introduction of independent economic cooperatives existing alongside state factories and industries, individual initiative in the cultural sphere seemingly should be encouraged as well. There are some early signs of movement in this direction. Authors are now publishing their own works at their own expense. An example of an independently produced publication was reported in *Moscow News*, in an article about the Consultative Cooperative Center's and the Moscow Cooperative Institute of the USSR Centrosoiuz's publication, in July 1988, of a cooperative newspaper entitled the *Cooperatives Herald*. The publishers of the new newspaper explained that "the cooperative publishes the paper with its own money. We paid over 2,000 rubles to print 20,000 copies."[59]

Likewise, it appears that independent theaters are now being allowed to use individual cost-accounting as a basis for their operations. This means that, in theory at least, theaters that are responsible for financing and producing their own plays are also responsible for the contents of the plays, removing the necessity of State financial support and approval by the Union for their productions. The new Irkutsk theater is already operating on such a cost-accounting basis and according to its producers "risks financial failure . . . if the public does not like their productions."[60] Although this particular theater is partially subsidized by the Irkutsk Region Department of Culture, if these and other experiments are successful, the USSR may soon have a number of experimental theaters that are no longer under the direct supervision of the Union of Theater Workers of the USSR.

There are, however, indications that the State is reluctant to allow independent artistic activity to run unchecked, and in an effort to control the process they have introduced a number of obstacles. For example, Gennadi Gerasimov, the official spokesperson for the Soviet Foreign Ministry, cited the paper and machinery shortages in the Soviet Union, as well as a decision not to have commercial competition, as the reasons behind the October 1987 decree of the Council of Ministers, halting independent publishing cooperatives. This decision was leaked and brought to public attention by the unofficial journal *Glasnost* in February of 1988.[61] General Secretary Gorbachev as well has shown support for some of these constrictive policies. In his address to Media Chiefs early in 1988, Gorbachev explained that "the Soviet press is not a private shop . . . Let us recall Lenin's premise that literature is part of the common cause of the Party. The service to society, to one's people has always been characteristic of our intelligentsia and our literature."[62]

THE LEGITIMATION OF POPULAR CULTURE

In the past, in order to avoid direct confrontation with authorities, Soviet writers and artists devised a number of clever stratagems to express their true viewpoints, through the use of indirect references and analogies, which Soviet audiences had learned to interpret and understand. According to one specialist of Soviet culture, "Over the years, Soviet historians, writers and literary critics have developed an intricate system of allusions and code words that educated readers readily understood . . . thus making it possible, with some connivance of the authorities, to discuss a reasonably wide variety of issues."[63] These literary devices have made it possible for Soviet writers to stay within the framework of the censors' tolerance and yet make critical observations about their own country. What has begun to change, however, is that it is no longer necessary to use these subterfuges; it is now possible to write and publish openly critical articles in the press and journals. In many cases, the policy of *glasnost* has moved the debate from "between the lines" to the front page.

Although the extent to which cultural reform will be allowed to flourish in the Soviet Union has not yet been determined, *glasnost* and the resulting willingness to address issues and historical topics long considered taboo have resulted in three important improvements on the cultural front. The first is the publication of authors whose works address political and cultural themes previously off-limits to the artistic world. Most of these works, in both literature and film, have been on the shelf awaiting release in the Soviet Union for a number of years. The second is the publication of émigré authors whose works have been considered antisocialist in nature. And finally, there is a new willingness to open the scope of the artistic world to include more contemporary and younger participants, such as the State's acceptance of rock and roll music and the publication of young authors and poets. These changes have resulted in a jump in circulation of the leading literary magazines and journals, a number of new television and radio programs that deal more honestly with contemporary social problems, and the presentation to the public of films, books and artistic pieces that challenge the accepted cultural mores of the last few decades.

The process of addressing the past in the Soviet Union involves the restoration of authors and artists who, for political reasons, have been excised from the Soviet artistic community, and whose works have been kept from the Soviet people. Most of these writers, directors, artists, and filmmakers are having their works published, produced, or displayed, and many have had their previously revoked memberships to artistic unions restored. In addition, contemporary social problems are receiving new examination due to the changes in cultural policy. Articles are now appearing in Soviet newspapers and books concerning such troubling problems as the environment, the fear of nuclear disaster, the resentment of the endless lines for scant provisions, natural calamities, the rampant abuse of alcohol, and the growing problem of drug abuse. Such issues as bureaucratic incompetency now headline evening television programs. One result of *perestroika* is the recognition that there are many difficult problems facing Soviet society and that such problems are now open to both literary and journalistic treatment.

The reexamination of Stalinism in both historical studies and artistic works in the Soviet Union today is beginning to, as Gorbachev has put it, fill in the "blank spaces" of Soviet history. Since the release of director Tengiz Abuladze's film *Repentance* at the end of 1986, the Soviet people have been exposed to a number of films, articles, and books that deal with the history of the Soviet Union under Stalin, and address sensitive issues including the prison labor camps, collectivization of the peasantry, and new interpretations of historical figures such as Bukharin, Trotsky, and Nicholas II. When the Georgian film *Repentance* was first shown in Moscow and Leningrad, it created a stir both inside and out of the Soviet Union. The film, which was made in 1984, describes a village run by a petty dictator, Varlam Aravidze, who bears a deliberate likeness to Stalin's notorious captain of the secret police, Lavrenti Beria. The plot of the film follows the bizarre tale of how the buried body of Aravidze keeps reappearing. The obvious point made with satiric humor is that such horrors cannot remain undergound, and that the truth of a brutal past cannot be covered over. As Abuladze points out, "Beria and Beriashivism had such deep roots among us that everything must be done to prevent its return . . . (its traces) are manifest even today, and this is what we have to struggle with."[64]

Works by prominent literary figures describing the difficulty of life under Stalin have been published in Soviet journals and magazines. In the spring of 1987, excerpts from Anatolii Rybakov's book *Children of the Arbat* began appearing in the weekly magazine *Ogonek*. The novel, which was completed over twenty years ago and finally published in *Druzhba naradov*, a literary monthly for several Soviet nationality groups, tells the story of Sasha Pankratov, who, like Rybakov himself, was a victim of Stalin's terror and was exiled to Siberia. The Stalin terror is also described in Anna Akhmatova's poem *Requiem* which is likewise based on personal experience. The poem describes the suffering that the mothers, wives, and daughters of the victims of Stalin's purges endured as their loved ones were imprisoned and killed. Also published in 1987 were Anatolii Pristavkin's novel, *A Golden Cloud Passed the Night*, in the monthly journal *Znamia*, and Iosif Gerasimov's *A Knock at the Door* in *Oktiabr*, the revitalized monthly journal published by the RSFSR Writer's Union. Pristavkin's book chronicles the forced resettlement of the Chechen, an ethnic minority group in the Caucasus mountains, under Stalin; while Gerasimov's novel focuses on the imposed resettlement of the Moldavians. Finally both Vasilii Grossman's novel *Life and Fate* written in 1980 and recently serialized in *Oktiabr*, and Vladimir Dudintsev's work *White Robes* which was published in early 1987 in *Neva*, the journal of Leningrad Writers Union, deal with aspects of Stalinism in realistic and harsh terms. In *White Robes*, Dudinstev narrates the debacle of Soviet science under the charlatan biogeneticist Trofim Lysenko, while Grossman's novel goes as far as to equate Stalinism with Nazism.

Besides Stalinism, other formerly taboo historical themes have been opened to Soviet intellectuals. Sergei Zalygen, a novelist and the editor fo Novui Mir, has written the novel, *After the Storm* which was published over a number of years on the journal *Druzhba naradov*. Zalygin's novel focuses on the political and economic situation in the Soviet Union in the 1920s, a period on economic innovation known officially as the New Economic Policy (NEP), and from which the present leadership seeks to draw justification for its current reforms. Another prominent cultural figure, Elem Klimov, who was elected first secretary of the Union of Cinematographers in 1986, has finally seen his film *Agony*, now renamed *Rasputin*, released. Klimov's film, made in 1975, was not shown publicly until 1985, and is significant for its representation of Nicholas II in a sympathetic light. In contrast, Vasilii Grossman's *All is Flux*, which *Oktiabr* has announced it will publish in 1989, depicts Lenin in an untraditional and highly controversial light, viewing him as the true founder of the Soviet totalitarian state.

In support of the charge to reexamine history, Mikhail Shatrov's recent plays, *The Peace of Brest* and *Onward, Onward, Onward*, are further evidence of a deeply felt cultural response. Soviet history is now being opened up to freer inquiry. Soviet historians, with the exception of dissident historians like Roy Medvedev, are only now following the lead of the authors and playwrights in their reexamination of the past. As Aleksandr Svobodin pointed out in his review of *The Peace of Brest* for *Moscow News*:

> It is a paradox that the dramatist has anticipated historians. We know next to nothing about the characters and careers of Lenin's closest allies Trotsky and Bukharin (who both appear in the play), and have little idea about Stalin's real, not mythological role in Soviet history . . . Shatrov does not retouch or simplify his characters. He offers us irrevocable facts, the history which ought to have long passed from the archives to the books and scholarly discussions open to every conscious citizen.[65]

Many believe that if Gorbachev is to be successful in changing political culture he must enable historians, artists, and journalists to document fully the previous political cultures, including the realities of Stalin, the early revolutionary period, and the 1920s in which Lenin's NEP flourished. As he stated in February 1987, the historiography of the past hasn't been history, but "artificial, time-serving constructions . . . we should not relegate to the shadows those who made the revolution. It is necessary to educate people by the example of those who laid down their lives for the revolution and socialism."[66]

In *Onward, Onward, Onward*, Shatrov examines the personal relationship between Stalin and Lenin and explores the idea that the direction in which Stalin moved the Soviet Union was not what Lenin would have chosen, suggesting that Stalin's course had harmed the interests of the Soviet

Union. The widespread reaction to Shatrov's play, which was published in *Znamia*'s first issue of 1988, serves as a good example of the mixed emotions many Soviets have to open criticism. Letters to the editor appearing in *Sovetskaia kultura*, written in response to the play, were mixed: some indicated disapproval of the play because it "puffed up the details" of Stalin's life, others praised the playwright's path-breaking work as a model leading the way into an area where historians have been hesitant to follow.[67]

An article published in *Sovetskaia Rossia* written by two historians criticized Shatrov's play, objecting to Shatrov's ignorance of "the significance of history's objective laws." They complained that Shatrov's advancement of the idea that Stalin was able to "oppose the natural laws and requirements of socialist building" does not agree with the "basic laws of social development," and they disagreed with one of Shatrov's major tenets, that individuals shaped the history of the Soviet Union after Lenin, not the inexorable movement of the Party.[68] This disagreement over the role of the individual highlights an important element found in Gorbachev's reform rhetoric. If Stalin misled the Party and the country, the true course of communism, and the intended direction of the State, lies in Lenin's "final testament" (i.e., NEP), not Stalin's revisions of them. Arguing in this way enables Gorbachev to make the case that his new economic reforms are soundly based on the precedent of successful past economic policies. Those who are in disagreement over Shatrov's play particularly question the suggestion that Stalin is responsible for the condition in which the USSR now finds itself, as well the "nihilism" that is expressed in describing the "degeneration of the Soviet State."[69] "Stalin and those who helped him certainly committed terrible illegal acts. This can neither be forgotten nor forgiven. But how is it possible to approach the whole history of our country after 1924 from this viewpoint, how is it possible to leave in the dark everything of which we are proud."[70]

The legitimation of popular culture has also meant the return to the fold of great Soviet authors, painters, dancers, musicians and directors who have been exiled or excommunicated. Pasternak's posthumous restoration to the Soviet Writers' Union and the publication of *Dr. Zhivago* is just one in a number of recent actions taken by the Soviet government in this regard. In the past two years *Novyi Mir* has published poetry by Iosif Brodskii and works by Osip Mandelshtam and Vladimir Nabokov. In July of 1988, *Ogonek* published a selection of poems by Iulii Daniel. Daniel is famous for publicizing the situation of the dissidents and for his trial, along with Andrei Siniavskii in 1966, which branded both men as traitors because their works were published abroad under the pseudonyms Tertz and Arshak. The readmission into the Writers Union of the popular songwriter and poet, Aleksandr Galich, who died while in exile in Paris in 1977, and the publication of a collection of his songs in the April 1988 edition of *Oktiabr*, is another example of the Soviet government's attempt to reincorporate into the mainstream some of the Soviet Union's true cultural heros.[71] The Pushkin Art Gallery sponsored an exhibit of the painter Marc Chagall in 1988, more than sixty-five years after he had emigrated from the Soviet Union. Vladimir Horowitz's triumphant return to the Soviet Union in the Spring of 1986 represents still another example of this trend. Invitations have also been extended to former greats of the Soviet ballet. The eminent ballerina Natalia Makarova, who defected to the West in 1960, was allowed to dance with her old company the Kirov ballet, in a performance of *Swan Lake* in London. There have been suggestions that she may be allowed to return for a performance inside the USSR. Also invited to perform in the Soviet Union is the current director of the American Ballet Theater, Mikhail Baryshnikov.

Changes in the Soviet artistic world are occurring rapidly. It is important to note, however, that these changes are not taking place solely because of State action. There have always been dissident works, and there have always existed in Soviet society officially sanctioned organizations like the Taganka theater that push the limits of acceptable "State art." The Taganka theater provides a good illustration of what has been artistically possible even in the pre-Gorbachevian Soviet Union, and gives an indication of how far an artist could push the limits of acceptable art before he or she would be punished or removed from an official position. The Taganka's exiled director, Iurii Liubimov, has unofficially returned to the theater and has taken over the direction of the play *Boris Gudunov*, ironically the very play for which he was unable to obtain official approval, and which was the cause of his forced exile from the Soviet Union. It has now been shown to enthusiastic audiences in Moscow. His office, which had remained unused for the four years that Liubimov lived in London, is now reoccupied by this controversial director of such works as *Crime and Punishment*, *Hamlet*, and *Wooden Horses*.[72] The fact that Liubimov has been able to return to his country and has been offered back his old position of director is remarkable in the face of his open skepticism of the Gorbachev reforms. Along with other prominent Soviet artists in exile, Liubimov signed a highly publicized open letter to the Soviet leadership which challenged the legitimacy of the new reforms, and called for a number of changes, many of which have subsequently taken place. In a harsh critique of the letter, *Pravda* said "those who sign this manifesto do not understand deep down how pitiful and isolated they are, how despised they are by the Soviet people."[73]

Permission to stage *Boris Gudonov* appears to be an example of one way to gain popular support, to move away from the "deadening dogmas" of Soviet society that prevailed until recently. As Liubimov himself noted in an interview reported in *Izvestiia* before his return to the Soviet Union, "it is important that the people are beginning to have their spiritual needs satisfied . . . Even back in the times which are now described as stagnant, our Taganka theater was breaking through to the human mind and opposing the bureaucratic suppression of individuality."[74]

Another extraordinarily popular cultural figure in the Soviet Union was the poet, actor and folk singer Vladimir Vysotskii. Vysotskii, who died in 1980 and is now the object a of wide popular cult following, sang about many of the themes so familiar to the ordinary Soviet citizen, such as the trials of everyday life, the problems of alcoholism, and corruption. All these themes are now officially acceptable to the present leadership as they relate to the Brezhnev years. The sanction of such popular performers as Vysotskii, whose songs have now been issued in four records by the Soviet musical publishing studio Melodiya, and which were recently performed publicly in Moscow, are further examples of Gorbachev's strategy to legitimate popular cultural heroes and to take advantage of the emotional sentiment they arouse in the Soviet population.[75] The cultural theme of proletarian internationalism is being replaced by Russian cultural heroes who speak to freedom and for a concern about the plight of the individual.[76]

Environmental issues, the problems of a disaffected youth, and the necessity for nuclear disarmament are also acceptable material for the Soviet artist. Recent films that have definite antiwar messages have been produced and supported enthusiastically by the new Cinematographers Union, such as Klimov's film *Come and See*, and Konstatin Loposhanksii's *Letters From A Dead Man*, both of which deal with the crisis of a world living under a nuclear threat.[77] The problems of drugs, national identity, and alienation of the individual are dealt with in Chingiz Aitmatov's novel, *The Executioner's Block*. Rolan Bykov's controversial film, *Scarecrow*, which was completed in 1981 and released just prior to Gorbachev's appointment to General Secretary, takes on the problems of rebellious youth and an insensitive educational system in a poignant tale of the sadistically cruel treatment by school children of one of their classmates. Part of the controversy surrounding this film, according to Ian Christie of the British Film Institute, is that the film lacks a "clear moral resolution" in its storyline. Art without an explicit moral conclusion is a rare experience for the Soviet filmgoer.[78] There are many other examples of films and books that consider the problems surrounding Soviet youth, such as Juris Podniek's film *Is It Easy To Be Young?* Valentin Rasputin treats the down-to-earth realities of daily Soviet life in his novella, *The Fire*, where he describes the scarcity of food and other basic needs.[79] All of these works are examples of art reflecting a society that is no longer forced to hide its internal problems.

The lively journalism presently evident in *Moscow News* is characterized by articles that encourage dissenting opinions. There are, of course, areas that are still off limits, such as the military, penal system, nationality issues (for example, A. Khodzhaev was dismissed as editor of *Komsomoli Tadzhikistan* for his part in the publication of three articles in January of 1988 that dealt with "national integrity"),[80] and any extensive discussion of alternative political parties. In fact, an effort by dissident groups to set up an independent party, the "Democratic Union," was unceremoniously broken up by the authorities when the KGB arrested sixty of the participants.[81] Criticism of Raisa Gorbachev or questions about the restructuring of the KGB remain sensitive areas that are generally not covered in the Soviet press. When Gorbachev's interview with Tom Brokaw was published in *Pravda*, the only section that was deleted dealt with Raisa and her role as her husband's confidante.

Publication of previously banned works is important in the reform of cultural policy, but at the same time it prevents publication of other, newer, works of contemporary Soviet artists. Behind the excitement that the publication of these once-suppressed works arouse, the reality exists that for each long-suppressed manuscript now "on the table" are the works of a number of new, young writers that remain unpublished. Due to the liberalization of publication controls, Soviet newspapers and journals have increased circulation by more than 19 million readers a year.[82] The journal *Znamia* has increased its circulation from 175,000 in 1985 to 500,000 in 1988. *Novyi Mir*'s circulation has increased from 496,100 in 1987 to 1,150,000 in January of 1988.[83] The sensationalism behind the publication of such works as Pasternak's *Dr. Zhivago* or Grossman's *Life and Fate* directly translates into higher circulation numbers, which in turn encourages editorial boards to repeat their successes with even more sensational, once forbidden works. To some extent the attention being paid to this latest group of formerly banned authors has taken publication space from young, relatively unknown authors who are experimenting with radical ideas and new forms of literature. A real move toward an awakening in the artistic world of the Soviet Union must require the publications of these artists of tomorrow. Such talented writers as Sergei Kaledin, Viacheslav Petsukh, and Tatiana Tolstaia are just now getting access to the Soviet public through the more adventurous literary journals.[84]

Another area in which cultural reform is evident is in the letters to the editor columns that now appear regularly in Soviet journals and newspapers. The newspaper *Izvestiia* now receives 1,500 letters a day, which is three times the amount received on average five years ago. This is an enormous number compared to major American newspapers like *The Wall Street Journal*, which receives about 100 letters a day.[85] Considerable discussion was engendered by the publication of the letter from the chemistry professor Nina Andreeva to *Sovetskaia Rossiia* in which many of Gorbachev's reform policies were criticized. The letter caused political reverberations felt throughout the Soviet Union. Most letters to the editor are filled with expressions of concern over recently addressed societal difficulties or are indictments of the villains of Stalin's era. These letters express concerns which, before Gorbachev, were often not mentioned, much less published with State approval.

The liberal intelligentsia is already taking advantage of the loosening of controls by publishing previously unpublishable material, reinterpreting Soviet history, and discussing issues in the press and literature that up until very recently were strictly taboo. But as Nancy Condee and Vladimir Padunov point out, "the reform of culture—liberal *perestroika*, the overhauling of cultural administration, the reorganization of artistic unions— has specific limits."[86] Opposition groups are finding an opportunity to make their opinions known, and this does not necessarily sit well either with the "liberals" or the authorities. What is emerging now in the Soviet Union is what Condee and Padunov call "conflicting *perestroikas*." That is to say that there are groups within the Soviet Union that are on the fringes of *glasnost*.

One example of cultural activity that is on the edge of State acceptability is the current explosion in youth culture. Increased tolerance in Soviet society has led to an emergence of new youth groups, such as hippies, punks, motorcycle gangs, and "heavy-metalists." *Glasnost* has incorporated parts of these movements by sanctioning rock and roll bands like Autograph and Aquarium. Boris Grebenshchikov, the leader of Aquarium, who up until 1987 had to perform underground, expressed his trepidation about becoming an accepted musician for the State. "We are so official now, so taken to heart, that the people that were with us before are not sure of us . . . Nobody believes that the system has changed. They think we must have changed."[87] There are still, however, many young people, as well as members of the older generation within the Soviet Union, who are repelled by the punk hairdos and loud music that has emerged in waves of increasing popularity among the Soviet youth.

Along with this freedom of expression in the young is a new effort by those members of the artistic community who work on the cultural fringes. These avant-gardes are experimenting with theater and creative writing in a fashion that is unique to the Gorbachev era and was impossible during the Brezhnev years. Examples of "parallel cinema"—independent filmmaking and alternative artists, as well as unofficial literary journals like *Epsilon-Salon*—simultaneously exist alongside officially reform-oriented art and journals. These unofficial journals have been very quick to take advantage of the present freedoms. *Epsilon-Salon* published émigré authors such as Brodskii and Nabokov months before *Novyi Mir* or other official journals. The independent artists' group "Hermitage" had showings of émigré artists in September and October of 1987, during which the established art world debated the prospect of doing it. And while official cinema critics are still debating whether to accept the late Andrei Tarkovskii, the unofficial cinema journal *Cine-fantom* has already published the screenplay for his last film, *Scarface*.[88]

There is also presently a strong pro-Russian nationalist movement in the Soviet Union that is becoming more outspoken and more visible. The unofficial *Pamiat* is a conservative, Russian-nationalist group that circulates its ideas in unofficial papers. It is ironic that this chauvinistic and reactionary group should come to the forefront of public attention as a result of the liberalization of publishing practices and the new freedom of discussion. There are also accepted Soviet authors who write in a nationalistic vein, such as Valentin Rasputin and Viktor Astafev. Socialist pluralism, which accepts and expects a diversity of opinion, is what eventually ties together groups like *Pamiat*, the "Lion Society," and *Glasnost*. Socialist pluralism is what teenage punks and the conservative Liubyte bodybuilders have in common, and it is what unites the more adventurous artists on the fringes of *glasnost* with the established intelligentsia.

Soviet culture is also changing in part because of the inevitable consequences of technological progress. Television now links the eleven time zones of the Soviet Union. It has the capacity to reach 90 percent of the Soviet population and has had a profound effect on the way Soviet people receive their news. It is estimated that up to 150 million people watch the news nightly.[89] The average Soviet television viewer switches on the set 365 times a year in contrast to visiting a museum once in six years, or going to the theater once every two years.[90] In the Soviet Union television is the most easily controlled medium. Whereas anyone with a pen and a paper can write, and anyone with a guitar can play music, only those shows or personalities with State approval can get on television. According to Ellen Mickiewicz, the fact that the State has full control over the television medium helps the authorities feel more comfortable about broadcasting the more daring programs. One of the first signs of *glasnost* in fact was a live debate on Soviet television where Margaret Thatcher was allowed to respond to a Soviet counterpart. There have also been "space-bridges" featuring *The Phil Donahue Show* and a similar show hosted by Vladimr Posner which claimed a Soviet audience of 150 million people. Likewise the *Capital to Capital* programs were shown to large Soviet audiences live and unedited.

Some of the television shows that are presently on the air are also significantly different from Soviet shows of previous years. Programs like *Perestroika Spotlight*, which airs after the evening news, challenges Soviet citizens to examine the new political thinking and incorporate it into their lives, and has received 80,000 letters in response to its broadcasts. The television show *Problems, Searches, Solutions* features audience members openly attacking bureaucrats with hostile questions concerning their official performance, and youth problems are dealt with openly on the show *The 12th Floor*.[91] The look and style of Soviet television has changed, with more graphics, skillfully packaged to make it easier to present to the population as a whole. What the Soviets hear and see about the United States on television is changing as well. Positive stories are being told about the United States, and recently a journalist who had been reporting from the United States to the Soviet Union explained on the air that some of his stories may have been too negative, that he might have shown a distorted view of life in the United States. Soviet citizens have also gotten a real taste of the American television, when they saw on Soviet television their first VISA and PEPSI commercials early in 1988.

Information can move across the Soviet Union in a matter of hours, and Western news sources are beamed to Soviet cities via the British Broadcasting Company and the Voice of America. The Soviet people have access now to an infinitely larger world than twenty years ago. In November 1988 the Soviet Union also stopped jamming Radio Moscow newscasts, an event American officials cited as strongly indicative of a new environment in foreign relations. News shots of the riots in Armenia and the aftermath of Chernobyl, as well as open and unedited discussions on television have left a lasting impression on the general public and would make any backward movement very difficult for the government to undertake. The argument that public opinion may now become a cohesive and meaningful force in the Soviet Union is substantiated by the importance accorded Academician Tatiana Zaslavskaia's All-Union Center for the Study of Public Opinion on Social and Economic Questions, which was set up as a result of a resolution of the Politburo.

There seem, at the moment, to be few official constraints on what Soviet artists may do. In an interview with the Spanish paper *Diaria*, the former Soviet Culture Minister Vasilii Zakharov, stated that "the Party and State are not abandoning culture. They will continue to guarantee its financial foundations but, in contrast to what happened previously, the artistic process is determined by people in the cultural world; it is they who will make the decisions on repertoire, works, and what should or should not be published—without bans."[92] In response to a question dealing with the viability of the Gorbachev reforms, Zakharov asserted that the "current changes are irreversible . . . they are the start of a process that will continue."[93] One of the best summaries of this new process is contained in a recent issue of *Litertaurnaia gazeta*, in which Viktor Karpov, First Secretary of the USSR Writers Union, described the union's efforts to "achieve full *glasnost*, to restore and bring back to our literature everyone who is worthy of it and who was driven out for subjective reasons, to fill in the "blanks" in our literature and history."[94]

Notes

1. As quoted in David Joravsky, *Soviet Marxism and Natural Science: 1917–1932* (New York: Columbia University Press, 1961), p. 24.
2. V. I. Lenin, "On Cooperatives," translated in Robert Tucker, ed., *The Lenin Anthology* (New York: W.W. Norton, 1975), pp. 709, 710.

3. Edmund Brown, *Russian Literature Since the Revolution*, rev. ed. (Cambridge, MA: Harvard University Press, 1982), pp. 139, 140, 171–173.
4. Zhores Medvedev, *The Rise and Fall of T. D. Lysenko* (New York: Columbia University Press, 1969), pp. 151– 220.
5. Nancy Whittier Heer, *Politics and History in the Soviet Union* (Cambridge, MA: MIT Press, 1971), Chapter 6.
6. Aleksandr Solzhenitsyn, *The Oak and the Calf* (New York: Harper and Row, 1979), pp. 1–3.
7. Robert C. Tucker in Congressional testimony before the House Subcommittee on Europe and the Middle East, 2 February 1988.
8. *XXVII s'ezd kommunisticheskogo partii sovetskogo soiuza: stenograficheskii otchet* (Moscow: Politizdat, 1986), vol. 1, p. 113.
9. *Pravda*, 15 July 1987.
10. As quoted in Roy Medvedev, *On Socialist Democracy* (New York: Alfred A. Knopf, 1975), p. 166.
11. Andrei Sakharov, *Progress, Coexistence and Intellectual Freedom* (New York: W. W. Norton, 1968), p. 29.
12. *Moscow News*, 9–16 August 1987, p. 4.
13. Mikhail Suslov, *Izbrannoe rechi i stat'i* (Moscow: Politizdat, 1972) pp. 650, 651.
14. *Pravda*, 19 December 1986.
15. *Kommunist* no. 8 (May 1987): p. 7.
16. *Pravda*, 19 February 1988.
17. Ibid., 5 October 1988.
18. Foreign Broadcast Information Service, *Daily Report: Soviet Union* (FBIS-Sov), 16 July 1987, p. R3.
19. *Izvestiia*, 7 May 1988.
20. *Pravda*, 1 July 1988.
21. Ibid., 5 October 1988.
22. Ibid., 1 July 1988.
23. FBIS-Sov, 16 July 1988, pp. R2, R3.
24. Mikhail S. Gorbachev, *Izbrannye, rechi i stat'i* (Moscow: Politizdat, 1985) p. 21.
25. *XXVII s'ezd: sten. otchet*, vol. 1, pp. 551, 552.
26. *Izvestiia*, 29 June 1986.
27. FBIS-Sov, 16 July 1988, p. R7.
28. Ibid., 17 February 1987, p. R3.
29. Ibid., 5 July 1988, p. 88.
30. *Sovetskaia kultura*, 20 June 1987.
31. *Pravda*, 25 September 1988.
32. Ibid., 13 January 1988.
33. FBIS-Sov, 28 August 1987, p. 19. In this same address, Ligachev urged that the pace of cultural reform should be moderated.

34. *Pravda*, 11 September 1987.
35. FBIS-Sov, 28 August 1987, p. 19.
36. *Pravda*, 25 March 1987.
37. *Sovetskaia kultura*, 15 July 1987.
38. *XXVII s'ezd: sten. otchet*, vol. 1, p. 236.
39. FBIS-Sov, 29 June 1988, p. 42.
40. Radio Free Europe/Radio Liberty (RFE/RL), *Research Bulletin*, 413/88, p. 5.
41. *Pravda*, 5 July 1988.
42. Pavel Litvinov, *The Demonstration in Pushkin Square* (Boston: Gambit, 1969), p. 125.
43. *Pravda*, 2 July 1988.
44. FBIS-Sov, 5 July 1988, p. 7.
45. *Pravda*, 2 July 1988.
46. FBIS-Sov, 6 July 1988, p. 15.
47. M. A. Fedotov, "Toward Conceptualization of the Law on Press and Information," as translated in *Soviet Law and Government*, vol. 27, no. 1 (Summer 1988): pp. 6–21.
48. *Moscow News*, no. 29, 27 July–4 August 1988, p. 13.
49. *Sovetskaia kultura*, 7 March 1987.
50. *Pravda*, 28 November 1987.
51. Nancy Condee and Vladimir Padunov, "Soviet Cultural Politics and Cultural Production," *IREX Occasional Papers Series*, (December 1987): p. 13.
52. As quoted in RFE/RL, 51/87.
53. FBIS-Sov, 4 May 1987, pp. R20–R23, and FBIS-Sov, 15 March 1988, pp. 52–54.
54. As quoted in Fedotov, p. 9.
55. *Izvestiia*, 3 November 1988.
56. M. K. Ivanov, "What Should be the Nature of the Law on the Press and Information," as translated in *Soviet Government and Law*, vol. 27, no. 1 (Summer 1988): p. 24.
57. *Moskovskie Novosti*, no. 43, 30 October–6 November 1988, pp. 12, 13.
58. RFE/RL, 495/88.
59. *Moscow News*, no. 31, 21 July 1988, p. 14.
60. *Moskovskie Novosti*, no. 47, 29 November–6 December 1987, p. 14.
61. *The New York Times*, 3 Feb. 1988, p. 7.
62. *Pravda*, 13 January 1988.
63. Maurice Friedberg, *Russian Culture in the 1980s*, Significant Issues Series, vol. 7, no. 6, (Georgetown: Center for Strategic and International Studies, 1985), p. 47.
64. As quoted in *The Washington Post*, 3 November 1986, p. B1, B4.
65. *Moscow News*, no. 46, 22–29 November 1987, p. 15.
66. *Pravda*, 15 February 1987.

67. *Sovetskaia kultura*, 16 January 1988.
68. *Sovetskaia Rossiia*, 29 January 1988.
69. Gerald M. Easter, "Gorbachev and the Ghost of Stalin: History and the Politics of Reform in the Soviet Union," American Committee on U.S.-Soviet Relations, Occasional Paper no. 5 (May 1988). See this for a fuller examination of Stalin and the reform of Soviet historiography.
70. *Sovetskaia Rossiia*, 29 January 1988.
71. RFE/RL, 311/88.
72. *The New York Times*, 11 May 1988, p. 1, 12.
73. *The New York Times*, 26 March 1987, p. 10.
74. *Izvestiia*, 30 March 1988.
75. *Moscow News*, no. 38 (18 September 1988): p. 15.
76. Friedberg, p. 2.
77. Nancy Condee and Vladimir Padunov, p. 10.
78. Ian Christie, "The Cinema," in James Cracraft, ed., *The Soviet Union Today* (Chicago: The University of Chicago Press, 1988), p. 290.
79. Nancy Condee and Vladimir Padunov, p. 10.
80. RFE/RL, 163/88.
81. FBIS-Sov, 9 May 1988, p. 49.
82. Ibid., 10 May 1988, p. 48.
83. RFE/RL, *Supplement*, 2/88.
84. Ibid.
85. *The Wall Street Journal*, 8 August 1988, p. 1.
86. Nancy Condee and Vladimir Padunov, "The Frontiers of Soviet Culture: Reaching the Limits?", *The Harriman Institute Forum*, vol. 1, no. 5 (May 1988): p. 1.
87. *The New York Times*, 9 April 1987, p. 1.
88. Nancy Condee and Vladimir Padunov, "The Frontiers of Soviet Culture," p. 2.
89. Ellen Mickiewicz, "The Mass Media," in James Cracraft, ed., *The Soviet Union Today* (Chicago: The University of Chicago Press, 1988), p. 296.
90. *Moscow News,* no. 15, 16–22 April 1988, p. 4.
91. Ibid.
92. FBIS-Sov, 15 March 1988, p. 53.
93. Ibid., p. 54.
94. *Literaturnaia gazeta*, 9 March 1988.

4 THE DILEMMA OF ECONOMIC REFORM IN THE SOVIET UNION

Timothy J. Smith and Eric F. Green

As the Soviet Union entered the 1980s, the country was led by a gerontocracy. Despite significant domestic and international changes, the Soviet system continued to function in ways largely unchanged from the patterns established by Stalin nearly a half century earlier. Nowhere was this growing contradiction between reality and the inflated promises of the Soviet system more apparent than in the Soviet economy, which had failed to respond to almost all attempts at significant reform, despite problems of declining growth rates, chronic shortages, and low-quality production. By the early 1980s, as economic growth rates reached all-time low levels, the Soviet leadership was confronted with the virtual stagnation of the Soviet economy and an outdated technological base, at a time when a technological revolution was unfolding in countries throughout Asia and the West. The death of Leonid Brezhnev in 1982, following a long illness, and the rapid succession of three new Soviet leaders in as many years, only heightened the impression that the Soviet Union was approaching a time of troubles which an aged, incompetent leadership was powerless to avoid.

Gorbachev's ascension to the highest office in the Soviet Union in 1985 was a watershed in Soviet politics. Not only was it a significant milestone marking the coming to power of a younger, more vigorous, and pragmatic generation of leaders in marked contrast to the slumbering leadership of Brezhnev, but, more importantly, the perceptions and ideas of the new generation differed substantially from those of their predecessors. Furthermore, they were far more pragmatic. In a remarkable speech nominating Gorbachev for the post of General Secretary, one of the older generation, President Andrei Gromyko, told the Central Committee:

121

You know, it often happens that problems—both internal and external—are very difficult to consider if you are guided by the law of 'black and white.' There may be intermediate colors, intermediate links, and intermediate decisions. And Mikhail Sergeevich [Gorbachev] is always able to come up with such decisions that correspond with the party line.[1]

Late in 1986 Gorbachev himself remarked:

There is a common understanding in the CPSU [Communist Party of the Soviet Union] and the country as a whole that we should look for answers to the questions raised by life not outside of socialism, but within the framework of our system, disclosing the potential of a planned economy. . . *But, we also cannot allow ingrained dogmas to cloud our eyes, to impede our progress and keep us from creatively elaborating theory and applying it in practice, in the given, concrete stage through which it is passing.*[2]

By 1985, it was probably impossible for the Kremlin Old Guard to hold out against the younger generation any longer, and many probably viewed the stagnation of Soviet GNP, agriculture, and other economic indicators during the early 1980s as proof that a solution to the country's problems could be delayed no longer.

When Gorbachev arrived in Moscow in 1978 and assumed the tasks of the Party official in charge of agricultural issues, he rapidly moved into a position of general oversight of the overall economy under the patronage of Andropov.[3] By the time he became General Secretary, Gorbachev had been considering the issue of economic reform for several years with various Soviet economists. Most notable among these economists were Abel Aganbegian, Leonid Abalkin, and Tatiana Zaslavskaia. As Gorbachev wrote in *Perestroika*,

I would like to emphasize here that this analysis began a long time before the April [1985] Plenary Meeting and that therefore its conclusions were well thought out. It was not something out of the blue, but a balanced judgment. It would be a mistake to think that a month after the Central Committee Plenary Meeting in March 1985, which elected me General Secretary, there suddenly appeared a group of people who understood everything and knew everything, and that these people gave clear-cut answers to all questions. Such miracles do not exist.[4]

According to American officials who met with the Soviet leader in early 1988, Gorbachev remarked that he had been working on the concept of *perestroika* for six years, from the time his mentor Andropov told the Soviet public that there were "many pressing problems" in the economy for which he could offer no "ready prescriptions."[5] When he became General Secretary, Gorbachev had already begun to map out the specifics of *perestroika*.

The last three years have made it clear that economic reform is one of Gorbachev's highest priorities, and that the success or failure of economic *perestroika* will determine whether the Soviet Union enters the twenty-first century as a world-class power. In contrast to previous leaders, Gorbachev has displayed a willingness to go beyond attempts to improve the economic mechanism which were tried in the past, noting that "there will be no progress if we seek the answers to new economic and technological questions in the experience of the 1930s, the 1940s, the 1950s, or even of the 1960s and the 1970s."[6] Instead, Gorbachev seeks "radical" and "revolutionary" changes in the economic system itself.[7] His campaign for *perestroika*, or restructuring, of the Soviet economy, while consisting largely of reform proposals that have been attempted in the Soviet Union earlier is unique both in its scope and depth. Gorbachev's process of reform aims to change political and social relationships as well as the economic system, and to make it more attuned to the demands of economic development in an era of rapid technological change.

THE NEED FOR ECONOMIC REFORM

International Pressures

In addition to the domestic pressures underlying the call for economic reform in the Soviet Union are the changes in the international environment which have led the new leadership to pursue a fundamentally new direction in economic policy. Perhaps most important is the failure of the Soviet economy to adapt successfully to the changing nature of economic development posed by the rapid development of high technology. The picture drawn by Gorbachev's advisors is that the rapid development of technology in the West is potentially dangerous. President Reagan's Strategic Defense Initiative (SDI) is perhaps the most visible new threat to the Soviet Union, though the increases in military spending which occurred during Reagan's administration certainly added to the feeling among some of these advisors that the American president was undertaking an aggressive military policy utilizing technological advances with the intention of "forcing the Bolsheviks to arm themselves to economic death."[8] Despite Soviet claims that such weapons systems can be countered inexpensively, there appears to be a real concern about the future of such programs and their effect on the strategic balance. Benjamin Lambeth and Kevin Lewis contend that a prominent worry of the Soviet leadership concerning SDI is that it "threatens to shift a major part of the arms competition away from an area in which the USSR holds clear advantages toward one in which the United States might gain leverage from its greatest strengths."[9] This concern is certainly a significant impetus to Gorbachev's call to reform the Soviet economy and to increase its ability to develop and absorb technological innovations. Leonid Abalkin, Gorbachev's Director of the Soviet Academy of Sciences' Economics Institute, expressed this fear bluntly:

> The challenge is more than another spiral of the arms race. Competition is becoming more fierce in the economy, in the technological application of the advances in the latest stage of the scientific and technological revolution, and in boosting production efficiency . . . . In many of these fields capitalism is ahead of the Soviet Union. That is the reality that cannot be ignored.[10]

The Soviet leadership sees economic reform as a necessary prerequisite of the future ability of the Soviet military to compete with the military forces of its adversaries. The Soviet leadership is not only concerned with military implications of the obsolescence of the Soviet economy and its slowness to adapt to technological change, but it also fears the very dynamics of international economic change. These changes are seen as a military challenge and as a possible threat to the intellectual foundation of the Soviet Union: the ideology of Marxism-Leninism. The writings and statements of prominent supporters of *perestroika* have gone so far as to argue that it is necessary to reevaluate the nature and development of capitalism. As one commentator has noted, "the possibilities of capitalism to adapt itself to the new historic environment have surpassed our expectations." He further argued that communist movements around the world have made little progress, and that the example of socialism has been tarnished, in part as a result of "failures, differences, crises and stagnations in the development of the Soviet Union and the other socialist countries and world socialism as a whole."[11]

Soviet writers have in the past used the concept of a "correlation of forces" to describe the competition between socialism and capitalism. It is a concept that encompasses economic, political, and military elements of strength and influence in its determination of the direction of the historical tide. For example, during the 1970s, many Soviet thinkers and writers on international relations held that the tide in world affairs was turning against capitalism, and that therefore the capitalist nations were willing to engage in a policy of détente toward the Soviet Union and its allies. Since the 1970s, this correlation of forces, as determined by Soviet scholars, has been seen as moving to favor the Soviet Union and its allies in the socialist camp. Any Soviet statement indicating a reversal in this trend would indicate a very serious reevaluation of Soviet economic and military progress. It is significant that the correlation of forces terminology was used by a prominent Soviet writer in warning against any failure to fully implement the policy of *perestroika*:

> We must clearly realize that if the *perestroika* fails or is substantially limited, narrowed and reduced again to placebos and jury-rigging, if the socialist countries do not embark upon a new level of development, if capitalism, and not socialism, succeeds in taking control over the new wave of scientific and technological revolution, then the balance of forces in the world may change in favor of capitalism. [12]

Such a view has also led the Soviet leadership to restructure foreign policy as a part of overall *perestroika*. Eduard Shevardnadze, the Soviet Minister of Foreign Affairs, stated this plainly when he told the staff of the Foreign Ministry:

> The time has come, so to speak, to 'economize' our foreign policy, if such an expression is permissible, since, until it is linked wholly with the economy, it will be unable to help in restructuring our domestic economy and society overall, which, in this manner, will be unable to participate on equal terms in the competitive political struggle for the attractiveness of our socioeconomic development model. [13]

The attempt of the current Soviet leadership to reform the Soviet economy has roots that are much deeper than a recognition that the economy has entered a period of stagnation. Both domestic and foreign policy have been damaged by inferior Soviet economic performance, and these policy concerns have had a profound impact on the evolution of Gorbachev's plans for *perestroika*. Political and economic pressures came together in the late 1970s and early 1980s, creating an overwhelming necessity to seek more daring and comprehensive changes throughout the Soviet system.

Gorbachev's Inheritance: Bureaucracy and Stagnation

When Gorbachev came to power,, he inherited an economic system that had continued to function along lines developed by Stalin. This system, created by Stalin in the late 1920s, was geared toward rapid industrialization. From the position of an industrially backward, predominantly agricultural society, the Soviet Union evolved into a powerful world economy, behind that of the United States, but with a military capability surpassed by none. This success was made possible not only by the priority accorded to rapid industrialization, but by the development of a highly-skilled workforce and the exploitation of abundant natural resources within the boundaries of the Soviet Union, an enormous country covering over twice the land area of the United States.

The success of such a development strategy, however, was more often than not measured only in quantitative terms. By the mid-1980s this policy attained notable successes: overall the Soviet economy had grown from less than half the size of the United States in the early 1960s to more than two-thirds of the United States; in certain products, such as coal, oil, and steel the Soviet Union leads world production. As Marshall Goldman observes, although Khrushchev was correct in his prediction that the Soviet Union could compete with the United States and even surpass it by 1980 in the production of some commodities, the Soviet Union has, in fact, "won the wrong race." While the Soviet economy continued to increase the volume of its production, the rest of the industrialized economies of the world had shifted from quantitative growth to intensive growth.[14] In general terms, *perestroika* is the result of a growing realization on the part of the Soviet leadership that, though successful in raising the Soviet Union in a short span of time to the level of a world superpower, the Stalinist model of development has been unable to meet the need for intensive growth. The Stalinist system focused on extensive growth, or the utilization of greater quantity of inputs to increase output, rather than intensive growth, the efficient use of inputs, and was by all accounts tremendously ineffectual and wasteful. During the decade following World War II, and to a lesser extent the 1970s, it was possible to exploit relatively cheap resources and to depend on constant increases in labor participation, but in the 1980s such a strategy was no longer viable for the Soviet Union. The Soviet workforce will grow much more slowly during the next several decades—estimates place the working population during the next fifteen years to be 20 million less than in the preceding fifteen years, and the rapid depletion of easily exploited reserves has meant that the rate of extraction of natural resources has fallen even as the cost and difficulty of exploitation of new reserves has increased. For example, fuel and raw material output increased only 8 percent during the last five-year plan, compared with increases of 25 percent and 10 percent in the ninth and tenth five-year plans, respectively.[15] The wastefulness of the Soviet economy has become a major concern of the

Soviet leadership, precisely because the sources of its rapid growth have largely been exhausted, and those that remain are much more costly. Soviet estimates assert that under current conditions it is two to three times cheaper to conserve one ton of natural resources than to extract it.[16]

Rapid industrialization and inefficient utilization of resources have taken a devastating toll on the natural environment of the Soviet Union. As in other developed countries, economic growth in the USSR has yielded ugly by-products such as acid rain, toxic water, and health-threatening air pollution. An official ideology which romanticized the conquest of nature as an integral element of the heroic task of building socialism reinforced the tendency to sacrifice environmental quality for economic growth. One slogan exhorted Soviet workers: "We cannot wait for favors from nature; our task is to take them from her." The Gorbachev leadership has been more attentive to ecological issues than its predessors. In early 1988 the leadership established a State Committee for the Protection of Nature (the rough equivalent of the American Environmental Protection Agency) and promised to endow it with enough authority to improve dramatically the treatment accorded the environment by Soviet enterprises and society as a whole. While the "new ecological thinking" now discussed in the Soviet Union seeks noble objectives, the problems posed by technological backwardness, structural inefficiencies, and ingrained wasteful habits will impede the progress of Soviet environmental protection efforts.

The increasing difficulties and cost involved in pursuing extensive development, which became apparent in the late 1970s, were compounded by the nature of the Soviet economic system, which had been geared toward rapid industrialization through the use of a highly centralized system of a command economy. The desires of the leadership for rapid growth were translated into specific and legally binding five-year plans for enterprises, State ownership of all property, and central control over inputs and outputs. The Soviet State and Party now exercise control over almost every aspect of economic activity through a system which has, over time, developed an enormous and complex bureaucracy. Of primary importance in the system are the State planning committee *Gosplan*, which drafts plans based on leadership preferences, the State supply committee *Gossnab*, which coordinates the distribution of goods, and the State bank *Gosbank*, which is in charge of financial implementation of the plan. The system was developed primarily to implement orders from the leadership, and has proven able to do so with sometimes remarkable results, as in the case of military and space programs. Obviously, only a few sectors or tasks can be designated as priorities, meaning that ill-defined goals and low priority sectors suffer. As a result, remarkable economic achievements are juxtaposed with serious shortages in consumer goods, distribution bottlenecks, and enormous inefficiencies.

The Stalinist economic system, geared toward rapid growth through extensive development and the attainment of greater output by means of greater inputs, led to troublesome problems for Soviet planners. Because it is beyond the ability of planners to collect and analyze, in a timely fashion, detailed information about enterprise production capacity, incentives, or the availability of inputs, planning and production has largely been carried out using aggregate indicators such as gross output. Planners base the current plan on the fulfillment of the previous year's plan, plus an increment. This policy of "planning from the achieved level" has led local agents to hide true production potentials from their ministries out of a fear that they will be given a more difficult plan to fulfill.[17] Because success and material rewards are measured by plan fulfillment, instead of from profit maximization through greater efficiency in cost reduction, Soviet managers tended to use more expensive inputs, since, if plan fulfillment is measured only in quantity, efficiency and waste are of little concern. For example, although the Soviet Union cuts down approximately the same number of trees as does the United States, the United States produces almost one third more timber than the Soviet Union.[18]

Waste and an inefficient supply system have led to widespread hoarding by managers who seek to guarantee that they will have the supplies necessary to fulfill their plan assignments. The drain on resources which such hoarding causes is significant in fostering shortages, which result in the virtual *diktat* of producers in the economy, because any product, no matter how poor the quality, is better than no product to a manager who needs the inputs for his production lines.

The increased size and complexity of the Soviet economy has made it even harder for the central government to manage economic policy comprehensively. One example which demonstrates the daunting task of the central bureaucracy is the job that the State Committee on Pricing has of administering a rational pricing policy for the country. It has been estimated that this involves the setting of approximately 200,000 prices each year, leading to the calculation that each staff member must approve one price every two hours.[19] Finally, because of its rigidly hierarchical nature, the system discourages innovation and risk-taking by enterprises or local authorities.

Smothering individual initiative has been disastrous for the agricultural sector. As conceived by Stalin, the collective and state farm system was not intended to meet economic criteria for efficiency. Rather, the leadership collectivized agriculture in order to finance the USSR's industrialization by imposing unfavorable terms of trade on the countryside[20] and to assert its political control over the peasantry. In the process the Soviets initiated a massive social experiment in which millions of family-based farms were consolidated into a few hundred thousand state-run farms, which were organized in the belief that state ownership would reduce social inequalities and that economies of scale could be achieved by applying techniques of industrial organization to agricultural production. Although inexcusably violent, collectivization did accelerate the industrialization process by increasing grain deliveries to urban areas during the early 1930s, as well as supplying the cities with labor. But in the process of reducing the peasant to the status of a day laborer, collectivization eliminated his incentive to cultivate productively and maintain the soil's fertility. Gorbachev, who was born and raised in a peasant family in the North Caucus region, has strong feelings on this subject: "We lost a lot by depeasantizing the land in the sense that we tore people away from the land and the means of production, thus delivering a major blow against all agrarian work and primarily against people's attitude to the land."[21] The system of forced state purchasing of output severed the link between effort and reward for members of collective farms. To this day peasants employed by insolvent farms earn equal (or even higher) wages than workers on more productive farms. As a consequence, peasants exhibit little enthusiasm for collective farm work and prefer to devote their energies to their small private plots, because they earn market prices for produce grown independently.[22] Indeed, the half-acre private plots produce about half of the country's fruit and vegetables although they occupy less than 5 percent of total farmland. The power structure that collectivization installed in the countryside also stifled productivity by allowing administrators to micromanage farms, deciding such matters as what crops to plant, when to sow, and when to harvest. "It is difficult," in the view of one peasant,

> to ascertain who has actually been the master [of the land] in our country for the last half century. The milkmaids? No. The *sovkhoz* directors? The specialists? They are not masters either. The regional apparatus is above them, and so it is at higher and higher levels; bureaucrats, whose planning figures long ago replaced the spirit of proprietorship. . . . It turns out that along the whole chain there was no master.[23]

In short, the collective farm structure effectively alienated peasants from the land by imposing a vertical command structure that denied peasants economic and administrative responsibility over their own activity.

Misguided planning and inefficient investment have compounded the inherent problems of collective farm organization; as a result, the rural Soviet Union is a difficult place to work productively and an unpleasant place to live. Unlike pre-industrial agriculture, which was largely self-sufficient, modern farming relies on a range of auxiliary goods and support services including genetically engineered seed varieties, chemical fertilizer, specialized veterinary expertise, and mechanical support for farm machinery. Modern farming as practiced elsewhere in the world also requires an advanced infrastructure capable of efficiently distributing huge volumes of goods and information across long distances. The centrally planned Soviet economy has shown itself chronically incapable of responding to these complex requirements. To begin wih, Soviet farming is under-mechanized; for every 1000 hectares of crop land, the USSR has twelve tractors while the US has thirty.[24] The lack of adequate service, spare parts and fuel supplies insures that farms face a perpetual shortage of equipment. In March 1987, in the RSFSR alone 100,000 tractors were out of commission awaiting delivery of spare parts.[25] Some farms use half of their equipment exclusively to strip down for parts. The lack of capital on Soviet farms is only part of the food problem. The food sector as a whole faces shortage of transport vehicles, storage facilities and refrigeration equipment. As a consequence, up to half of the harvest of some crops rots or is wasted before it reaches the consumer. These conditions are more remarkable in light of the fact that the Soviets direct 26 percent of their capital investment expenditures (up from 20 percent in the early 1960s) to the agricultural sector.[26] Consequentely, the returns on investment in agriculture in the Russian republic have declined by over 60 percent since the mid-1960s; in 1965 each ruble invested yielded slightly more than a ruble increase in agricultural output, fifteen years later each ruble invested produced only 38 kopeks in output.[27] Instead of directing resources to storage and transport, which produce immediate improvements in the amount of food available to consumers, planners have wasted untold billions on land improvement schemes and large-scale construction projects. The eleventh five-year plan invested R45 billion on land improvements, producing a return of only R378 million.[28]

The USSR's rural infrastructure, which effects both agricultural productivity and the quality of life, remains remarkably primitive. Two-thirds of Soviet farms are not accessible by paved roads and less than 15 percent of rural households have running water and central heat. Entire rural raions (the rough equivalent of a county) lack telephone service. In Gorbachev's words, the dismal condition of rural schools, medical centers and cultural institutions is "beneath all criticism."[29] These problems conspire to degrade living conditions; for example, poor health care in the provinces is exacerbated by low quality roads which impede ambulance service from the cities. The isolation from adequate medical treatment has produced death rates in rural areas 20 percent higher than in the cities, among children the rate is 50 percent higher.[30] The harsh living conditions compel thousands of peasants — particularly young people — to abondon the countryside every year, leaving behind ghost towns and fields overgrown with weeds. Despite the fact that over one-third of the Soviet population still lives in the countryside, the leadership actively encourages young people to return to rural regions where millions of hectares of arable land have been neglected due to the exodus of able-bodied manpower.

The Economy and Sociopolitical Goals

Attempts to explain the policies of *perestroika* being introduced by Gorbachev have led some Western scholars to conceptualize a "social contract" between the Soviet leaders and population.[31] It is argued that the post-Stalin leadership created a contract through policies that granted the middle class, primarily blue-collar workforce, stable social and economic guarantees, in exchange for popular support of the leading role of the Communist Party and its policies. In fact, the needs of society and the economy have shifted in a significant way since the current system was put in place. The stress now, in the context of intensive development, is less on work than on productivity, and less on manual labor than on creative, innovative, technological developments. As Jerry Hough argues, "The Soviet Union has reached the point of diminishing returns from a policy that grants privileges to blue-collar workers, especially privileges that permit them to work without discipline."[32] Considering questions about how such a social contract may have functioned in the Soviet Union, and the ways Gorbachev seems to desire to change it — because of the close interaction between the economic and social spheres — reveals much about Gorbachev's assessments of what changes are needed. Understanding social policy in the Soviet Union is integral to understanding the program of economic reform being undertaken by Gorbachev.

Gorbachev recognized that Soviet society had become much more complex, more educated, and politicized, and that a fundamental conflict between state and society had arisen. Gorbachev had apparently come to realize that the interaction between social policy and economic policy is of great importance and has been grossly neglected. The thrust of Gorbachev's *perestroika* in many ways seems to be aimed at the goal of attaining a closer correlation between individual interests and those of the state, to make the Soviet worker "the keeper of his own home." As such, economic reforms in the Soviet Union should be considered in light of the profound changes that have taken place in Soviet society.

During the 1970s many Soviet citizens lost faith in the capacity of the system to fulfill their material needs. Their changing perceptions had severe implications for the economy. As people lost faith, morale deteriorated and drunkenness and absenteeism increased, thus compounding the economy's inability to respond to consumer demands. Gorbachev expresses the need for change in society when he writes that,

> The need for change was brewing not only in the material sphere of life but also in public consciousness . . . . Perplexity and indignation welled up that the great values born of the October Revolution and the heroic struggle for socialism were being trampled underfoot. All honest people saw with bitterness that people were losing interest in social affairs, that labor no longer had its respectable status, that people, especially the young, were after profit at all cost.

He concludes this statement by noting that "the energy for revolutionary change has been accumulating amidst our people and in the Party for some time."[33] The criteria by which the Soviet economy is being judged, in the international arena and, no less importantly, by its citizens, have changed.

During the 1950s and 1960s the Soviet public had confidence and optimism about the future. Advances in Soviet sciences, most remarkably the launching of Sputnik, convinced many, even abroad, that the Soviet Union was capable of competing with, if not surpassing, the West. One need look no further for an example of this confidence than to Khrushchev's boasts of overtaking the United States, or the claims of the Program of the Soviet Communist Party, which asserted that communism would be basically achieved by the year 1980. The average Soviet consumer was undeniably better off in the 1960s than ever before; certainly for those who had lived through the hardships of the wartime economy the return to a peacetime economy meant a much improved standard of living. Economic development was occurring so rapidly during this period, for example, that two American economists studying the Soviet economy in the early 1960s actually projected that although the Soviet economy was half the size of the United States' economy in 1960, the faster growth and greater investment in the USSR would permit the Soviet Union to reach the level of U.S. gross national product between 1973 and 1996, depending on the average annual growth rate in each country.[34]

Significant progress has been achieved by the Soviet leaders in supplying the population with consumer goods. In 1960, for example, only one family in 100 owned a tape recorder, only four in 100 a washing machine or refrigerator, only eight in 100 a television set, and fewer than fifty in 100 a radio, while by the beginning of 1987, nine out of ten families owned a refrigerator, seven out of ten a washing machine, and almost all households owned a television and radio.[35] Although living standards improved in the Soviet Union during the 1950s and 1960s, the expectations of the population had begun to rise, spurred on, undoubtedly, by the boasts of Khrushchev, and by the comparisons with the living conditions of previous decades in Soviet history. As an integral part of this transformation, the Soviet consumer began to place much greater emphasis on the quality of these products. As basic needs were fulfilled, a family previously thankful for the opportunity to buy *any* refrigerator or television set began to demand products that worked better and lasted longer.[36] The inability of the Soviet economy to provide quality goods has been the focus of much public criticism, and not infrequent cynicism. Recently, a Soviet journalist inquired of his readers,

> Why on one side of the city is [the television model] "Elektronka" produced, which is exported, while on the other side . . . the pitiful "Raduga," which in good conscience can be offered to the consumer only in a package with an on-duty repairman and a fire guard?[37]

According to one survey, Soviet consumers found fault with one-sixth to one-third of such basic consumer durables as clothing and footwear that they have purchased.[38]

This is not to say that the issue of quality has completely replaced the problem of shortages, for the Soviet economy is also well-known for its inability to fulfill even the most basic needs. A particularly troublesome area of shortages has been, and continues to be, the food sector. Here, despite massive government investment and a comparatively large ratio of farmers per capita in relation to the United States, long lines and even rationing are not uncommon phenomena. Such a state of affairs, particularly when considered in context of rapidly rising expectations, has led to serious social problems, the growth of an extensive underground economy, and corruption. One Soviet writer, describing the poor position of the consumer in the economy, wrote that the situation is such that, "[consumers] will buy shapeless frankfurters and sausage made out of poorly mixed meat. And they will even say thanks for it."[39]

Copious anecdotal evidence can be cited to illustrate that the issues of quality and quantity in the Soviet economy have been far from solved. No one can deny that the advances made by the Soviet Union in raising the standard of living of all classes since the war have been truly remarkable, but it is clear that the rapid development of the consumer goods industries sacrificed quality of production for quantity. This is clearly in the minds of the current Soviet leadership, whose plans call for increases of 150 percent in consumer goods production, as well as new mandatory requirements of improved quality and greater variety. The Soviet Prime Minister has stated that, "a more complete satisfaction of the purchasing power of the population is of principal significance in the social policy of the Party."[40]

Health care, education, public services, and housing, all important parts of the social contract between state and citizen, have come under attack for failing to meet the needs of the public. Gorbachev has referred frequently to "the acute problem of housing."[41] According to Aganbegian, the housing sector has been significantly shortchanged in recent years; in 1960 residential construction constituted 23 percent of the State budget, while in the past five years it has fallen to less than 15 percent.[42] While there has been a solid improvement in housing since World War II,[43] and one of the early pronouncements of the Soviet government was that each person would be provided with a minimum of nine square meters of living space, a Western analyst has computed that for many Soviet citizens this modest goal has yet to be fulfilled.[44] The problem is further compounded by the practice of distributing new housing to the upper levels of the bureaucracy, at the expense of better housing for the middle class. The system of universal health care which is guaranteed by the Soviet government has also been the focus of growing dissatisfaction. Aganbegian notes that in this sector there has been no significant improvement in the last fifteen years, and that the situation may have deteriorated.[45] The Soviet Union resumed publication of life expectancy statistics in the mid-1980s after there was an upturn in the figures (which was attributed to the reduction of alcohol consumption), but the figures given in 1987 reveal that the average life expectancy in the Soviet Union during 1985–1986 is still slightly below the average for 1969–1970.[46] This is a troublesome statistic when compared to the levels attained in other developed countries.

These phenomena have been acknowledged by the leadership as significant social problems which must be given immediate attention. Gorbachev clearly intends to pursue "a genuine revolution in the entire system of relations in society."[47] A reflection of the awareness that serious economic reform will, in the words of Hough, involve "a fundamental change in social policy," Gorbachev has, unlike his predecessors, developed a comprehensive program that recognizes the importance of the interaction between social and economic policy.[48] The importance of social change in Gorbachev's plan for *perestroika* is apparent in his assertion that "In the long run the purpose of restructuring is to take [individual and collective] interests into account, to influence interests, and to effect control over them and through them."[49]

Gorbachev's views on social change and its influences on the economy can be traced in part to the ideas and analyses of Tatiana Zaslavskaia, who has become one of the Soviet leader's closest advisors. While working as a socioeconomist at the Siberian Institute for Economics and the Organization of Industrial Production, Zaslavskaia received a great deal of attention in the West when a confidential discussion paper she authored was obtained by Dusko Doder and reported in *The Washington Post* in 1983.[50] Zaslavskaia has been the leading proponent of the need to redefine "social justice," suggesting a return to the socialist diction. "From each according to his ability, to each according to his work." Zaslavskaia argues that during the last two decades, inequalities in the system of social distribution have increased, and this is reflected in "the inability of the system to make provision for the full and sufficiently effective use of the labor potential and intellectual resources of society."[51]

Zaslavskaia's analysis stresses the interaction of personal with social interests, and blames the highly centralized structure of the Soviet economic system for engendering "an indifferent attitude to work . . . and its low quality, social passivity, a low value attached to labor as a means of self-realization, an intense consumer orientation, and a rather low level or moral discipline." She concludes that "at present the mechanism is 'tuned' not to stimulate, but to thwart the population's useful economic activity."[52] Zaslavskaia argues that fundamental changes have occurred in the Soviet economy which have made the inherited Stalinist economic system inappropriate for current social conditions. The Stalinist system treated workers as "cogs" in the economic machinery. During the 1930s workers' education levels were low and the absence of a social safety net meant that wages were the principal source of income for most families.

The situation has changed significantly since the 1930s. Zaslavskaia contends that workers "have become a much more complex object of management" due to the expansion of individual rights, a sharp improvement in the standard of living, the introduction of social welfare for the ill and elderly, and the growing shortage of labor. In addition to these changes, Zaslavskaia focuses on the rapid qualitative change in technology that has increased the productive potential of every worker, but at the same time notes that it means "the scale of damage inflicted upon society through careless labor, violations of labor and technology, discipline, irresponsible attitudes to technology, etc., have also risen."[53] Widespread dissatisfaction and cynicism manifested themselves through an indifferent attitude toward work and responsibility. This cynicism is largely due to the failure of well-publicized attempts of previous leaderships to improve the economy. Particularly during the Brezhnev period, when corruption and cronyism were widespread, the inability of the leader ship to improve economic performance led to increased apathy about the possibility that the system would be reformed. As a result, black market activities increased and those who were less enterprising relied on the guarantees provided by the socialist State to fulfill their basic needs and worked less productively. Gorbachev has made it clear that, while the State will uphold the social guarantees that have been provided to the population, the linkage between effort and reward will come to play a greater role. As he told members of the Central Committee in early 1988,

> [T]he standard of social protection in our society depends on the magnitude of the national wealth and it, in its turn, depends on the correct, consistent application of the socialist principle "from each according to his abilities; to each according to his labor." In line with their principle, a person's well-being and living conditions are directly dependent on the application of his abilities and talent and his contribution to the common cause. This is the foundation of socialism's vitality.[54]

GORBACHEV'S REFORM AGENDA

Personnel Changes and Enhanced Worker Discipline

By the time he was elected to the position of General Secretary, Gorbachev already had some conception of the direction in which he was going to lead the country. At his first Central Committee Plenum as General Secretary, he noted:

> Now the main issue is how and by what means the country will be able to achieve an acceleration of economic development. In reviewing this issue in the Politburo we unanimously came to the conclusion that there are real opportunities to achieve this. The tasks for accelerating the growth rate and by a considerable

degree are quite achievable if the intensification of the economy and the speeding up of the scientific and technical progress are placed in the center of all of our work, if management and planning are restructured, if the structural and investment policy is restructued, if the level of organization and discipline is everywhere raised and the style of activity is radically improved.[55]

This passage, which includes references to discipline and acceleration (*uskorenie*) as well as to restructuring (*perestroika*), offered a preview of the main themes of the first few years of Gorbachev's economic policy. The slow evolution of the program of reform has elicited different explanations: either no plan existed until late 1986, or Gorbachev was merely biding his time and strengthening his political position. Gorbachev's comments above, and the powerful memory of Khrushchev, who attempted to make changes at a faster pace than that acceptable to the conservative bureaucracy, lend credence to the latter interpretation. During the two years leading up to the June 1987 plenum, at which economic reform was approved, Gorbachev and his advisors devoted considerable time and energy to arguing for the need for economic reform. The actual policies implemented, however, were largely confined to stress on the "human factor," which encompassed not only vast changes in personnel, but also a call to better and more work.

Gorbachev's first actions as General Secretary were not radical. They were aimed at improving the performance of the economic system which he inherited. His call for the intensification of the "human factor" combined an earlier effort by Andropov to increase productivity with an administrative shake-up of his own making. By placing greater pressure on workers and managers, Gorbachev sought to expose "hidden reserves" in order to bring about a reversal of the falling rates of economic growth, and provide a springboard for more extensive economic changes. Gorbachev stressed this approach in April 1985:

A relatively rapid return can be obtained if one puts into use organizational-economic and social reserves and if, in the first instance, one puts the human factor into action and ensures that everyone in his place works conscientiously and wholeheartedly . . . Such reserves exist at every enterprise and building site, in every collective farm.[56]

The desire to further accelerate growth was similarly reflected in Gorbachev's call for an ambitious revision of the targets for the twelfth five-year plan (1986–1990), which, as amended, anticipates that by the year 1990 the growth of gross national product will rise to over 5 percent per year, and that industrial and agricultural output will also increase dramatically. The fact that many of the targets in this plan, if reached, would return the economy to rates of growth not achieved since the 1960s or 1970s, is significant. The goal of intensification, also reflected in the amended thirteenth five-year plan, is to completely replace one-third of capital stock and quadruple the percentage of modern Soviet machinery, both by 1990.

To support such optimistic plans, Gorbachev has sought to encourage greater desire and enterprise from workers and managers who previously lacked any incentive to work harder at their jobs. At higher levels, sudden personnel changes were used to motivate complacent officals. One month after coming to office, Gorbachev gave notice at a Party meeting that he would not tolerate leaders who had been in positions of power who were either unable or unwilling to aggressively support his policies. As Gorbachev noted in early 1988, "The tasks of restructuring must be solved in such a way as to ensure the maximum possible incentive for people's initiative and independence and to overcome their passiveness, civic indifference, apathy, and lack of independent thinking, all of which are defects directly attributable to the bureaucratic system of leadership."[57]

Upon assuming office in March 1985, Gorbachev wasted little time in solidifying his position in the Soviet leadership; since that time the Soviet Union has witnessed the most rapid change of top cadres since Stalin's purges. Gorbachev has also sought turnover at lower levels of political and economic management. He called for *democratizatsiia,* meaning that workers would be entitled to elect their own bosses. Even though the Party would control the nomination process, Gorbachev clearly believes that greater worker productivity and initiative is dependent upon worker control over working conditions and benefits. Indeed, Gorbachev takes this view seriously, particularly as the conditions introduced by such legislation as the Law on the State Enterprise increase the number of decisions to be made by local units. In addition, such elections for factory leadership positions may benefit Gorbachev's program since the mechanism for nominating candidates would be controlled by Party officials, who tend to more accountable to Gorbachev than government officials.[58]

In addition to making personnel changes, Gorbachev used his first two years in office to confront some of the most serious economic problems facing the Soviet Union. First, following Andropov's refrain that "although everything cannot be reduced to discipline, it is with discipline that we must begin," Gorbachev attacked the widespread alcoholism that had come to have an increasingly negative effect on worker productivity. In May 1985, a decree introducing measures aimed at restricting alcohol sales and consumption was published. Not only was vodka production reduced, but the production of cheap wines was to be completely phased out by 1988 and retail outlets for alcohol were moved farther away from factories. Gorbachev also cracked down on theft, bribery, and corruption, a trend that had grown under Brezhnev, moreover, in an initial attempt to bring the large second economy into the legitimate sphere of economic activity, he also issued a decree widening the legal boundaries of individual labor activity. By legitimizing to such activity, however, Gorbachev showed that some of his changes were going to go beyond mere reshuffling of personnel. Although these new forms of economic activity have spread very slowly because of public caution and the opposition of some local authorities, Gorbachev and his advisors have not relented in their calls for individual and cooperative forms of production to play greater roles in the economy. Aganbegian predicts that these two forms of labor organization could potentially meet half of all services and one-fourth of all consumer goods demands by the public.

During the first years of the Gorbachev leadership, the government moved aggressively to reorganize the central bureaucracy. A guiding principle of Gorbachev's overhaul of the system of economic management is "democratic centralism," which Lenin described as follows:

> Centralism understood in a truly democratic sense, presupposes the possibility, created for the first time in history, of a full and unhampered develoment not only of specific local features, but also of local inventiveness, local initiative, of diverse ways, methods and means of progress to the common goal.[59]

Lenin considered the balance between centralized leadership and local autonomy as a great strength of socialism. Gorbachev's economic reforms, as is evidenced by the 1987 Law on the State Enterprise, have redefined the rights and responsibilities of the central management apparatus and the local economic agents. As one of Gorbachev's economic advisors argues,

> Today both [centralism and democratism] must be reinforced: centralism—by overcoming departmental and localistic approaches while depending on heightened creative activity of the public, work collectives, and local bodies; democratization—by encouraging self-dependence and initiative on the part of enterprises (amalgamations), and by extending their rights and responsibility in the interest of the national economy at large.[60]

Gorbachev is clearly intent on reducing the size and influence of the bureaucracy which reached enormous proportions under Brezhnev. This reflects his desires to devolve as much responsibility and initiative to the local levels as possible and to limit the ability of the bureaucracy to slow or reverse *perestroika*. The role of ministries, for example, will change as enterprises assume more operational duties such as setting prices and wages. However, the Basic Provisions make it clear that the ministries still carry overall responsibility for the performance of enterprises in areas of production, technical standards, quality, and the implementation of programs for scientific-technological development. In these and other duties involving supervision of enterprises, the ministry is still to play an active role in the operation of the economy.

One clear objective in Gorbachev's efforts to combine administrative entities is to reduce the number of bureaucrats, and to change the administrative structure so that bureaucratic obstacles and foot-dragging will not obstruct the implementation of reform. Nationwide, the numbers of workers in the bureaucracy is estimated to be around 14 million, excluding engineers and technicians, which comprise 12 percent of the workforce in the Soviet Union. The portion in the State apparatus is 2.5 million.[61] However, bureaucrats in all systems possess very strong survivalist instincts, and the Soviet bureaucracy is certainly no exception; reports in the Soviet journals assert that even the attack on the bureaucracy has become bureaucratized.[62]

Significant streamlining of the bloated economic bureaucracy started in the fall of 1985 when there were some significant changes in the organizational structure of central economic organs. These changes seemed to foreshadow a more widespread movement toward the consolidation of ministries and State committees charged with specific industries or sectors. First, a superministry was created for the agro-industrial sector, which required the abolition of some ministries, the absorption of parts of departments of some surviving ministries, and the subjugation of control of still others. The new entity, *Gosagroprom*, included all ministers and State chairmen whose responsibilities involved agricultural issues. Similar reorganizations have occurred, resulting in the creation of the State Committee for Construction, the State Committee on Foreign Economic Relations, a Bureau for Machine Building, a Bureau for the Fuel and Energy Complex, a Bureau for the Chemical and Timber Complex, and a Bureau for Social Development.

Gorbachev hopes that such reorganizations will, in addition to encouraging local autonomy, make the central apparatus better able to carry out its primary function: planning the general direction of the economy. The Soviets claim that *Gosplan* now directly administers the production of only 415 products, down from over 2,000.[63] In addition to such changes, there has been a call for enhancing the role of regional government, centering primarily on the activity of local Soviets, which will be responsible for ensuring the development of local needs in socioeconomic development.

Enterprises are required to remit a "tax" to these local bodies to provide them with the means to support such development.

In retrospect, the first two years of Gorbachev's leadership leading up to the June 1987 Plenum of the Central Committee were important in allowing the Soviet leader to establish supportive leadership cadres, as well as to instill a general "reform-mindedness" in the public at large.[64] In the short term, Gorbachev's strategy focused on exploiting existing capacities and reserves through more efficient use of existing resources. These two policies, acceleration, or increased growth, and intensification, more efficient use of what is available, have been evident in Gorbachev's pronouncements and policies aimed at better work discipline, personnel changes, and some changes in areas of organizational structure; improvement of management and planning, and the reallocation of investment priorities. During this period, however, the rhetoric of Gorbachev's speeches was not matched by implementation of policies, giving rise to a skepticism that Gorbachev was intending less than a "radical" reform of the economy. Many analysts expressed the view that Gorbachev seemed to be content with campaigns to increase work discipline and efficiency, much as had taken place during Andropov's short tenure, and with minor tinkering with the economic system to address the most obvious shortcomings. This perception changed abruptly in mid-1987 when, at the June plenum, Gorbachev introduced and gained support for a comprehensive package of reforms which are to be implemented during the next several years. This is certainly not to say that the final outcome is clearly planned, for Gorbachev and his advisors have frequently stressed the need for a continuous evaluation of progress, and the further revision of policies which fail to give the desired result. But, according to Aganbegian, work has been in progress during the last couple of years on the development of a framework of an ideal economic system, and that there is now a more or less coherent model at which the reforms are being aimed.[65]

Restructuring Management and Creating Incentives

The blueprint for reform of the Soviet economy is contained in a document entitled "Basic Provisions for Fundamentally Reorganizing Economic Management," as well as the "'State Law on the Socialist Enterprise," which were approved by the Central Committee at the June plenum and, subsequently, by the Council of Ministers.[66] The Basic Provisions unambiguously declare that the economic system as a whole will be centrally administered and will be guided by policies originating from the Party leadership, and stop far short of the scope of decentralization attempted by such planned economies as Hungary and China. However, the intent is clearly to create a new economic system in which market forces are to be balanced with state directives. In the reform outlined, the priorities of the state would be maintained through target figures and state orders that would direct general economic activity, while greater initiative and independence at lower levels would be carried out through a "socialist" market. The essence of the new system was described by Aganbegian:

> This market will play a major role but it will be a socialist market. It will not be a free-for-all market . . . we will not have unemployment; and there will not be a market dominated by capital in our country. We will not have shares or bills of exchange, so this market will not include the whole of the economy, but only part of it connected with the sale of goods and paid services . . . the market will be regulated by the fact that the price of the most important products and of means of production will be in the hands of the State. The prices of other goods, many of the goods, will be free and subject to agreement, but the State will monitor them to prevent them from rising excessively.[67]

In general, the intention of the reforms is to allow the central planners to guide individual enterprises in their choice of annual plans through the use of "economic levers," suggestions in the form of normatives, price policies, and other financial controls, rather than the "administrative levers" that were present in the previous system. This strategy focuses on the enterprise as the key link in the economic system, and seeks to formalize enterprise rights while at the same time increasing their accountability and allowing them greater independence. This is actually an admission that in the modern stage of scientific and technological progress it is very difficult, if not impossible, to foresee or implement technological innovations from the center, but that much of the success of economic development takes place at and below the enterprise level.

Significant changes in the Soviet system were introduced by the enterprise law, which came into effect in 1988. This law is based on an experiment, begun selectively by Andropov, which simultaneously gave enterprises greater independence and greater responsibility. The greater independence is reflected in the ability of the management to decide all activity at the enterprise based on self-financing, wholesale trade, and government orders. The law is a significant departure from previous Soviet economic practices because of the stress it places on indicators of financial success;

it even suggests the possibility of bankruptcy for enterprises that are unable to sustain themselves financially. Each enterprise is required to be "self-financing," meaning that it must meet its own expenses, including salaries, from revenues.

To create the conditions favorable for enterprise initiative as envisioned by the law, the June plenum also passed a document entitled "Basic Guidelines for the Radical Restructuring of Economic Management," which endorsed the need for fundamental changes in the economic system. Included are provisions for expanding direct producer-consumer relations through a network of wholesale trade. While *Gossnab* is charged with the development of such a network, it is allowed to intervene directly only in the case of scarce goods and those which are required by the State to assure the fulfillment of State orders. The stress is on the formation of long-term ties between buyers and sellers, and the transition has been mandated to grow from a current level of 5 percent of deliveries, which *Gossnab* now controls, to 60 percent by 1990 and 100 percent by 1992.[68]

The Basic Provisions also contain a decree on pricing, which provides for the implementation of a radical price reform to be completed by 1990. Notably lacking was any mention of a reform in retail prices, although Gorbachev has indicated that this is to be part of the overall reform, and may occur in the early 1990s. The number of prices independently set through operation of the wholesale trade system is to increase, although the state will continue to set prices for raw materials, energy resources and other importance commodities. While price reform may introduce more rational prices, particularly as concerns raw materials, it is improbable that market-clearing prices will result because it seems likely price setting will continue to rely on cost-based rules rather than scarcity values. Furthermore, even the prices which are to be set by agreement between buyer and seller will be closely followed by the State Pricing Committee (*Goskomtsen*), which is likely to revise any prices that it deems unjustified.

The wage reform is aimed largely at giving greater independence to managers to set salaries and award bonuses, and to increase the proportion of a worker's income that is based on salaries while making bonuses a less necessary supplement to wages.[69] Gorbachev's call for an end to wage-leveling will reward workers for increased productivity and quality of production. It is also expected that white-collar workers will benefit more, on average, than blue-collar workers.

The most detailed legislation of Gorbachev's economic reform is the "Law on the State Enterprise," which was adopted by the Supreme Soviet following extensive public discussion of a published draft. This law, which took effect on 1 January 1988, and is to be fully implemented at all enterprises in 1989, sets forth the rights and responsibilities of enterprises. Among the most important provisions of the new law are the rights of an enterprise to draft its own five-year and annual plans based on stable normatives, state orders, customer contracts, and control figures which are to be provided by the central authorities but are not compulsory. The law also seeks to increase the authority of the labor collectives in enterprises by providing for the election of labor councils as well as managers, although the latter are to be subject to the approval of superior authorities. The goal of the law is to bring about a change in the functioning of the economic system by which the center will be limited to strategic planning, while day-to-day operation is placed under the control of the individual economic enterprises. According to Aganbegian, "The State will no longer be responsible for the economic results of the enterprises. The enterprise will have no responsibility based on its commitment to the State. The enterprise will get control data, but it will be in the character of a suggestion."[70] At the center of the law, which grew out of decentralization experiments conducted over several decades, is the concept of *khozraschet*, or cost-accounting, which makes each enterprise responsible for meeting its costs from income. For this to be a reality, the enterprise managers must have autonomy in decisionmaking in operational matters, and the ability to seek profits, requiring that managers be able to control employment and the allocation of surplus funds.

Gorbachev has sought to apply the principle of *khozraschet* to agriculture as well by encouraging State and collective farms to finance themselves by raising productivity and reducing waste. Yet despite increased capital investment and some changes in labor organization, the food problem showed no signs of dissipating during the first four years of Gorbachev's tenure. In mid-1988, Gorbachev launched a serious effort to break the established cycle of low productivity, massive government subsidies, and shortages by proposing that peasants be given the option of taking out long term leases—up to fifty years in duration—on farm plots. At a Central Committee plenum in March 1989 Gorbachev gained approval for this proposal and an ambitious program that will shift much of the burden for the production, transport, and marketing of food from state enterprises to peasant farmers and private cooperatives. Leasing, as well as the gradual introduction of freer trade in agricultural products and price deregulation, plays a key role in the reform. The plenum resolution declares that "the restructuring of socialist productive relations in the countryside, returning the peasant to the position of the master of the land," occupies the central place in the new agrarian policy.[71]

Under the plan, leasing contracts will be based on the "free will and equal rights of both sides"; a typical leasing contract involves an agreement in which a collective farm permits a family or group of peasants to take responsibility for a plot of land or a herd of livestock as well as farm buildings and domiciles. Peasants will have the option of passing on leases to their children. In exchange for the land, the peasants are obliged to pay an annual rent or deliver a specified amount of output at state prices. Peasants are free to dispose of production above this quota as they choose; they can consume it, sell it to the state a negotiated prices, or market it themselves in farmers' markets. In the current system collective farmers are essentially paid by the hour, hence there is little incentive for consciencious cultivation or higher productivity.

The implementation of this reform has already engendered fierce struggles in the countryside over who will control agricultural activity. In principle, long-term leases should shift the balance of power away from the bureaucrats, who have had the authority to micromanage agricultural production, to the producers themselves, who will gain the right to choose what to plant and where to sell their surplus production. Consequently, collective farm directors and *Gosagprom* (the Ministry of Agriculture) officials will resist encroachments on what has been literally their turf since the 1930s.[72] In an attempt to undercut this opposition and improve the provision of inputs (e.g., capital, chemicals) to the agrarian sector, the leadership formally abolished the *Gosagprom* at a Central Committee plenum in March 1989. In the opinion of many Soviet reformers the changes announced at the plenum do not go far enough. The local agricultural apparatus and the collective farm directors can still dictate their will to the peasants by manipulating the terms of lease agreements or placing binding state orders on farms. If the reform succeeds, the long-beleaguered agricultural sector could, after five to ten years, constitute an asset rather than a liability to the Soviet economy. A similar agrarian policy in China drastically improved the food situation and ultimately led to the breakup of the collective farms, an outcome that Soviet conservatives will resolutely oppose.

CONCLUSION

The significance of the program for economic reform which has been launched by Gorbachev lies not only in its urgency, but also in its scope. As one American scholar on the Soviet Union has written, "So much is being proclaimed, launched, and undertaken that we must talk not only of Gorbachev's policies but of a 'Gorbachev phenomenon.'"[73] Yet, Gorbachev faces a very rough ride, even if his plans for a restructured economy are achieved. The difficulty, aside from the content of the proposed reforms, is largely in the transition from the current economic system to that which Gorbachev seeks to bring into existence, since it is during the transition that elements of both systems will be in operation. It is a confusing situation in which *perestroika*, in the words of one American economist, "amounts to a blanket injunction not to operate in old ways, but gives little concrete indication how to operate without them."[74]

Much of the urgency of Gorbachev's economic reform is a result of his desire to have introduced the fundamental aspects of the reform by 1990, if not earlier, since the expectation is that the new system will serve as the basis of the thirteenth five-year plan, which will cover the years 1991–1995. Soviet economists have expressed such an urgency, noting that the economic predicament is so severe that it is imperative that the reformed system operate during the thirteenth five-year plan since the Soviet Union cannot afford to wait until 1996. Abalkin remarked in late 1986 that the reform should be laid out by 1988, to be followed by "a couple years of tinkering, fixing the major flaws, so that a somewhat workable and unified system" is in place by 1991, or at least so that the planners will "know the general direction in which movement is to be sought" in drafting the thirteenth five-year plan.[75]

The transition period, a troublesome phase in the best circumstances, is further complicated in Gorbachev's strategy by the ambitious targets set for the current five-year plan. Not only is he demanding that the system considerably improve on its performance in comparison with the last several years, but at the same time work out and implement wide-ranging reforms.[76] Several troublesome contradictions have appeared in the reform as detailed in the numerous laws and documents of the last few years, which appear to indicate the complexities involved in combining market and planned economic processes into what Oleg Bogomolov has referred to as a "plan-regulated socialist market."[77] On the one hand, ministries have been ordered not to interfere in the operational activities of the enterprises which they supervise, although they still hold responsibility for results. Similarly, despite calls for decentralization, the independence of enterprises has been limited by a torrent of central directives, which are virtual commands to implement various policies, such as to introduce multiple-shift work, and to support the development of cooperative activity. Meanwhile, the enterprise has been released from many central directives, and is required to be self-supporting within an environment of irrational prices, which makes economically prudent decisionmaking almost impossible. Such contradictions will only serve to increase the confusion and dysfunctional economic activity which will make the fulfillment of plans increasingly difficult. In the face of such confusion, managers are trying to secure as many State orders as possible, since the State is responsible for guaranteeing necessary inputs.[78] Similarly, there are serious inequalities between enterprises; some will have few problems thriving in the new economic environment because the state has supplied them with modern equipment and generous investment resources. Other enterprises will have difficulties competing, given long periods of mismanagement and neglect by central planners. Some economists advocate the confiscation of windfall profits arising from such disproportions, but this would necessitate increased interference by the center. In addition, according to one reform-minded Soviet economist, the impact of economic accountability is declining, rather than increasing, because of continued interference from the center and the continued redistribution of profits from profitable work collectives to unprofitable ones. Pavel Bunich, for example, cautions economic accountability loses its capacity to promote efficient and good work; instead, under such conditions, enterprises will use increased independence to "make life easier," by understating plans and making larger than needed claims on State funds.[79]

Managers who have gained new independence under the current reforms, including the Law on the State Enterprise, even if they seek to maximize their production and operate economically and efficiently, will be set loose in an environment that reflects poorly, if at all, the true opportunity costs of any decision they make. In addition, even the best-planned and implemented reform contains loopholes that will be found and used by managers for the benefit of the enterprise. It will take some time for such loopholes to emerge, and the success of the reforms will depend to a large extent on actions taken by the center to correct such problems. One cannot discount the possibility that the system will be in such disarray that the pressure for a return to the policies of the early 1980s will prevail.

In the short run, help should come from the redirection of investment to machine-building sectors, the stress on renovation rather than new construction, increased utilization of existing plants, and the introduction of more advanced and productive technologies, particularly those which require fewer labor inputs. A revision of prices, scheduled to be in operation by the start of the thirteenth five-year plan, could help if adjustments bring prices into closer correspondance with actual opportunity costs. In addition, a more assertive attempt to attract foreign technology and know-how through the legislation on joint ventures, as well as through closer cooperation with CMEA members, could give a boost to the Soviet economy.

A fundamental reform of the Soviet economic system demands, first of all, a significant devolution of authority and responsibility to the local economic agents in the system, which possess the information required for efficient economic decisions. Firms must have the independence to set their own plans, choose their own partners, and have some control over prices. Such increased independence must further be accompanied by the responsibility of accepting the consequences of their decisions. This applies to the benefits, such as being able to retain significant portions of their profits, and to the negative implications, such as bankruptcy. In essence, enterprises must determine their own fate. This model is a far cry from the current situation in the Soviet Union, even though such previously unthinkable possibilities, such as bankruptcy, have been introduced. In order to function effectively in more competitive, marketized conditions, state enterprises will require new management skills. It will take a major effort to instill an economical mindset among the managers who have been trained to function in the present economic system. As Goldman notes, "To operate in a centrally planned system requires one set skills—the ability to procure supplies and produce quantity, whereas to operate in a market environment requires another—the ability to cater to and generate demand, and to produce quality and variety."[80] A decisive aspect of this will also be the trimming of the bureaucracy and the limiting of the ability of superiors to make demands on managers.

The extent to which these policies are implemented will determine the shape of a fundamental realignment of authority in the Soviet economic, as well as political system. There would be a weakening of the power of the central organs, including the Party, a paradoxical situation in which Gorbachev would be asking the bureaucracy to implement and enforce reforms that will weaken their power, an action that is now being opposed by the middle level of the bureaucracy. Furthermore, the security which Soviet citizens have come to expect from the system will be undermined. There is a delicate balance between central control and economic equality on one hand and stimulation of greater initiative and efficiency on the other.

To a significant degree, Gorbachev's ability to lead the Soviet Union through the difficult period of transition will depend on the strength of public and institutional support. This, too, presents a problem for Gorbachev. On the one hand, it is necessary to show workers and managers some tangible benefit from the reform, while at the same time much of Gorbachev's strategy seems to be aimed at producers' goods sectors while demanding greater effort and discipline. Without raising living standards, calls for improving the performance of the "human factor" will do little to lessen public skepticism and apathy. As Schroeder notes, "Creative, conscientious work effort cannot be elicited and sustained through pressure tactics; it must come voluntarily from workers who see some payoff reasonably close at hand and who expect even greater payoff in the future."[81]

Economic reform in the Soviet Union poses numerous dilemmas, managerial, technological, social, political, and environmental. Gorbachev has launched a reform that is fraught with difficulties, even assuming the most favorable domestic and international circumstances. If Gorbachev had known initially how far he had to go, he might not have started at all. And yet despite setbacks, his determination to forge ahead with *perestroika* appears as urgent as ever. One thing is certain about *perestroika*: even if it fails, it will provide the foundations for future reforms, much like the efforts of the 1960s. Feodor Burlatskii and other reformers associated with Gorbachev have referred to themselves as "children of the 20th Congress." Even if Gorbachev fails, he has already given birth to his own "children of the 27th Congress."

Notes:

1. Archie Brown, "Gorbachev: The New Man in the Kremlin," *Problems of Communism,* vol. 34, no. 3 (May–June 1985): p. 9.
2. *Pravda,* 2 August 1986. (emphasis added)
3. Brown, p. 13.
4. Mikhail Gorbachev, *Perestroika* (New York: Harper & Row, 1987), p. 24.
5. I. V. Andropov, *Izbrannye rechi i stat'i* (Moscow: Politizdat, 1985), p. 212.
6. Gorbachev, speech at Khabarovsk, *Pravda,* 2 August 1986.
7. Mikhail S. Gorbachev, "Political Report of the CPSU Central Committee to the 27th Congress of the Communist Party of the Soviet Union," 25 February 1986, in Gorbachev, *Selected Speeches and Articles* (Moscow: Progress, 1987), pp. 368, 371.
8. Aleksandr Iakovlev, as cited in Radio Free Europe/Radio Liberty (RFE/FL), *Radio Liberty Research Bulletin* 332/87, p. 5.
9. Benjamin Lambeth and Kevin Lewis, "The Kremlin and SDI," *Foreign Affairs,* vol. 66 no. 4 (Spring 1988): p. 758.
10. Leonid Abalkin, *The Strategy of Economic Development in the USSR* (Moscow: Progress, 1986), p. 25.
11. A. Bovin, "Perestroika and Socialism's Future," *Moscow News* no. 35 6–13 September (1987): pp. 2–3.

12. Ibid.
13. Eduard Shevardnadze, as translated in Foreign Broadcast Information Service: Daily Report, Soviet Union (FBIS-Sov), 3 November 1987, p. 89.
14. Marshall I. Goldman, The USSR in Crisis (New York: W. W. Norton, 1983), p. 33.
15. Abel Aganbegian, as translated in FBIS-Sov, 5 December 1987, p. 68.
16. A. Aganbegian, Make the Economy Responsive to Innovation (Moscow: Novosti, 1986), p. 20.
17. Igor Birman, "From the Achieved Level," Soviet Studies vol. 30 (April 1978): pp. 153–172. See this for an insightful discussion of this phenomenon in Soviet planning practice.
18. Sotsialisticheskaia industriia, 21 April 1988.
19. Sotsialisticheskaia industriia, 3 April 1987.
20. While some scholars question whether or not collectivization actually achieved this objective, there is no doubt that Stalin intended collectivization to effect a transfer of resources from agriculture to industry. See M. Ellman, Socialist Planning (Cambridge, 1989), pp. 92–107.
21. Pravda, 15 January 1989, translated in FBIS-Sov, 26 January 1989, p. 76.
22. H. Aage, "Labor Allocation in the Soviet Kolkhoz," Economics of Planning vol. 16 no. 3 (1980).
23. Izvestiia, 20 December 1988.
24. Pravda, 13 March 1989.
25. U.S. Department of Agriculture, USSR: Agriculture and Trade Report, 1988, p. 8.
26. Narodnoe khoziaistvo 1985 (Moscow, 1986), p. 260.
27. Alec Nove, "Soviet Agriculture: The Brezhnev Legacy and Gorbachev's Cure," unpublished manuscript, April, 1987, p. 9.
28. Pravda, 8 September 1988.
29. Izvestiia, 16 March 1989.
30. Ibid.
31. Peter Hauslohner, "Gorbachev's Social Contract," Soviet Economy vol. 3 no. 1 (January–March 1987): pp. 54–89.
32. Jerry Hough, Opening Up the Soviet Economy (Washington, D.C.: The Brookings Institution, 1988), p. 18.
33. Mikhail Gorbachev, Perestroika: New Thinking for Our Country and the World (New York: Harper & Row, 1987), pp. 24–25.
34. Morris Bornstein and Daniel R. Fusfeld, The Soviet Economy: A Book of Readings (Homewood, IL: Irwin, 1962), p. 2.
35. Narodnoe khoziaistvo SSSR za 70 let (Moscow: Financy i Statistika, 1987), p. 472.
36. Abalkin, p. 19.
37. Oleg Petrichenko, "Tron Pozitrono" Ogonek no. 1 (January 1988): p. 2.

38. O. Latsis, *"Kak shagaet uskorenie? (How is acceleration faring?)"* Kommunist no. 4 (March 1987): p. 58.
39. *Moskovskie Novosti*, no. 6 (14-21 February 1988): p. 4.
40. *Pravda*, 4 March 1986.
41. *Pravda*, 26 February 1986.
42. Abel Aganbegian, "Up the Steps of Acceleration," FBIS-Sov, 22 February 1988, p. 78.
43. *Narodnoe khoziaistvo*, (*Nar. Khoz.*), p. 517. In 1986, official Soviet statistics noted that 85 percent of urban families were living in their own apartments.
44. Micheal V. Alexeev, "Soviet Residential Housing: Will the 'Acute Problem' Be Solved?" in Joint Economic Committee, *Gorbachev's Economic Plans* (Washington, D.C.: Government Printing Office, 1987), vol. 2, p. 284.
45. Aganbegian, "Up the Steps," p. 79.
46. *Nar. Khoz.*, p. 409.
47. *Pravda*, 2 August 1986.
48. Hough, p. 13.
49. Gorbachev, p. 10.
50. *The Washington Post*, 3 August 1983, p. A1.
51. Tatiana Zaslavskaia, "The Novosibirsk Report," as translated in *Survey* (Spring 1984): p. 88.
52. Ibid., p. 106. (Compare this with Gorbachev's statement that "A whole system of weakening the economic tools of government emerged and there took shape a mechanism of braking socioeconomic development and hindering progressive change which made it impossible to tap and use the advantage of socialism," in his speech to the Plenum of the CPSU Central Committee, *Pravda*, 28 January 1987.)
53. Ibid., pp. 91–92.
54. *Pravda*, 19 February 1988.
55. *Pravda*, 24 April 1985.
56. Ibid.
57. *Pravda*, 19 February 1988.
58. Hough, p. 33.
59. V. I. Lenin, "Original Version of the Article 'The Immediate Tasks of the Soviet Government,'" as cited in Leonid Abalkin, p. 134.
60. Leonid Abalkin, "'The Economic Mechanism in Soviet Society," *Socialism as an Economic System:* p. 45.
61. *Pravda*, 21 January 1988.
62. Georgi Matiukhin, "Combatting Bureaucracy by Bureaucratic Means," *Moscow News*, no. 8, 28 February–6 March 1988, p. 3 and A. Nuikin, "Idealy ili interesy (Ideals or Interests)," *Novyi Mir* no. 1 (1988): pp. 190–191.
63. *Pravda*, 18 August 1987.
64. Abraham S. Becker, "Report on Panel 2: Economics," in *The 27th Congress*

of the Communist Party of the Soviet Union: A Report from the Airlie House Conference (Santa Monica, California: Rand, CSSIB Joint Notes Series, 1986), p. 39.

65. Alec Nove as cited in "A Report on the Proceedings of 'The International Conference on the Gorbachev Initiatives,' 30 October–1 November 1987, Washington D.C., The American Committee on U.S.-Soviet Relations," p. 26.
66. *Pravda*, 27 June 1987.
67. Interview with Abel Aganbegian carried by Prague Television Service, in FBIS-Sov, 10 July 1987, p. R20.
68. *Pravda*, 18 July 1987.
69. Gertrude E. Schroeder, "Anatomy of Gorbachev's Economic Reform," *Soviet Economy* vol. 3 no. 3 (July–September 1987): p. 228.
70. Interview with Abel Aganbegian carried by *Die Zeit*, in FBIS-Sov, 21 September 1987, p. 42.
71. *Izvestiia,* 1 April 1989.
72. FBIS-Sov, 26 August 1988, p. 41. Viktor Tikonov acknowledged the pervasiveness of the resistence in a speech in Tashkent in August 1988. For a description of a particular example of opposition to leasing by local bureaucrats, see *Izvestia*, 28 August 1988.
73. Moshe Lewin, *The Gorbachev Phenomenon: A Historical Interpretation* (Berkeley, California: University of California Press, 1988), p. *x*.
74. Gregory Grossman, "The Second Economy: Boon or Bane for the Reform of the First Economy?" *Studies on the Soviet Second Economy,* Paper no. 11 (December 1987): p. 2.19.
75. Leonid Abalkin, *Ekonomicheskaia gazeta*, no. 46, November 1986.
76. Gertrude Schroeder, pp. 231–233. See this for an insightful account of the demands being placed on the various agencies charged with reform.
77. *Moscow News* no. 30, 1987, p. 8.
78. *Pravda*, 18 April 1987.
79. *Sotsialisticheskaia Industriia*, 7 March 1988.
80. Marshall I. Goldman, "Gorbachev and Economic Reform," *Foreign Affairs* vol. 64 no. 1 (Fall 1985): pp. 68–69.
81. Gertrude Schroeder, "Consumer Malaise in the Soviet Union: Perestroika's Achilles' Heel?" *PlanEcon Report* vol. 4 no. 11 (18 March 1988): p. 12.

5 MIKHAIL GORBACHEV AND THE FOREIGN POLICY OF THE SOVIET UNION

William F. Brazier

During the late 1970s and the early 1980s, the Soviet Union faced serious declines in economic production. The traditional emphasis on extensive growth, command planning from the center, and rigid political controls that Moscow relied on to direct its economic system resulted in the serious stagnation in economic performance that became evident in the latter half of the last decade. The drawn out process of leadership succession of 1982 to 1985, and the infirmities of the three General Secretaries who reigned during those years, only contributed to and symbolized the failing state of the economic and political systems of the Soviet Union, which continue to employ burdensome control measures to enforce production and performance directives.

In the last years of Brezhnev's rule and continuing into the mid-1980s, it became clear to those in the highest levels of the Soviet leadership that changes in the economy and political system were necessary if the USSR was to enter the next century as an effective superpower rival to the United States. The widening technology gap between East and West continues to cause serious concern in the Kremlin, and appears to be one of the primary factors contributing to the consensus among the present Soviet leadership of the need for reform of the economic system. General Secretary Mikhail Gorbachev assumed the top leadership post in this atmosphere of critical concern, and has, since his ascension to power in 1985, proven himself a strong advocate of economic reform. He has made *perestroika*, or reconstruction, the watchword of new Kremlin policies to invigorate economic performance and long-range growth, and has overseen the passage of new laws on State enterprises that are aimed at creating incentives for improved production performance at lower levels of plant and firm activity.

The present ideological formulations in Soviet foreign policy, as outlined primarily by General Secretary Gorbachev, focus on the interrelationship between the requirements for domestic reform, the success or failure of Soviet reform efforts, and the dynamic of international politics. Gorbachev said that the "main task" of Soviet reform policies is

> to make the economy more efficient and dynamic, to make the lives of the people spiritually richer, more full-bodied and meaningful, to develop the system of socialist self-government by the people.[1]

Gorbachev has also noted that "the main thing that will ensure us success [in accelerating the economy] is the living creativity of the masses."[2] In order to allow this "creativity" to do its work, Gorbachev has asserted that the USSR needs a stable international environment.[3] It is in this way that Soviet domestic objectives have shaped the Kremlin international outlook and Soviet foreign policy ideology. As Gorbachev said:

> I state with full responsibility that our international policy is more than ever determined by domestic policy, by our interest in concentrating on constructive endeavors to improve our country. This is why we need lasting peace, predictability and constructiveness in international relations.[4]

In his speech to the Soviet people after his return from the December 1987 Washington summit, Gorbachev expressed the view that benefits in the international realm would come to the USSR once progress was made in domestic restructuring:

> for all of us there is still one thing to keep in mind, that the more successful we will be in carrying out the revolutionary affairs of *perestroika*, the more success will come to affairs in the international arena.[5]

Having identified the connection between economic and bureaucratic efficiency in the domestic arena and "success" in international politics, Gorbachev outlined a theoretical world outlook that expands traditional Marxist-Leninist ideology. Within his new ideological framework, it appears that what he and his colleagues consider to be "success" for "affairs in the international arena" is different from the notions of success of previous Soviet leadership groups. From Stalin to Chernenko, Soviet General Secretaries and their advisors explained world events and different international phenomena as instances of the classic Marxist-Leninist conflict between socialism and capitalism. Stalin led the institutionalization of the "two-camp" approach to world affairs, which was based on the view that if a country was not communist, with a Soviet-style form of government, then it was an enemy of socialism and the USSR. This confrontational view was maintained during the reigns of Khrushchev and Brezhnev, although it was gradually tempered by the theories behind peaceful coexistence and détente. But despite the moderating influence of détente and peaceful coexistence, the two-camp approach still compelled both Soviet and American strategic thinkers to view the East-West competition as a win-all or lose-all struggle.

Gorbachev's theoretical formulations have by no means completely replaced the USSR's two-camp, theoretical approach to international politics. They have, however, added to it what Gorbachev has called a recognition of the interdependence of all nations of the world. This interdependence of nations, Gorbachev has said, is compelled by the present dangerous stage of the nuclear arms race, and the proliferation of contemporary "global problems."

In his speeches and public statements, Gorbachev has focused attention on the threat he says is posed by the existence of nuclear weapons. The Soviet Union's proposed nuclear testing moratorium of 1986–1987, the Soviet program for the elimination of nuclear weapons by the year 2000 announced on 15 January 1986, the Gorbachev leadership's conciliatory overtures on the arms control issues—such as the invitation to U.S. congressmen to inspect the controversial Krasnoyarsk radar installation, and the USSR's acceptance of intrusive, on-site inspection for treaty verification purposes, the proposals for radical cuts in both nuclear and conventional forces, all strongly support the view that arms control issues are at the top of the Soviet leadership's international policy agenda, and constitute a primary element in the present Soviet world outlook. Gorbachev himself has said as much on numerous occasions in words such as these:

> Now that the world has huge nuclear stockpiles and the only thing experts argue about is how many times or dozens of times humanity can be destroyed, it is high time to begin an effective withdrawal from the brink of war, from the equilibrium of fear, to normal, civilised forms of relations between the states of the two systems.[6]

Gorbachev and his advisors owe much for their views on "global problems" to the thinking of Soviet political scientists Georgii Shakhnazarov, Vadim Zagladin, and others, who wrote in the 1970s on the topic referred to by the Soviets as "globalistics." These scholars developed theories on the dialectics of global problems and international interdependence. They wrote that certain problems that are global in nature—such as those concerning the international economy, global security, and the world's environmental problems—increase the interdependence of nations and peoples, while the solutions to these problems *require* international interdependence and joint approaches.[7] Gorbachev has expressed views that parallel those of the globalist political scientists, and has appointed some of those theoreticians to important foreign policy positions. In his foreign policy speeches, Gorbachev has repeatedly called for unified international approaches to problems that he says threaten the very survival of the human race:

> In view of the rising danger of a new spiral in the arms race and of the drastic exacerbation of regional and, what we call, global problems, we must waste no more time trying to outplay each other and to gain unilateral advantages. The stake in such a game is too high—the survival of humanity.[8]

Gorbachev first summed up the modified Soviet world outlook in his address to the 27th Congress of the CPSU in 1986. To this forum, the highest-ranking ideological, political, and economic leadership body in Soviet society, Gorbachev claimed that humanity can survive as long as the communists of the world, who are aware of the phenomenon of international interdependence, make progress in spreading their view of the world's interconnectedness. His final observation regarding the present dynamics of international relations noted the world's contradictions, as well as the evolution of those contradictions taking place under the conditions of interdependence:

> The prevailing dialectics of present-day development consists in a combination of competition and confrontation between the two systems and in a growing tendency toward interdependence of the countries of the world community. This is precisely the way, through the struggle of opposites, through arduous effort, groping in the dark to some extent, as it were, that the controversial but interdependent and in many ways integral world is taking shape.[9]

The Soviet world outlook as Gorbachev has explained it, has also served as the Party line for members of the Soviet foreign policy establishment whose job it is to disseminate the Soviet viewpoint on foreign relations to the outside world. Foreign Minister Shevardnadze and Director of the Institute for World Economy and International Relations Evgenii Primakov have repeatedly expressed their views on the essence of the new Soviet approach to foreign policy. They have said that the Soviet Union proceeds from the fundamental assumption that the enduring conflicts between socialism and capitalism are present in contemporary international relations, but that these conflicts are counteracted in part by the interdependence of countries and the interconnectedness of nations.[10]

The qualitatively new stage in the dynamic of international relations, wherein conflicts and opposition are tempered by the need for cooperative measures and the necessity for interdependence, requires, according to the Soviet leadership, "new political thinking" on the part of world leaders and individual citizens. Proceeding from this conclusion, Gorbachev and his foreign policy spokesmen have focused on what they view as the world's interconnectedness through economic, political, cultural, and ethnic ties, in putting forward their recommendations for the kind of "thinking" in which international actors ought to engage. The "new thinking," according to Gorbachev, calls for joint action to help solve international problems, a recognition of the interdependence of all countries, and a discarding of "old" approaches to foreign relations that put "selfish, national interests" above the interests of the world community. For example, in order to resolve regional conflicts, Gorbachev has said that the USSR favors joint action to reach political settlements[11]; regarding international and bilateral security issues, he claims that the Soviet Union believes one nation's security is dependent on the feeling of security attained by another, and that all security questions must be viewed as they affect, in toto, and in both the economic and political realms, the nations concerned;[12] and regarding any country's national interests, both Gorbachev and Politburo member Aleksandr Iakovlev have publicly decried the "selfish" pursuance of "national interests." Gorbachev has gone so far as to say that all nations must put aside their "class narrowmindedness" in order to work together on global problems.[13]

These lofty ideals constitute the basic tenets of the new Soviet theoretical formulations on international relations as they have been put forward by Gorbachev. It became clear in 1988 that differences exist among members of the Communist Party Politburo about where the Soviet Union should emphasize in its new "contradictory yet interdependent" framework. Although Gorbachev, Shevardnadze, and Iakovlev appear to have been able to push their interpretation of the "contradictory yet interdependent" framework as the center of policy, Politburo member and Central Committee Secretary Ligachev has challenged that view and has clearly stressed his own, somewhat different views on interdependence and "all-human values. " During the summer of 1988, Ligachev responded to a speech by Politburo member and Foreign Minister, Eduard Shevardnadze, with his own observations on the world class struggle and international interdependence.

The Shevardnadze address, given in the wake of the 19th Communist Party Conference and the Central Committee plenum of July, 1988, was directed at the *aktiv* in the Foreign Ministry, and dealt with the overall direction of Soviet foreign policy. In that address, Shevardnadze described, as both he and Gorbachev had in the past, how the Soviet Union's foreign policy hinges on the new historical stage of international relations where international interdependence works to determine much of the dynamic of world politics, and helps to counteract the conflicting tendencies engendered by the existence of two different social systems. Shevardnadze went so far as to say that "the struggle between two opposing systems is no longer a determining tendency of the present era," and that the promotion of tendencies such as the increasing "democratization and demilitarization" of world affairs, and "the exploitation of scientific-technical potential for the cooperative resolution of global problems" constituted "our main calling" in world politics.[14] Shevardnadze added as well that "peaceful coexistence," as defined by Gorbachev to include the new tenets of interdependence, should serve as the "universal principle" of international relations, and that it should never be linked with the Marxian class struggle. Although Gorbachev's notion of peaceful coexistence still recognizes that there are class differences, as well as the class' determining role in the policy making of a state for that class which enjoys supremacy, it demands that all nations *and* national-liberation movements recognize the all-human, universal values that are wider than their own narrow interests, Shevardnadze said.

One week after Shevardnadze delivered his speech, Politburo member and Central Committee Secretary Egor Ligachev delivered a speech in the Russian city of Gorkii, and made statements that were clearly intended to address some of the issues raised by Shevardnadze. He stressed the point that all-human interests and proletarian, or class, interests could overlap, and that the two interests are not mutually exclusive. He also clearly implied that class struggle can most certainly be identified with the principles of coexistence, because it is the proletarian class that holds as its fundamental value "the liberation of man and mankind from all types of exploitation and oppression." "The struggle for peace and for the survival of mankind," he said, "is indeed also the struggle for the root interests of the working class."[15] Further, Ligachev[*] reasserted the view that "international relations

---

* It should be noted also that Ligachev said that one of the best ways for the national-liberation movements to "fetter the forces of imperialist militarism" is to contribute to the process of the *political* settlement of regional conflicts of all kinds" (emphasis added). See footnote 15 for citation. This view is still a rather sharp departure from the policy that held the day for an extended period during the Brezhnev era, that of assisting so-called national-liberation movements with *military* assistance at various levels.

are particularly class in character" and that "[a]ctive involvement in the solution of general human problems, and primarily the struggle against the nuclear threat, by no means signifies any—I would say—artificial braking of the social and national, national liberation, struggle."[16]

On the heels of Ligachev's remarks, Politburo member and Central Committee Secretary Aleksandr Iakovlev made a speech in the Soviet Republic of Lithuania responding to Ligachev's comments. He said, in agreement with Ligachev, that proletarian interests are indeed a part of the body of all-human interests and that the two are not mutually exclusive. But he stressed, as did Shevardnadze, that the nuclear threat and other global problems to unite mankind with links of interdependence. He said, in a clear rebuff to Ligachev, that the global problems of today's world were capable of assisting mankind in overcoming international phenomena that have heretofore divided humanity. The modern world, where "individual" interests merge with mankind's overall interests, said Iakovlev, constituted a case of "opposites converging."[17] Such language, especially when used by a Communist Party Politburo member, is significant, because the term "convergence" holds particular meaning to adherents of Marxist thought, referring to the "*bourgeois*" theory that socialism and capitalism can unite through a metamorphic process of interaction and conflict. As a theoretical formulation of Marxist philosophy, "convergence" has historically been out of favor in the Soviet Union. It marks a significant new direction in ideological debate when a Politburo member, with a background in ideology, who clearly knows what the term implies, uses it in a public address relating to issues of foreign policy. Iakovlev's statement is a clear rejection of Ligachev's emphasis on the class nature of Soviet foreign policy.

Readers of the Soviet press have been able to witness in the publication of these Politburo members' statements very different emphases given by different leaders to overall foreign policy ideology. Ligachev pushes one aspect of the official foreign policy line, while Shevardnadze pushes another, yet the choice each Politburo member has made to stress different aspects of the framework indicates the deep disagreement among them. Quite clearly, both Ligachev's and Shevardnadze's statements are consistent in some important respects with the general guidelines propagated by Gorbachev as a framework for Soviet foreign policies. Gorbachev, in his 27th Party Congress speech, described the contemporary world as one containing class and other contradictions, but stressed that these contradictions are tempered by ties of interdependence. Shevardnadze's position emphasizes interdependence, while Ligachev concentrates on class conflict. Both points of view fit into the parameters laid down, by way of consensus decision making, by the General Secretary. This is a familiar pattern in all Soviet policy and/or sociopolitical debates. What is most striking is that underlying, fundamental tenets of the Soviet Union's foreign policy ideology are being discussed in public by the highest-ranking members of the Kremlin leadership. Those who read the press—including foreigners—can observe in detail what transpires. That the policy of *glasnost* has extended even to the Politburo members' differences on such an important subject as foreign policy is, in itself, significant.

Although the Gorbachev/Shevardnadze/Iakovlev position may have been challenged in debate and in some areas of policy, their view has clearly emerged as the dominant view determining policy and Soviet international ideology. The September 1988 personnel shake-up of the CPSU apparatus certainly supports this point. As a result of this reshuffling, Iakovlev was given an expanded role in the Secretariat to oversee the Party's role in foreign policy-making, while Egor Ligachev has been separated from any supervisory role in foreign policy ideology and put in charge of the domestic agricultural sector. In addition, Vadim Medvedev, an ally of Gorbachev, was promoted to full Politburo membership at the September Central Committee meeting, and was given the ideology portfolio in the reorganized Secretariat. Only a few days after his promotion, Medvedev asserted an ideological viewpoint on foreign affairs that clearly supported the Shevardnadze/Iakovlev emphasis on international interdependence. Although he did rule out the idea of the convergence of socialism and capitalism, he said that "universal values" occupy the "foreground of international relations and constitute the nucleus of the new political thinking."[18]

ECONOMICS AND SOVIET FOREIGN POLICY

The influence of economics on the formulation of Soviet foreign policy has always been strong. During the tenure of Iurii Andropov, however, changes in Soviet foreign policy has already taken on a new, officially sanctioned direction, due largely to the practical limitations of the Soviet economy. Influenced by soviet thinkers such as Karen Brutents, a Deputy Chief of the Central Committee International Department, as well as a number of scholars at other institutes of the Soviet Academy of Sciences, General Secretary Andropov expressed the view in a 1983 Central Committee speech that the USSR should not automatically assist, economically or militarily, revolutionary governments or movements in the developing world simply because these groups call themselves "Marxist-Leninist" in nature. In this speech, he emphasized that a certain level of "productive forces" must be attained in the developing countries before Soviet assistance to these countries can have any long-term staying power. In effect, he said that the Soviet Union was going to be careful about which "revolutionary" movements it would give generous assistance, because the USSR could no longer afford to sink political *and* economic capital into countries that offered little hope of long-term political stability or self-reliance in their economic development strategies.[19]

This line of thinking, which emphasized limited support for unstable and unreliable Marxist movements and regimes, in conjuncton with a cultivation of relations with large, stable countries of the developing world with capitalist-oriented economies, had been under discussion in the academic and scholarly communities in the Soviet Union for some time. Karen Brutents and Evgenii Primakov, the present director of the World Economy and International Relations Institute, were both writing as early as 1976 about the success that capitalism was having in the developing countries, and were clearly of the opinion at that time that the Soviet Union should take steps in its foreign economic relations to avoid being left behind or closed out of the economic ties that continued to develop between the less-developed countries (LDCs) and the "imperialist" nations.[20]

Arguments similar to those made by Primakov and Brutents are still evident today in the Soviet scholarly journals. Recent articles have even gone so far as to recommend an overhaul of the entire *study* of developing nations, claiming that the presently accepted framework for undertaking research on the LDCs is ill-defined and outmoded. In a recent article in *Mirovaia Ekonomika i Mezhdunarodnye Otnosheniia (MEMO)*, R. M. Avakov, Department Head of Economics and Politics of Developing Countries at the Institute of World Economy and International Relations (IMEMO), in a veiled but cutting manner criticized the enforced ideological orthodoxies that the study of the LDCs has been forced to accept. He also claimed in this article that national-liberation movements obviously do not automatically develop into Marxist-Leninist social systems, and said that the people who believe that this development can occur are really applying wishes, and not objective observation, to actual events.[21]

Although Andropov introduced the officially sanctioned policy of examining political and economic costs before investing in new LDC clients, General Secretary Gorbachev has further encouraged such methods, and has in fact directed an emphasis on the economic determinants in Soviet foreign policy. He first began to set the tone for his new policies at a June 1985 Central Committee meeting, asserting that, "both in domestic and foreign affairs the objective of accelerating the country's development has become of primary political, economic, and social importance."[22] Two years later at the June 1987 Central Committee plenum, Gorbachev continued, in his report to the Committee, to emphasize the primary importance of accelerating the development of Soviet society economically and politically. He consistently referred to the policy of *perestroika* as a "strategic" task before the country, and plainly viewed the reform process as an imperative for the maintenance of the USSR's great power role in world affairs:

> It should be clearly understood that we see the aims of accelerating social and economic development not only in overcoming the lag that has accumulated and the deformations that have appeared in various fields of society's development. Dictated by historic necessity and the altered conditions of an internal and international nature, cardinally altered at that, they are directed at the attainment of a new qualitative state of socialist society.
>
> History has not left us much time to solve this task. The possibilities of socialism, what it gives a person in practice, how socially effective the society is will be judged exactly by the progress of the restructuring drive, by its results.[23]

Taking up the tasks put before him and the entire Soviet people by Gorbachev at the June 1987 plenum, Foreign Minister Eduard Shevardnadze issued new directives and guiding principles to his own staff at a meeting of the Foreign Ministry *aktiv* held 4 July 1987. He emphasized the need to further the acceleration and restructuring drive that Gorbachev is pushing in the Soviet economic sphere, and described certain specific tasks that the foreign policy establishment under his direction should seek to complete. In this address Shevardnadze not only called for a rejuvenation and redirection of Soviet foreign economic relations, but actually insisted on the infusion of economics and economic goals into the overall direction of Soviet foreign policy. The reasons for this he stated quite plainly. The USSR's position on the world stage will be negatively affected if all those who work to implement Soviet foreign policy do not keep the goals of economic restructuring at the top of their priority list. He said, in part,

> The time has come, so to speak, to "economize" our foreign policy, if such an expression is permissible, since, until it is linked wholly with the economy, it will be unable to help in restructuring our domestic economy and society overall, which, in this manner, will be unable to participate on equal terms

in the competitive political struggle for the attractiveness of our socioeconomic development model.[24]

In no uncertain terms, Shevardnadze's address to the Foreign Ministry *aktiv* in July 1987 expresses the view that improvement in Soviet economic performance is, in fact, a political task. Moreover, Shevardnadze makes plain that the USSR's domestic economic performance has significant international political ramifications since it is seen as one aspect of the Eastern economic development *model* toward which LDCs may be attracted. Indeed, there can be no clearer expression of the view that the success or failure of Soviet domestic economic reform will have profound international consequences than the inclusion of the task of economic *perestroika* among the primary objectives to be sought by the *aktiv* of the Ministry of Foreign Affairs. In Shevardnadze's own words, "the embassy [i.e., Soviet embassies throughout the world] is called upon to play the role of forward patrol that follows everything new in the realm of scientific and technical progress, everything that could be of interest to the national economy, not only now, but in the future as well."[25] In accordance with the Marxist principle that economics determines politics, Shevardnadze has thus asserted that the most important political task of the Ministry of Foreign Affairs is to find ways in the international sphere to improve the domestic Soviet economy.

The Foreign Ministry has not been the only institution involved in the implementation of the new Soviet economic foreign policy. By promoting a fresh corps of cadres well-versed in economics and trade, the Gorbachev leadership has dramatically changed the structure, functions, and emphasis of the Soviet foreign trade apparatus. Most notable among the new cadres is Ivan D. Ivanov, now Deputy Chairman of the State Foreign Economic Commission created by Gorbachev in early 1987. Ivanov has long advocated the kinds of reforms in foreign trade that the Soviet Union is now undertaking, having first proposed Soviet entry in the GATT (General Agreement on Tariffs and Trade) in 1984, subsequently suggesting Soviet participation in the IMB (International Monetary Fund) and calling for a convertible ruble in incremental stages. Ivanov also has an extensive background in trade issues, having been graduated from the Institute of Foreign Trade in 1957, and later serving as a section chief at the Institute for World Economy and International Relations (IMEMO).[26]

Ivanov, in his capacity as Deputy Chairman of the new Commission, and even before that agency's creation, has been the most visible Soviet spokesperson on the issue of foreign trade. As early as 1986 he publicly discussed the bureaucratic changes in the trade apparatus of the Soviet Union, and was in charge of almost all of the Soviet press conferences on the topic of foreign economic relations.[27] Most recently, Ivanov published an article describing the bureaucratic changes taking place in the Soviet foreign trade establishment in the American journal, *Soviet Economy*.

First, to fulfill Shevardnadze's recommendation that the embassies become outposts of information for the domestic economic researchers and managers, the Soviets have created a special position of "Counselor on Foreign Economic Affairs" in overseas embassies located in countries that are the USSR's major trading partners.[28] At home in Moscow, the bureaucratic agencies dealing with trade were left in place, but their functions were changed, and in some instances, drastically. The Ministry of Foreign Trade, the State Committee for Foreign Economic Relations (GKES), and the USSR Chamber of Commerce and Industry all remain as institutions, but they are, ostensibly, now to receive their overall direction from the new State Commission on Foreign Economic Relations where Ivanov is a Deputy Chairman. The new Commission's Chairman, Vladimir Kamentsev, has the rank of Deputy Prime Minister. The Commission itself is charged with "managing economic relations with foreign countries as a single 'external economic complex.'" It is assigned the task of supervising external economic relations by coordinating the activities of ministries and organizations involved in foreign trade. "Its major task is to formulate and implement the country's foreign economic strategy so as to enhance its potential contributions to *uskorenie* [acceleration], strengthen the Soviet position in the world economy, and promote structured and organized development of economic cooperation with all groups of countries."[29] What this means in practice is the infusion of foreign economic/trade concerns into the planning procedures for the entire Soviet economy. The Commission will have a right to assert its interests in the planning process, thereby attaining for the foreign trade concerns increased influence and heightened prestige—at the expense of the existing bureaucratic planning interests.

Another agency that has had its influence circumscribed by the structual changes being made in the foreign economic bureaucracy is the Ministry of Foreign Trade. As Professor Jerry Hough of Duke University has pointed out, the Ministry, which exercised a monopoly in policy and direction of the USSR's foreign trade until recently, has lost supervision of a large part of Soviet trade. In 1986, responsibility for trade in manufactured goods was transferred from the Ministry to twenty-one industrial ministries and seventy industrial enterprises.[30] Many Soviet enterprises will now have the right to establish direct ties and trading contracts with foreign firms, and will be able to spend their profits in hard currencies according to their own determinations.

One of the most well-publicized aspects of Soviet economic reforms consists of the new joint ventures with socialist and non-socialist countries. Although Moscow has recently announced that under certain circumstances the majority of stock shares can be held by the foreign company in a joint venture, the original rules stipulated that 51 percent of a joint firm's stock had to be owned by the Soviet enterprise, and the Chairman of the Board and the Director-General both had to be Soviet citizens. Presently, foreign employees can be hired by joint enterprises and can repatriate their wages in hard currency after a 13 percent tax. In addition, the joint ventures are to receive priorities in the procurement of construction materials, and are "entitled to an accelerated depreciation on their capital equipment."[31] This last point is rather significant because it indicates the priority Moscow has attached to direct foreign ties, the influx of technology, and interaction with foreign economic management. It is well-known that in the USSR at present there are serious shortages of capital resources and construction materials. Giving priority to the joint ventures' requests for equipment illustrates well the need that the Soviet leadership feels for foreign economic interaction. This, it seems, is the most important lesson to be learned by the West from the new Soviet policies. As Professor Hough points out in his new study of the Soviet economic reforms, the present leadership in the USSR wants to open the Soviet economy to foreign markets and investments for the same reasons that leaders in the United States and other capitalist countries criticize protectionist trade policies. That is, that the exposure of a domestic market to the practices of firms operating effectively in the world economy can have enriching consequences for the domestic economies—thanks to competition and active cooperation. The Soviet economy has historically been the most "protectionist" in the world. But starting in the late 1970s and early 1980s, the leaders of the USSR recognized the negative consequences of their protectionist policies.[32] Ivan Ivanov expressed this view very well when he said,

> Around the beginning of the eighties, rather unfavorable features began to appear in our traditional form of foreign trade . . . We started to lose out on prices and our exports began increasing in volume more than in value, and so on. We were in no way able to exceed 4 percent of world trade. That is to say, we had become a great industrial power and accounted for 20 percent of world output, and yet in this sphere we have been unable to become a big foreign trade power. Analyzing why this was so, we found that the main reason was—and we are now rectifying this—that our producers, and incidentally consumers also, were isolated from

the foreign market, and therefore did not have experience of operating in it or indeed have any great interest in operating in it.[33]

It is indeed difficult to imagine how the new Foreign Economic Commission under Kamentsev and Ivanov will achieve its goal of making foreign trade an important facet of domestic economic *perestroika*. Many Soviet economists have said that main problem of the Soviet economy up to now has been its inability, due to the over-bureaucratized and over-centralized political system, to encourage individual initiative and produce efficiently on a nationwide scale. The creation of a new bureaucracy ostensibly to synchronize and coordinate the other inefficient bureaucracies involved with foreign trade appears to be a dubious method of encouraging enterprise independence and foreign interaction. Only time will tell whether or not the new foreign economic agency can make a contribution to the Soviet economy's acceleration by not interfering in a plant's direct ties with foreign companies or by preventing other bureaucracies from doing so as well. If the new bureaucracy seeks to increase its own influence and authority in this heated political atmosphere of reform, it would not bode well for the success of the effort to stimulate individual initiative by plant managers that Gorbachev and the top leaders are trying to cultivate, and could result in even lower rates in growth of Soviet foreign trade.

The USSR has taken concrete political steps to cultivate international economic ties. The internal directives and changes within the Foreign Ministry constitute one economically motivated reform in foreign policy, but the changes in diplomatic style and direction aimed at developing countries are perhaps more significant from a foreign policy point of view. As has been discussed in the Avakov article referred to previously, as well as in many other publications, there has been, for the last six to seven years, a reluctance on the part of the Soviets to rush to the assistance of self-proclaimed Marxist movements or regimes, while at the same time the USSR has increased its activity in relation to developing capitalist countries with growing technology sectors. The Soviets have also been energetically promoting ties with multilateral economic organizations primarily made up of capitalist countries, both developed and developing. They have expressed a desired to become a full-fledged member of the GATT,[34] have proposed vigorously the opening of direct relations between the European Economic Community (EEC) and the Council for Mutual Economic Assistance (CMEA),[35] have sent Foreign Minister Shevardnadze to Australia, Brazil, and Argentina,[36] and have hosted a high-level Mexican delegation in Moscow. [37] They have also supported OPEC in its recent pricing policies,[38] and have shown a special interest in establishing closer ties with Asian and Pacific countries. Ivan D. Ivanov's hopeful economic report on the Asian/Pacific region, commissioned by the top party leadership in 1986, would tend to support the view that Moscow is seriously interested in this part of the world for economic reasons.[39] This heightened interest in Asia has taken the form of proposals to establish deeper ties between the Association of Southeast Asian Nations (ASEAN) and the USSR, fishing agreements with Pacific island nations,[40] increased cultivation of economic ties to the Republic of Korea,[41] and proposals for the establishment of at least forty science joint ventures with Thailand.[42]

The emphasis that the Soviet Union is presently putting on the new relationships that it is establishing with the capitalist-oriented, developing countries is clearly economic. Even a small sampling of the capitalist countries with which the Gorbachev leadership has been cultivating ties reveals this economic slant to Soviet diplomacy—especially in the area of joint ventures for the production of industrial equipment. When the Presdient of Argentina Raúl Alfonsin visited the USSR in October 1986, he met with General Secretary Gorbachev, while his Economic Minister, Mr. Sourrouille, met wth the new Chairman of the State Commission on Foreign Economic Relations Kamentsev. Alfonsin announced in Moscow that there was beginning to be a long-term shift in the structure of Argentine-Soviet trade in the direction of "mutual supply of industrial equipment and the establishment of mixed Soviet-Argentine business ventures with a view to operations on the markets of third countries."[43] A year later, in October 1987, when Soviet Foreign Minister Shevardnadze visited Argentina, he issued a joint communiqué with Argentine Foreign Minister Caputo that outlined similar hopes for trade relations between the two countries. The communiqué emphasized the need to introduce "new forms of cooperation, particularly industrial production sharing, and create joint enterprises and mixed firms. In this respect the sides will promote a mutual exchange of production processes based on advanced technology and the organization of ties between enterprises in the two countries for the purpose of producing and marketing products."[44]

This same emphasis on industrial production sharing and joint enterprises can be seen in Soviet statements and communiqués issued in relation to ties with Brazil, Australia, and Thailand. At a meeting of Brazilian and Soviet business circles taking place in June of 1987 in Rio de Janeiro, it was announced that the aim of the meeting was to "map out specific directions for stepping up Soviet-Brazilian commercial ties and making fuller use of the potential of industrial cooperation, including the creation of joint enterprises."[45] Similarly, during Shevardnadze's visit to Brazil in

October 1987, the joint communiqué issued there made special note of the significance of "commodity exchange operations, license trade, and the establishment of joint enterprises and mixed firms."[46] In Moscow in May of 1987, the Soviet-Australian Trade Promotion Committee and the Australia-USSR Businessmen's Council issued statements on the continued export of raw materials to the Soviet Union and Soviet exports of ships and equipment to Australia, but what was clearly the Soviet hope for the meeting was agreement on Australian involvement in the modernization of Soviet industries. The spokesmen announced that this topic would be explored in future talks, and so would the subject of possible Australian assistance in the development of the Far Eastern regions of the USSR.[47] Finally, when the Thai Foreign Minister Sitthi Sawetsila visited Moscow in May 1987, he met with Chairman of the new State Commission, Kamentsev, also. He signed, with Soviet Minister of Foreign Trade Aristov, a protocol establishing an intergovernmental Soviet-Thailand Commission on Trade. A group of Thai businessmen visited Moscow concurrently with Sawetsila's delegation, and were, apparently with the Foreign Minister himself, pressed to establish closer ties with Soviet production firms. The reportage on the meetings says nothing about a Soviet suggestion for direct ties, yet it quotes Sawetsila's unequivocal statements on the difficulty of developing ties with a planned economy such as the Soviet one, and the hope he has for the reform process underway in the USSR.[48]

Judging from this evidence, Ivan Ivanov appears to be speaking candidly when he says that Soviet firms and industries will continue to be unable to develop intensively at a quickened pace without also developing extensive ties with international markets and foreign production enterprises. Ivanov, as well as the Soviet leadership that appointed him, recognizes that Soviet managers and factories can substantially improve production and efficiency through international competition and integration, as well as through the sharing of industrial technologies.

INTERNATIONAL SECURITY AS BOTH A MEANS AND AN END

From the Soviet point of view, there is a need for a division in national security policy between issues that constitute a direct threat to the security of the Soviet homeland, such as conflict or crisis situations on or near Soviet borders, and those that undermine security in regions geographically far from the Soviet State. For the purpose of discussion, these latter concerns are defined as those seats of tension that threaten to alter in some way the present international security equation, or adversely affect the Soviet Union's interests as a reigning superpower.

At the 27th Congress of the Communist Party of the Soviet Union in February 1986, General Secretary Gorbachev outlined what he called a "comprehensive system of international security." Since that time, Gorbachev and his lieutenants in the foreign policy establishment have stressed this "system" as a major tenet of Soviet foreign policy. The system consists of four areas: military, political, economic, and humanitarian. In the military sphere, the Soviets have stated that military doctrines should be adjusted in the direction of a purely defensive posture, and that the military capabilities of each contending country should be reduced to the level of what Moscow has termed "reasonable sufficiency"; that is, levels that allow the United States and the USSR enough firepower to defend against an attack but not enough to launch an overwhelming surprise attack. In the political realm, the system proposes that priority be given to finding peaceful political solutions to regional conflicts, the principle of inviolability of frontiers, and the establishment of international measures to combat terrorism. In the economic area, the Soviets propose the exclusion of discriminatory trade practices and sanctions, joint actions to solve the problem of debt in the developing world, and the reduction of military budgets so that funds can be transferred from the procurement of military hardware to the improvement of the individual LDC economies. In the field of human rights, Moscow has proposed the "extirpation" of genocide, apartheid, and discrimination; decision in "humane" fashion on questions of the reuniting of families, and cooperation in culture, science, and education, etc.[49]

These lofty proposals on international security sound not unlike the platitudes that Soviet foreign policy spokesmen have historically put forward as "concrete" proposals aimed at ensuring peace and equality in international affairs. Indeed, many of these measures to promote international security appear to be empty phrases, and can only remain empty until actual steps are taken that are consistent with their spirit. It should be noted, however, that recent Soviet statements and policies regarding the implementation of this system of international security through the organizations of the United Nations (UN) suggest that the USSR is interested in the practical implementation of some aspects of their proposed system. A series of statements by key Soviet leaders and foreign policy personnel regarding the usefulness of the UN and the validity of its Charter, as well as recent Soviet actions such as the payment of the USSR's past dues to the international organization, testify to a renewed Soviet interest in promoting their own version of international security through the United Nations.[50]

The idea of promoting international security through the UN has roots in the USSR that extend back before Gorbachev's rise to power. Vladimir Petrovskii, who is presently a Deputy Minister of Foreign Affairs, published a book in 1985 which called for a more active security role for the United Nations. In his chapter on international security, Petrovskii emphasized the UN's role in the preservation of peace, and stressed the need for the UN Security Council to be energetically involved with the defusion of international tension in all regions of the globe. He further pointed out that the General Assembly, the International Court of Justice, and the Secretary-General's office should not in any way be entrusted with duties that are reserved by the Charter for the Security Council. In very clear terms, Petrovskii expressed the view that the Security Council should act as the primary UN guardian of international security.[51]

In September of 1987, General Secretary Gorbachev published a statement addressed to the UN General Assembly, wherein he proposed joint international actions to safeguard security on a global level, and recommended that the UN act as the primary body through which all actions for the preservation of international peace and stability be taken. In his own words, today's world is "increasingly interdependent" in its complexity, and its main protagonists need to operate through the UN because the international stage "increasingly needs a mechanism which is capable of discussing its common problems in a responsible fashion and at a representative level and provides a place for the mutual search for a balance of differing, contradictory, yet real, interests of the contemporary community of states and nations."[52] Gorbachev also expressed in his address his view that the UN should adopt the "system of international security" framework he proposed at the 27th CPSU Congress. According to Gorbachev, there are many steps that the UN can take, such as the setting up of a crisis hotline between the Security Council member states, the UN headquarters, and the chairman of the Non-Aligned Movement, in order to implement his security system in the military, political, economic, and humanitarian spheres. Gorbachev, like Petrovskii, expressed the view that the Security Council has a key role to play in defusing regional and international tension and conflict, and thereby in ensuring international security in general.[53] Soviet Foreign Minister Shevardnadze expressed these same views when he addressed the UN General Assembly one week after Gorbachev's statement was released. He, too, highlighted the role of the Security Council in the settlement of crisis situations, and reiterated the view that the Soviet Union's proposed system of international security should provide the framework for the UN's peace-keeping and security efforts.[54]

It should come as no surprise, however, that Soviet policies regarding national and international security have not been limited to proposals for enhancing the role in the UN. Moscow naturally views its relations with countries located on the Soviet Union's borders as vital to its security and will not rely solely on any multilateral organization to guarantee that security. Relying on geography to identify the most immediate threats to Soviet territory, and starting from the Far East regions and working west, there appear to be six "threats" to Soviet security of varying intensities. First, there is Japan, an economic superpower with territorial claims against the USSR and in alliance with the United States; second, there is China, a rapidly developing communist giant with economic ties to the West; third, there is the multifaceted threat posed by the complex interrelationships in the Subcontinent—such as Afghanistan's continuing civil war, with Pakistani and American support for the rebels there; India's close relationship with the USSR but its enmity with China; fourth, the threat posed by Islamic fundamentalism in Iran and the effects that could have on the Moslem republics of the Soviet Union; fifth, there is the extremely complicated, tense, and violent situation in the Middle East, where the Arab-Israeli conflict focuses the competing interests of many nations on a crucial geostrategic location; and sixth, the central European front where NATO and the Warsaw Pact have together created the most heavily armed frontier in the world.

Viewing these various threats to Soviet security from Moscow's perspective, these threats can be prioritized in descending order of importance— "importance" being defined as a situation of a high level of political volatility, as well as a Soviet perception that the USSR, alone or in concert with other nations, possesses the capability to strengthen in a positive way an existing security problem. In the words of the Reagan administration, some of these important situations are identified as regional "hot spots." Soviet leaders have said that they view the situations in the Middle East, the Persian Gulf, and the Subcontinent as a first level of urgency, while their problems with China and Japan, in that order, would be on a second level.

For the USSR, issues relating to the Subcontinent, Iran/Iraq and the Persian Gulf, and the Middle East are closely interconnected. Islamic fundamentalism rooted in Iran will clearly have some effect on the political situation in Afghanistan and the Arab countries of the Middle East, as well as the Moslem republics in the Soviet Union. How the Soviet Union deals with the countries of the Middle East will affect, in turn, its state-to-state relations with Iran, with whom it wants good relations. Iran is a large, powerful, and volatile regional power on its border, as well as one that might have influence on certain factions of the Moslem population in Afghanistan. Soviet relations with China are also understood to be conditioned by how Moscow handles the Afghan situation, as well as its relations with Iran, which is supplied with military hardware from Peking. It is worth noting that the Soviet withdrawal from Afghanistan has been one of the Chinese "conditions" for improved relations with Moscow. Gorbachev's visit to Beijing in May 1989 could not have taken place as long as Soviet troops remained in Afghanistan.

There are both friends and foes of the USSR in the Subcontinent. India clearly has a very close relationship with Moscow and relies on it for military supplies and assistance to meet the perceived threats from China and Pakistan. Although India may not be able to operate with total confidence in the belief that the Soviet Union will come to its aid in the event of Chinese pressure or aggression,[55] India remains one of the Soviet Union's most important trading partners with political influence at both the regional and geostrategic levels. Gorbachev's first trip abroad outside of Europe was to India, and, excluding Europe and Japan, India stood in 1986 as the country with the highest level of trade with the USSR.[56] The domestic political situation in India is clearly not as favorable for the Soviet Union as is its state-to-state relationship with New Delhi. India remains an ethnically divided nation, with many open political wounds that can be aggravated by the sometimes violent tactics of both the government and opposition. In Rajiv Gandhi, Moscow has found a friend, but many of his most powerful opponents are not as favorably disposed to the Soviet Union as he is.

In Afghanistan, the Soviet Union continues to face a more difficult situation than it does in India. The problem of Afghanistan remains an important factor for the politics the Subcontinent. The civil war in the wake of a Soviet withdrawal continues to make the situation difficult from the Soviet point of view. Iran's influence continues in Afghanistan now that the Soviet troops are out, and the unconventional and independently minded Iranian regime is one toward which Moscow feels some apprehension. Gorbachev has succeeded thus far in cultivating better relations with Iran than the United States has, yet the situation with Afghanistan and its neighbors to the west remains complicated in the aftermath of the USSR's withdrawal from Kabul. The strife that could result in an unstable Afghanistan due to Iran's assistance to the Mujaheddin, its occasional encouragement of Islamic fundamentalist beliefs to the detriment of political pragmatism, and the tribal, factional consciousness that could be furthered by these factors must be a particularly distasteful scenario for the Kremlin to envisage given the political, economic, military, and human costs it has already incurred in Afghanistan.*

Gorbachev first expressed his displeasure with the situation in Afghanistan at the 27th Party Congress, and then later in a speech in Vladivostok in July 1986. In Vladivostok, he announced the withdrawal of six Soviet regiments from Afghanistan. The removal of these regiments did not change the military or political situation, and some Western diplomats claimed that the regiments were quickly replaced, but the action indicated that Gorbachev believed that the mounting political and economic costs of the Soviet Union's Afghan policy required a change.

Serious attempts by the Soviets to remove themselves from the war in Afghanistan were first seen when Babrak Karmal was removed as Afghan Party leader in early 1986, Najibullah was installed in his place, and then took a trip to Moscow in December 1986. During this trip, Gorbachev claimed that the Soviet Union would "not abandon our southern neighbor to a difficult situation,"[57] and upon Najibullah's return to Kabul, the latter announced the policy of "national reconciliation." This "reconciliation" policy was a step taken by the Soviets and Najibullah to try to broaden the Afghan government's base of support by granting amnesty to those rebels who gave up fighting and agreed to work to rebuild the country.[58] Their aim was to put the People's Democratic Party of Afghanistan (PDPA) on a stable footing that would have some staying power once the Soviet troops returned to the USSR.

At the beginning of 1988, both Foreign Minister Shevardnadze and General Secretary Gorbachev said that the Soviet Union would be willing to withdraw its troops from Afghanistan before an agreement on the makeup of the subsequent Afghan government could be reached.[59] They agreed to do so under the auspices of the UN-sponsored agreement reached between Pakistan and Afghanistan, the United States, and the Soviet Union in Geneva. The Afghan government has continued to assert that its dominant position will remain in any government formed after the Soviets leave their

---

* Mikhail Gorbachev, "M. S. Gorbachev's Speech at the UN Organization," *Pravda*, 8 December 1988, pp. 1–2, as translated in FBIS-Sov, 8 December 1988, pp. 11–19. Gorbachev's December 1988 address to the United Nations certainly bears out this analysis. His proposals for a UN peacekeeping force in Afghanistan, and his appeal for a UN-sponsored conference on the "neutrality and demilitarization" of the country indicate his concern for the Afghan situation in the wake of his country's military withdrawal.

country, but the Soviets clearly indicated in early 1988, to both the outside world and the Afghan authorities themselves,[60] that the UN-sponsored talks mediated by UN Under Secretary General for Political Affairs, Diego Cordovez, were not geared to solve the problem of the Afghan government's makeup, and that Soviet forces planned to carry out their withdrawal on the conclusion of the UN-sponsored agreement regardless of the governmental situation in Afghanistan. This new position constituted a major change in Soviet policy. In January of 1988, Gorbachev was no longer saying that he would not "abandon" his southern neighbor, rather he was telling Najibullah that the latter would have to survive without Soviet troops in his country.

This fact takes on even more significance given the provisions included in the side agreement on the Afghan conflict between the United States and the Soviet Union. In this agreement, the Soviet Union conceded that the United States has the right to supply arms to the Afghan rebels as long as the USSR supplies the Najibullah government with military equipment. As an agreement on a Soviet withdrawal from Afghanistan drew near, the United States had added the issue of Soviet arming of Najibullah's government as a negotiating point, and insisted on the right to arm the rebels if Soviet military assistance to the Afghan government was to continue. It was a last-minute American condition, pressed on the Reagan administration by U.S. supporters of the Afghan rebels, and was at first rejected out of hand by Foreign Minister Shevardnadze. Approximately one week after the initial rejection, in April 1988, upon consultation with Gorbachev, and after having pressured Najibullah into agreeing to the U.S. condition, Shevardnadze sent a letter to Secretary of State Shultz indicating Moscow's assent to the American condition.[61] The side agreement between Moscow and Washington was settled in mid-April 1988, and accordingly, the UN-sponsored agreement providing for the nine-month withdrawal of Soviet troops from Afghanistan was reached and signed by the United States, the Soviet Union, Pakistan, and Afghanistan in Geneva on 14 April 1988.

Although the Soviets temporarily halted their withdrawal from Afghanistan in November 1988, they resumed their pullout in the new year and completed it according to schedule on 15 February 1989. Moscow has continued to arm the Najibullah government and to supply Kabul by air, but it is at this point unclear whether or not their allies in Afghanistan will prevail—or even survive—in the face of the bold and well-provisioned opposition coming from the U.S.-backed Islamic rebels. In any event, the completed withdrawal of Soviet troops from Afghanistan has provided Gorbachev and his colleagues in the Kremlin with significant political capital in the international arena, with which they can gain some of the economic and political interstate ties necessary for their policy of *perestroika*.

What is interesting about the USSR's policies toward Afghanistan is that the new leaders in Moscow have shown an increased desire to use the UN to help further their interests there. They continued to press for an agreement that was negotiated with the crucial assistance of a UN mediator, having steadfastly supported the efforts that Mr. Cordovez was making, yet they had no desire to have the Afghanistan question discussed in the UN General Assembly.[63] They still view UN General Assembly involvement in international security issues as being unhelpful, and even damaging from a public relations point of view. This conclusion would certainly be consistent with previous statements by Shevardnadze, Petrovskii, and even Gorbachev that emphasized the role of the Security Council over that of other UN organizations and institutions.

Turning eastward from Afghanistan to Iran, the Soviet leaders clearly recognize the pivotal role played by that country. Its potential influence with the Afghan rebels, and its power position stemming from its Islamic identification, as well as its size and location make Tehran an important actor in both Asia and the Middle East, and in the geostrategic picture as well. Moscow views good relations with Iran as a goal worth pursuing because Tehran can exert influence over issues that are crucial to Soviet international security interests. Afghanistan, the stability or instability of certain Arab countries, energy pricing and supply, and travel through strategic transportation channels are all issues or situations about which the USSR cares deeply and over which Iran can exert its influence.

Given the Soviet interest in good relations with Tehran, it should not be surprising that Moscow has never criticized Iran as strongly as it has Pakistan and the United States for "interfering" in the internal affairs of Afghanistan. Vocal attacks on the United States have been harsh, and the Soviet Union has even put military pressure on Pakistan, while Soviet condemnation of Iran's assistance to the Afghan rebels has remained in the rhetorical sphere and at levels that are comparatively lower in intensity than those applied to Pakistan.[64] This policy toward Iran by the Soviet Union has met with some success from the Soviet point of view. In August of 1987, Soviet Deputy Foreign Minister Vorontsov capped a series of consultative meetings he had been carrying on with the Iranians since at least November of 1986 by signing an agreement with Tehran on economic cooperation, and for the construction of a railroad link and an oil pipeline connection. The aim of this agreement, according to the Soviet news agency TASS, is partly to "deepen political relations."[65]

Moscow has continued with this kind of conciliatory policy toward Iran, and has also successfully managed to maintain businesslike relations with those countries that are either enemies of, or feel threatened by, Tehran. This much is clear from an examination of Soviet statements and policies regarding the Iran-Iraq war, as well as the war's consequent effects on Persian Gulf shipping. The USSR consistently resisted the UN Security Council resolution sponsored by the United States calling for sanctions on any party refusing a cease-fire in the Iran-Iraq war. This, at least until July 1988, pleased Tehran, because Iran had wanted the international community to brand Iraq as the aggressor before any settlement on the conflict was reached. Yet, Moscow has worked toward good relations with those nations that are fearful of Iran as well. When the United States first rejected the Kuwaiti request to escort oil shipping in ther Persian Gulf in conjunction with the Soviet Union, the Soviets accepted. This forced the U.S. to meet the Kuwaiti request since it was clearly unwilling to cede to the Soviet Union a unilateral naval role as protector of shipping in the Gulf.

Regarding the Iran-Iraq war itself, the Soviet Union claimed a position of neutrality when the war began eight years ago, and has sought to maintain that position since 1980. The Soviet position on the U.S.-proposed sanctions in the UN Security Council is one illustration of Moscow's attempts to appease the Khomeini regime, while its continued arms assistance to Iraq at quite substantial levels. This example gives some indication of the lengths to which the Gorbachev leadership was willing to take in order to balance its objective of maintaining businesslike relations with both Iran and Iraq.

Although the Soviets resisted efforts by the United States to impose an arms embargo through the UN Security Council on Iran and Iraq, this should not necessarily be interpreted as lack of support for a UN role in the settlement of the conflict. Soviet officials have, on numerous occasions, suggested that the Security Council continue, and step up, its efforts to end the fighting, and have even come out in favor of Secretary General Perez de Cuellar's attempts to hold a UN Security council session at the Foreign Ministerial level to discuss questions involved with the ending of hostilities between Iraq and Iran.[66] Iran's announcement in July 1988 that it intends to go along with a UN-sponsored cease-fire vis-à-vis Iraq was seen as an opportunity for the Soviet Union to translate into policy its long-touted support for the cessation of the Iran-Iraq conflict through UN-sponsored negotiations.

Soviet attempts to balance the conflicting interests in the Persian Gulf are also evident in Moscow's policies toward the Middle East and the Arab-Israeli conflict. The Soviet Union has attempted, during the last three years, to cultivate and maintain friendly and businesslike relations with all disputing parties in the Middle East. Moscow dispatched a consular delegation to Tel Aviv in the summer of 1987 in an attempt to open diplomatic relations with this solid U.S. ally, and also rescheduled the long-standing debt that Egypt owes to the USSR. The Gorbachev leadership has continued the USSR's military and political support for Syria, supported OPEC's recent pricing changes, and played a key diplomatic role in maintaining the union of differing factions of the PLO.

The most significant change in policy made by Gorbachev in the Soviet Union's Middle East policy has been the recent series of diplomatic overtures to Israel. Although Soviet policy under Gorbachev has maintained a position of support for the PLO and Syria, Gorbachev himself has indicated publicly to both President Assad of Syria and Yasir Arafat of the PLO that Israel not only has a right to exist, but that its security concerns are no less legitimate than those of either the Syrians or the Palestinians.[67] It is with this attitude that Gorbachev has said the Soviet Union approaches the idea of an international conference on the Middle East under UN auspices. Recent statements concerning an international conference by top Soviet officials have stressed the participation of "all sides concerned, including the PLO, and the permanent members of the UN Security Council." They have also indicated that the member nations of the Security Council should play a catalytic role at the conference, assisting the Arabs and the Israelis to overcome "hurdles of mistrust."[68]

Soviet intentions regarding the exact nature of the PLO's status at the international conference have not yet been made completely clear. Foreign Minister Shevardnadze has made statements implying a Soviet position whereby the PLO would participate on a completely equal footing with the other participants, instead of as part of the U.S.-favored joint delegation with Jordan,[69] but no concrete proposal regarding the status of the PLO at an international conference has come from Moscow as yet.

Both Gorbachev and Shevardnadze have expressed the view that relations with Tel Aviv cannot be formally established until an international conference with the participation of the UN Security Council has been convened. It nevertheless appears that Moscow would like formal relations with Israel. It has eased restriction on Jewish emigration, and it declined to prevent Hungary and Poland from establishing interest sections in Tel Aviv, and at the UN in the fall of 1987, Foreign Minister Shevardnadze proposed to establish USSR-Israeli interest sections when he met Israeli Foreign Minister Shimon Peres.[70] Shevardnadze's unprecedented overtures to the conservative Shamir ruling faction in Israel in early June 1988 also tend to support the view that the Soviet Union would like to have formal relations with Tel Aviv in the near future, yet they are tempered by statements of both Shevardnadze and Gorbachev regarding the timing for the establishment of diplomatic relations with Israel. At his press conference after the May/June 1988 summit meeting with President Reagan, Gorbachev said that there would be no formal relations with Israel until an international peace conference with the full participation of all concerned parties is convened, and Shevardnadze expressed that same position after his meeting with Shamir at the UN. Judging from statements like these, the Soviet Union is attempting to put pressure on Shamir to give up his adamant opposition to the convening of an international conference on the Middle East. It is as yet unclear how well this strategy will work, given the resistance from the Shamir government in Israel that still does not want the USSR to become an influential actor in the region.

In addition to its diplomacy toward Israel, the Soviet Union has encouraged Arab unity in relation to the negotiating positions the Arab countries should take at an international conference on the Middle East conflict. Moscow has encouraged and assisted the reunification of different PLO factions under Yasir Arafat, and has stressed on numerous occasions the need for developing a unified Arab approach to security questions in the Middle East before an international conference on the region is convened.[71] The Soviets have attempted to cultivate Arab unity on these important security questions by conferring directly with representatives of Saudi Arabia—another country with which the USSR does not maintain diplomatic relations. Gorbachev and the Soviet leadership appear to have learned from the Camp David experience that it does not serve the interests of a superpower to be excluded from multilateral diplomatic processes.

Soviet proposals for a UN role in the Middle East peace process are evidence that Moscow does not intend to be shut out of any settlement between the Arab countries and Israel, as it was excluded from the Camp David Accord. Gorbachev's insistence on an international conference to settle the Middle East conflicts, and his government's suggestions that the UN Security Council play a central role in that conference, combine Soviet participation in the settlement of the issue with international legitimacy for any solution that would result, both of which enhance the USSR's strategic and regional interests.

Soviet policies toward Southern Africa, Vietnam/Cambodia, and Nicaragua do not include—or even suggest—the active participation of the UN or its Security Council for the settlement of these hot spots. In February of 1988, when Soviet Foreign Minister Shevardnadze met with Indonesian Foreign Minister Kusumaatmaja, who is naturally concerned with the status and outcome of the war in Cambodia, the UN was called upon to play an international peace-making role in their joint statement, but the UN was mentioned in reference to the situations in the Persian Gulf and Afghanistan, and not the conflict in Southeast Asia.[72]

This does not mean, however, that the Soviets are not interested in settling these conflicts. Vietnam's war in Cambodia is certainly one hot spot that Moscow would like to defuse, because its support for Hanoi complicates its relations with China and the ASEAN states. These are two large, economically expanding nations in Asia with which Soviet leaders would very much like to interact economically, but China's and ASEAN's fear and distrust of a Vietnam allied with the USSR poses a serious obstacle to any desire they might have to improve economic relations with the Soviet Union. With this in mind, it is easier to understand Moscow's encouragement of Hanoi's policy of "national reconciliation" for Cambodia, as well as the latter's announcements of troop withdrawals from that country. Chinese Premier Li Peng's positive assessment of Gorbachev and his reform efforts, as well as Peng's expressed desire to see the Soviet Union remove the obstacles to improved Sino-Soviet relations, speak well of Soviet efforts in this regard, especially since Peng's statements most complimentary to the USSR came on the heels of Vietnam's own announcement that its Command Staff was turning over the direction of the Cambodian military to the Cambodians themselves, and that 50,000 of Hanoi's troops would leave Cambodia by January 1989.[73]

The reasons Moscow has not proposed active UN involvement in Southeast Asia are straightforward. UN involvement, particularly Security Council involvement, would not please the Vietnamese. They would most likely view it as an unwanted interference in affairs that they are presently handling in their own way. Vietnamese displeasure is especially troubling to Moscow, as Hanoi has shown in the past a clear willingness to undertake independent policies and actions in the world arena without consulting the Soviet Union. Any action taken by Moscow that displeases the Vietnamese could jeopardize the Soviet naval bases leased from Vietnam in the warm-water Pacific. Secondly, Security Council involvement in the Southeast Asian conflict would mean direct Chinese involvement in the settlement. The People's Republic of China (PRC) is a permanent member of the Security Council and a key disputant in the political problems that led to the Vietnamese invasion of Cambodia. Moscow values an independent and powerful Vietnam as an ally because such a Vietnam can check the influence of the PRC and prevent it from again dominating its smaller neighbors to the south. As the PRC is a permanent member of the Security Council, a Soviet proposal to deal with Southeast Asia in that body would give back influence to the PRC that the USSR has thus far successfully kept out of Chinese hands.

As the July 1988 positive turn in Sino-Soviet relations evidenced, the USSR prefers to keep its relations with Peking in its own hands and bilateral in nature—at least when the conflict in Cambodia is on the agenda. The Soviet-supported, Indonesian-sponsored talks on the Cambodian question that began in July 1988, in conjunction with the Chinese statements to the effect that a Sino-Soviet summit meeting could take place as long as the USSR was taking a "positive" diplomatic role in settling the Cambodian/Vietnamese conflicts, and the Vietnamese stated intention to remove its troops from Cambodia by 1989, testify to the success Moscow has had in improving relations with Peking while still preventing it from having direct input into the negotiations on a Cambodian settlement.[74]

Regarding the remaining two hot spots of Southern Africa and Nicaragua, the Soviet Union has expressed its support for its allies in these regions in a measured manner. Boris Eltsin, formerly one of Gorbachev's chief lieutenants, visited Managua in March of 1987 to display Soviet support for the Sandinistas, but three months later, it was learned from sources in Managua that the Soviet Union was drastically cutting its oil exports to Nicaragua by more than one-half.[75] And in April of 1987, Gorbachev met in the Kremlin with the leaders of the "Frontline" African states who are under fire from South Africa and U.S.-supported rebels, yet the latest figures show that Soviet exports to such states as Mozambique have drastically declined, and that Nicaragua receives more easy-term exports than any of the "Frontline" states.[76]

These facts, combined with the observation that the Soviets consistently push UN involvement in crisis situations where their interests are most concerned, lead to two conclusions. First, that Moscow is, indeed, interested, as recent press reports have claimed, in using the UN in a more active and constructive manner than they have in the past.[77] Second, that although the Soviets appear to want to infuse their system of international security into UN processes and practices, this system has its priorities. Those priorities are, clearly, the interests of the Soviet state. This conclusion is supported in the first instance by examination of the conflict areas where Moscow has proposed or supported some type of UN involvement. These conflict areas, notably, are those that are located on the Soviet borders and thereby involve direct threats to Soviet security. For the Middle East and the Persian Gulf, Moscow has suggested an international conference under UN Security

Council auspices to discuss settlements in these regions and deal with area security problems as they arise. Regarding Afghanistan, the Soviets supported the mediation efforts of Under Secretary General Diego Cordovez, hinge their withdrawal from Afghanistan on the maintenance of the UN/ Cordovez agreement, and hope to secure a UN-sponsored agreement on the Afghan situation with the assistance of UN peacekeeping forces. Secondly, this conclusion is supported by an examination of *how* the Soviets have wanted the UN to be involved with the conflicts in question. As noted in the statements of Petrovskii, Shevardnadze, and Gorbachev, Soviet policy clearly expresses a preference for Security Council participation in international disputes. Moscow apparently prefers to keep UN member participation limited in dealing with issues that affect its own national security, such as those in the Middle East and Afghanistan. This is confirmed by Moscow's support for Diego Cordovez's role in Afghanistan, but its condemnation of the General Assembly resolutions on Afghanistan, as well as discussion of the problem in that body.

What this says about Soviet motivations in its international security policy should not be surprising. Through its change in attitude regarding a UN role in creating and guaranteeing international security, the USSR shows that it is primarily concerned with its own security. The UN Security Council can play a useful role in the pursuance of Soviet security because it lends international legitimacy to any negotiating process, yet it limits the influential participation of international actors in its security arrangements because of its limited membership and the veto powers of its permanent members. Finally, and perhaps most importantly, a willingness to use the UN to settle disputes helps create an atmosphere of trust and stability in world affairs, and as noted in our preceding section, such an environment is essential for Soviet international integration and economic revitalization. This aspect of Soviet security policy should not be underrated. Much of what Gorbachev's "new thinking" in the security realm is ultimately concerned with is in the economic sphere. As evidence of this, it should be recalled that progress along the road to a settlement in Afghanistan, and a UN-sanctioned agreement on the conflict in that country, served to stabilize one major security issue for Moscow, but they also helped to eliminate key obstacles to improved relations with countries possessing developing technological sectors such as the ASEAN states and the People's Republic of China. It is important to keep in mind that Gorbachev has stated, on numerous occasions, that success for the USSR in international affairs will affect in fundamental ways his priority program for the Soviet Union: *perestroika*, or reconstruction of the Soviet economic system.

SOVIET POLICY TOWARD THE UNITED STATES

Among the important issues that shape the bilateral relationship between
Moscow and Washington are the major areas of arms control and human
rights. A third area, which is most relevant to United States domestic politics, is the issue of Soviet "expansionism." The perception is strongly held by
many American citizens and public officials that the USSR is persistently
pursuing political domination of the globe owing to its Marxist ideology,
and that its actions in Afghanistan, Vietnam, Nicaragua, Southern Africa,
and Ethiopia testify to its objectives in this direction. Diplomatic efforts in all
three of these areas have seen varying degrees of progress, that is, certain
levels of agreement between the United States and the USSR that contribute in a positive way to the overall U.S.-Soviet relationship, since the assumption of power of Mikhail Gorbachev. In the area of arms control, the US and the
Soviet Union reached an agreement eliminating intermediate and short-
range missiles stationed in Europe in December 1987. The Soviet Union had
adhered steadfastly to positions unacceptable to the United States on important points in arms control negotiation until 1984–1985, but the Gorbachev
leadership helped to make the INF agreement possible by modifying the
USSR's previously uncompromising stand a number of times in the course
of two years of negotiation. First, Gorbachev announced with finality in
early 1987 that the Soviet Union would be willing to negotiate and conclude
an agreement on the INF (intermediate-range nuclear force) in Europe apart
from the strategic or space weapons negotiations. Second, Soviet negotiators
accepted the principle that intrusive verification measures were required for a
successful INF agreement, and accepted the complete elimination of all INF
missiles in Europe. Third, Moscow agreed to include short-range missiles
in the agreement, as well as their SS-20 force deployed in Asia. In sum,
the USSR accepted the approach favored by the United States known as a
"global double-zero." The Western alliance was, in some respects, caught
off guard by this accommodating policy coming from Moscow, having first
proposed the so-called "zero-option," that is, the symmetrical U.S. and Soviet
elimination of intermediate-range missiles from Europe, largely because it
was believed that the Soviets would never accept it.

In the area of human rights, progress has been made due to changes in
Soviet policy. The Soviet Union has recently made what might be viewed by
some observers as concessions to American demands in this area, but these
concessions were most likely undertaken by Moscow because it recognized
that certain famous human rights cases were obstacles to improved U.S.-
Soviet relations in other fields. Examples of these cases are Andrei

Sakharov, who is now visibly taking part in international forums in the Soviet Union, and was allowed to travel outside the Soviet Union for the first time in November 1988 to the United States as a board member of a new international foundation; Iurii Orlov and Anatoli Shcharansky, who have been permitted to leave the USSR; and Naum Meiman, who had been denied emigration papers because of alleged knowledge of military secrets, who was finally permitted to emigrate to Israel in early 1988.

The Gorbachev leadership may consider, in contrast to previous Soviet ruling groups, that some human rights questions are legitimate concerns of Soviet citizens, and is thereby willing to deal with public discussion of them without resorting to suppression, retribution, or defensive measures. The reforms aimed at streamlining the emigration processes and the reorganization of the Soviet bureaucratic agency overseeing the processing of emigration papers may be evidence of a new Soviet attitude in this direction. While there are an increasing number of hopeful signs of more moderate policies, however, evidence that would support the view that a long-lasting change in the human rights field is taking place in the USSR is not at this time conclusive.

Regarding the so-called Soviet proclivity toward expansionist policies, it is important first to note that a certain amount of expansionist behavior is due in part to the tendency demonstrated by great powers to seek to exert influence in areas of the world far beyond their borders. Certainly Britain's international policies in the eighteenth century and those of the United States during the Theodore Roosevelt period could, to many analysts, be viewed as expansionist, but these policies clearly cannot be attributed to a Marxist doctrine of world conquest. Second, much of the Soviet activity in Africa, Asia, and specifically Afghanistan during the 1970s was viewed by Moscow as in accord with the superpower "rules of the game" established by Moscow and Washington in the early 1970s, and was to be tolerated, Moscow believed, under the rubric of East-West détente. The détente policy, to the USSR, amounted to agreement between the superpowers to freeze their own direct competition while continuing the worldwide ideological and political competition in regions not directly threatening to the security interests of either the United States or the Soviet Union.[78] Analysts of international affairs in both the United States and the USSR have come to this conclusion; several Soviet figures have claimed that it was hardly consistent for the United States to criticize Moscow for invading Afghanistan while the SALT II treaty was under Senate consideration, because the United States bombed North Vietnam while the original SALT treaty was being negotiated.[79]

These observations are not meant to convey the idea that the USSR was in any way justified in its undertaking of assertive policies in different regions of the world during the 1970s. Rather it should be viewed as an attempt to adjust the political analysis of U.S.-Soviet relations so that much of what is presently viewed as expansionist policy can be seen as partly traditional Great Power behavior, and partly a difference in leadership interpretations of the rules governing a superpower's international behavior.

Finally, and most importantly, some progress has been made by the Gorbachev leadership to implement a foreign policy for the Soviet Union that does not appear to the West to be so blatantly expansionist as Soviet foreign policy did during Brezhnev's leadership. Moscow's support for its clients in the developing world has continued under Gorbachev (for example, in Southern Africa, Southeast Asia, and the Middle East), but its military and political support for new revolutionary movements in the LDCs has been reduced below the 1970s level of activity. Moreover, Gorbachev has encouraged processes of "national reconciliation" in Cambodia and Afghanistan, and has also taken a number of political steps that reveal how long-standing and genuine his desire has been to remove the Soviet troops from Afghanistan. Most important among these recent steps are, first, his announcement that the makeup of the Afghan government in place after the Soviet forces return home is not an issue that the Soviet government necessarily wants to have settled before their military withdrawal begins;[80] and second, his assent to "symmetrical assistance" in military supplies to the Afghan government by the USSR, and to the Afghan rebels by the United States.

Clearly, progress has been made in U.S.-Soviet relations in both arms control and human rights, and this is due in large measure to the Soviet leadership's new approaches to these problem areas. Similarly, progress has been made by Moscow in creating a popular image in the United States and Western Europe as a less threatening, less expansionist power, owing to Gorbachev's political style and apparent willingness to compromise on issues that were formerly considered nonnegotiable by the Soviet leadership.[81] It follows from this that the change in U.S. public opinion about the Soviet Union has contributed to a certain warming and increased dialogue in the overall U.S.-Soviet relationship. But does an increased Soviet willingness to accommodate U.S. interests necessarily indicate a primary desire on the part of Moscow to stabilize relations with the United States? If so, to what end? And what does this say about where the United States stands in the general direction of Soviet foreign policy?

The progress made in the arms control and human rights fields does not automatically lead to the conclusion that the primary foreign policy interest of the USSR is to improve relations with the United States. Both the INF agreement and the increased emigration record in the Soviet Union are as much directed toward Western Europe as they are toward the United States, for the missile agreement removes from deployment the nuclear weapons that are the most directly threatening to Europe, while relaxed Soviet emigration requirements placate the large numbers of human rights advocates in Western Europe as well as those in the United States. Additionally, the withdrawal from Afghanistan was taken because of the great economic and political costs that the USSR was incurring there. In Southeast Asia as well, Gorbachev appears to believe that important political benefits from the People's Republic of China and the ASEAN nations will result if he succeeds in convincing Hanoi to withdraw completely from Cambodia.

These facts provide evidence to support the view that the present Soviet foreign policy is not solely oriented toward the United States. Further evidence is found in the theoretical arguments of Gorbachev's chief lieutenants and recent statements made by Soviet foreign policy officials. As an example, one ranking Soviet official is reported to have commented rather expressively on what he regarded as the overemphasis on the U.S. in Soviet foreign policy under former Foreign Minister Gromyko. As much of Gromyko's foreign outlook was colored by the East-West rivalry and the power position of the United States, this official remarked, soon after Gorbachev's assumption of power, that the time had come to "put an end to the United States exercising a veto over our foreign policy."[82]

For evidence of Gorbachev's most trusted advisors' opinions regarding the need to deemphasize the role of the US in Soviet foreign policy formulation, it is only necessary to look at a 1986 article in *Kommunist* by CPSU Secretary and Politburo member Aleksandr Iakovlev. Here Iakovlev stressed the increasing importance on the world scene of other "centers of power" such as Japan and Western Europe. His article is partly an appeal to the foreign policy establishments in his own as well as other countries, to recognize the growing role of regional powers and the trend in today's world away from a bipolar power structure. A careful reading of this article gives the clear impression that Iakovlev considers the increasing contradictions between world capitalist centers as a factor that will contribute to a lessening in importance of the United States in world affairs.[83]

Gorbachev's speech to the 27th Party Congress of February 1986 conveyed similar ideas. At the very beginning of the speech, which is the theoretical section devoted to trends in international affairs in the modern world, Gorbachev uses phrases and ideas identical to those used by Iakovlev in his *Kommunist* article. He refers to the three "main centres of power," and the consequent lessening of U.S. influence among its allies, and expresses the belief that the allies of the United States will not follow blindly its *diktat* any longer.[84] This is particularly significant when contrasted with Leonid Brezhnev's speech to the 26th Party Congress in 1981. In 1981 Brezhnev not only avoided a discussion of theoretical formulations in the section of his speech devoted to foreign policy, but followed the traditional Soviet categorization of topics relating to international affairs. Most importantly, in the sections of the Party Congress speech traditionally devoted to the capitalist countries and détente and peace, Brezhnev's comments were directed at what he called the "futile attempts" of the United States to gain military superiority.[85] In this speech, Brezhnev clearly indicated that the USSR was not only watching carefully the actions of the United States in the world arena, but that those actions determined to a large degree the nature and direction of Soviet foreign policy.

While it is evident that for the USSR under Gorbachev, the United States does not play the overarching, defining role in Soviet foreign policy today that it did under Gromyko and Brezhnev, nonetheless Gorbachev continues to accord the United States a most important position in his foreign policy. For example, many of his key advisors are American specialists. Aleksandr Bessmertnykh and Iulii Vorontsov are two Americanists who presently hold key positions in the Foreign Ministry, and Anatolii Dobrynin, who is the former Ambassador to the United States served, until recently, as the head of the Central Committee International Department and still serves as an advisor to Gorbachev. Georgii Kornienko, Dobrynin's one-time deputy in the United States, has also served as Dobrynin's assistant in the International Department. Aleksandr Iakovlev, who is one of Gorbachev's closest colleagues and advisors, is a former ambassador to Canada, and was at one time a student at Columbia University in New York.

The question now arises, does this in any way lessen the veracity of the view that the United States is playing a less-substantial role in the process of Soviet foreign policymaking? The answer to this question is a conditioned yes. The Soviet Union can deemphasize the "vetoing" role played by the United States but still consider the United States its primary security threat. Under this new formula, the United States is assigned the primary position in the hierarchy of Soviet foreign policy concerns but not an all-encompassing one. According to the view now prevailing in Moscow, knowledge of the United States and careful analysis of its actions are still of vital importance, because the United States is presently the only power that can frustrate Soviet international objectives in almost every area.

Finally, Gorbachev, Iakovlev, and many in the Soviet leadership hold that other centers of power are crucial parts of the modern international environment, and they believe that these centers will increasingly demand more of the USSR's foreign policymaking resources as the world enters the twenty-first century. Recognition of this new multipolar emphasis makes the Soviet interest in the United Nations more easily understood. For if Soviet foreign policy is shifting to take into account other centers of power and a concomitant lessening of U.S. influence in the world, then the investment by Moscow of more resources, attention, and confidence into the UN, an organization with international legitimacy that will most likely last into the next century and at the same time allow consistent Soviet interaction with almost all emerging nations, makes political sense. Thus a new foreign policy agenda appears to have emerged in Soviet thinking, one that attempts to take account of the present international "objective realities" compelling nations to act in response to new trends in contemporary world economics and political power variables.

WORLD OUTLOOK AND PRACTICAL POLICY: A SHIFT IN THE SOVIET AGENDA

Two sets of questions regarding the Gorbachev leadership's foreign policy remain to be addressed. First, if the Soviet Union is now attempting to stabilize international politics and promote peaceful economic interaction due to the failing condition of its domestic economy, what does this say about the relationship between the theoretical world outlook that Gorbachev has outlined and the USSR's practical policy actions. Are the two in any way connected? How are they connected? Can the two be said to share the same, or similarly oriented, philosophical attitude? Second, how do the answers to these questions help the observer to come to conclusions about the present overall direction of Soviet foreign policy? Can any substantial conclusions in fact be made in only the fourth year of Gorbachev's rule?

In order to answer the first set of questions, it is useful to outline policies and proposals that would be consistent with the announced world outlook. Thus in the economic sphere, the Soviets should display an interest in joining the world market as it is presently structured, not in changing its nature as Lenin and Stalin insisted. It would also follow, if they mean what they say about economic and security interdependence, that they would take steps to open their domestic economy for foreign investment, make information such as production statistics more readily available to world economic organizations such as the GATT, and take steps to make the ruble convertible. In the security realm, application of Gorbachev's new doctrine would require Moscow's willingness to take a multilateral approach to regional and international security questions, as well as its acceptance of all legitimately interested parties' participation in regional security negotiations. Finally, in its relations with the United States, Gorbachev's pronounced doctrines would require that the USSR willingly engage in dialogue with the United States on a broad range of contentious issues dividing the two countries. Gorbachev's rhetorical emphasis on the need for political solutions to problems rather than military solutions would also require that he consider and devote attention to the security concerns of the United States, and not simply and solely publicize Soviet security concerns as the USSR often did when Leonid Brezhnev was General Secretary.*

The question of a relationship between Gorbachev's international theoretical formulations and his foreign policy actions naturally arises, and indeed there appears to be a degree of consistency. In the area of economics, the Soviet Union under Gorbachev has indeed sought to enter the world market. It continues to call for direct ties between the European Economic Community (EEC) and the CMEA, and has shown interest in joining multilateral economic organizations and treaties such as the GATT and the Pacific Economic Cooperation Council (PECC). It has in no way sought to change the nature of the world market, instead it has extolled the virtures of foreign economic competition. In addition, Moscow has begun opening its economy to foreign investors. The joint venture law is a clear manifestation of this policy. Also, the convertible ruble is continuously referred to by experts such as Ivan D. Ivanov as something that will have to be introduced, although incrementally, into the world monetary system. It is as yet unclear how cooperative the USSR will be in supplying economic statistics for multilateral economic groupings such as the GATT, because the question of Soviet membership has thus far not reached the stage where statistical information would be required of Moscow.

In the area of international security, Moscow's record is not as consistent as it has been on international economic issues. In the Middle East and Afghanistan, the Soviets have been willing to accept a multilateral approach

---

* The original negotiations for the Conference on Security and Cooperation in Europe (CSCE) in 1973-1975 provide a good example of this trend in Soviet diplomacy.

to negotiated settlements, displaying an eagerness for the UN to play a role in these regions. But Moscow envisions a primary role for the limited-membership Security Council in these negotiations, and in Southeast Asia, has not proposed a UN role at all. Moscow's reluctance to include the PRC in a negotiated settlement for the Cambodia-Vietnam issue marks a departure from its own appeals for negotiated settlements and recognition of the modern international realities of security interdependence.*

The USSR's policy toward the United States has shown a higher degree of consistency with the Gorbachev leadership's theoretical formulations and doctrines than some of the USSR's actions elsewhere in the international security sphere. Gorbachev has certainly shown himself willing to maintain dialogue with the United States, having taken part in five summit meetings with President Reagan, has concluded a major arms agreement, the INF Treaty, and has proposed drastic cuts of both conventional and nuclear forces. In addition, Gorbachev has unilaterally withdrawn forces from Europe, and has removed Soviet troops from Afghanistan. In addition, Gorbachev and his lieutenants appear to have taken account of the security concerns of the Untied States when they have felt it necessary, having acceded to the U.S. demand for symmetrical arming of the Afghan rebels and the Afghan government in the aftermath of a Soviet withdrawal from that country, and having agreed to the intrusive verification measures for the INF treaty that had long been an American condition for the conclusion of a European arms agreement. There is little doubt that Gorbachev agreed to these moves for his own reasons, yet his willingness to discuss them, especially when compared to previous Soviet rejections of even the mention of them in negotiation (i.e., Afghanistan and intrusive verification), suggests that he understands the nature of some American security concerns, and may respond to them as long as overall Soviet security is not adversely affected by doing so.

Having established a connection between the new Soviet international theory and doctrine and Moscow's present foreign policy, what can be said about the nature of that connection? First, as a regime born out of, and committed to maintaining, an ideological mission, the Soviet government and Party must provide a theoretical basis and justification for every major action or policy it undertakes. The Soviet leader's statements on

---

* Gorbachev proposed a conference on Asian security in his 1986 Vladivostok speech that would include Chinese participation, but that conference would not deal specifically and solely with the Southeast Asian conflict, and it would not involve the UN or its Security Council, of which China is a permanent member.

questions of world social, political, and economic phenomena become the official doctrine of the moment. Gorbachev's infusion of "interdependence" into the long-held "contradictory" world view not only provides justification for his policy but helps to explain, in part, the motivation behind the policy to his own followers.

This does not mean that Soviet decisionmakers all look to the speeches and writings of Gorbachev and the top leaders on foreign affairs before they set about creating a policy toward a certain country. It does mean, however, that their modes of expression, and even their thinking, are subtly affected as they are made to conform to the policies and statements made at the top levels of the Soviet leadership. By according their statements and actions, at least on the surface, with the new thinking, globalistics, interdependence-yet-contradictory* outlook established by the top leadership, Soviet policymakers are still pursuing the USSR's interests above all else in the international arena, but the new doctrine coming from above can and does change, albeit in small, incremental ways, the methods employed by them in looking out for Moscow's international interests.

To the extent that they do not adversely affect or blatantly compromise Soviet interests on the world stage, the theoretical explanations of world affairs that the Gorbachev leadershp has put forward need to be taken seriously. Where Moscow has felt it necessary to depart from the "interdependence of security" tenet, for example, it has, as in the case of Southeast Asia and the implicitly attempted exclusion of the PRC from any negotiation specifically dealing with that region. Yet, this departure from the presently prevailing theory and doctrine of the Soviet Union reveals something else. It shows that where Soviet policy is consistent with Soviet statements of principle on international affairs, those policies can be interpreted as authentic. There is thus substantial reason to consider the Gorbachev leadership seriously interested in opening the Soviet economy and integrating it more fully into the market-oriented international system. Soviet actions and statements of intention have not only been consistent with each other on this matter, but are supported as well by the widely held negative assessment of Soviet economic performance in both West and East bloc countries. Indeed, the role played by the declining Soviet economy in determining Moscow's present foreign policy is immense. The "economizing" of the USSR's foreign policy, as Shevardnadze expressed it, and the improvement of Soviet economic performance, are absolutely essential if the Soviet Union is to maintain

---

* I am indebted to William G. Miller for pointing out the new thinking, globalistics aspect of this concept.

its great power status. The "one-dimensional" military superpower that the USSR had become in the early 1980s,[86] and the sealing off of the USSR from the rest of the world that both Lenin and Stalin encouraged,[87] have compelled the Gorbachev leadership to reassess that which is supposed to put the USSR on a higher historical plane than the rest of the world: its economic system. The leadership's resulting conclusions have produced a new economically oriented agenda for Soviet foreign policy that will likely last until the next century.

Notes

1. Mikhail S. Gorbachev, "Address to the French Parliament, 3 October 1985," in *A Time for Peace*, (New York: Richardson & Steirman, 1985), p. 265.
2. Mikhail S. Gorbachev, "Political Report of the CPSU Central Committee to the 27th Party Congress, 25 February 1986 (in Russian)" (Moscow: Novosti Press, 1986), p. 28.
3. Mikhail S. Gorbachev, "Address to the Forum, 'For a Nuclear-Free World, For the Survival of Humanity,' " in *Foreign Broadcast Information Service: Daily Report, Soviet Union* (FBIS-Sov), 17 February 1987, p. AA17, and Gorbachev, "Address on French Television," 30 September 1985, in *A Time for Peace*, pp. 243–244.
4. Gorbachev, 'Address to the Forum,' p. A17.
5. Mikhail S. Gorbachev, "Vystuplenie M. S. Gorbacheva po sovetskomu televideniiu," *Literaturnaia gazeta* (16 December 1987): p. 1.
6. Gorbachev, "Political Report," p. 14.
7. William F. Brazier and Joel S. Hellman, "Gorbachev's New World View," *Social Policy* vol. 18 no. 1 (Summer 1987): pp. 6–7.
8. Gorbachev, 'Address to the Forum,' p. A24.
9. Gorbachev, "Political Report," p. 24. (emphasis in original)
10. Eduard A. Shevardnadze, "*Perestroika* in Soviet Diplomacy," Report at a Conference of Diplomatic Staff, *Bulletin of the Ministry of Foreign Affairs of the USSR*, as excerpted in *Moscow News* no. 48 (6–13 December 1987): pp. 4–5; and Evgenii Primakov, "Novaia filosofiia vneshnei politiki," *Pravda*, 10 July 1987, p. 4.
11. Gorbachev, 'Address to the Form,' p. AA22.
12. Gorbachev, "Political Report," pp. 79–80.
13. Mikhail S. Gorbachev, "Speech in Vladivostok," *News and Views from the USSR*, Soviet Embassy in the United States (28 July 1986): p. 5, and "From Russia with Glasnost: A New Look at What is to Be Done," an interview with

Aleksandr Iakovlev, *New Perspectives Quarterly* vol. 4 no. 2 (Spring 1987): p. 33.

14. Eduard A. Shevardnadze, "Nauchno-Prakticheskaiia Konferentsiia MID SSSR, 'XIX Vsesoiuznaiia Konferentsiia KPSS: Vneshniaia Politika i Diplomatiia,' " *Bulletin of the Ministry of Foreign Affairs of the USSR* no. 15 (15 August 1988): pp. 24–46.

15. Egor K. Ligachev, Speech in Gorkii, from *Vremia* newscast in FBIS-Sov, 8 August 1988, pp. 40–43.

16. Ibid.

17. Aleksandr N. Iakovlev, Speech in Lithuania, TASS report, "In the Interests of the Country and Every People," *Pravda*, 13 August 1988, in FBIS-Sov, 17 August 1988, pp. 28–32.

18. TASS, "The Contemporary Concept of Socialism. International Scientific Conference," *Pravda*, 5 October 1988, p. 4, as translated in FBIS-Sov, "Medvedev on Socialism at International Forum," 6 October 1988, pp. 4–6.

19. Iurii V. Andropov, "Speech at a Plenary Meeting of the CPSU Central Committee, 15 June 1983," in I. V. Andropov, *Speeches & Writings* (New York: Pergamon Press, 1983), p. 356, as well as Francis Fukuyama, "Patterns of Soviet Third World Policy," *Problems of Communism* vol. 36 no. 5 (September–October 1987): pp. 1–13, and Elizabeth Valkenier, "New Soviet Thinking about the Third World," *World Policy Journal* vol. 4 no. 4 (Fall 1987): p. 658.

20. Elizabeth Kridl Valkenier, *The Soviet Union and the Third World: An Economic Bind*, (New York: Praeger, 1983), pp. 57–58.

21. R. M. Avakov, "Novoe Myshlenie i problema izucheniia razvivaiushchikhsia stran," *MEMO* (11/87): pp. 48–62.

22. Mikhail S. Gorbachev, "The Key Issue of the Party's Economic Policy," 11 June 1985, in *Selected Speeches and Articles* (Moscow: Progress, 1987), p. 101.

23. Mikhail S. Gorbachev, "On the Tasks of the Party in the Radical Restructuring of Economic Management," 25–26 June 1987, in *Report and Concluding Speech by the General Secretary of the CPSU Central Committee* (Moscow: Novosti Press, 1987), p. 6.

24. Eduard A. Shevardnadze, "An Unconditional Requirement—Turn to Face the Economy," Speech by USSR Minister of Foreign Affairs E. A. Shevardnadze at a Meeting of USSR Ministry of Foreign Affairs Workers' Aktiv on 4 July 1987, in *Vestnik Ministerstva Inostrannykh Del SSSR* (10 September 1987): pp. 3–6, as translated in FBIS-Sov, 3 November 1987, pp. 88–92.

25. Shevardnadze, "An Unconditional Requirement," p. 91.

26. J. L. Scherer, *Soviet Biographical Service*, vol. 3 no. 1 (January 1987): p. 33.

27. Conversations with John Hardt, Senior Specialist on the Soviet Economy and

Associate Director for Senior Specialists, Congressional Research Service of the Library of Congress, April 1987.

28. Ivan D. Ivanov, "Restructuring the Mechanism of Foreign Economic Relations in the USSR," *Soviet Economy* vol. 3 no. 3 (July–September 1987): p. 198.
29. Ibid., p. 197.
30. *Pravda*, 24 September 1986, as cited in Jerry F. Hough, *Opening Up the Soviet Economy* (Washington, D. C. : Brookings Institution, 1988), p. 64.
31. Ivanov, p. 212.
32. Hough, pp. 1–26, 54–77.
33. Moscow Television Service, "Repercussions—The Problems of Economic Security," with Viktor Komplektov, Ivan D. Ivanov, Ernest Obminskii, Petr Koshelev, and Ivan Korolev, as cited in FBIS-Sov, 18 February 1988, pp. 81–84.
34. Hough, p. 65.
35. Anders Aslund, "The New Soviet Policy Towards International Economic Organizations," *The World Today* vol. 44 no. 2 (February 1988): p. 28.
36. Melbourne Overseas Service, as cited in FBIS-Sov, 4 March 1987; *Pravda*, 1 October 1987; *Pravda*, 5 October 1987.
37. *Pravda*, 6 May 1987.
38. Aslund, p. 29.
39. Conversations with John Hardt.
40. "Asia & Pacific," FBIS-Sov, 29 January 1987.
41. "Moscow TV Notes Month of Solidarity with S. Korea," FBIS-Sov, 29 June 1987, p. C1.
42. "Asia & Pacific," FBIS-Sov, 3 March 1987.
43. FBIS-Sov, 16 October 1986, p. K2, and FBIS-Sov, 17 October 1986, p. K2.
44. FBIS-Sov, 5 October 1987, p. 46, originally in *Izvestiia*, 5 October 1987.
45. FBIS-Sov, 9 June 1987, p. 13, originally a TASS report in *Izvestiia*, 4 June 1987.
46. FBIS-Sov, 1 October 1987, p. 43, originally in *Pravda*, 1 October 1987.
47. FBIS-Sov, 27 May 1987, p. E9.
48. FBIS-Sov, 13 May 1987, pp. E1–E10.
49. Gorbachev, "Political Report," pp. 92–93.
50. "A Breath of Fresh Air," *Moscow News*, no. 6, 14-21 February 1988, p. 1.
51. Vladimir Petrovskii, *The Nuclear-Space Age: The Soviet Viewpoint* (Moscow: Progress, 1987), pp. 187–189 (originally in Russian by *Mezhdunarodnye otnosheniia*, 1985).
52. Mikhail S. Gorbachev, "The Reality and Guarantees of a Secure World," *Pravda*, TASS, 17 September 1987, as translated by TASS Report (17 September 1987): p. 1.
53. Ibid., pp. 5–6.

54. Eduard A. Shevardnadze, *"Soobshcha stroit' vseobshchuiu bezopasnost',"* statement at the 42nd Session of the UN General Assembly, 24 September 1987 (Moscow: Izdatel'stvo politicheskoi literatury, 1987), pp. 5, 12.

55. Jyotirmoy Banerjee, "Moscow's Indian Alliance," *Problems of Communism* vol. 36 no. 1 (January–February 1987): p. 9.

56. Ministry of Foreign Trade of the USSR, *Vneshniaia Torgovlia SSSR v 1986 g.*, Statistical Collection (Moscow: Finansy i statistika, 1987), pp. 9–14.

57. Mikhail S. Gorbachev, "In a Friendly Atmosphere: Comrade M. S. Gorbachev's Speech," *Pravda*, 14 December 1986, p. 2, as translated in FBIS-Sov, 15 December 1986, p. D3.

58. TASS International Service, 1 January 1987, as printed in FBIS-Sov, 2 January 1987, p. D1.

59. "Interv'iu agenstvu Bakhtar," TASS, *Pravda*, 7 January 1988, p. 4, and Gorbachev, "Statement on Afghanistan," TASS, 8 February 1988.

60. Ibid.

61. "U. S. and Moscow Agree on Pullout from Afghanistan," *The New York Times*, 12 April 1988, p. A1.

62. Paul Lewis, "Pakistan Pressed to Accept Terms for Afghan Accord," *The New York Times*, 15 March 1988, p. A3.

63. Vadim Okulov, *"Realisty i ekstremisty,"* *Pravda*, 12 November 1987. This gives a negative Soviet assessment of discussion of the Afghan situation in the General Assembly.

64. "Iranian 'Interference' in DRA Affairs Noted," FBIS-Sov, 29 September 1986, p. D2. This gives an example of the Soviet Union's tame rhetoric in regard to Iranian involvement in Afghanistan.

65. Philip Taubman, "Iran and Soviet Draft Big Projects, Including Pipelines and Railroad," *The New York Times*, 5 August 1987, p. 1.

66. TASS, "Near East: The Time for Talks Has Come," *Izvestiia*, 28 April 1987, p. 4, as translated in FBIS-Sov, 1 May 1987, p. H1.

67. TASS, "Gorbachev, Arafat Meet," in FBIS-Sov, 11 April 1988, p. 26, and Gorbachev, "In a Friendly Atmosphere," TASS, *Pravda*, 25 April 1987, in FBIS-Sov, 28 April 1987, p. H7.

68. Eduard A. Shevardnadze, "Shevardnadze Dinner Speech," *Pravda*, 21 May 1988, in FBIS-Sov, 23 May 1988, p. 45.

69. Ibid.

70. *The New York Times*, 2 October 1987, p. A8.

71. Jim Muir, "Soviets, Saudis aim to unite Arab world in bid for Mideast meeting," *The Christian Science Monitor*, 11 May 1987, and Gorbachev, "In a Friendly Atmosphere," pp. H5–8.

72. TASS, "Zavershenie sovetsko-indoneziiskikh peregovorov," *Pravda*, 7 February 1988, p. 4.

73. Keith B. Richburg, "Hanoi Cuts War Role in Cambodia," *The Washington*

Post, 1 July 1988, p. A1, and Daniel Southerland, "Beijing Presses Case for Soviet Summit," *The Washington Post*, 5 July 1988, p. A10. Gorbachev's performance at the Soviet 19th Communist Party Conference, and his own political situation that emerged intact from that meeting, also contributed to the Chinese government's willingness to encourage Gorbachev's foreign policies in Southeast Asia and keep alive the prospects for a Sino-Soviet meeting at the highest political levels.

74. Don Oberdorfer, "China, Soviets Agree to Hold Special Talks on Cambodia," *The Washington Post*, 21 July 1988, p. A18.

75. Julia Preston, "Soviet Delegation Visits Nicaragua to Reaffirm Support," *The Washington Post*, 8 March 1987, p. A34, and William A. Orme, Jr., "Soviets Expected to Reduce Oil for Nicaragua," *The Washington Post*, 4 June 1987, p. A1.

76. TASS, "Gorbachev Receives Frontline States Delegation," 29 April 1987, as translated in FBIS-Sov, 30 April 1987, p. J1, and Ministry of Foreign Trade of the USSR, *Vneshniaia Torgovlia*, pp. 9–14.

77. *The New York Times*, 8 October 1987, section I, p. 1, col. 5.

78. Marshall D. Shulman, "U.S.-Soviet Relations and the Control of Nuclear Weapons," in Barry M. Blechman, ed., *Rethinking the U. S. Strategic Pos ture: A Report from the Aspen Consortium on Arms Control and Security Issues*, (Cambridge, MA: Ballinger, 1982), p. 80.

79. Raymond L. Garthoff, *Détente and Confrontation: American-Soviet Relations from Nixon to Reagan*, (Washington, D. C. : The Brookings Institution, 1985), p. 1076.

80. *Pravda*, 9 February 1988, p. 1. See, among others, Gorbachev's statement.

81. Marttila & Kiley, a Boston-based polling firm, *Americans Talk Security—A Survey of American Voters: Attitudes Concerning National Security Issues*, 17 November 1986, Washington, D.C., pp. 3–13.

82. Conversation with USIA official, 10 November 1986.

83. Aleksandr Iakovlev, "Mezhimperialisticheskie protivorechiia—sovremennyi kontekst," *Kommunist* no. 17 (November 1986): pp. 3–17.

84. Gorbachev, "Political Report," pp. 18–19.

85. L. I. Brezhnev, "The Report of the CPSU Central Committee to the 26th Congress of the Communist Party of the Soviet Union and the Party's Immedi-ate Tasks in the Fields of Domestic and Foreign Policy," *Pravda*, 24 February 1981, pp. 2–9 as translated in *Current Digest of the Soviet Press*, vol. 33 no. 8 (25 March 1981): pp. 3–8.

86. Zbigniew Brzezinski, *Game Plan: How to Conduct the U.S.-Soviet Contest* (Boston: The Atlantic Monthly Press, 1986), pp. 99–144.

87. Jerry Hough, pp. 11–12.

6 SOVIET NATIONAL SECURITY POLICY UNDER GORBACHEV

Linton H. Bishop

In an article written to commemorate the forty-first anniversary of the allied victory over Nazi Germany in World War II, General of the Army Iurii Maksimov, Chief of the Soviet Strategic Rocket Forces and a Deputy Minister of Defense, remarked

> I did not think during those first hours of peace that every day after 9 May 1945 would demand from us huge efforts and constant exertion of will to ensure that victory was defended by high combat readiness, vigilance, and martial labor.[1]

Maksimov's lament is an expression of a deep and widespread sense of frustration and dissatisfaction with the results of World War II. Victory in the war was achieved at a horrifying price, but to many in both East and West, the world that emerged in its wake seems not to have justified the sacrifice. Instead of ushering in an era of peace and international cooperation, the great military success was followed by political failure, as mutual suspicion created divisions between the wartime partners. These divisions gradually hardened into a rigid bipolar confrontation which was most sharply expressed in a peacetime military competition of unprecedented magnitude.

Postwar international history has been dominated by the dynamics of the Cold War. Two elements have served to make this phenomenon particularly intractable and dangerous. The first and most fundamental of these is the tendency of both sides to perceive their opposition to one another as absolute. Paul Fussell has suggested that the habit of distinguishing in absolute terms between "us and them" was born out of the experience of the Great War of 1914–1918, as a result of which

> the mode of gross dichotomy came to dominate perception and expression else-where, encouraging finally what we can call the modern versus habit: one thing opposed to another, not with some Hegelian hope of synthesis involving a dis-solution of both extremes (that would suggest a "negotiated peace", which is anathema) but with a sense that one of the poles embodies so wicked a deficiency or flaw or perversion that its total submission is called for.[2]

The mutual hostility which Fussell describes has been expressed in ideo-logical, geopolitical, and sociocultural terms and has been an enduring feature of the postwar international system. President Reagan's well-known "evil empire" speech was, for all its notoriety, no more than a rather blunt expression of the psychological orientation underlying the rhetoric and policies of both sides throughout the postwar period.

The considerable tensions generated by a relationship based on this built-in habit of hostility are compounded by the second basic element of the post-war world: the centrality of military security, and its corollary, the primacy of the military instrument in international politics. In an anarchic interna-tional system military security is accorded the highest priority. International efforts to "manage" the security problem tend to be far less successful than efforts in nonsecurity areas, because, as Robert Jervis has pointed out, "the primacy of security, its competitive nature, the unforgiving nature of the arena, and the uncertainty of how much security the State needs and has" made international cooperation difficult to achieve.[3] In these circumstances, states rely on "self-help" measures for the provision of security, and relative military power becomes the most important and widely sought-after currency in international politics.[4] The enormous arsenals in existence today—above all those of the United States and the Soviet Union—are stark testimony to the power of this systemic tendency.

Together, these two elements—the perception of absolute opposition and the centrality of military security—form the core of what can be referred to as the Cold War paradigm of international security. In addition to its two core elements, this paradigm contains a number of principles that have helped drive the Cold War for the past four decades. Among these, two of the most important are the idea that war remains an instrument of politics, and the belief in the utility of military superiority and in the possibility of achieving a meaningful margin of such superiority. The Cold War paradigm has served as the conceptual basis for the foreign and security policies of both blocs and has contributed to the development of a highly militarized, zero-sum approach to international relations in which military superiority is a constant goal, and every conflict around the world is considered in the context of the superpower rivalry. This approach is manifested most clearly in an arms race which is at once a product of bipolar confrontation and a principal source of its continuation and intensification.

But implicit in Maksimov's reminiscence of "the first hours of peace" is the notion that there was, at the close of World War II, an expectation that victory would produce a world based on other principles, a world in which measures such as "high combat readiness, vigilance, amd martial labor" could be relegated to the periphery of national security policy. The early hopes for the creation of a new international security system were dashed by the emergence of the Cold War paradigm as the dominant conceptual force in international politics. But that dominance has not gone unchallenged. It has, in fact, been subjected to the scrutiny of government leaders, scholars, and others on both sides of the ideological divide who have persisted in questioning the tenets of the paradigm, and the policies it has spawned.

Challenges to the Cold War concept of international security, if frequently implicit and limited in scope, have played a major role in the development of Soviet policy throughout the postwar period. In the 1950s, Soviet Premier Malenkov sanctioned debates on such fundamental issues of security as the utility of war in the nuclear age, and the economic priorities (usually expressed in terms of heavy versus consumer industry) of the Soviet Union.[5] After initially opposing Malenkov on these issues, Nikita Khrushchev gradually incorporated much of his predecessor's thinking into his own emerging conception of international security. The propositions put forth by Khrushchev at the 20th Party Congress in 1956 on the noninevitability of war and on the necessity and possibility of peaceful coexistence between different social systems are indicative of his efforts to modify Cold War thinking in order to bring it into line with the changing conditions of the age. Although his pursuit of new approaches to security was sporadic, and in some notable cases such as the Cuban missile crisis, contradictory, Khrushchev made a significant contribution to the development of Soviet thinking on the nature of security in the nuclear age. For Khrushchev, as for Malenkov, the key questions facing the Soviet Union in the 1950s concerned the impact of nuclear weapons on international relations and the relationship between the requirements of security and the development of the domestic economy. These themes have remained at the heart of the Soviet security debate.[6]

The period between the 23rd Party Congress in 1966 and the 24th Congress in 1971 was marked by the emergence of new concepts such as "military détente" and global interdependence. These new departures were combined with existing concepts like peaceful coexistence, marking the beginning of what was described by a number of Soviet international affairs specialists as a restructuring of international relations.[7] These new ideas were the foundation for later policy breakthroughs such as détente and the successful negotiation of the first Strategic Arms Limitation Talks (SALT I).

Challenges to Cold War perspectives continued to be generated within the Soviet leadership in the middle 1970s despite the difficulties that plagued détente from its inception. The conceptual initiatives of the Brezhnev leadership in the field of international security reached an apex in January 1977 when Brezhnev stated in a speech at Tula that the Soviet Union had as its primary objective the prevention of war, and that toward this end it would pursue not military superiority, but only a defense capability "sufficient to deter anyone from disturbing our peaceful life."[8] At that time it appeared, at least at the level of declaratory policy, that parity began to take the place of superiority as the criterion of military sufficiency.

The movement toward a new framework for international security slowed, however, in the last years of the decade. There were several major reasons for this. First, the dynamism of the early Brezhnev years diminished with the serious slowing down of the Soviet economy and the physical infirmity of the leading members of the ruling group. These developments made vigorous pursuit of bold initiatives in the security field difficult, a difficulty that was compounded by the fact that in 1977, NATO began what was to be a two-year debate over the modernization of its nuclear weapons program. During this period, Brezhnev came under increasing pressure from the Soviet military to take strong action to maintain the economic and technological support of the military at a level they deemed adequate, while refraining from making concessions to NATO. Brezhnev disappointed the military on both counts. First, the economy continued its slide, thus making the technological-industrial support of the military difficult to achieve. Second, Brezhnev resisted military pressure and attempted to dissuade the NATO leadership from adding to its European-based nuclear arsenal by offering Soviet reductions in conventional forces. In October 1979 he made a speech in Berlin in which he announced the unilateral withdrawal of 20,000 Soviet troops and a tank army from East Germany.[9] The discomfort that this caused within the Soviet military was sharply increased when, two months later, NATO announced its intention to add two new weapons systems to its nuclear arsenal in Europe. From 1979 until his death in 1982 Brezhnev was on the defensive in his relations with the Soviet military—a fact that was made clear by his extraordinary speech before the military leadership shortly before his death — and further movement away from the Cold War approach to international relations was halted.[10] The experience of the Brezhnev years illustrates how domestic and international factors can combine to increase the difficulty inherent in overcoming a firmly entrenched paradigm, but it also reveals the resiliency and evolutionary character of Soviet thinking on international security. Challenges to the dominant paradigm have not always been successful, but they have been a part of the agenda, at least implicitly, of all postwar Soviet leadership groups.

The international security program set forth by General Secretary Mikhail S. Gorbachev is very much a part of this evolutionary process. Gorbachev's approach, however, is distinguished from those of his predecessors in a number of important ways: by its comprehensiveness, by the boldness of its innovations, by the determination and urgency with which it is being advanced, and by the sophistication and thoroughness with which its conceptual foundation is being laid. These characteristics add up to what can be described as a framework of principles and concepts that collectively bear the seeds of an international security paradigm that is profoundly different from that evident in the Cold War.

THE PROCESS OF PARADIGM CHANGE

In his important work, *The Structure of Scientific Revolutions*, Thomas Kuhn wrote:

> Political revolutions are inaugurated by a growing sense, often restricted to a segment of the political community, that existing institutions have ceased adequately to meet the problems posed by an environment which they have in part created.[11]

This passage depicts very well the driving force behind the Gorbachev reform movement. Gorbachev's initiatives are rooted in the belief that existing institutions, and by extension, ways of thinking, are no longer adequate to deal with the dilemmas posed by the modern age. Bureaucratic inertia and a blind adherence to outdated approaches to the problems facing Soviet society resulted in a period of stagnation that reached, by the late Brezhnev years, what Gorbachev refers to as a "pre-crisis" level. The impending domestic crisis is paralleled, in the view of Gorbachev, by growing contradictions in the realm of international security. At the 27th Party Congress in 1986 he told the delegates that

The situation has reached a turning point not only in internal but also in external affairs. The changes in current world developments are so deep going and significant that they require a reassessment and a comprehensive analysis of all factors. The situation created by the nuclear confrontation calls for new approaches, methods, and forms of relations between the different social systems, states, and regions.[12]

Gorbachev's call for "new approaches" to international relations, for "new political thinking" (*novaia politcheskoie mishlenie*), in matters of international security, is based on the perception that the Cold War paradigm—its core principles, institutions, and psychological orientation—is out of step with the requirements of security in an age of nuclear weapons and rocket delivery systems, and that the existing lack of correspondence between the challenges of the nuclear age and the mechanisms available to meet them constitutes a source of great danger. "New political thinking" is advanced by the Soviet leadership as a means of reducing this danger through the introduction of concepts and principles which may in time be developed into policies and institutions capable of effectively managing the problems of the age.

A large number of experts representing a diverse cross section of the Soviet national security establishment appear to concur with General Secretary Gorbachev's assessment of the dangers inherent in contemporary international relations, and are currently engaged in a thorough analysis of the nature of international security. Deputy Foreign Minister Vladimir Petrovskii noted in a recent book that the character of the nuclear age had made

the problem of security. . .the focal point of world politics and assurance of security is connected with the need for a radical reorganization of international relations. Nuclear missile reality demands a new approach to the problem of security and to a definition of its parameters.[13]

Petrovskii struck at the heart of the Cold War paradigm when he expressed the view that nothing less than a "new psychology" of international relations is needed if the catastrophe of war is to be avoided. He stated that the old psychology, the psychology of the Cold War, is "imbued with national egotism . . . and based on the concept of the inevitability and even the permissibility of wars as an instrument of politics," and that it is "conclusively outdated."[14]

Military leaders have joined their civilian counterparts in expressing an appreciation of the profound changes that have taken place in the nuclear age and of the need for a reassessment of traditional modes of thinking in the security field. Marshal of the Soviet Union S. F. Akhromeev, former Chief of the General Staff, wrote in 1987 that contemporary conditions require an active policy of peace, and that the pursuit of such a policy requires in turn a "fundamental break in the types of thinking and action which have existed for centuries in the international arena."[15] While differences clearly exist between the civilian and military segments of the Soviet national security establishment (and within the respective segments), they appear to be united in a belief that important changes have taken place in the world and that these changes require serious attention.

The recognition of crisis, the call for "new political thinking," and the translation of this thinking into policies and institutions together form a three-stage process of paradigm change that appears to be operating within the Soviet Union today. The first stage—crisis recognition—has been completed, and the second stage—the development of concepts and principles—is well underway. The third stage—the translation of concepts into policies and institutions—has begun, but remains in a preliminary phase. This process provides a useful framework for the analysis of changes in Soviet national security policy under Gorbachev. While there are undoubtedly many sources of change in Soviet national security policy, two stand out as being of particular, perhaps decisive, importance: the economic crisis and the dilemmas posed by developments in the technology of war.

THE ECONOMIC CRISIS AND SECURITY

The most pervasive theme in the Soviet reform movement is the need for drastic action to halt the slide toward a debilitating economic crisis. Gorbachev's response to the impending crisis has been the call for a fundamental restructuring of the economic, social and political institutions and mechanisms of society. A far-reaching program of reform such as the one envisioned by Gorbachev raises important questions for the Soviet defense establishment. As one of the largest consumers in the Soviet economic system, absorbing some 15 to 20 percent of the gross domestic product, the military is vulnerable to any reform that entails large-scale spending cuts and major reallocations of resources. This vulnerability is particularly acute in the case of the military because "the armed forces do not possess an internal economic source and function at the expense of the nation's economy."[16] At the same time, the defense sector is critically dependent on the general economy, and has a vested interest in any reform that promises to improve the performance of the economy, and by implication, to expand and improve the quality of the industrial-technological base so important to the defense effort. The traditional approach to the question of the relationship of economic strength and economic reform to defense capacity focuses on the issue of how economic performance can be improved in order to increase the military power of the State. The emphasis here on increased military power as one of the principal *ends* of economic reform is clearly linked to the Cold War paradigm of international security and its core concepts: the unremitting opposition of the competing social systems and the centrality of military security.

But there is emerging within the Soviet national security establishment a new conception of the relationship between economic conditions and security. In this conception, military power is not viewed as a victim of economic weakness and a chief beneficiary of economic reform, but instead as part of the problem itself. Military power is thus transformed from an end to a means, in the sense that it can be manipulated in the effort to reach a new, more compelling objective. Such a transformation implies a radical redefinition of the concept of security itself. Evidence suggests that within the Soviet national security establishment there is currently a mix of traditional and new approaches to the issue of economoc reform and its relationship to security. How contradictory elements of these approaches are reconciled will determine the degree to which the economic factor will contribute to, or conversely, hinder the movement toward a new paradigm of international security.

THE ECONOMY AND NATIONAL SECURITY: THE TRADITIONAL VIEW

Friedrich Engels stated in *Anti-Duhring* that

the triumph of force is based on the production of arms, and this in turn on production in general; therefore on "economic power," on the "economic order," on the material means which force has at its disposal.[17]

Engels' conception of the relationship between economic might and military power has served as a guide to generations of Soviet leaders, both civilian and military, who have been involved in the formation and implementation of national security policy, and for whom the "triumph of force" has been the governing concept. Soviet military success has traditionally been attributed to the inherent correctness of the Marxist-Leninist approach to war, which emphasizes the importance of a large and efficient economic base as the indispensable foundation of defensive capability. The issue of economic reform and its relationship to the military has thus figured prominently throughout Soviet history. The drastic economic initiatives of Stalin in the early 1930s, for example, are frequently cited as having led to the rapid development of the Soviet economy which in turn made possible the "technical reconstruction of the armed forces."[18] The accomplishment of this task is considered to have been one of the most crucial elements in the Soviet victory over Nazi Germany.

The relationship of economic power to military strength has continued to receive attention in the postwar years. The rise of the Soviet Union to the status of a nuclear power, and its leadership in ballistic missile technology in the 1950s, was directly linked by Khrushchev to the postwar recovery of the Soviet economy, and at the 23rd Party Congress, Kosygin made use of the linkage of economics and military power in support of the economic reform program of the late 1960s. In what appears to have been in part an attempt to enlist military support for the program, he pointed out to the delegates that the military would indeed be a chief beneficiary of reform, saying that

> The defense power of a state also depends on the state of economics. This is especially true in our time, when armies have become much more complicated and expensive, and a high level of science and technology is needed for its production. In developing our economy, we are thereby strengthening the defense capability of the Soviet Union, the power of the entire socialist camp.[19]

In the 1960s and early 1970s, the dynamism of the Soviet economy contributed directly to the "scientific-technical revolution" in military affairs. This phenomenon was the practical foundation on which the Soviet drive toward strategic parity with the United States was built.

The issue of national security and economics came to the fore again in the late 1970s and early 1980s as a result of the downturn in the performance of the Soviet economy. The deepening economic crisis, as Harry Gelman has pointed out, placed the Soviet leadership in the difficult position of having to choose between a pair of far from ideal alternatives: a substantial redirection of resources away from the military sector, or a program of fundamental reform involving significant steps toward economic decentralization.[20]

Unwilling to undertake such a reform program and unable to successfully challenge the military over resource allocations by the late 1970s, the Brezhnev leadership did nothing, thus adding to the mounting economic woes of the Soviet Union. Decisive action on this issue was also avoided during the brief tenures of Andropov and Chernenko as General Secretary, as "muddling through" substituted for decisive action. This reluctance or inability to face the deteriorating situation head-on ended with the elevation of Gorbachev to the top of the Party leadership in March of 1985.

The military has for the most part expressed cautious support for the restructuring campaign of General Secretary Gorbachev. It appears that this support stems primarily from the traditional view that a strong economy means a strong military. This view is reflected in an unattributed lead article that appeared in a Soviet military journal in 1986:

> The Party considers the development of the economy as one of the decisive factors of strengthening the State's defense capability, the combat capabilities of the Armed Forces, and of ensuring military victories. Only a strong and modern economic basis can ensure the possibility for perfecting the Armed Forces.[21]

In another issue of this same journal, a Soviet military writer pointed to the positive relationship between the radical program of reform initiated by Gorbachev and the strengthening of Soviet defensive capabilities by citing Lenin's statement that "it is impossible to make the nation capable of defense without the greatest heroism on the part of the people who carry out boldly and decisively great economic transformations."[22] The ultimate purpose of economic reform, according to this writer, is compliance with the Leninist principle of "maximum satisfaction of Army and Navy material requirements."[23] This theme is sounded by military writers in practically every article dealing with the issue of national defense and appears to confirm the view of a leading Western analyst who has concluded that military support for reform can be expected as long as the military leadership feels that reform is "enlarging the pie" from which its slice of economic resources will be drawn.[24]

Military proponents of the traditional approach to the economy-security relationship are apparently aware of nonmilitary considerations that are relevant to the issue, but they are understandably loathe to grant to these issues a status equal to that of military security. In an interview with the Spanish newspaper *Diario*, Army General Iurii Lebedev, a deputy chief of the Soviet General Staff, was asked if the high percentage of the Soviet gross domestic product dedicated to defense is an important factor in the country's low living standard. Lebedev replied that indeed this is the case, and that if so much were not devoted to defense it could be allocated to other social needs. But, he added, in what might be taken as a standard warning to anyone considering intemperate cuts in defense spending, the Soviet Union cannot risk a repeat of the disasters of 1941, which he attributed to a lack of attention to the needs of the Army.[25]

But support within the defense establishment for reform is not simply a matter of what the economy can do for the military. On the contrary, there has developed within the military a realization that the seriousness of the economic situation makes it necessary to take steps that would reduce costs while maintaining an adequate level of defense preparedness. Measures such as increasing training efficiency and the institution of cost reduction measures are among those being discussed.[26] Military sent support for, and participation in, Gorbachev's program of *perestroika* has centered on issues related to efficient management, troop discipline and morale, and increased combat readiness, all of which can be seen as elements of an effort to achieve the greatest results at the least expense. Indeed, General Iazov's selection for the post of Defense Minister was undoubtedly due in no small part to his reputation as a strict disciplinarian who stresses effective leadership and individual morale as key factors contributing to military efficiency.

The magnitude of the problem, however, is such that a more comprehensive approach to the problem of economic crisis and military power is required. M. A. Gareev, a deputy chief of the Soviet General Staff, indicated as much when he wrote that

> military-theoretic thought should be working constantly on how to most rationally utilize the means allocated for military needs within the limits of strict necessity so that defense be reliable and at the same time not too burdensome for the State.[27]

Gareev links three concepts in this statement: the limits of strict necessity, reliable defense, and the capacity of the State to carry the burden of defense. In the traditional view, reliable defense would be elevated to the supreme position in this scheme, while the other two elements would be relegated to supporting roles. The new conception of economics and security focuses on the limits of strict necessity and the tolerance of the economy for military expenditures. It does not disregard the requirement for reliable defense, but redefines the concept of security. Military power no longer is an end in itself, but one means among others, such as a sound economy, for achieving the desired end of security.

THE ECONOMY AND SECURITY: THE NEW THINKING

The "new thinking" on the relationship of the economy to security is based on the assumption that the nature of international relations is changing, and that as a result, the nature of the threat to security is also changing. In contrast to the conception of international relations imbedded in the Cold War paradigm, which portrays a world of rigid divisions maintained by military power, the emerging conception is based on the belief that the world is becoming increasingly interdependent and that all nations face a spectrum of global problems that require cooperative global solutions. Gorbachev described this new condition in his speech marking the seventieth anniversary of the October Revolution, saying that

> for all the profound contradictions of the contemporary world, for all the radical differences among the countries that comprise it, it is interrelated, interdependent, and integral. The reasons for this include the internationalization of world economic ties, the comprehensive scope of the scientific and technological revolution, the essentially novel role played by the mass media, the state of the earth's resources, the common environmental danger and the crying social problems of the developing world which affect us all.[28]

These are essentially nonmilitary conditions and problems that call, according to Gorbachev, for nonmilitary responses. He pointed out in this speech that the technical perfection of the military instrument has, paradoxically, increased the importance of the nonmilitary aspects of security, because the impossibility of defense against such weapons means that security is becoming an increasingly political matter.[29] In the new conception of international relations, the "nonmilitary aspects of international security are not seen . . . as secondary or subordinate to the military aspects, they are considered to be fully independent and no less important than the military aspects."[30]

The relationship of the economy and society as a whole to defense is beginning to be discussed in the Soviet Union in new ways. There appears to be a growing willingness to question the once sacrosanct priority granted to defense, and calls are being heard for a shift toward a more rational utilization of resources. L. Semeiko, a specialist at the Soviet Institute for the Study of the USA and Canada, has provided an interesting historical perspective on the impact of military spending on societies in an article published in *Izvestiia*.[31] He noted that historical experience confirms that "the law of diminishing returns operates in raising the level of military confrontation: increasingly reduced efficiency of arms increments and increasingly large expenditures on them." Referring to this situation as "absurd," Semeiko went on to state that throughout history, the pursuit of military surpluses has always resulted in the slowing of socioeconomic and techno-logical processes. Although he cited as examples of this process the Roman Empire and the contemporary Pentagon, Semeiko made no explicit reference to any class bias in this historical phenomenon, and concluded this section of the article by saying "We do not want this practice either for the United States, or for ourselves, or for anyone else."

In a recent interview, a Soviet economist offered some concrete examples of the impact of military spending on domestic economics.[32] The economist V. M. Krivosheev, a sector chief at the Institute of Economics of the World Socialist System, stated that currently on a worldwide basis the rate of development of the military sector is now twice the rate of the development of the world economy as a whole. To illustrate this, he said that with the money being devoted to the world military industry, enough high-quality apartments could be constructed over the next thirty years to house virtually everyone in America, Europe, and Africa. Krivosheev admitted that the diversion of funds from social programs to the military sector is doing serious damage to the Soviet economy, just as it is in the United States. In making this admission Krivosheev went on to cite a precedent from the Soviet past to illustrate how changes in resource allocation patterns could alleviate serious socioeconomic problems within the Soviet system. He said that

> Many socioeconomic problems could be resolved were it not for the forced diversion of resources for the arms race. In the late fifties the Soviet Union unilaterally reduced its Armed Forces by 1.2 million men. This made it possible to build 100 major house building combines. In a comparatively short space of time housing construction was doubled in the country, and the old-age pension was doubled.[33]

Krivosheev underscored the seriousness of his prescription for a program of rediverting resources back into the nonmilitary sector of the economy by cal-ling for the development of a new economic field, the "economics of disarm-ament," which would have the responsibility for directing the transfor-mation of military industries and organizations into effective nonmilitary ones.[34]

The view that massive military expenditures interfere with the satisfactory functioning of domestic economic systems applies, within the new concep-tion, to the international economic and social arena as well. The comprehensive system of international security, reflecting the new thinking in the security field, includes as a central aspect the resolution of the emerging global problems referred to by Gorbachev at the 27th Party Congress. These problems include the preservation of the environment, the fight against economic backwardness and the attendant struggle against hunger and disease, the search for new sources of energy, and the equitable and efficient use of the world oceans. Former Soviet Ambassador to the United States and key advisor to General Secretary Gorbachev, Anatolii Dobrynin, has written that these global problems do indeed require global solutions, and that the economic and technical prerequisites exist in modern civilization to effectively deal with them within the span of two generations. But Dobrynin asserted that the achievement of this goal will be possible only if economic priorities are altered. He stated that

> It is quite obvious that progress in solving such problems will require, above all, tremendous investments on the part of all countries within a global program for action. A true global community can obtain and use such substantial funds only if essential changes are made in the area of disarmament and in reducing military expenditures.[35]

Dobrynin illuminated in this article another fundamental difference between Cold War concepts and the emerging security paradigm when he pointed out that such a shift of resources can occur, and a solution to global problems be found, only "through the collective efforts of all members of the global community of nations."[36] "Collective efforts" and the "global community of nations" stand in stark contrast to the Cold War conception of international relations.

Gorbachev provided a concise overview of his understanding of the relationship of military power to global problems in his January 1986 statement on international security.[37] He stated that ending the arms race and the reduction of military arsenals are prerequisites for coping with emerging global problems. Attributing a significant measure of blame for the world's ills to the militarized state of contemporary international relations, Gorbachev said,

> The pattern imposed by militarism—arms in place of development—must be replaced by the reverse order of things—disarmament for development . . . . The Soviet Union wants each measure limiting and reducing arms and each step towards eliminating nuclear weapons not only to bring nations greater security, but also to make it possible to allocate more funds for improving people's life.[38]

The common prescription for dealing with the socioeconomic problems of both the Soviet domestic system and the international system is to shift resources away from the military into productive nonmilitary sectors. Soviet "new thinkers" have developed a concept which provides a basis for this process: the principle of reasonable sufficiency.[39] Reasonable sufficiency is referred to by Soviet leaders and writers as the basis for the building of the Armed Forces.[40] One of the expressed purposes of this concept, and the one most germane to the linkage between economics and security, is to facilitate efforts to "demolish the logic of the arms race" and thereby provide a basis for the progressive reduction of military arsenals.[41] This change would be accomplished by the creation of military forces that are sufficient to reliably defend a state against attack, but which are not sufficiently powerful or appropriately structured to enable the state to carry out an attack. Reasonable sufficiency therefore implies an objective standard of defensive power which creates an opportunity to move away from the symmetrical, tit-for-tat dynamic that has fueled the postwar arms race. The pursuit of this principle can lead beyond the stabilization of the arms race to a reversal of the arms race, since the requirements of sufficiency would be progressively reduced as the force levels of the sides are lowered.[42] The ultimate objective of arms reductions based on reasonable sufficiency is the production of a stable balance of forces at the lowest possible level,[43] and though the principle remains somewhat ambiguous, it implies a rational criterion for the structuring of armed forces which may in time have significant implications for policy and facilitate substantial reallocations of resources.

The Soviet perception of "pre-crisis" conditions in both the Soviet domestic economy and the international economic system has stimulated the development of a new conception of the relationship between economics and security. The contrasts that are evident between the old and new approaches to the economics-security relationship are important and do reveal something of the nature of the emerging paradigm. But a desire to reduce the burden of defense in a time of economic stagnation is not necessarily an indication that something as profound as paradigm change is taking place. The proponents of the new approach to security advocate the reduction of military forces but they do not deny that military power still plays an important role in international relations, and the Soviet leadership clearly takes its responsibilities in this area seriously. The Party's oft-repeated pledge to provide everything necessary for the reliable defense of the Soviet Union could, of course, be inconsistent with the goal of reducing military spending.[44] But there is evidence that this apparent contradiction is being addressed by a new concept of security that is changing the defense requirements of modern states. This new concept has emerged in response to radical developments in the technology of war.

SECURITY AND THE TECHNOLOGY OF WAR

Soviet military science is based on the Marxist-Leninist system of dialectics in which development is achieved through the recognition and reconciliation of dialectical contradictions. Former Chief of the Soviet General Staff, Marshal of the Soviet Union Nikolai Ogarkov, described this process:

> Thus, investigation, discovery, and the resolution of contradictions and conflicts in military realities are a most important condition for advances in military theory, the task of which consists precisely in promptly spotting imminent contradictions, seeking the most effective measures to resolve them, and thus influencing the development of military affairs.[45]

Ogarkov cited the tension between offense and defense, the requirement for massing of forces versus the need for troop dispersal, and the need for modern weapons in sufficient numbers versus the economic capabilities of the State to produce them as examples of dialectical contradictions that drive the process of military development.[46] But developments in military technology have introduced a new and overarching contradiction into the national security equation. This contradiction is grounded in the inherent tension between the requirements of defense (traditionally thought of in terms of war-fighting capabilities) and the need for military stability.

In the view of many Soviet leaders and thinkers, efforts in the security field must increasingly focus on the issue of stability, even if this means relegating traditional defense issues to a secondary place. According to Gorbachev, this is because in the nuclear age war raises the transcendent issue of human survival.[47] Military leaders have echoed this sentiment. Minister of Defense Iazov, for example, said in a speech before a Kremlin meeting commemorating the seventieth anniversary of the Soviet Army and Navy that

> Comprehension of the realities of the nuclear missile age and the interests of humanity's survival dictate the need for the new political thinking. This stems from the utter unacceptability of war as a political means, the futility of striving for military superiority and the senselessness of the arms race. Never before have the problems of war and peace been posed so urgently as at the present.

Never before has peace been identical with the very possibility of the existence of human civilization, and war with the inevitable destruction of all that lives on earth.[48]

While the primary cause of concern for these Soviet spokesmen is nuclear war, conventional warfare is also being examined in a new light, and not simply because of the long-recognized hazards of escalation to the nuclear level. Recent developments in the means of conventional war-fighting, especially in the areas of weapons accuracy, penetrability, and destructive power, have been described by Soviet analysts as amounting to a "qualitative leap," which has carried them to levels of effectiveness approaching those of weapons of mass destruction.[49] The use of such weapons in Europe, where population density is exceptionally high and where there are numerous high-risk targets such as chemical and nuclear power facilities, could have, as Iazov has put it, "catastrophic consequences comparable with a nuclear cataclysm."[50]

Advances in the technology of war have thus brought the issue of survival itself into the calculations of civilian and military leaders. As a result, increasing attention is being paid to the idea of stability, or the aversion of war, as a strategic imperative. According to V. V. Zhurkin, head of the recently formed Institute of Europe,

the irreversible fact that nuclear war will signify the end of human history has brought the problem of the stability of the strategic situation to the central place in the political and military thinking of the contemporary epoch.[51]

The pursuit of stability implies a conception of the problem of military security that is different in significant ways from traditional approaches. The phenomenon of war itself, rather than traditional "enemies," is increasingly seen as the object of national security planning. Evidence that this approach is having an impact on Soviet military thinking can be found in an article by Deputy Chief of the General Staff M. A. Gareev, in which he compared the struggle against nuclear war to the joint efforts of the anti-Hitler coalition in World War II, and wrote that "the threat of nuclear war leaves the contemporary world no alternative but to join efforts to prevent a nuclear catastrophe."[52] An important result of the emergence of this "war as the enemy" line of thinking has been the assignment of war aversion as a strategic task, a development that has in turn led to a blurring of the traditional distinction between the political-military and military-technical aspects of military doctrine.

The entry on military strategy in the 1986 Soviet Military Encyclopedic Dictionary, an authoritative reference work published by the Ministry of Defense, concludes, "The most important task of Soviet military strategy in contemporary conditions is the working out of the problem of averting wars."[53] The development and implementation of a strategy for war aversion poses a formidable challenge for the Soviet security community, especially its military contingent, because the requirements of war aversion appear in a number of cases to conflict with military rationality as traditionally conceived. This is because those military strategies considered by military planners to offer the best chances for victory in war have frequently been strategies that have made war more likely; that is, strategists have traditionally preferred offensive strategies that give, in theory, a decisive advantage to the side that strikes first. In the past, a fairly rigid compartmentalization of military and political aspects of security has been maintained in the security establishments of most countries, and military planners have not been significantly constrained in their operational planning by political considerations. But the unique threats posed in the nuclear-missile age do not, according to the "new thinking," allow for such divisions of labor. Instead, there is a merging of the political and the military aspects of security, a union which, though perhaps necessary, will not be easy to produce.

In a critique of American strategic policy, Soviet scholar G. A. Trofimenko admitted that some Soviet theorists display a "devil-may-care" attitude toward nuclear war, and stated that such attitudes spring from adherence to obsolete stereotypes. Trofimenko went on to write, in what appears to be a passage aimed at domestic opponents of the new approach to security, that while it "would have been much simpler to resort to the cliché that only capitalism will die while socialism survives," the Soviet leadership

> faced the facts and has frankly informed its own people and the "potential adversary" of the consequences of war, stating that their prevention will necessitate a change in customary ways of thinking and the renunciation of cessitate a change in customary ways of thinking and the renunciation of common stereotypes. This will also entail the revision of some theoretical premises, which were correct at one time but cannot be considered valid in the nuclear age.[54]

It is in the process of revising theoretical premises engaged at operational levels of military affairs that the distinction between military-technical and political-military aspects of military policy begins to break down. Sir

Michael Howard has described the transformational impact of nuclear weapons by pointing out that, historically, military thinkers and practitioners have struggled against human and technological constraints in the pursuit of the ideal of "absolute war."[55] But the technological realization of this ideal changed the requirements of security, and the barriers between the political and the military began to weaken, for, as Howard has written,

> Whereas in Clausewitz's day human effort had been necessary to *transcend* the limitations imposed on the conduct of war by the constraints of the real world, now that effort is needed to *impose* such limits.[56]

Historically, overcoming constraints was largely a military-technical task, but the imposition of limits on the means and conduct of war demands a broader, politically-oriented approach. This condition has led, according to one Soviet specialist, to "a deep and sharp politicization of traditional military questions" that has extended down to the level of military tactics.[57] One of the most daunting tasks facing Soviet security specialists is how to combine political and military-technical approaches to security in ways that enhance stability and also meet the requirements of defense. This requires above all an effective mix of what have in the past been contradictory concepts and policies. A recent article in the Ministry of Defense daily newspaper *Krasnaia zvezda* described the current task in the following way:

> today maintaining security is above all a political task, since the character of present-day weapons do not permit any government the hope of defending itself by military-technical means alone. Hence it follows that the real problem is the search for the proper relationship of political and military means of securing the hope of defending the USSR and its allies.[58]

The search for the proper balance between political and military means of maintaining security is an inherently complex task. Any sound security policy requires a sound conceptual foundation. The development of such a foundation appears to be underway in the Soviet Union today.

A conceptual framework composed of three tiers has emerged from the work of Soviet security specialists. The first tier of this new conceptual framework is the idea that military-strategic parity is the basic prerequisite for peace and stability. The intermediate tier carries parity a step further: parity at the lowest possible force levels with forces structured exclusively for defensive purposes. This tier is operationally expressed in the concept of "reasonable sufficiency." The third tier is the principle of defensive defense which provides for the strategic, operational, and tactical implementation of reasonable sufficiency. This three-tiered conceptual framework is the intellectual means by which the fundamental contradiction between military utility and military stability is being addressed in the Soviet Union. The success of efforts to deal with this dilemma will depend on the degree of political consensus that can be reached.

PARITY AS THE BASIS OF STABILITY

In a 1985 book, Marshal Ogarkov stated that the Soviet Communist Party had come to the conclusion that "wars are not fatally inevitable."[59] He attributed this condition not to any change in the nature of capitalism, but to such factors as the deepening crisis of capitalism, the growing power of the world socialist system, and "the increased defense capability of the countries of the socialist community to the level of guaranteed destruction of any aggressor." Ogarkov echoed the view of other Soviet experts when he concluded that

> under modern conditions the sociopolitical and military-technical prerequisites are being created for the prevention of a new world war and, in the future, for the complete eradication of wars from the life of society even before the complete victory of socialism on earth, while capitalism still remains for some time in a number of countries. Of course, during this period the military threat still remains, *but it will be possible to neutralize it.*[60]

According to Soviet experts, the primary prerequisite for the neutralization of the continuing military threat posed by capitalism is the existence of military strategic parity between the Soviet Union and the United States, the Warsaw Pact, and NATO. Colonel-General Dimitrii Volkogonov, the recently appointed head of the Soviet Ministry of Defense Military History Institute, referred to parity as *the* factor blocking war, when he wrote that currently "there is but one objective material basis for holding back war: socialism's ability to maintain strategic parity in nuclear arms."[61] He stated that this was the case because parity "deprives imperialist politicians and strategists any real hope of achieving victory," and concluded therefore that a "dialectical interconnection between the balance of strategic forces and the guaranteeing of international security" has emerged that constitutes "one of the laws governing the preservation of peace."[62] Civilian specialists on international relations appear to share this view of the importance of parity to stability; indeed, Vladimir Petrovskii has devoted an entire chapter of a book to this relationship. The chapter, entitled "Strategic Balance—The Basis of a Secure World," begins

> The realities of the nuclear-missile age require recognition of the fact that strategic military balance (approximate parity) between the USSR and the USA, between the Warsaw Pact and NATO is the most important precondition for a reliable system of international security. It is a matter of the optimal state of a system of military confrontation in the area of nuclear as well as conventional arms.[63]

But despite the broad consensus on the importance of military strategic equilibrium for international stability, some Soviet specialists have reached the conclusion that "the stabilizing role of parity is not absolute," and have expressed the concern that parity's stabilizing effects are undermined as force levels rise.[64] A representative statement of this concern can be found in an unattributed lead editorial which appeared in *Krasnaia zvezda* in January 1988. The editorial stated that

> military-strategic parity in itself still does not guarantee the full security of any country or rule out the potential danger of war. The Warsaw Pact states proceed from the premise that the contemporary balance of military forces is inadmissibly high. And this harbors a tremendous threat to peace. It is obvious that the further continuation of the arms race will still further increase the danger and could bring it to the point where even military-strategic parity will cease to be a deterrent factor.[65]

Parity seems to be viewed as an essential strategic principle that implies a move away from the Cold War pursuit of military superiority, but it should not be considered, in Petrovskii's words, "a panacea against nuclear war and a reliable safeguard for security."[66] It is instead seen as a necessary, but not a sufficient, condition for the maintenance of stability. Parity is indispensable. But parity alone does not achieve military stability.

THE SECOND TIER: PARITY AT THE LOWEST LEVELS OF FORCES AND THE PRINCIPLE OF REASONABLE SUFFICIENCY

The emerging Soviet framework for international security has two main goals: the halting and reversal of the arms race, and the creation of military force structures which are more stable than those existing today.

Military strategic parity is considered by many Soviet specialists to be an inadequate guarantor of international security if it is linked to high force levels and an expanding arms race. The Cold War paradigm has provided what some Soviet scholars refer to as the "logic" of the arms race. This logic requires that the sides involved not only preserve their force levels, but also believe there is a necessity to increase them.[67] The contending logic argues that if the arms race is unregulated, there is a danger that it will reach a level that makes control difficult, if not impossible, to achieve. General Secretary Gorbachev elaborated on this theme in his January 1986 statement on international security when he said that the logic of the arms race

> has to be resolutely rejected. We are making yet another attempt in this direction. Otherwise the process of military rivalry will assume gigantic proportions and any control over the course of events would be impossible. To yield to the anarchic force of the nuclear arms race is impermissible. This would be acting against reason and the human instinct of self-preservation. What is required are new and bold approaches, fresh political thinking, and a heightened sense of responsibility for the destinies of the peoples.[68]

Central to the logic of the arms race is the belief in the utility of military superiority. The new approach to security rejects this notion as obsolete and dangerous. Volkogonov has made the point that beyond certain limits arms buildups cease to play a decisive military role, while Marshal Akhromeev has stated that developments in the technology of war, particularly in nuclear weapons, have made further efforts to increase and improve them "absurd and criminal."[69] The concept of parity at the lowest possible levels of forces and its operational principle, reasonable sufficiency, have emerged in response to problems created by a continued reliance on superiority as the criterion of military development.[70]

There are several ways in which reasonable sufficiency might facilitate stopping the arms race. First, the principle presupposes the existence of strategic parity as the basis for reductions to lower levels. Acceptance by the involved parties means, by definition, a move away from the principle of superiority, allowing the sides to reassess force levels. This, in practice, means that the standard of sufficiency is not the number of weapons possessed by the adversary, but the number required to carry out specified tasks. Linkage of weapons requirements to such a standard breaks the action-reaction cycle, and makes reductions possible. For example, Zhurkin, Karaganov, and Kortunov have stated that the proposed 50 percent cuts in strategic arms are both desirable and possible because current levels of strategic parity have what they refer to as a "large surplus of stability"; that is, the numbers of weapons systems needed to assure that unacceptable damage will be wreaked in retaliation (which is the strategic-nuclear criterion of sufficiency) in case of attack are far in excess of what is actually required.[71] Reasonable sufficiency could, in the estimation of the Soviet specialists, have a similar impact across the entire spectrum of military forces, as surpluses associated with offensive strategies and structures are eliminated.

Kokoshin and Kortunov have speculated further that the process of reducing force levels within a framework of strategic parity could initiate a reverse action-reaction mechanism, in which each reduction of forces could lead to further reductions by progressively lowering the levels of sufficiency, by reducing the element of risk involved for the sides engaged in reductions, and by gradually improving the politico-psychological environment within which policies are developed.[72]

As important as the halting and reversal of the arms race is in enhancing strategic stability, it is not in itself a sufficient guarantee of peace. Arms races do tend to create a momentum of their own, but national military forces are, for the most part, structured according to leadership views of threats to the security of the state or bloc. Attempts to reduce military forces will fail if the new levels of forces do not correspond to perceived threats to security. The principle of reasonable sufficiency deals with the issue of how lower levels of forces should be structured to assure security. Through this conceptual innovation, Soviet thinkers have taken a step toward bridging the gap between political and military-technical approaches to security.

The new Soviet emphasis on stability, or war aversion, as a strategic task, is reflected in the principle of reasonable sufficiency. Reasonable sufficiency requires military forces that provide reliable defense, but are incapable of large-scale offensive action. Its implications for the development of Soviet military affairs are profound, because force structures and strategies implied by reasonable sufficiency appear to fly in the face of some of the most fundamental principles of Soviet military art, such as the requirement for superiority in men and equipment, the necessity for offensive action on the territory of the enemy at the outset of conflicts, the importance of surprise in seizing the initiative in war, and the employment of massive combined-arms forces in deep penetration operations. Soviet theorists have recognized the radical implications for military planning. Semeiko, for example, has referred to the objective of reasonable sufficiency as "revolutionary because it proposes for the first time that the sides mutually reject a type of military activity such as the offensive, which is traditionally considered to be fundamental."[73] It is here that the "politicization of traditional military questions" that Kokoshin referred to, begins.[74]

But challenges to traditional military principles (as reflected in attempts to cut and/or restructure forces) are difficult to sustain if they raise doubts about the ability of the armed forces to fulfill their primary mission, the preservation of the security of the state. Soviet political and military leaders have repeatedly stressed that the Party and the military will always maintain the military at a level which guarantees the reliable defense and security of the Soviet State and the socialist community.[75] A question, therefore, arises about the compatibility of reasonable sufficiency and military security.

Soviet proponents of these new approaches to security have responded to this question by pointing out that as the essence of security has changed in the nuclear age, so have the requirements for its safeguarding. In these circumstances new threats arise and old ones recede, and concepts, policies, and institutions must keep pace. This requires conscious effort because, as three leading Soviet security specialists have stated,

> Human thought as is well known, naturally lags behind quickly changing political reality. Exactly by this is explained the natural inclination of the ordinary consciousness to concentrate basic attention on traditional threats, with which one has already had to contend, and to underestimate the new and unforeseen, which has already or soon will become reality.[76]

For strategic planners faced with the traditional threat of war—the authors of this article employ the case of June 1941 as an analogy—the measures implied by reasonable sufficiency appear intolerably risky. But, according to the authors, important changes have taken place in recent years that greatly reduce the risk of a repeat of 1941. First, they assert that the great destructive power of modern weapons, both nuclear and conventional, raises the cost of war to such a high level that resort to military means for the resolution of some conflict would be most unlikely. In addition to this constraint, the authors point to the existence of serious problems within the capitalist states which could in no way be remedied by military aggression against socialism, and they concur with many other Soviet experts when they state that the existing strategic parity consititutes a most formidable obstacle to aggression.[77]

What this adds up to, in the opinion of these specialists, is a situation that requires, and can accept within tolerable limits of risk, a shift away from traditional military-technical approaches to the maintenance of security, in favor of a more strongly political approach. This process will demand in turn significant changes *within* the military-technical realm itself.

> The qualitatively different character of the threat assumes also a qualitatively new reaction to the threat. Previously, the level of sufficiency of Soviet military power in the European theater was determined by the demands to repel any aggression, to crush any possible coalitions of enemy governments. Now, the task is set in a principally different manner: to deter, to prevent war itself. This task demands, in turn, a rethinking of any traditional postulates of military strategy and operational art, beginning with a reevaluation of the quantitative requirements of one or another type of weapons (for example, tanks) or of the character of the maneuvers that are conducted, etc.[78]

Consistent with this Soviet assessment of the current situation is the analysis of Michael MccGwire, a leading Western analyst of Soviet military affairs, which holds that the Soviet military has changed its views in recent years on the principal threat to the Soviet Union and that, as a result, Soviet military requirements have changed.[79] MccGwire argued in a 1987 article that in 1982–1983, the leadership of the Soviet military concluded that the primary objective of military policy must be "to avoid escalation from regional to world war," and that if this policy requires a defensive Soviet force posture in Europe, then such changes would have to be accepted. This led to a relaxation of the requirement for a large-scale Soviet offensive in Europe in the event of war.[80] MccGwire has made the very useful point that this change signaled an end to the condition existing in the 1960s and 1970s in which the offensive strategies and structures of Soviet forces in Europe acted as a serious constraint on Soviet foreign policy.[81] The relaxation of this constraint adds a degree of flexibility to Soviet policy that has heretofore been lacking.

The principle of reasonable sufficiency is an important element in the Soviet new thinking because it provides a conceptual basis for policy which links arms reductions and reliable defense. This linkage is made possible by a fundamental redefinition of the concept of security which holds that political approaches to security should take precedence. But military-technical factors remain important, both in terms of their impact on stability and their capacity for effective defense. According to Soviet theorists, reasonable sufficiency requires that military forces be structured for purely defensive purposes. The concept of defensive defense provides a means of studying how that requirement can be fulfilled in practice.

THE CONCEPT OF DEFENSIVE DEFENSE

In a major statement on Soviet military doctrine published in *Pravda*, Defense Minister Iazov provided the following operational definition of reasonable sufficiency:

> When we speak about maintaining the armed forces, our military potential, within the limits of reasonable sufficiency, we mean that at the present stage the essence of adequacy for the strategic nuclear forces of the Soviet Union is determined by the necessity of preventing an unpunished nuclear attack in any, even the most unfavorable, circumstance. As far as conventional weapons are concerned, sufficiency refers to a quantity and quality of forces and arms which would be enough to reliably guarantee the collective defense of the socialist community.[82]

The nuclear component of this formula is relatively clear-cut: the maintenance of a secure retaliatory capability under any conditions. This requirement is absolute and is accepted by virtually all civilian and military leaders. Soviet leaders appear to have high confidence that their existing strategic nuclear forces are capable of meeting this requirement, though there is concern in some quarters that U.S. progress in the area of strategic defense could at some point cast doubt on this capability. In these circumstances, and assuming the absence of any major technical breakthrough in strategic defense, the Soviet military will probably concentrate on improving the survivability and reliability of its strategic strike forces, but it is unlikely that any fundamental changes will be called for in either force structure or strategy.

The situation is very different, however, on the conventional side of this equation. Strategic stability at the conventional level involves a different set of factors and considerations than those which operate at the nuclear level. With nuclear weapons, the threat of inevitable retaliation at unacceptable levels of damage serves as the basis of stability. But at the conventional level "an analogous threat is practically and materially unrealizable."[83] A major task facing Soviet security specialists is, therefore, achieving stability in nonnuclear conditions. The basis for this is provided by the concept of defensive defense.

Stability is not enhanced by political and military doctrinal statements about the "defensiveness" of a state's orientation in the international system, unless these statements are evident in strategies and force structures. Soviet leaders have always insisted that the military doctrines and forces of the socialist states are strictly defensive, because the Marxist-Leninist laws of the class struggle make it impossible for them to be otherwise. Such declarations provide little comfort, however, to Western leaders who hear the Soviet words, but see massive forces structured and deployed for offensive warfare. This was clearly the case in the 1970s, when major developments in the Soviet military posture in Europe heightened NATO leaders' already considerable sense of threat.[84] Apparent contradictions between expressions of national intentions and military planning are not the result of characteristics inherent in any particular state or political system, but spring instead from the profound difficulty of consistently integrating military means with political ends. This is a universal dilemma, and contemporary Soviet military planners would no doubt find much to commend in the statement made by United States Secretary of the Navy Benjamin F. Tracy in his 1889 annual report, that "a war, though defensive in principle, may be conducted most effectively by being offensive in operations."[85] But as concern for stability increases, the implications of this contradiction become more serious.

The destabilizing impact of the gap between doctrine and strategy has been explicitly recognized by Soviet security analysts, two of whom stated in a 1987 article that, in the interests of security,

> the military concepts and doctrines of the military alliances have to be based exclusively on defensive principles. This places corresponding demands on strategy and tactics. The exclusively defensive character of military doctrines assumes corresponding measures in the areas of armed forces construction, including questions on their strength, structure, arms, deployment, combat readiness and training of personnel, and military planning.[86]

Defensive defense, as the basis of military strategy, operational art, and tactics, is intended to enhance stability through the creation of forces capable, and demonstrably so, only of defensive actions. The first, and perhaps most difficult, task facing Soviet specialists engaged in the developent of this concept is to make a case for defensive defense as a *militarily* rational approach to security. The military audience to whom this case must be presented is imbued with the traditional principles of Soviet military art—offense, surprise, the seizure and maintenance of initiative, et cetera—

and will resist all but the most compelling arguments. Despite the difficulties involved, an effort is being made to develop and present the case for defensive defense as a serious strategy for stability *and* defense.

Important civilian work to elaborate a concept of effective defensive defense has been undertaken by Andrei Kokoshin of the Academy of Sciences Institute for the Study of the USA and Canada, and his collaborator V. Larionov, a retired military officer and a respected analyst of security affairs. These two security specialists have produced over the past year three articles that examine some of the central issues related to defensive warfare.[87] These articles represent an attempt to give historical legitimacy to defensive strategies, and to evaluate their applicability to the contemporary period.

Kokoshin and Larionov began this series with an analysis of the World War II Battle of Kursk, which they describe as the first battle in history in which the stronger side chose to assume a defensive posture because it was deemed to be operationally advantageous.[88] The authors appear to have drawn two major inferences—one positive, the other negative—from their study of the Kursk engagement, which have important implications for current policy. The positive inference is that defense can indeed by the stronger form of warfare. Kokoshin and Larionov maintain that the success of the Soviet forces at Kursk was due to a timely decision to adopt a plan of *premeditated* defense which effectively combined strategic and technological innovations. The battle plan revolved around the building of an echeloned defense network composed of eight defense zones extending to a depth of 300 kilometers. This network was conceived and developed primarily as an antitank defense, and was constructed around natural barriers (the premeditated use of which is considered to be one of the great strengths of the defense), and obstacles built by the Soviet engineering corps. The engineers also produced an extensive system of communications trenches throughout the zones, which were of great value during the battle.

Several innovations in the application of military technology are cited by the authors as being of significance at Kursk. A layered system of antitank mine fields was established that produced unprecedented results. The mine fields were linked throughout the defense network with antitank artillery forces deployed at a rate of twenty-three guns per kilometer of front. In addition to mines and artillery, the defenders at Kursk were supported by tank armies configured and deployed as antitank forces, and by aircraft equipped with new antitank, hollow-charge bombs, which were capable of penetrating the thick armor of the German Tiger and Panther tanks.[89] The result of this strategically sound employment of technology in defense

was victory in one of the largest land battles ever fought. For Kokoshin and Larionov, this result refutes doubts about the capacity of well-planned, prepositioned defenses to stand firm in the face of powerful offensives by enemies utilizing diverse means of attack.[90]

If the positive inference drawn by Kokoshin and Larionov is that premeditated defense can succeed, then the negative inference is that the absence of defensive planning can lead to disaster. The debacle of the summer 1941 campaigns is offered by the authors as a vivid example.[91] According to Kokoshin and Larionov, the major defeats of the early war period were largely the result of a lack of adequate attention to matters of strategic defense. Without an existing plan for strategic defense the Soviet forces were left to improvise in the face of a well-organized and rapidly moving enemy offensive. The combination of factors that proved decisive at Kursk—a premeditated defense plan, the use of natural and artificial barriers, clear intelligence, and the effective integration of diverse technologies—was almost entirely lacking in the Western campaigns of 1941 and 1942.

Kokoshin and Larionov suggest that inadequate attention to strategic defense was not the result of any lack of Soviet military thinking on the subject, but that such thinking had been for the most part ignored by political and military leaders who were "beguiled" by the idea of the necessity of transferring war at its outset to the territory of the enemy through the large-scale offensive actions. This obsession with offense led to a situation in which "the possibility of conducting operations on one's own territory was practically excluded."[92]

The Battle of Kursk cannot be considered in the opinion of Kokoshin and Larionov, as directly analogous to a contemporary Warsaw Pact-NATO relationship based on a mutual acceptance of the principle of defensive defense. The massive scale of the forces involved in that battle, as well as the great significance of Kursk as a classic example of a strategic counteroffensive action does not appear to be consistent with the goals of Soviet military reformers.[93] Indeed, as Michael MccGwire noted at a recent conference on conventional stability in Europe, if the transition to defensive defense means the prospect of future Battles of Kursk, then perhaps we need to return to the drawing board.[94] But the authors assert that the defense plan at Kursk was developed under particular wartime conditions and driven by considerations that differ greatly from those now motivating military planners primarily concerned with the strengthening of strategic stability.[95]

The value of the Kursk experience for contemporary thinkers lies in its illumination of the dialectical relationship between offense and defense. Kokoshin examined the history of this relationship in the second of the three articles.[96] According to Kokoshin, the struggle between offensive and defensive methods and means of warfare has been a persistent feature of military affairs for hundreds of years. This struggle has been characterized throughout history not by any one-sided dominance of one form of warfare over the other, but by a continual shifting of dominance which reflected the action of the basic law of dialectics: the negation of the negation. Negation in military affairs has for the most part been a function of technological development; that is, during periods of apparent offensive dominance, methods and means of defense were developed to offset any advantage, and vice-versa.[97]

The significance of the tension between offense and defense has extended far beyond the battlefields of the world, because *political* estimations of the relationship of the two basic modes of warfare can have a direct impact on the likelihood of war. Belief in the dominance of offense gives political leaders hope that decisive goals can be achieved through the application of military power, and that in these conditions the side striking first gains an important advantage, pushing leaders toward war in crisis situations. Kokoshin points out that there is frequently a substantial gap between leaders' estimations of the offense-defense relationship and the military reality, and cites World War I as a case in which practically all sides were convinced that offense was supreme and that decisive aims could be attained by resolute military action, only to discover that their views were grossly inaccurate. The tragic results of this mistake are well known.[98] Kokoshin repeats in this article much of the criticism of Soviet military thinking in the pre-World War II period that was put forth in the "Kursk" article and adds that the lessons of the early tragedies of the war have not been sufficiently grasped.

> We must note that down to the most recent times, our postwar literature about the military art of the Great Patriotic War has focused on the experience of conducting strategic offensive operations in the second half (1943–1945). Often authors did not even mention that such operations became possible only after costly, tremendous sacrifice, largely on account of fundamental mistakes in the development of military doctrine and strategy, only then making it possible to wrest the strategic initiative away from the perilous enemy. There is no doubt that if the question of strategic defense had been given sufficient attention before the war, the price which we were forced to pay for victory would have been significantly smaller.[99]

It is particularly important, in Kokoshin's view, that these lessons be considered today, because recent developments in the struggle between offensive and defensive methods and means of warfare are making efforts to regulate the process imperative.

According to Kokoshin, the current period is one of both opportunity and risk. Opportunity springs from the fact that the postwar period has witnessed a number of developments in military technology that have served to balance the means of attack and defense.[100] In support of this view, Kokoshin cites the effective application of new antitank and anti-air weapons during the 1973 October War. The use of weapons systems such as mobile antitank and anti-aircraft guided rockets, deployed both with infantry and on helicopters, could lead to a situation in which the combination of tanks and fighter bombers, which dominated the battlefield of World War II, would begin to lose its decisive tactical role. This tendency is strengthened by the fact that these developments have made it possible to use relatively inexpensive weapons to put out of action aircraft and heavily armored vehicles that cost considerably more.[101]

But true to the law of the negation of the negation, Soviet theorists believe that technology now threatens to reverse this situation. Kokoshin asserts that the rapid development of new weapons systems is now underway, which could once again upset the balance between offense and defense and, in the process, destabilize the military confrontation between the Warsaw Pact and NATO. Highly accurate long-range strike systems deployed in "reconnaissance strike complexes," automated command and control systems, and mechanized infantry possessing great mobility could, if left unregulated, combine to produce a situation in which political leaders would once again have to face crises under military conditions that would reward the side striking first.[102] According to Kokoshin, this threat must be countered by effective defensive postures, as well as through measures such as arms control agreements, which could help to ratify and consolidate the dominance of defense over offense.[103]

Kokoshin indicates in this article that the ultimate goal of defensive defense is to make large-scale offensive war impossible, and he cites Clausewitz's statement that "Absolute defense stands in complete contradiction to an understanding of war" as support for this proposition.[104] But the transition to a defensive posture is difficult to achieve in practice. Kokoshin and Larionov appear to have recognized this problem and, in the third and final article in their series, attempt to provide some guidance to those pursuing this complex conceptual matter.[105]

Kokoshin and Larionov set forth four hypothetical variants of war ranging across a continuum from purely offensive to purely defensive. They assert that this construct should be considered an analytical tool. The value of this tool is measured by the thinking it may stimulate on how to move across the offense-defense continuum toward a more stable defense. The first variant, described by the authors as the basis of traditional military thinking, finds each of the sides orienting its military strategies and force structures for immediate offensive or counteroffensive operations at the outset of war. The second variant, identified with the Kursk defense, requires the sides to adopt a defensive posture at the beginning of the conflict, but to prepare for decisive, unlimited counteroffensive operations at some later point. The third variant envisions premeditated defense, but with strictly limited counteroffensive capabilities. The authors define "limited" here as the lack of a capability for carrying the counteroffensive beyond one's own borders. The final variant, pure defense, consists of a premeditated defensive posture that does not possess the "material possibility of conducting offensive or counter offensive operations." The strategic objective in this variant is simply the restoration of the status quo ante.[106]

Kokoshin and Larionov seem to be aware of the considerable problems involved in moving from one end of the offense-defense spectrum to the other, even where hypothetical variants exist to guide the process. One practical step proposed is the categorization of weapons systems according to their offensive and defensive characteristics. Among the main factors determining a weapon's "offensiveness" or "defensiveness" are the speed and range of the weapon, its mobility, the possibility of its multiple-function use, and its defensibility and invulnerability. The authors suggest that it might be possible to achieve agreements on a system by system basis, and in this way take steps toward enhancing stability.[107] But military technology cannot be easily categorized as offensive or defensive. This problem is highlighted when the approach of the Soviet military to defense in war is examined.

In 1985, Deputy Chief of the Soviet General Staff Gareev added an influential voice to the military discussion of strategic defense when he stated in his book on M. V. Frunze that in the future, strategic defense will be one of the most important types of military operations.[108] Gareev's call for increased attention to the problems of strategic defense appears in part to stem from his reading of the Soviet experience in World War II. Gareev, in an argument that Kokoshin and Larionov drew on extensively, asserts that the lack of a well-prepared strategic defensive plan prior to the Nazi invasion led to the early disasters. He stated that the possibility of an enemy attack should have led to the development of carefully elaborated plans for strategic defense "since the repelling of an offensive by superior enemy troops would be impossible incidentally as a merely intermediate task."[109]

Gareev points out that Soviet military planners responsible for staff training considered defense to be a kind of combat activity to which one resorted only temporarily and in secondary sectors in order to set the stage for going over to the offensive.[110] This serious deficiency in Soviet military thinking prior to the war, according to Gareev, was due to an obsession with the (purely offensive) idea of shifting operations to the territory of the enemy at the outset of the conflict.[111] In his view, this had a negative impact not simply on the preparations for the defensive, but on the entire theater of operations which extended deep into Soviet territory.[112]

The main lesson of June 1941 for Gareev appears to be that

> The experience of the war demonstrated that a combination of the offensive as the main type of military action and the defensive is an objective pattern of warfare and, like any pattern, it operates with the force of necessity and it is very dangerous to disregard it.[113]

Gareev's interest in defensive strategies seems to be motivated in part by a concern for stability. In citing the need for a high degree of combat readiness and a capacity to respond to an attack under any conditions, bad as well as good, he points out that the early strategic deployment of forces is not always feasible because of "military-political considerations."[114] Gareev appears to be making the point that such early strategic deployment—the type that would, it seems, be necessary for an offensive operation—would be destabilizing, since

> A mobilization, let alone the entire range of measures related to strategic deployment, has always been considered tantamount to a state of war and it is very difficult to achieve a return from it back to a peacetime status.[115]

But even if one assumes that Gareev's obvious concern with defense as a strategic and operational issue and his apparent interest in stability as a military responsibility are reflections of the concerns and interests of the military as a whole (and it is not clear that they are), there are difficulties in integrating the military's approach to defense with the concept of defensive defense as it has been put forth by civilian security specialists like Kokoshin and Larionov. The problem arises from the fact that the way that the military strategists think about defensive operations is inconsistent with some of the essential requirements of the new concept. In order for defensive defense to be a stabilizing factor, forces must be structured and strategies articulated in ways that will reduce to a minimum concerns that a side may have about the offensive capabilities of its adversary. It is therefore of the utmost importance that the defensive qualities of a force posture be clearly apparent. Soviet military discussions of defense, however, do not yet conform to this requirement.

For example, in contrast to the new interpretation of the Battle of Kursk offered by Kokoshin and Larionov, military analyses tend to focus on the importance of Kursk as an example of a strategic counteroffensive operation.[116] Even though defense is recognized as an essential element in the campaign, it is generally viewed as a temporary expedient whose structure is determined to a significant extent by the requirements of the transition to the offensive. According to a leading military historian, the purpose of the Kursk operation was to

> meet the Hitlerite attack with a well-organized defense, to exhaust and bleed white the enemy, to go over to the counteroffensive, after which, to go over to the general offensive.[117]

These tasks required the employment of preemptive artillery strikes, the creation of powerful second echelon tank groups for use in counteroffensive strikes, the massing of reserves behind defensive lines to support these strikes, and the use of aircraft to carry out deep strikes against enemy reserves. These elements together project an image of "offensive defense."

The fact that weapons such as tanks, rockets, and aircraft appear to retain, in the view of some Soviet military analysts, considerable value as defensive systems points up the problems inherent in creating categories for weapons based on their "defensiveness" or "offensiveness." This in turn illustrates the substantial difficulties facing the analyst or planner responsible for the development of a defensive strategy and force structure that is seen by one's own side as militarily reliable, while at the same time appearing unambiguously non-threatening to the other side. Civilian analysts like Kokoshin and Larionov have not denied that these serious difficulties will persist. They have instead attempted to reveal a way out of this situation by demonstrating through military-historical analysis that defense is not inherently inferior to offense and that steps taken in the direction of a more clearly defensive force posture will not jeopardize Soviet security.

The existence of inconsistencies between civilian and military approaches to defensive warfare should not obscure the fact that the efforts of Soviet analysts to give military reality to reasonable sufficiency through concepts like defensive defense represent an extraordinary effort to reconcile the requirements of military utility with those of military stability. Gorbachev set the agenda for the reassessment of Soviet security policy in his January 1986 statement on international security, and civilian and military specialists have responded vigorously. This process is clearly still underway, and further development will undoubtedly take place, but the conceptual foundation of parity, reasonable sufficiency, and defensive defense will, in all likelihood, continue to serve as a guide.

The recognition that there is a crisis in the economy and that military stability is an increasingly urgent requirement has led to the development of concepts such as reasonable sufficiency and defensive defense. The Soviet security establishment has already traveled a considerable distance toward a new security paradigm. Interdependence instead of rigid opposition, strategic parity instead of military superiority, and a defensive orientation that reaches down to operational and tactical levels instead of blind adherence to offense all suggest that the Cold War paradigm is coming under increasing pressure. But it remains to be seen what impact these conceptual advances will have in practice, and this, of course, is the most important test of the Soviet new thinking.

THE TRANSLATION OF CONCEPTS INTO POLICY

Efforts to reduce the level of arms competition in order to enhance security can take a number of forms. A government can, for example

> choose to shift military expenditures from offensive to defensive weapons in the hope that this will solve the "security dilemma" by increasing its security without decreasing that of its opponent. It can attempt to convince its rival of the futility of increased arms expenditures by announcing that it will henceforth spend neither more nor less on defense than the rival. Or it can propose that the two sides initiate formal arms talks.[118]

The Soviet leadership appears to be employing forms of all three of these strategies, individually or in combination, in its efforts to translate the concepts of the new thinking into policy. Proposed changes in Soviet military doctrine and corresponding adjustments in force levels and weapons procurement and deployment constitute one step in this process.

Military doctrine is defined in the Soviet Union as

> an accepted system of views of a state at a given time on the essence, aims, and possible character of a future war, on the preparation of the country for it, and on the methods of its conduct.[119]

Soviet military doctrine is a comprehensive, overarching body of principles that guides the development of defense policy. It performs this function by analyzing and describing the security problem facing the country, and by prescribing, on the basis of this analysis, a course of action. When security concepts are incorporated into military doctrine in the Soviet Union, they become, in effect, elements of policy. This is because Soviet military doctrine expresses official State and Party views on the nature and requirements of security, and because doctrinal statements serve as the principal instrument for disseminating these views to all levels of the military establishment. Doctrinal developments can be considered an informative, if sometimes complex, guide to Soviet military thinking, because it is unlikely that the Soviet leadership would sacrifice the crucial communication and education functions of doctrine in order to deceive foreign audiences.[120]

At the international level, military doctrine can have a significant impact on stability because, as Barry Posen points out,

> the offensive, defensive, or deterrent quality of a military doctrine . . . affects states' perceptions of, and reactions to, one another. International politics is a competitive arena. Because offensive doctrines appear to make some states more competitive, they encourage the rest to compete even harder. Defensive and deterrent doctrines should tend to produce more benign effects.[121]

This dynamic highlights the fact that military doctrines have international, as well as domestic, functions and consequences. Military doctrines are seen as indicators of intentions. As a result, offensive doctrines are equated with aggressive intent, while defensive doctrines lead to more sanguine interpretations. International stability is thus significantly affected by the military doctrines of states.

Since Gorbachev assumed the position of General Secretary of the Soviet Communist Party, the subject of military doctrine and its impact on security has received considerable attention. At the June 1986 meeting of the Warsaw Pact Political Consultative Committee in Budapest, the participants declared that the maintenance of security in Europe requires that "the military concepts and doctrines of the military alliances must be based on defensive principles."[122] In Budapest, and at subsequent Political Consultative Committee meetings in Berlin in May 1987 and in Warsaw in July 1988, the leadership of the Warsaw Pact continued in the development and refinement of the idea of defensive military doctrines.[123]

At the Budapest meeting, the focus was on how to structure forces in a way that makes surprise offensive action a less feasible military option. Toward this end, the Pact leaders proposed a broad package of arms reductions. These proposals included an initial cut of between 100,000 and

150,000 troops from each side, which would be followed by a further 25 percent reduction in troop strength by the early 1990s that would bring the total decrease in force levels to around 500,000 troops for each alliance. It was proposed that troop cuts be supplemented by reductions in weapons systems considered to be particularly destabilizing, for example, tactical nuclear weapons and tactical air power. The problem of surprise attack was addressed through calls for the creation of zones with limited weapons deployments, and for the development of a strict and reliable verification regime.

The approach taken at Budapest was reaffirmed by the Pact at the 1987 meeting in Berlin. The leaders of the Pact presented a more fully developed concept of their defensive military doctrine and stated that it would serve as the basis for Pact military activities. They explained that the basic precepts of their doctrine, precepts which conditioned the character of their arms reduction proposals, included: a pledge never to initiate military action against others unless attacked first, continued adherence to their commitment to a policy of no first use of nuclear weapons, respect for the territorial integrity of all states and rejection of the use of force as a means of resolving disputes, a commitment to maintain an adequate level and structure of military forces to repel an attack on any of the members of the Warsaw Pact, and to deliver a "crushing strike against the aggressor."[124] It was asserted at the meeting that in fulfilling the requirements of defense the Pact states would adhere strictly to a standard of defensive sufficiency and would not maintain forces beyond the level necessary to meet these requirements.[125]

In reaffirming the results of the two previous Political Consultative Committee meetings at Warsaw in July 1988, the Pact leaders stressed the priority of efforts to reduce radically the military potentials of NATO and the Warsaw Pact in accordance with the principles of defensive defense.[126] They identified three issues of major importance that should be dealt with in the first phase of "Atlantic to the Urals" arms talks: parity at lower levels, the prevention of surprise attack, and a program for an exchange of data and a supporting verification regime. Pursuit of parity at lower levels would involve, they asserted, an elimination of force asymmetries followed by the 25 percent cut proposed earlier, and ultimately, further reductions that would render the forces of both sides strictly defensive in nature. Surprise attack capabilities would be reduced through the creation of reduced weapons zones and confidence-building measures designed to increase transparency in military operations. The agreement of the Pact to take geostrategic factors into consideration in establishing the depth of the reduced weapons zones appears to indicate flexibility and a willingness to pursue compromises. An earlier proposal for symmetrical zones of 150 kilometers on each side had been rejected by NATO leaders as a proposal that would exacerbate the problems they face due to the lack of operational depth in the European theater. The exchange of verifiable data is considered by the Pact leaders to be essential to the success of future negotiation. The experience of the Mutual and Balanced Force Reduction negotiations serves as a vivid reminder of the potential of the data issue as a disrupting force. This experience prompted a proposal at the Warsaw meeting for a verification system based on national technical means of observation and international measures including intrusive, on-site inspection as a means of ameliorating the difficulties inherent in establishing and maintaining a baseline for comparisons.

The doctrinal pronouncements and the comprehensive package of arms proposals put forth at the past three Political Consultative Committee meetings appear to form the Soviet policy agenda in the security realm for the coming years. It can be argued that these developments are largely rhetorical, and that they bear little relation to current policy. But several recent events indicate that changes in the Soviet approach to security have already begun to have an impact on international security relations.

First, a mandate for new conventional arms talks in Europe has been adopted. These "Atlantic to the Urals" negotiations will focus on the concept of stability at lower force levels that has been so prominent in Soviet conceptual and policy discussions. In support of this effort senior Soviet military officials announced, in recent talks with their American counterparts, forthcoming changes in Soviet force structure which will be based on the new defensive doctrine.[127] In addition, progress is continuing in the negotiations for a 50 percent reduction in strategic nuclear arms.

The Soviet reversal of its long-standing opposition to verification through on-site inspection and the apparent desire to move to increase transparency in military activities in Europe cleared the way for the successful completion of the Conference on Confidence and Security-Building Measures and Disarmament in Europe negotiations in September 1986. This agreement is intended to reduce substantially the risk of surprise attack and thus enhance stability in Europe by requiring a forty-two day advance notification of major military activites, providing for mandatory international observation of these activities, constraining unannounced large-scale activities, and by establishing a verification system that includes on-site inspections to ensure compliance with these terms.[128]

The signing of the Treaty On the Elimination of Intermediate and Shorter Range Missiles (INF) in December 1987 provides an illustration of the impact of changing Soviet perspectives on security. Important breakthroughs in the negotiations came when Gorbachev agreed to delink INF from strategic and space arms talks, and when the Soviet Union accepted the U.S. "double zero" proposal. These shifts in the Soviet stance indicate a new flexibility that seems to be grounded in a belief that the issues being addressed are of transcendent significance, and that the treaty enhances Soviet security by contributing to military stability without adversely affecting defense capabilities.[129] Stability has been directly strengthened by the removal of two classes of weapons whose technical characteristics and deployment patterns made them particularly well-suited to first-strike missions, and in an indirect way by the improvement of the political and psychological atmosphere which resulted from the successful negotiations, an improvement which is expected to facilitate progress in forthcoming talks.

Support from the Soviet military for the treaty seems to be based on the view that the elimination of the intermediate and shorter range systems removed "a direct and serious threat to the territory of the USSR and its allies."[130] Indeed, the treaty can be seen as a stage in an evolutionary trend toward the acceptance, *by the military*, of more stable ways of dealing with what has been one of the greatest threats to Soviet security in the postwar period: the existence of European-based nuclear weapons capable of striking targets inside the Soviet Union. Instead of relying on a policy of nuclear preemption, as in the 1960s, or conventional preemption under a powerful nuclear umbrella, as in the 1970s, the Soviet military accepted, in the INF treaty, a political approach through which these highly threatening systems were negotiated away.[131] This case illustrates the emerging potential of arms control as a means of managing the problems of stability *and* defense. Gaining military support for arms control has been compared to persuading "shoemakers . . . to agree on the suppression of shoes," but the emergence of war prevention as a central strategic task for national security has fundamentally altered the manner in which leaders, civilian and military, approach their responsibilities.[132]

Perhaps the most dramatic example of the Soviet effort to translate new thinking into policy was the announcement by Gorbachev at the United Nations in December 1988 of a major unilateral reduction of the Soviet armed forces. Gorbachev told his UN audience that a decision had been made to reduce the armed forces by 500,000 troops worldwide. He said that this unilateral reduction in manpower will be accompanied by substantial cuts in conventional armaments. Of particular note is Gorbachev's statement that the cuts will include six tank divisions (approxiately 5000 tanks and 50,000 troops) currently deployed in the German Democratic Republic, Czechoslovakia, and Hungary. In addition to these units, Gorbachev cited assault landing and crossing troops as other candidates for reductions.[133]

This major Soviet decision appears to have been prompted by considerations of stability and economy. Soviet concern for stability is indicated by Gorbachev's pledge that forces remaining after the reductions will be reorganized in such a way as to make them clearly defensive. If this pledge is fulfilled, stability could indeed be enhanced, particularly if, at an appropriate point, NATO becomes engaged in the process. The economic aspect of the reduction decision is revealed in Gorbachev's discussion of the "economy of disarmament." While asserting that Soviet defense capabilities will be kept at a reasonable and reliable level, Gorbachev said that reductions, unilateral and negotiated, are now possible, and that money and resources released as a result should be funneled into productive areas of society. He stated that the Soviet Union is preparing a plan for the conversion of defense facilities to civilian functions and that such conversions would be iplemented on an experiental basis at two or three Soviet plants in 1989. Although details of the reduction program have yet to be revealed and their impact on Soviet military capabilities determined, the Gorbachev initiative, apparently undertaken in the face of significant military opposition, must be considered an important step in the development of a new approach to the problem of international security.

These doctrinal changes—unilateral reductions, arms proposals, and arms agreements—are consistent with the new conception of security that has been emerging in the Soviet Union under General Secretary Gorbachev. The belief that there is an urgent need to avert war, the stabilizing impact of parity at lower levels and defensive force structures, the possibility of effectively employing political means to strengthen security, the acknowledgment that contemporary conditions have shifted the concept of security away from traditional ideas of national security toward a new notion of common security, and the recognition of economic benefits that can be derived from arms reductions are all important elements of the new approach to security evolving in recent Soviet doctrine and policy. It is too early to come to any conclusion about the long-term impact of the new thinking on policy, but these initial results indicate considerable promise.

The passage to a new paradigm of international security is a long and difficult process, and despite considerable progress, it is not yet completed.

Mutual suspicion persists, and there are serious issues which continue to divide East and West. Force postures, with the notable exception of the systems eliminated by the INF treaty, have not changed noticeably. But it appears that a common ground for discussion of concerns and principles has formed. This common ground is not so much the result of any State policy, but reflects the fundamental changes that have taken place in the postwar world, and as such it is beginning to condition State policy. The value of the Soviet new thinking lies in recognition of these changes, and in the development of concepts and policies in response to them. The fundamental question is whether it will be possible for East and West to be linked together in a relationship that is based on cooperative, political efforts in the pursuit of *common security* instead of continuing the pattern of unilateral military efforts to increase *national security*.

The two elements driving the process of reform in the security realm in the Soviet Union—the military-technological "crisis" and the economic crisis—are also significant factors in the West. These factors compel both sides to seek better ways of preventing war and reducing the military burden on their respective economic systems without lessening real security. This search has resulted in the formulation, at least at the declaratory level, of remarkably similar security objectives by NATO and the Warsaw Pact. For example, the 1986 NATO Brussels Declaration on Conventional Arms Control states that NATO philosophy holds that

> Military forces should exist to prevent war and to ensure self-defense, not for the purpose of initiating aggression and not for purposes of political or military intimidation.[134]

The Declaration states that the objectives should be: stable force levels that eliminate disparities, gradual reductions in which undiminished security for both sides is assured at each stage, the elimination of surprise attack and large-scale offensive capabilities, measures to improve openness and calculability about military behavior, the redressing of regional imbalances, and the establishment of an effective verification regime.[135] These objectives are to be sought through negotiations

> to eliminate existing disparities from the Atlantic to the Urals, and establish conventional stability at lower levels, between the countries whose forces bear most immediately on the essential security relationship in Europe, namely those belonging to the Alliance and the Warsaw Pact.[136]

Although differences between the two sides remain over the specific steps required to strengthen stability, it is nonetheless clear that a considerable degree of agreement exists between NATO and the Warsaw Pact on the character of the problems facing the alliances today.

In explaining the 100 years' peace of 1815–1914, Karl Polanyi cited the decisive importance of a new factor. This factor was "the emergence of an acute peace interest."[137] In the nineteenth century this "peace interest" was international trade and finance, which required international peace. The new approach to security being developed in the Soviet Union might be said to be based on compelling new peace interests—physical survival and economic development. The primary task facing governments, both East and West, is the defense of this peace interest through joint efforts to increase stability while reducing military expenditures. The concepts and principles that are emerging from the Soviet discourse on security can make an important contribution to the international effort to accomplish this task.

Notes

1. Iurii Maksimov, General of the Army, *Trud*, 9 May 1986, in Joint Publications Research Service (JPRS), UMA-86-033, pp. 30–33.
2. Paul Fussell, *The Great War and Modern Memory* (Oxford: Oxford University Press, 1975), p. 79.
3. Robert Jervis, "Security Regimes," in Stephen Krasner, ed., *International Regimes* (Ithaca: Cornell University Press, 1983), p. 175.
4. See Kenneth Waltz, *Theory of International Politics* (Reading, MA: Addison-Wesley, 1979).
5. Raymond Garthoff, *Soviet Strategy in the Nuclear Age* (New York: Praeger, 1958), ch. 2.
6. Ibid., and Nikita Khrushchev, *Khrushchev Remembers*, translated by Strobe Talbott (Boston: Little, Brown, 1970).
7. Raymond Garthoff, *Détente and Confrontation: American-Soviet Relations from Nixon to Reagan* (Washington D.C.: The Brookings Institution, 1985). The emergence of détente is covered in detail.
8. *Pravda*, 19 January 1977.
9. *Pravda*, 7 October 1979.
10. *Pravda*, 28 October 1982.
11. Thomas Kuhn, *The Structure of Scientific Revolutions*, (Chicago: University of Chicago Press, 1970), p. 92.
12. Mikhail S. Gorbachev, *Selected Speeches and Articles*, 2nd ed. (Moscow: Progress, 1987), p. 343.
13. Vladimir Petrovskii, *Bezopastnost v iaderno-kosmicheskuiu eru* (Moscow: Mezhdunarodnie otnosheniia, 1985), p. 83.

14. Ibid., pp. 111–112.
15. Sergei Akhromeev, Marshal of the Soviet Union, "Bolshaia Pobedii," *Krasnaia zvezda* (9 May 1987).
16. A. Musychenko, Major-General, "Comprehensively Develop the Theory of Military Economics," *Military Thought* no. 8 (1971).
17. Friedrich Engels, *Anti-Duhring* (New York: International, 1976), p. 184.
18. M. M. Kiryan, Lieutenant-General, *Istoriia voennovo iskusstva* (Moscow: Voenizdat, 1986), p. 98.
19. Alexi Kosygin in his speech to the 23rd Party Congress, as cited approvingly by Marshal Malinovski in "The Terrible Lesson of History," *Military Thought* no. 6 (1966).
20. Harry Gelman, *The Brezhnev Politburo and the Decline of Détente* (Ithaca: Cornell University Press, 1984), p. 191.
21. Voenno-istoricheskii zhurnal, no. 4 1986, in JPRS, UMA-86-048.
22. V. A. Zubkov, Colonel, *Voenno-istoricheskii zhurnal* no. 3 (March 1986) in JPRS, UMA-86-047, pp. 1–6.
23. Ibid.
24. Timothy Colton, *The Dilemma of Reform in the Soviet Union* (New York: Council on Foreign Relations, 1984), p. 57.
25. Foreign Broadcast Information Service Daily Report: *Soviet Union* (FBIS-Sov), 20 August 1987, p. H2.
26. Admiral Sorokin in FBIS-Sov, 1 July 1987, p. V1 and the 4 February 1986 *Krasnaia zvezda* editorial, "To Learn Thriftiness," in JPRS UMA-86-025, pp. 1–3.
27. M. A. Gareev, Colonel-General, *M. V. Frunze: Voennii Teoretik* (Moscow: Voenizdat, 1985), p. 425.
28. Mikhail S. Gorbachev, "October and Perestroika: The Revolution Continues," 2 November 1987, released by the Soviet Embassy Information Department, 4 November 1987, p. 43.
29. Gorbachev, *Selected Speeches and Articles*, pp. 419–420.
30. V. Zhurkin, S. Karaganov, and A. Kortunov, *Kommunist* no. 1 (1988), p. 50.
31. L. Semeiko, "Vmesto gor oruzhiia," *Izvestiia*, 13 August 1987, p. 5.
32. FBIS-Sov, 3 February 1988, p. 5.
33. Ibid.
34. Ibid.
35. A. Dobrynin, "Za beziadernii mir, navstrechi XXI veku," *Kommunist* no. 9 (1986), p. 29.
36. Ibid.
37. *The New York Times*, 5 February 1986, p. A13.
38. Ibid.
39. A. Kokoshin and A. Kortunov, "Stabilnost i peremeni v mezhdunarodnikh otnosheniiakh," *SShA: ekonomika, politika, ideologiia* no. 8 (1987); Zhurkin, Karaganov, and Kortunov, "O razumnou dostatochnosti," *SShA: ekonomika,*

politika, ideologiia no. 12 (1987); and Semeiko p. 5. Sufficiency has an economic aspect and a military stability aspect. The former has been addressed here.

40. Semeiko, p. 5.
41. Zhurkin, Karaganov, and Kortunov, p. 13.
42. Kokoshin and Kortunov, P. XX.
43. Semeiko; Kokoshin and Kortunov
44. Gorbachev, statement at the April 1985 Central Committee Plenum, *Selected Speeches and Articles*, p. 30.
45. N. V. Ogarkov, Marshal, "Always in Readiness to Defend the Homeland," *United States Air Force*, Selected Translations nos. 9 and 10, 1982, p. 317.
46. Ibid., p. 316.
47. Gorbachev, "October and Perestroika," p. 43.
48. D. T. Yazov, Army General, in FBIS-Sov, 23 February 1988, p. 69.
49. V. Nazarenko, Colonel, "Na puti k mandati," *Krasnaia zvezda* (2 March 1988).
50. Yazov, p. 69; see also Nazarenko, ibid.
51. V. Zhurkin cited in A. Arbatov, A. Vasilev, and A. Kokoshin, "Iadernoe oruzhie i strategishchekaia stabilnost," *SShA: ekonomika, politika, ideologiia* no. 9 (1987): p. 3.
52. Gareev, Colonel General, "A Great Victory in the Name of Peace and Progress," *Partinaia zhizn* no. 9 (May 1986), in JPRS, UMA-86-050, pp. 1–8.
53. *Voennii Entsiklopedicheskii Slovar* (Moscow: Voenizdat, 1986), p. 712.
54. G. A. Trofimenko, "Novie realnost i novoe mishlenie," *SShA: ekonomika, politika, ideologiia* no. 2 (1987), p. 4.
55. Michael Howard, *Clausewitz* (Oxford: Oxford University Press, 1983), p. 70.
56. Ibid. (emphasis in original).
57. A. A. Kokoshin, "Razvitie voennovo dela i sokrashchennikh sil i obichnikh vooruzhenii," *Mirovaia Ekonomika i Mezhdunarodniie Otnosheniia* (MEMO), no. 1 (1988): p. 20.
58. G. Mukhin, Colonel, "Chemu otdat prioritet," *Krasnaia zvezda*, (7 June 1988).
59. Ogarkov, *Istoriia uchit bditelnost*, (Moscow: Voenizdat, 1985), p. 85.
60. Ibid. (emphasis added).
61. Dimitri Volkogonov, "Questions of Theory: War and Peace in the Nuclear Age," *Pravda*, 30 August 1985, in JPRS, UMA-85-059, pp. 3–8.
62. Ibid.
63. Petrovskii, p. 84.
64. Zhurkin, et al., "O razumnou dostatochnosti," p. 13.
65. *Krasnaia zvezda*, 15 January 1988.
66. Petrovskii, p. 86.
67. Zhurkin, et al., "O razumnou dostatochnosti," p. 11.

68. Gorbachev, 15 January 1986, statement on international security, *The New York Times*, 5 February 1986, p. A13.
69. Akhromeev, "Bolshaia pobedii," *Krasnaia zvezda*, 9 May 1987.
70. Semeiko, p. 5.
71. Zhurkin, Karaganov, and Kortunov, "Vizozi bezopastnost-starie i novie," *Kommunist* no. 1 (1988), p. 47.
72. Kokoshin and Kortunov, pp. 10–12.
73. Semeiko, p. 13.
74. Kokoshin, p. 20.
75. "Na puti k beziadernomu miru," *Krasnaia zvezda*, (20 December 1987).
76. Zhurkin, et al., "Vizozi," p. 43.
77. Ibid., pp. 43–47.
78. Ibid., p. 46.
79. Michael MccGwire, "Update: Soviet Military Objectives," *World Policy Journal* (Fall 1987), pp. 726–727.
80. Ibid.
81. Ibid.
82. Yazov, "Voennaia doktrina Varshavskovo Dogovora-doktrina 'zashchiti mira i sotialisma," *Pravda*, 27 July 1987.
83. Kokoshin, p. 29.
84. Christopher Donnelly, "Soviet Operational Concepts in the 1980s," in European Security Study, *Strengthening Conventional Deterrence*, (Boulder, CO: Westview Press, 1985).
85. Russell F. Weigley, *The American Way of War: A History of United States Military Strategy and Policy*, (New York: Macmillan, 1974), p. 182.
86. A. Kokoshin and V. Larionov, "Kurskaia bitva v cvete sovremennou doktrinii," *MEMO* no. 8 (August 1987), pp. 32–33.
87. Kokoshin and Larionov, Kokoshin, "Razvitie," Kokoshin and Larionov, "Protivostoianie sil obshevo naznacheniia v kontekste obespecheniia strategiskii stabilnost," *MEMO* no. 6 (1988).
88. Kokoshin and Larionov, "Kurskaia bitva," p. 36.
89. Ibid., pp. 37–39.
90. Ibid., p. 39.
91. Ibid., p. 37.
92. Ibid.
93. The 1986 *Voennii entsiklopedicheskii slovar* entry on Kursk divides the 1943 battle into two distinct phases: the defensive operation of 5–23 July, and the offensive action of 12 July – 23 August (p. 385).
94. Michael MccGwire, at the American Committee on U.S.- Soviet Relations "Conference on Alternative U.S. and Soviet Conventional Defensive Postures," Washington, D.C., 19 May 1988.
95. Kokoshin and Larionov, "Kurskaia bitva," p. 39.

96. Kokoshin, "Razvitie."
97. Ibid., p. 21.
98. Ibid., pp. 21–22.
99. Ibid., p. 24.
100. Ibid., p. 25. Kokoshin cites the estimation of Marshal Ogarkov here.
101. Ibid., pp. 26–27.
102. Ibid., pp. 27–29.
103. Ibid., pp. 29–30.
104. Ibid., p. 30.
105. Kokoshin and Larionov, "Protivostoinie."
106. Ibid.
107. Ibid., pp. 29–30.
108. Gareev, *M. V. Frunze*.
109. Ibid., p. 230.
110. Ibid.
111. Ibid., p. 231; see also V. N. Lobov, Colonel-General, "Strategia pobedii," *Voenno-istoricheskii zhurnal* no. 6 (1988): pp. 5–6.
112. Gareev, *M. V. Frunze*, p. 231.
113. Ibid.
114. Ibid., p. 242.
115. Ibid.
116. S. Ivanov, Army General, "The Influence of the Battle of Kursk on the Development of Strategy and Operations," *Military Thought* no. 1 (1969); Kiryan, *Istoriia voennovo iskutstva*, pp. 209–219; and John Erickson, *The Road to Berlin* (Boulder, CO: Westview Press, 1983), pp. 97–122.
117. Krikunov, Colonel and Matveev, Colonel, "Iz opita armeiskikh oboronitelnikh operatsii," *Voeeno-istoricheskii zhurnal* no. 2 (1988), pp. 67–75; and on the role of tanks, see the review article by Marshal O. Losik, "Issledovanie opita tankovikh armii," *Krasnaia zvezda*, 8 March 1988.
118. George Downs, David Rocke, and Randolph Siverson, "Arms Races and Cooperation," *World Politics* (October 1985): p. 118.
119. *Voennii entsiklopedicheskii slovar*, p. 240.
120. *Soviet Strategy in the Nuclear Age*, p. 270. Raymond Garthoff has maintained for many years that open doctrinal writings are important, reliable sources of information.
121. Barry Posen, *The Sources of Military Doctrine* (Ithaca: Cornell University Press, 1984), p. 16.
122. Documents of the Meeting of the Political Consultative Committee of the Member States of the Warsaw Treaty Organization, Budapest, 10–11 June 1986 (Moscow: Novosti Press, 1986), p. 11.
123. Budapest documents, ibid.; the documents of the Berlin meeting are cited here

as they were published in *Pravda*, 30 May 1987, and the Warsaw documents as they were published in *Krasnaia zvezda*, 17 July 1988.

124. Berlin documents.
125. Ibid.
126. Warsaw documents.
127. Walter Pincus, "Soviet Pledges Military Changes," *Washington Post*, 13 July 1988, p. A13.
128. *Arms Control Today*, November 1986.
129. The testimony of Soviet leaders at the 9 February 1988 INF Ratification committee meeting, "Ot konfrontatsii k mirhomu sosushchestvovaniiu," *Krasnaia zvezda*, 10 February 1988.
130. The discussion with Colonel-General Chervov in *Krasnaia zvezda*, 19 December 1987. It can also be argued that Soviet military support for the INF Treaty was based above all on a belief that its provisions make it more likely that the Warsaw Pact could fight and win a war if one should break out.
131. Stephen Meyer, "Soviet Theatre Nuclear Forces," Adelphi Papers nos. 187 and 188, International Institute for Strategic Studies, London, Winter 1983–84 on the development of Soviet military policy in the 1960s and 1970s; Michael MccGwire, *Military Objectives in Soviet Foreign Policy* (Washington, D.C.: The Brookings Institution, 1987).
132. Alfred Vagts, *A History of Militarism* (New York: Meridian Books, 1959), p. 400.
133. The *New York Times*, 8 December 1988, p. A16 for excerpts from Gorbachev's speech.
134. "Documentation," in *NATO Review*, (December 1986), p. 28.
135. Ibid.
136. Ibid.
137. Karl Polyani, *The Great Transformation: The Political and Economic Origins of Our Time* (Boston: Beacon Press, 1957), p. 7.

7 CONCLUSIONS

THE COLD WAR HAS LOST ITS RELEVANCE

George W. Ball

A century and a half have passed since that remarkable young Frenchman, Count Alexis de Tocqueville, made the now familiar observation that there are "two great nations in the world which seem to tend toward the same end, although they started from different points. I allude," he wrote, "to the Russians and the Americans."

> Both of them have grown up unnoticed; and while the attention of mankind was directed elsewhere, they have suddenly assumed a most prominent place among nations; and the world learned of their greatness at almost the same time. All other nations seem to have nearly reached their natural limits, and only to be charged with the maintenance of their power . . . but these are proceeding with ease and celerity along a path to which the human eye can assign no term.

It was an extraordinary prescient comment for a French aristocrat who at the age of twenty-six had visited our country for less than a year and a half. Nor were his conclusions any less provocative, for, of the two nations Tocqueville wrote:

> Their starting point is different, and their courses are not the same; yet each of them seems to be marked out by the will of Heaven to sway the destinies of half the globe.

He was, of course, referring to the Tsarist Empire, yet ever since 1835 when Tocqueville published his seminal work, the implications of that comment have remained in the murky attic of our thinking regarding Russia and, more recently, the Soviet Union. If America and Russia could each exercise a dominant influence over half the globe, then, by combining their efforts and objectives, could not America and the USSR keep the peace throughout the world? But so long as they seem unable to agree on common objectives and continue to live in that state of mutual tension and antagonism known as the Cold War that question must remain rhetorical.

Yet today, to a greater extent than ever before, many informed and thoughtful people on both sides of the Iron Curtain are beginning to ask themselves: "Need the Cold War always persist? Must we accept it as a permanent condition that poisons world politics and forces men and women to concentrate their energies on the infliction of death rather than the improvement of life?"

To be sure, a state of rivalry between the prevailing great powers is a phenomenon as old as time, and no doubt it will continue, but what, of course, gives special menace to the Cold War is the existence of obscenely destructive nuclear arsenals on both sides. That development could obviously not have been foreseen by Tocqueville or by the leaders of the then major nations who, from the Napoleonic era to 1914, sought to keep the peace by combining their efforts in the name of the Concert of Europe.

Particularly after the shock of Sputnik, the ghastly meaning of the bombs dropped on Hiroshima and Nagasaki, reinforced by the Chernobyl disaster, led perceptive men and women in both America and the Soviet Union to recognize the imperative need to avoid a major conflict between the two nuclear superpowers. Although America and the Soviet Union might continue to compete in nonstrategic areas of the world, they must avoid direct conflict in any area of strategic importance so great that their quarrel might lead to a nuclear escalation.

But as the two sides built their nuclear arsenals and both developed intercontinental missiles capable of delivering those warheads across the wide ocean, the policy of the Western allies came more and more to be shaped by the sullen threat of the Soviet menace. That menace drove our political leaders into inflexible and sterile patterns of thought. Meanwhile, the Cold War was marked by periodic crises, such as over Berlin and over missiles in Cuba; yet on each occasion when there was even desultory talk of a direct superpower clash, both sides averted cataclysmic actions by preventing the competition of their interests from escalating too far.

That need seemed well-understood even though the early years of the Reagan administration were marked by an increasingly strident rhetoric that tended to give respectability to talk of Armageddon as more than a Biblical place name. There were serious discussions regarding the utility of nuclear warheads as instruments for warfighting; military leaders and even civilian cabinet members straight-facedly debated limited nuclear conflicts as though they were a feasible option; and some even argued that if the United States were to invest sufficient effort and resources it might "win" a nuclear war.

Politicians and the public have short attention spans, and such talk had only a transient effect. Thus, even today one can hardly conceive of a situation in which either superpower would deliberately launch a nuclear attack against the other or pursue an adventure likely to trigger a nuclear response.

Both experience and logic should make clear that the practice of designing foreign policy almost exclusively in Cold War terms is no longer obligatory or even useful. Indeed, there is a growing body of opinion that the nuclear standoff has thus effectively destroyed the threat of another world war—a view that should drastically change the shape and emphasis of our foreign policy. Moreover—and this point should not be overlooked—the conclusion that the Cold War has lost its relevance does not depend either on the continuance in power of Mr. Gorbachev or on the advent of a similar sensible Soviet leader. It seems almost certain that whoever may succeed Gorbachev will be equally wary of actions that might well produce a superpower clash, not because of that leader's special prudence or statesmanship but simply because he will react to the universal reflex of self-preservation. Even Hitler, mad as he was, rejected the use of Nazi supplies of poison gas because he had a whiff of it in World War I and understood that, if the Germans were to initiate its use, the Allies could envelop Germany in a gas cloud with cataclysmic effect.

All this does not suggest, of course, that the Soviet Union and the United States are about to cease their active rivalry; almost certainly their interests may conflict—particularly in areas in the Third World as they have in Afghanistan, certain parts of Africa, and even Nicaragua. But, in view of the compulsion each side has shown, repeatedly, to avoid a head-on clash, those problems should be amenable to solution through diplomatic rather than military means.

It will not be easy for America to conform its foreign policy to the recognition that the Cold War is effectively ended, since, among other reasons, many political leaders, including President Reagan himself, formed their view of the Cold War in the vicious days of Iosif Stalin and have never since altered that frozen impression, in spite of the fact that President Reagan has, in the last year of his administration, displayed a marked change at least in the tone and manner of his relations with the Soviets.

Nevertheless, in spite of the President's recent conversion, the rhetoric emanating from Washington still often reminds me of a poignant news item that periodically appeared in the American press as late as the 1970s—the report of a lonely Japanese soldier discovered hiding in a cave on one of the more remote Pacific Islands. He was still cowering in fear of discovery for no one had ever come by to tell him that World War II had long been over.

Just as the Japanese soldier was kept in ignorance is it not possible to assume that no one has yet penetrated the cavernous chancelleries on both sides of the Iron Curtain to tell the harassed leaders that the Cold War is effectively ended? And, if that be so, should we not now revise our thinking in consonance with a new set of realities?

Such a revision will certainly not be easy. Our nuclear scholastics and hardened communist-bashers may not be the only group to find the new realities hard to accept; even our most flexible-minded political leaders may find difficulty in adjusting to the thought of intellectual liberation and be appalled at the prospect of breaking their well-entrenched habit of regarding the Cold War as the fundamental framework in which policy must be formulated. I have learned from my own experience that, in shaping almost any aspect of foreign policy, trained American diplomats, by conditioned reflex, automatically seek the answer by first asking the elementary question: how much will the initiative in question advance or discourage the expansion of Soviet interests? The officials at the top of our government will have to provide firm directives to persuade our foreign policy bureaucrats to abandon a shibboleth that has served them so long as a device to avoid hard thought and complex decisions.

There is thus a built-in fear of the proposition I am urging: fear not merely that its underlying assumption may be mistaken, but fear also of having to face the perplexing problems that flow from the greater freedom of choice permitted in the new environment. Our statesmen will not find it easy to break old habits and carefully craft new policies without the current simplifying Cold War guidelines.

But if the new environment offers increased complexity it for the first time assures access to overwhelming opportunities—provided we are sufficiently alert and incisive to exploit them. The most important is that we should finally feel free to make common cause with the Soviets in developing solutions to problems that affect not only our two countries but the welfare and future of the world.

By fully exploiting the nuclear standoff, we should still move forward with increased speed and confidence to reduce the superpowers' hypertrophied nuclear arsenals—a prospect facilitated by the fact that we will have far greater latitude in the scope of our bargaining. America's most prudent course, as I see it, is not to seek either to abolish all nuclear weapons or to try to build a "Star Wars" shield that would render such weapons, in President Reagan's words, "impotent and obsolete."

Neither option makes sense. The nuclear weapon exists and, so long as humanity continues to remember its technology and has access to essential raw materials, new weapons can always be built. Nor can we afford the dubious alternative of a fabulously expensive device that might—if everything worked perfectly—theoretically destroy nuclear weapons in midflight. What it would be more likely to destroy is the American economy. Already burdened with debts at home and abroad, our country is in no position to underwrite what would, at a minimum, be a 4 trillion dollar effort offering only slight chances for even limited success.

Contrary to pious press disclaimers, except for President Reagan himself, the most that even the extreme zealots of the Strategic Defense Initiative have ever hoped to accomplish—and this has now been confirmed by the Pentagon—is to deploy a defensive system designed not to protect America's civilian population but to shield merely a fraction of its land-based nuclear launchers. That, they contend, should reduce the percentage of Soviet missiles able to get through to target. But, since their advocacy is driven more by passion than logic, even the fiercest proponents of the SDI shrug off the obvious objection that such a system would merely compel the adversary to multiply the number of its offensive missiles—or, in other words, would provide an incentive to escalation. At the same time, they scornfully dismiss any thought that it might be converted to deadly offensive uses—a prospect which acutely worries Moscow.

The issue of the SDI is more academic than real, because the project seems highly likely to fail either for technical or financial reasons. Our government would be far better advised to bargain it away for some useful Soviet concession than to remain beleaguered in an ideological bunker which time will almost certainly overrun. Instead of trying to abolish all nuclear weapons, we should concentrate on maintaining on both sides the least possible number to provide reasonable deterrence, which, so the experts generally admit, is only a fraction of our current arsenal.

In contemplating the possibilities offered by this new sense of affairs, I find it difficult not to indulge fantasies. Is it not at least possible that the nuclear standoff may mark the end of major wars between powerfully armed great powers and that the world can at long last look forward to facing its problems without the distracting consciousness of an overhanging sword of Damocles?

There are many recent developments that suggest how times seem to be changing—of which the most important are signs that the Soviet Union is anxious to reduce its revolutionary commitments abroad. That is reflected in its diminished aid to Nicaragua, its withdrawal from Afghanistan, its reduced role in Angola, Ethiopia, and South Yemen, its gestures of civility toward Israel, and its pressure on Syria and the PLO to adopt a more accommodating stance regarding Middle East peace negotiations.

Yet one need not be bemused by apocalyptic prophecy to recognize the implications of the Cold War's fading relevance. Even if habit disguised as caution requires us to thrust aside our more spacious hopes, we can tentatively make common cause with the Soviet Union with respect to those areas where there appears to be an overlap in the interests of our two countries. By closely consulting, America and the Soviet Union may be able to develop parallel courses of action and together exploit the promise of a new order.

Of course, such common action must be approached with sensitivity; otherwise, leaders of other nations might regard it as a cabal of the superpowers to impose their condominium on poorer and weaker nations. So, to avoid inciting such suspicions, we should, wherever possible, take pains to envelope the agreed action in an institutional context, so that our common action appears not as a connivance of the superpowers, but rather as an initiative of all peoples acting together under the reassuring flag of the United Nations.

These days it is easy to forget that, when its framers drafted the United Nations Charter against the background of experience with the Concert of Europe and the League of Nations, they centered the peacemaking function in the Security Council. They empowered that body to adopt resolutions binding on all members and made those resolutions enforceable through the imposition of a specified range of sanctions, not excluding military action.

But, unfortunately, this machinery was never tested, for, soon after the UN Charter was adopted, the emerging Cold War contest between the Soviets and West undercut the basic assumption that the great powers would be able to make common cause; and for four decades thereafter Cold War calculus has led each superpower to use its veto to block initiatives by the other, thus rendering the Security Council of only marginal utility.

Confronted with the Council's impotence, our government mindlessly yielded to the easy option of preempting for itself the role of world policeman, while at the same time trying assiduously to exclude the Soviet presence and influence from large portions of the world.

The result was easily predictable. By letting itself be represented as what some congressmen sanctimoniously called the "conscience of the world," America has by its appearance of presumptuous imperialism created antagonism and resentment. Such resentment might have been avoided—or at least substantially mitigated—had our actions and policies been invariably fair and evenhanded, based on considerations more uplifting than mere anti-communism combined with a slavish support of a variety of despotic regimes whose only discernible distinction was that they were not Russian henchmen. But we all too often adopted a posture of self-righteous unilateralism even when our actions violated Thomas Jefferson's commandment that we should show "a decent respect for the opinions of mankind."

It is time to put aside our unilateral posturing and begin once again to use the United Nations in the manner its framers originally intended. Even for our own countrymen such an abrupt change in our national conduct would pose a considerable challenge but it would also open vast new possibilities. We Americans have become so addicted to unilateralism that the practice of resorting to the United Nations would require a major reorientation in our thinking and a substantial reconsideration of our strategy. It is a truism of physiology that when a human organ ceases to fulfill its intended function, it tends to atrophy, and, because the East-West conflict has for four decades effectively paralyzed the principal organ of the United Nations—the Security Council—that whole institution has fallen into disrepute among wide sectors of American opinion.

But that does not mean, as many academic critics solemnly assert, that the Wilsonian concept of institutionalized diplomacy is unworkable. It means rather that it has never been tried under conditions where it could possibly be effective; first, because the United States failed to ratify the League of Nations and, second, because the Cold War has, up to now, precluded the superpowers from making the common cause. Now, by finding areas of common interest with the Soviet Union—creating, as it were, an alliance of adversaries or concert of the powerful—we at last have the chance to test Wilsonian principles pragmatically. It is important that we do so, for, if we neglect that chance, America will continue to pursue unilateral policies at high cost, great danger and with dubious results.

When the United States undertakes an initiative by itself rather than through an international institution we limit rather than expand our freedom of maneuver while running the grave risk of widening the conflict. Once we commit our prestige to the achievement of even a discrete, well-defined and temporary objective and we either fail in our effort or find it too costly to pursue, we cannot reverse course for fear that world opinion will interpret such action as a failure of our national will. By taking much the same measures through the United Nations, however, we could denationalize the operation, diminish its hazardous implications, and preserve freedom of maneuver.

I recognize that one explanation for the United States' addiction to unilateralism is our national shortage of patience and the presumptuous tendency of inexperienced leaders of a large, rich nation to adopt the simplest solution which, in practical terms, means arrogating to America the responsibility for world peacekeeping while discouraging interference from other countries — even from those which may have equal interests in the area.

Unpopularity is not the only price America is paying for its dogged folly in going it alone. Within recent memory there have been at least two cases in the Middle East where our country could have saved itself anguish and injury by agreeing with the Kremlin on common action through the Security Council.

One is America's decision to commit its marines to Lebanon in 1982; the second is its more recent action in deploying its national naval units to the Persian Gulf.

During the 1982 Israeli invasion of Lebanon, our negotiator Ambassador Habib was seeking the establishment of a peacekeeping force to maintain order while the PLO leaders complied with Israel's demarche to withdraw. But, instead of agreeing to a United Nations force, as the Soviet Union was proposing and key members of Congress were suggesting, the Administration yielded to Israeli pressure and committed a unit of American marines to an improvised peacekeeping force.

At that time I urged the Senate Foreign Relations Committee not to commit American troops, pointing out that "We would imprudently hazard the lives of our marines to commit them to an area where anti-Americanism is a dominating sentiment." And I added further that although America might facilitate the removal of the PLO leaders, there would still "be plenty of frustrated Palestinians left behind and they may be driven to desperate acts of terrorism by the atmosphere of death and violence that has enveloped the city." If, therefore, there must be some third party intervention, I contended: "Let the troops of other nations undertake it — young men who are not Americans and hence not the natural targets for assassins." But the Administration ignored this cautionary counsel and the tragic denouement is still painfully remembered; on 23 October 1983 the Beirut Embassy was destroyed by a truck bomb that killed 239 Americans.

A second opportunity for common action through the Security Council appeared more recently in connection with fighting in the Persian Gulf where each superpower had expressed its willingness to protect a limited number of Kuwaiti tankers. Here again, the Soviet Union called for the creation of a United Nations naval force to maintain the traditional right of free passage through Gulf waters, but once more our government rejected that sensible proposal.

Surprisingly few have noticed that the effort to exclude the Soviets from the Middle East runs counter to the teachings of history, which tells us that no single outside nation has ever been able to maintain unilateral hegemony in the Middle East for more than a brief period. Sooner or later we will discover—in spite of our national penchant for turning a blind eye towards history—that America will have no more luck trying to exclude both the Soviet Union and our Western European allies from active participation in Middle East politics than have its predecessors in the past.

Thus, I do not advocate that the United States should abandon its policy of "containment," but rather that we should redefine that term to accord with current circumstances. When Ambassador George Kennan first put forward the "containment" concept in 1946, the communist parties, both in France and Italy, were, as he put it, "under the total control of the Stalin regime in Moscow." Under those circumstances he feared that Moscow might succeed "in taking over one or more of the Western countries or Japan by ideological-political intrigue and penetration." But, except in the Warsaw Pact nations, local communist parties are now almost everywhere in a wretched state of decline and Moscow has so far shown no willingness (except in its now failed adventure in Afghanistan) to risk larger conflict by utilizing its own armed forces beyond the territories of the Warsaw Pact system.

Once there is a general understanding that the Cold War has lost its relevance, we Americans should be able to concentrate on the major problems haunting humanity, such as the emerging phenomenon of a fanatical and widely destructive Shiite fundamentalism (often accompanied by terrorism), a worldwide population crisis, a rapid depletion of the world's nonrenewable energy resources, a wasteful Third World arms race, the depletion of the ozone layer, and the increase and spread of acid rain coupled with a threatened water shortage—problems which, if left unresolved, could lead to a rapid and catastrophic deterioration of the earth as a support system for humanity.

Meanwhile, we must keep closely in touch with the Soviet leadership in order to play a restraining role in dealing with the explosive forces that could be let loose by an abrupt change in Europe's political geography, as Moscow's grip over Eastern Europe progressively relaxes and historic forces of irredentism and ethnic hatred are unleashed within the Soviet Bloc and even within the boundaries of the Soviet Union itself.

The agenda for the years ahead will be crowded. We must push forward with our efforts to bring about a major reduction in—though not the complete abolition of—nuclear weapons (for the nuclear standoff does not require more than a fraction of the now overblown arsenals on both sides). At the same time, we should accept the Soviets' willingness to negotiate and press hard to conclude the agreements that now seem possible to scale down substantially both sides' conventional arsenals. Such discussions are indispensable, it seems to me, not merely to reduce the number of instruments of destruction in the world, but, equally important, to sustain the momentum of conversations between the superpowers that can enable us to avoid crises and to resolve them peacefully should they occur.

Finally, if I am right in my thesis that the Cold War has lost its relevance and if we show skill and diligence in developing areas of common interest with the Soviets, we may finally realize—or at least test—the Wilsonian ideal, by seeking for the first time to exploit the full potential of the United Nations and thus to render it, as its founders intended, the central instrument for maintaining the world's peace and stability.

THE MORE WE KNOW

William E. Colby

"Mr. General Secretary, the more we know about each other, the safer we all will be," I said to Leonid Brezhnev in 1973 when President Nixon presented me to him as the new CIA chief. I hoped he would agree, but

after the translation he turned without comment to the next person in the receiving line in the White House.

General Secretary Gorbachev might agree with the comment today, although he would surely have some reservations. Despite *glasnost*, the Soviet Union will probably never be a totally open society (and of course the U.S. also tries to keep some secrets, albeit not too effectively). But the key to "knowing" about another society is more than information, it is also understanding what the information means.

For centuries, all nations have endeavored to learn what they need about other nations from which they perceive a threat. In addition to depending on their diplomats and publicly available information from travellers and the media, they have for centuries organized intelligence services to conduct the kinds of secret operations that will tell them what is transpiring within another nation's decision-making system; the United States and the USSR are no exceptions to this process. They have also used such open means as they could to collect information about the other nation, listen to what it tells its own people by reading its press and recording its radio programs, and seek the assistance of friendly foreigners and allies.

Even before Mr. Gorbachev took office, there have been steps taken to improve the knowledge of each of the two superpowers about the other. In the United States, the turn to technology to overcome Soviet secretiveness revolutionized American intelligence. The first major step in this direction was taken when the U-2 first overflew the vastnesses of the Soviet Union from which foreign information gathering had been excluded for centuries. When that aircraft was shot down, the United States turned to other technologies to accomplish the necessary mission that we know what types of weapons the Soviets possess and are developing. Space opened a new dimension of capability, and electronics, photography, and acoustics all have provided precise information on subjects in the USSR beyond imagination only a few years ago. The result can be seen in examples such as the fact that the CIA was the first to issue accurate maps of the Soviet Union, correctly locating whole cities and rivers that had been carefully falsified on Soviet public maps or precisely delineating the streets and major buildings of Moscow itself in a fashion never before known to Soviet citizens. The CIA's economists and order of battle specialists were able to testify to Congress on the Soviet defense budget with a comprehensiveness and precision not available to senior Soviet officials who found these expenditures so dispersed within the many elements of the Soviet budget that no full description of them was possible. Gorbachev has only now begun to fill this information gap.

The Soviet Union has also developed its own technologies to assist their military to cover those aspects of American forces which are not known to the public, such as the locations of major American naval forces. But perhaps more important, probably under the stimulus of Iurii Andropov while he headed the KGB, it developed a series of serious area research institutes such as the Institute for the Study of the USA and Canada. Adapting the pattern of the CIA's analytical staffs and the many other centers of research among the universities and think tanks of America, these institutes devoted themselves to serious study of the mass of information available on the free U.S. society in order to understand it. They also recruited and trained the "best and the brightest" of Soviet society to learn the languages, the cultures and the manners of the West, and particularly the United States, rather than only to explain developments there according to the dogma of Marxism-Leninism.

In addition to these actions by each side on its own, there have been a number of conscious steps taken in collaboration by the two powers in recognition of the needs of each for certain types of information to improve confidence against surprise moves by the other or to avoid dangerous suspicions and confrontations. Visiting teams of attachés from NATO now attend Warsaw Pact maneuvers, as do WP attachés to NATO maneuvers. Regular conferences take place between the United States and the Soviet navies, to discuss the actions of these navies which can produce "incidents at sea" between them, trying to end the unwise temptation of some destroyer captains to play "chicken" by holding to collision courses until the last possible moment. The "hotline" between Moscow and Washington has been upgraded to ensure rapid communication between the heads of the two governments during tensions and crises, replacing suspicions by explanations of what appear to be signals of hostile intent. Arms control agreements require declarations of the forces of each side covered by them (SALT II, INF), arrangements for inspection visits (INF, Peaceful Uses, Threshold Test Ban), and joint commissions to discuss and resolve questions of compliance (ABM, SALT I, INF), all designed to provide additional reassuring information to the other side that the agreement is being complied with.

These various actions have completely changed the knowledge by the two powers of what *is*, but they only partially assist in the even more important question of what *will be*, that is, the intentions of the other nation about the future. This has always been such a difficult challenge that good generals of many nations have based their plans on their potential adversary's capabilities, that is, what he *could do*, rather than risk being fatally wrong on what he *will do*.

To a degree, this question can be answered by what the adversary *did do* in the past, but this is not at all reliable, as the United States discovered when its analysts noted in 1962 that the USSR had never deployed nuclear weapons outside the Soviet Union and concluded that they would never do so, only to be surprised by their appearance in Cuba. Such changes can come from changes of policy stemming from internal political developments (especially in the United States) or be the result of deliberate deception or secrecy. And fear of being fooled by deceptions can even create doubts that an apparent shift in policy by an adversary is truly a feint, as it was for those Americans who considered the Sino-Soviet differences in the early 1960s as only a deceptive maneuver by the two communist powers. Announced doctrine can be of great importance, such as Nikita Khrushchev's pledge to support "wars of national liberation" throughout the world or Leonid Brezhnev's "doctrine" that a socialist state would never be permitted to throw off its socialist orientation, but such doctrines frequently have more continuing impact on the nation listening to them from outside than they perhaps mean to a successor government in the nation whose previous leader enunciated them. John Foster Dulles' pledges to "liberate" Eastern Europe lingered on in the minds of many long after Dulles has passed from the scene. The need to simplify issues for public understanding can make it easy to believe that an action was deliberate when it in truth might have been at least in part inadvertent and caused more by fear and confusion at lower levels than by the international decision of national leaders, as in the downing of KAL Flight 007 and Iran Air Flight 655.

The rise of Mikhail Gorbachev to the leadership of the USSR marks a major advance in this process of what the two nations can "know about" each other, and he deserves great credit for his innovative approach to this problem as well as to the other changes he has called for. The major steps made to establish monitoring and inspection teams in the two countries in the INF Treaty are a fundamental recognition that each has legitimate needs, and that they should be met through agreement. They also recognize that the substantial benefits to each nation which can come from mutual arms control and reduction can only occur if confidence can be established that the agreements will be complied with, and that this must be built on knowledge, not "trust." The loosening of restrictions on public discussion within the Soviet Union, much of which can also be heard by foreigners, is not only a contribution to understanding elsewhere, it is a recognition that in the modern information age no nation can seal itself off from the world without halting needed progress which has occurred in those which have tried (even futilely) to do so, as in Burma, Albania, and the Soviet Union itself.

Thus the understanding of the Soviet Union in the United States, and the understanding of the United States within the Soviet Union, can exponentially increase over the coming years if the Gorbachev policies continue. There will still be some secrets, some suspicions and some misunderstandings, but the process of reducing these is now open, and the opportunities are immense. The result can be better confidence on each side in its relations with the other, a normalization of the passage of information which in the past has only been the exception (or even nonexistent), and a resulting increase in collaboration between these two powers in the work of improving the chances of the future of the small sphere hurtling through space on which we both now live, precariously. Both nations must seize this opportunity, and open new windows for each other to see—and understand—that no threats lie hidden behind them.

THE END OF THE COLD WAR

Arthur Macy Cox

The forty-five year old Cold War between the Soviet Union and the United States is about to end. The diplomacy will probably require several years of negotiation, but the political framework has already been established. The leaders of the Soviet Union have decided to terminate the Cold War. They are in the process of destroying the terrible legacy of Iosif Stalin. The terror, the tyranny, and the totalitarian government which Stalinism represented fueled the Cold War as it was manifested in both the internal and external affairs of the Soviet Union. The liquidation of Stalinism is already liberating dynamic forces within Soviet society that are reversing Cold War policies and ideology.

After Stalin died in 1953, Nikita Khrushchev gave a secret speech condemning the "cult of personality." Khrushchev advocated measures to de-Stalinize Soviet society, but they didn't go very far. In fact, despite overtures for détente advanced at the Geneva summit in 1955 the Cold War continued unabated. This was reflected dramatically by Soviet tanks crushing the Hungarian revolution of 1956 and by the Cuban missile crisis of 1962.

When Khrushchev was ousted and replaced by Leonid Brezhnev many of the totalitarian mechanisms of Stalin were restored to Soviet life.

In fact, the fate of Khrushchev has given weight to the opinion of those Americans who claim that it is too early to talk about an end to the Cold War. They believe that the new thinking represented by Mikhail Gorbachev and his supporters may be a short-lived and tenuous phenomenon. There remain within the Communist Party leadership members who are very conservative and neo-Stalinist in their thinking. It is speculated that Gorbachev is moving too far, too fast and may suffer the same fate as Khrushchev. But this appears most unlikely because the public exposure of Stalin's evil and the damage his actions caused for Soviet society has been so pervasive that it will be impossible to put the genie back into the bottle. Very few Soviet citizens desire to return to the tyranny of Stalin or the stagnation of Brezhnev.

In addition to the rejection of Stalinism there are other fundamental changes that have reversed forever the nature of U.S.-Soviet competition. The Cold War received its name because the destructive capabilities of nuclear weapons forced both sides to avoid direct military confrontation and hot war. Despite the nuclear realities politicians and military leaders on both sides continued to plan for war based on the lessons learned from World War I and World War II. The Soviet military planners, especially, continued to rely on massive ground forces armed with tanks, artillery and fighter bombers. Both sides continued to give blind obeisance to the strategic theories of Clausewitz who had asserted that war was merely the continuation of politics by other means. It was not until 1956 that Khrushchev and the Soviet Communist Party reversed Lenin's theory of the inevitability of war. War should be avoided, it was maintained, because nuclear weapons threatened the destruction of the Soviet State.

Despite the wisdom implicit in ruling out the inevitability of war, the two superpowers continued to seek military superiority over each other. The mistrust of each other's aggressive intentions was so great that both sides asseted the requirement to build the capability to fight and win a nuclear war. The process of preparing to fight a nuclear war became ever more dangerous as technology produced nuclear weapons with such speed, accuracy, and power that it was possible to contemplate war-winning, first-strike attacks. As this capability grew both sides took incredible risks testing each other's early warning systems.

Now, that suicidal race is being reversed. Mikhail Gorbachev and his associates have concluded that further competition between the powers must exclude war as a political option. General Secretary Gorbachev and President Reagan agreed at the 1985 Summit meeting in Geneva that "a nuclear war cannot be won and must never be fought." They reiterated this conclusion on several subsequent occasions. The Soviet government has initiated a series of proposals to stop the arms race and to reduce the risk of war, both nuclear and conventional, which demonstrate new thinking about the risks of war and the need to change the rules of competition. Though the INF Treaty is the only concrete achievement so far, there is growing evidence of the seriousness of Soviet intentions to negotiate large scale reductions in both strategic and conventional military forces.

Though direct military confrontation between the forces of the superpowers has been avoided during the Cold War, there have been numerous instances of direct or indirect use of military force. The Vietnam War, fought to halt the advance of communism in Asia, became a political, military, and economic debacle for the United States, the most divisive event in U.S. history since the Civil War. Dragged out for years after U.S. public opinion had turned decisively against it, the war produced psychological and political repercussions that continue to affect American life adversely. Though Soviet forces did not participate in the Vietnam war, Soviet military supplies provided to North Vietnam were instrumental in killing thousands of Americans.

The Soviet invasion of Afghanistan, though on a smaller scale than the U.S. involvement in Vietnam, was a disaster for the Soviet Union of similar proportion. The Soviet decision in 1988 to withdraw its forces from Afghanistan, like the U.S. decision to withdraw from Vietnam, represented the acknowledgment of a tragically misguided policy. U.S. forces did not participate in Afghanistan but U.S. weapons provided to the Afghan resistance fighters were responsible for killing many young soldiers of the Red Army. In both wars the results were the same, pointing to the conclusion that there should be no more Vietnams and no more Afghanistans.

The roots of the Cold War were established by the results of World War II and the emergence of two victorious superpowers with antithetical political and economic systems. World War II also marked the decline and gradual dissolution of the colonial empires of Europe and Japan leaving a power vacuum that the United States and USSR would compete to fill. World War II also left Germany, Korea, and Vietnam dangerously divided and politically unresolved. The war had drastically crippled the economy of Western Europe and there were large communist parties in France and Italy. The United States responded with the European Recovery Program (the Marshall Plan) and established the clandestine services of CIA to battle the spread of communism.

As the Cold War burgeoned with the consolidation of Soviet power in Eastern Europe marked by the overthrow of the Benes government in Czechoslovakia, alarm spread through the United States. An examination of some of the theory of Marxism-Leninism demonstrated that the Soviets intended to advance their power and influence throughout the world, not by war, but through conspiracy, secret political penetration, agitation, and propaganda. The main arm of the Soviet conquest was to be the political apparatus of international communism. For most Americans it was frightening to contemplate that members of indigenous communist parties, for example, in France, Italy, Indonesia, Algeria, or the United States, were loyal not to their own nations, but to the Soviet Union—and that they had a goal of taking power in their countries to become part of an international communist bloc run by Moscow.

In 1947 Congress passed the National Security Act which, among other things, created the National Security Council and the Central Intelligence Agency. In 1949 President Harry Truman established the Psychological Strategy Board which was assigned to develop a strategic concept for waging the Cold War. In 1950 the president signed NSC-68 setting policy for U.S. assets and operations to contain the spread of communism throughout the world. The policy called for a vast expansion of U.S. military power capable of blocking any Soviet military aggression, but it also called for waging a struggle against international communism by covert political, psychological, and paramilitary operations. The policies set in NSC-68 have been pursued throughout the Cold War.

The fear of communism and disloyalty in the United States was exploited by unscrupulous politicians who gained power and influence by making wildly exaggerated claims about the penetration of the U.S. government by U.S. citizens allegedly acting as Soviet spies, and about the size and influence of the American Communist party. This phenomenon, known as "McCarthyism" after Senator Joseph McCarthy, who led the political exploitation, caused a kind of hysteria which temporarily impaired the functioning of the government until the facts were exposed by the media and Senator McCarthy was censured by his fellow members of the U.S. Senate.

The principal role for waging the Cold War was assigned to the clandestine arm of the CIA. After Dwight Eisenhower became president in 1953 the Cold War policy was largely developed by Secretary of State John Foster Dulles and implemented by his brother Allen Dulles, the director of the CIA. The NSC decided that to succeed in winning the Cold War it was necessary "to fight fire with fire." This meant fighting a totalitarian system with totalitarian means. It meant employing all of the black arts of deception, including the big lie and the employment of corrupt, double-dealing politicians. It meant a vast increase in espionage and counterespionage. The treachery of Stalin was to be confronted with the treachery of secret U.S. operations.

In the early years, starting in the late 1940s, there were some very sophisticated and successful operations. In association with the Marshall Plan the CIA was instrumental in exposing and defeating Soviet operations with the Italian, French, and Greek Communist parties, as well as Soviet operations in Berlin and Vienna. The CIA helped the social democratic and socialist parties of Western Europe to defeat the communists. But after the struggle for Western Europe the Cold War shifted to the Third World where a wave of nationalism was filling the vacuum created by the freeing of the European colonies. For a while the Soviets successfully exploited this opportunity by supporting anticolonial leaders who were struggling for national liberation.

Secretary of State Dulles, on the other hand, proclaimed a U.S. policy for supporting only those Third World politicians who would "stand up and be counted as fighters against communism." No U.S. support would go to neutralists or socialists, he said. The result was that the military supplies and clandestine assets of the United States frequently supported unpopular, right-wing dictators. There was no question about their anticommunist credentials, but their dictatorial methods made them vulnerable to overthrow from communist-supported liberation movements.

Winning the Cold War was such a popular bipartisan objective that virtually no American politicians questioned the extraordinary secret powers granted to the CIA. In fact, for almost twenty years, there was virtually no congressional oversight of CIA secret operations. A few members of Congress, carefully chosen by the Executive Branch, were given limited briefings on aspects of the CIA program and budget. But it wasn't until the late 1960s when some CIA operations involving illegal links to domestic enterprises were exposed in the press. The ensuing investigation led to the creation of Senate and House intelligence committees to provide a greater degree of congressional review and accountability.

The forty-five-year record of covert operations, on both sides, is not impressive. In fact, the impact of these operations has often caused serious setbacks to the national security of the USSR and the United States. The Soviets were thrown out of Yugoslavia, Egypt, Ghana, and Guinea in large measure because of the exposure of covert operations attempting to take over or control indigenous politics. In the case of Egypt the Soviets lost a powerful base in the Middle East when it was discovered that the head of Egyptian intelligence was a KGB agent planning a coup to overthrow the government leaders. The United States has sponsored numerous failed secret operations with disastrous consequences, including the Bay of Pigs invasion of Cuba, and the Iran-Contra fiasco.

Even the so-called covert successes have often produced horrendous negative repercussions. For example, an East German spy, directed by the KGB, was successfully infiltrated into the offices of Willy Brandt, Chancellor of the Federal Republic of Germany. When the spy was discovered, Brandt was compromised and decided to resign. During this period the most important Soviet foreign policy objective was the successful completion of negotiations with Brandt of the so-called *Ostpolitik* leading to improved relations and, most especially, to the recognition of the government of East Germany. The resignation of Brandt, caused by the KGB operation, could have wrecked the sensitive political fabric of the negotiations.

In 1969 when Chinese and Soviet forces engaged in serious border clashes the Soviets demanded that the Chinese come to the negotiating table. The Chinese refused. The KGB immediately launched a black propaganda operation planting rumors in the press that the Soviets were about to launch a preemptive strike to eliminate the Chinese nuclear capability. The Chinese were intimidated. Soon the "ping-pong" diplomacy began, Kissinger made his secret trip to Peking, and President Nixon arrived to sign the agreement reestablishing relations between the United States and China. Thus, a successful Soviet covert operation helped pave the way to U.S.-Chinese rapprochement.

A covert operation claimed to be one of CIA's greatest successes was the overthrow of President Mossadeq of Iran and the restoration of the Shah to the throne. Mossadeq had been a popular figure and the Shah was not. The Shah's power was ensured by the military, the secret police, and U.S. government assistance, especially sophisticated weapons. When the revolution ensued, forcing the retirement of the Shah, he was replaced by the religious radicalism represented by the late Ayatollah Khomeini. Relations between the United States and Iran reached an all-time low. This unfortunate turn of events for the United States was rooted in a so-called successful CIA operation.

Someday there may be a joint U.S.-Soviet examination of covert operations during the Cold War. There is already enough public evidence to speculate that such an examination would produce a joint conclusion that such operations have produced a net loss to the national security of both sides. Covert operations have also created a major barrier to diplomatic negotiations attempting to seek greater stability in U.S.-Soviet relations. The Cold War has produced such fundamental distrust between the superpowers that attempts to reach agreement are faced with unusual fragility. Both sides use as a litmus test of true intentions the secret operations of the other side. There have been numerous occasions when Soviet or U.S. intelligence discovered covert operations of the other side which were used to demonstrate that the peaceful assertions made by the United States on Soviet leaders were false. Thus, covert operations on both sides tended to reinforce each other and to block progress toward ending the Cold War.

Moreover, there are important political problems for the United States in conducting covert operations. The decision to fight Soviet totalitarianism with totalitarian methods raised serious questions for our democratic system because we have learned during the course of the Cold War that foreign affairs, even when conducted secretly, cannot be separated from domestic affairs. Totalitarian methods are incompatible with our democracy. Furthermore, despite some Congressional oversight it has always been very difficult to ensure the essential checks and balances called for in the Constitution. The Constitution makes no provisions for covert operations. In fact, the National Security Act of 1947 which created the CIA makes no mention of covert operations. The Iran-Contra affair is the most recent evidence of the desirability of a full congressional review to determine whether U.S. covert operations should be terminated.

Espionage had some of the same negative impact on diplomacy, but was generally accepted as inevitable so long as both sides believed that there was a real risk of war. Especially since first-strike nuclear weapons were deployed by both sides it became essential for national survival to have the best possible intelligence of intentions, capabilities, and command and control systems. The arms control negotiations have produced a breakthrough that in time may dramatically change the military intelligence requirements. Both sides have now agreed to workable arrangements for on-site inspection of certain military facilities in order to verify agreement to destroy or stop producing certain nuclear weapons. There are also on-site inspections of some nuclear tests. There are numerous other confidence-building measures that are being implemented and that will permit each side to openly observe the military deployments and equipment of the other. As on-site inspections increase, becoming progressively more intrusive, trust will be enhanced and there will be less need for reliance on espionage.

All of these issues may become academic during the next decade because of the expressed intention of General Secretary Gorbachev and the Soviet government to bring the Cold War to an end. The most important evidence for this conclusion is the sweeping measures being pursued in the Soviet Union to eradicate the dark stain of Stalinism and the totalitarian methods which it represented in both domestic and foreign policy. Another very important change is the Soviet conclusion that war must be totally ruled out as means to attain political objectives.

In fact, Gorbachev has stated that all future competition must be limited to political, economic, and psychological measures. He has expressly ruled out direct and indirect military intervention in support of wars of national liberation—a reversal of Soviet policy during the Cold War. A concrete manifestation of this shift in policy is the decision to withdraw Soviet forces from Afghanistan, and the negotiations to withdraw Cuban troops from Angola, and Vietnamese troops from Cambodia. Soviet indirect and direct intervention in the Third World to support anticolonial struggles is a thing of the past.

Portugal was the last European government to free its colonies. Angola represents the last important Cold War contest rooted in colonialism. The warfare in Nicaragua has been called a national liberation movement by the Soviets, some of whom claim that the Samoza regime was the same as a U.S. colony. In any case, there is a basis for a solution of the U.S.-Soviet contest in Nicaragua. The Soviets have indicated a willingness to stop their military assistance to the Sandinistas as soon as the United States agrees to cut off military assistance to the Contras.

The Soviet arms control proposals calling for deep cuts in nuclear and conventional arms provide further evidence of their desire to end the cold war. The seriousness of their intentions has been demonstrated by their willingness to accept intrusive on-site inspection to verify compliance of arms control agreement. Furthermore, Gorbachev's policy of *glasnost* has begun to open up Soviet society. Gorbachev has condemned the cult of secrecy. He says that the actual details of the Soviet defense budget will soon be published.

Gorbachev frequently asserts that he intends to end the Cold War and the action he has been taking provides clear evidence that he is serious—this is not a propaganda smoke screen. Now, the United States must also launch the process and seize the opportunity to negotiate the final resolution of the Cold War.

CHANGE, REALITY, AND INSTITUTIONAL TRUTH*

John Kenneth Galbraith

Essays on international affairs almost always open with a reference to change: "I write in a time of great political, economic, and social change." I am firmly in this tradition, and my subject here is the very great forces in modern life and government that refuse to accept changed realities. Specifically, our overriding preoccupation with international and military policy has been resistant to change because of our commitment to what I would call institutional truth.

The changes that have occurred are in the internal character and external manifestations of the two great economic, social, and political systems that for seventy years have been dominant on the world scene. The institutional truth with which I deal is strikingly revealed in the resistance to accept that change.

The change or changes in the socialist *cum* communist world dominated by the Soviet Union and in the capitalist world epitomized and led since World War II by the United States, are not in doubt. They are visibly obtrusive. In the case of some, there is an element of déjà vu in mentioning them. All, nonetheless, are in conflict with and, in striking degree, denied by institutional truth.

For many years after Lincoln Steffens returned from Russia in 1919 to tell Bernard Baruch, "I have been over into the future and it works"—one of the more spectacularly premature economic observations of all time—there was an uneasy feeling that, in our relations with the Soviet Union, we were contending with a dangerously compelling economic order. This was made evident even in the impassioned oratory that condemned the Soviet system. Beneath the rhetoric was a legacy of fear. And in the years between the wars the Soviets built a powerful industrial base, avoided the unemployment and general economic disaster of the Great Depression, and then sustained

---

* This article is adapted from an address given at the Department of State on 29 March 1988.

the vast armies that defeated Hitler. All this contributed notably to one of our most common social phenomena: the compelling belief of fortunate Americans, rejoicing greatly in their good fortune, that somewhere there lurks an infinitely powerful, deeply insidious design for its expropriation.

Paranoia, in turn, had its Russian counterpart. The 1918 military interventions by Western powers, the onslaught of Hitler, the years of exuberant capitalist success following World War II, all were seen as a threat to the Socialist system. Capitalism was not thought disposed to tolerate a rival system; it was awaiting the opportunity to obliterate it.

There was similarly a source of fear for both Soviets and Americans in what appeared to be a common commitment to international influence — to Soviet expansionism as it was called by the West, to American capitalist imperialism as it was denoted by Moscow. And here too there was substance. In 1961, when I went to India as a point man for American imperialism, Soviet power seemingly stretched undiminished from the Brandenburg Gate in Berlin to the port of Haiphong. The Eastern European satellites, the most visible evidence of Soviet expansionism, seemed solid, successful, and secure. There were outposts of marked importance in North Africa, Indonesia, and in the Western Communist parties. The Korean conflict had, in the general view, made evident this commitment to expansion as did the overt promise of support to wars of national liberation. There was a formidable concern in Washington as to how we could prevent India from falling under communist control, a misfortune I've often thought no perceptive communist would wish to contemplate.

Similarly evident was the American influence — SEATO, CENTO, NATO, the web of John Foster Dulles's bilateral treaties, a strong moral position in Central and South America and much of Africa. The Soviets saw this, not surprisingly, as evidence of the American imperialist intention or, at a minimum, of a determined policy of encirclement.

Finally, there was the military experience. In World War II there was our vision of the enormous power of the Soviet armies as they drove the Wehrmacht back to Berlin and beyond and the combination of gratitude and fear that this engendered. And again there was the counterpart concern of the Soviets — our evident advantage in naval and aerial strength and above all in nuclear weaponry. Here, along with economic achievement and imperial ambition, was the third source of reciprocal fear and tension.

It is a mistake, I believe, to make light of these fears in their time — to say, as some have said, that they were invented for military and political purposes. They were, or certainly they seemed, very real. And it was inevitable, accordingly, that they would become the foundation of foreign and military policy in both the Great Powers. In doing so, they became, I suggest, the sources of the institutional truth that now controls belief and guides policy to this time. And the singular and inescapable fact is that the substance of all of these sources of fear have almost completely disappeared.

The aspect of reciprocal and threatening economic success has totally disappeared. The Soviet Union, China, and the satellite countries, their considerable past achievements notwithstanding, are now openly struggling with grave, perhaps even intractable, economic problems. The confidence of an earlier time has been all but lost. The present preoccupation is with bureaucratic status and strategies of reform, and with a somewhat neglected point, the difficulty that a planned economy has in meeting the diverse needs of the modern high-consumption society. A primary concern in all the socialist world is how concessions can be made to the market without surrendering the basic fabric of socialism.

Similarly in the capitalist world and especially in the United States. We sustain our living standard only by creation of massive internal and external debt. In our traditional areas of industrial achievement we are no longer competitive. For each speech in the Congress on the economic threat of the Soviet Union, there are at least fifteen on the threat of Japan. The dollar, once above challenge as the reference currency of the world, is now viewed with caution and sometimes with disdain.

No one can suppose that either American capitalism or Soviet socialism any longer projects the image of success that once induced fear in the other country. We do indeed have the normal manifestation of conservative paranoia about socialism, but increasingly we recognize it as such.

The change has been even more spectacular as regards the once-avowed dangers of Soviet expansionism and capitalist imperialism. Here the retreat has been massive and inescapable. The Soviets have experienced the traumatic break with China; a visibly weakened position in Eastern Europe; the loss of all effective influence in Egypt, Algeria, Ghana, and Indonesia; the shrinkage or near disappearance of the Western European Communist parties; also the disaster in Afghanistan, and now the dissent of the ethnic communities within the USSR itself.

Our experience viewed over the last twenty-five years has not been different. Central and South America are no longer on call. Only Grenada and perhaps Honduras are now ours for the asking. SEATO and CENTO have gone with the wind of which they so largely consisted. So also most of the bilateral treaties. NATO survives, but it no longer accords us the automatic support we once enjoyed. No one for some years has suggested that NATO meetings are intellectually demanding. And there was the traumatic experience and lesson of Vietnam.

To a remarkable extent we and the Soviets have run into the same two problems. One has been the intense, unrelenting desire of all countries and their governments to be free from external authority; this certainly is one of the most powerful influences in our time. The second is the manifest inapplicability of the model of either mature socialism or developed capitalism in the Third World. The socialist disaster there, evident in Afghanistan, Ethiopia, and Mozambique, is particularly great. And this should not have been to any good socialist's surprise. On nothing did Marx insist more adamantly than that socialism could come only after the preliminary socializing influence of capitalism. But we have also suffered from the supposition that what is sound economic policy in the United States must somehow be right for India, Africa, or even Latin America.

Finally, there has been the massive change in the military relationship. Here one risks a rapid descent into the tediously trite. Any modern conflict brings the unacceptable risk of nuclear exchange. This neither capitalism nor communism, both highly sophisticated designs for ordering economic process, would survive. Accordingly, capitalism and communism now sit on the same side of the table facing the common threat of nuclear war.

There is a further possible change in the larger military nexus. That concerns the question of whether the modern industrial state can be an object of successful military action and occupation. From the earliest times agricultural regions were a useful fruit of conquest. Farmers or peasants, whatever their ethnic or other objection, would perform more or less equally well whoever their ultimate masters. No one can suppose this to be so of the modern, complex, intricately demanding industrial economy. Can the Russians really imagine that they could take over and operate the Japanese economy, a thought that, as they contemplate military expenditure, has almost certainly occurred to the Japanese? Or the Italian economy, as we hear alarming references to the undefended "southern flank" of NATO? Or do we wish to have responsibility for the Polish economy? I mention these matters not as final judgment but as things we should be discussing. Do we need armed troops along every frontier? Is what lies behind any longer that enticing? Reading of the alarm over the withdrawal of those F16's from the environs of Madrid, I wondered if the worry was not over a new Ottoman onslaught against the Knights of Malta.

But I turn from these matters—from the great and largely undisputed changes I have cited—to the role of institutional truth.

A certain stability in public thought and policy is not to be deplored. This is especially so under our system, where, every four or eight years, the White House and the departments of government, especially the former, are invaded by men and women with an unduly imaginative vision of what is theirs to change. But we must also recognize that all great organizations have a deeply intrinsic resistance to change, and both our public and private life today are dominated by great organizations.

The organizational factors resisting change are five. There is, first, in all organization the need for a unifying system of thought, commonly called a policy or in military organization a military doctrine. To this, all participants must in some measure adhere. The alternative—everyone proceeding on his or her independent, undisciplined course—would, indeed, be chaos.

There is, second, both a release from mental effort and a measure of pride in accepting the ruling idea or doctrine. Tolstoy tells in *War and Peace* of the relief, even pleasure, in surrendering all decision to the rule of the regiment. Institutional truth is likewise an alternative to painful thought.

Third there is a safety in such surrender. It is a hard but inescapable fact that in all organized effort it is safer for the individual to be wrong with the majority than to risk being wrong alone.

Fourth, there is a strong tendency of all organization to exclude the inconvenient voice. Here I venture to cite personal experience. In the earlier stages of our involvement with Vietnam I was more than marginally concerned with our policy there. I felt, from some personal knowledge of the larger region, that, as in India, while capitalism and communism were concepts irrelevant to most of the population, foreign intervention (Vietnamese, Chinese, French, Japanese, and now ours) was not. I also perceived, from some background in agriculture, that herding people into strategic hamlets, so-called, was a particularly efficient design for alienation. Moreover the governments we supported were oppressive, corrupt, and incompetent. Finally, I later saw that our sophisticated military establishment was badly designed for the elementary warfare there required, where only the most discerning ideologist could tell a capitalist jungle from a communist jungle.

But I learned in those years that urging these matters was far from being a formula for popularity. Or even inclusion. "We know where Galbraith stands. He is not useful." And there is a more disagreeable thought. Perhaps the individual motivated to dissent has fallen under some adverse external influence. "Maybe they have got to him." Such in organizations is the frequent fate of the individual who challenges institutional truth.

Finally, there is vested personal and pecuniary interest. Not many of us wish to deny our past or admit to past error. And there can be great pecuniary rewards in established policy—in the accepted institutional truth. No one doubts the great financial interest in present military policy. It was implanted in our thought by Dwight D. Eisenhower and his enduring reference to the military-industrial complex.

All of the foregoing factors come to bear as institutional truth on U.S.-Soviet relations. Especially as they come to bear on the military nexus. On the one hand, the change: on the other hand, the strongest manifestation in our time of the resistances to change—of the power of institutional truth and the vested economic interest therein. The consequence is the present and highly visible anomaly in our foreign and military action and policy. We have a dual policy or, at least, a wonderfully bifurcated policy. Through the force of the changes I earlier cited in the relations between the two great systems and their two principal exponents, we have the compelling pressure for association and compromise. Here the reality asserts itself. This is made evident in the summits, the closer working relationships between Secretary of State and Foreign Minister, the INF Treaty and an unprecedented increase in scientific, artistic, and other association. These, to repeat, are in response to the underlying changes—changes that no leader and certainly none in our politically responsive democracy can wholly resist.

At the same time, and notably on military matters where doctrine rules most strongly, where vested economic interest is great and perhaps decisive, we still have the full force of institutional truth. The two great systems, ours and that of the Soviet Union, remain in bitter conflict. Expansionism is still assumed. Military parity, if not preeminence, is still sought. All frontiers are deeply vulnerable.

We accept that change has altered the basic relationship between the two superpowers, as by courtesy they are still called. Institutional truth, as reflected especially in military doctrine or force disposition, effectively denies that there has been any change. We have one policy in response to reality; we have another policy in response to institutional truth.

It will perhaps be evident that I regard the case for reality as being stronger than that for institutional truth. It is also abundantly evident that in the arena of U.S.-Soviet relations there is a dangerous disparity between institutional truth and reality. But it is not my purpose here to urge a particular course of action. It is to identify the wonderfully conflicting forces which, in a world of great organization and great change, come to control attitudes, speech, and action.

PERESTROIKA AND THE U.S.-SOVIET RIVALRY

John Lewis Gaddis

There is little that we in the United States can do to ensure the success — or, for that matter, the failure — of *perestroika*. But this does not mean we should refrain from having attitudes about it, or from considering how the remarkable set of reforms Mikhail Gorbachev is now attempting to implement within the Soviet Union might affect something over which we do have some control: the future of Soviet-American relations. So far, our attitudes have been somewhat confused. We cannot seem to decide whether we want *perestroika* to succeed or not. Few if any of us want a return to the bad old days of the Cold War at its height; but neither are we particularly eager to see the Soviet Union become, for the first time, an efficient military and economic competitor. One of the good things about the Russians as adversaries over the years, after all, has been their chronic inefficiency.

It is, of course, unrealistic to expect that the Soviet Union could ever evolve into what we would consider a liberal democratic state. Nor has it ever been the goal of United States policy to seek to bring such a thing about: the architects of containment did look forward to an eventual "mellowing" of Soviet society, but at no point did they hold out as an objective the replication of American political institutions along the banks of the Moskva or beneath the walls of the Kremlin.[1]

[1] John Lewis Gaddis, "The Evolution of U.S. Policy Goals Toward the USSR in the Postwar Era," in Seweryn Bialer and Michael Mandelbaum, eds., *Gorbachev's Russia and American Foreign Policy* (Boulder: Westview Press, 1988), pp. 313–318.

And yet, the past four years have witnessed far more movement toward democracy in the Soviet Union than anyone would have thought possible at the time Gorbachev took power. We, like the Russian people, find ourselves eagerly scanning the newspapers every morning to see what new manifestation of *glasnost* has taken place overnight; the cumulative effect of what has happened already—even if the process should abruptly end tomorrow—is worthy of comparison with such historic reforms as those attempted by Peter the Great, Aleksandr II, Petr Stolypin and, in his own self-contradictory way, Nikita Khrushchev. Events have been moving so rapidly as to out strip our ability to analyze them: there has been little effort, as yet, to think precisely about what stake the United States might have in *perestroika*, or what it might mean for the future of our relations with the USSR.

It has long been a staple of American rhetoric about foreign affairs that we would like to see democracy spread as widely as possible throughout the world. But why? Apart from the self-gratifying flattery that imitation brings, are there hard-headed, practical reasons for holding this position? Ideological homogeneity is not, after all, a necessary requirement for geopolitical stability, or for national security, or for economic prosperity: if it had been, we would be far worse off than we are today. In particular, are there hard-headed, practical reasons why we should want to see democracy expand inside the Soviet Union? I believe that some do exist, although we do not as yet seem to talk about them very much.

The first and most important reason has to do with the avoidance of war—a priority that, in a nuclear age, must override all others. Ever since Thucydides, students of the causes of war have tried to determine why it is that nations fight. There is still no very good answer to that question, but we do at least know something about what kinds of nations tend to fight each other. It is not the case, for example, that nations actively involved in trade, cultural exchange, and people-to-people contacts tend not to fight: the most cursory glance at the history of Europe during the first half of this century should be sufficient to show that familiarity can breed contempt as well as harmony, and with disastrous results. But there is a related generalization that holds up much better to historical scrutiny: it is that liberal democracies tend not to fight each other.[2] Now, admittedly there have not been many such states in world history, so our basis for analysis is limited;

---

[2] Michael A. Doyle, "Kant, Liberal Legacies, and Foreign Affairs," *Philosophy and Public Affairs* (Summer and Fall, 1983): pp. 205–235, 323–353, is the best analysis.

but such states have been present in increasing numbers over the past two centuries, and it is striking that there has yet to be a major war between any two of them. It is also important to stress that the Soviet Union, even under Gorbachev, has a long way to go before it can legitimately qualify as such a state. But if one effect of *perestroika* is to widen the circle of decisionmakers on for policy inside the Kremlin—and to ensure that those decisionmakers are better informed than their predecessors about the world in which they function— then that is a start. And it is farther than almost all of us thought we would be four years ago.

Second, democratization should make for a more efficient Soviet economy. To be sure, there is some reason to wonder whether we really want that: the economic inefficiency of the Soviet State over the years has been a major constraint on Moscow's ability to function as a world power.[3] But even a state with a third-rate economy will maintain world power pretensions if it has nuclear weapons in abundance: the question we should consider—both for the Russians and for ourselves, for that matter—is whether global stability is best served by having great powers that combine nuclear overkill with crippled economies. Once again, history would seem to suggest that states behave most irrationally, not when they are weak, but when they see themselves as *beginning to weaken*;[4] although possessing nuclear weapons in great abundance probably does help stave off visions of decline, we ought not to rely on that crutch to do so indefinitely. This would suggest, then, an American interest comparable to that of Gorbachev himself in a healthier Soviet economy.

Third, even moderate democratization inside the Soviet Union would go far toward removing major sources of antagonism that have bedeviled Russian-American relations since before the Bolshevik Revolution. I refer here, of course, to such questions as the treatment of minorities and dissidents within Russia, and the extent to which Russian leaders have felt it necessary to impose their control over neighboring states.[5] The human rights issue is already a less divisive factor in Soviet-American relations than it

[3] Paul Kennedy, *The Rise and Fall of the Great Powers: Economic Change and Military Conflict from 1500 to 2000* (New York: Random House, 1987), pp. 488–514.

[4] Richard Ned Lebow, *Between War and Peace: The Nature of International Crisis* (Baltimore: Johns Hopkins University Press, 1981), pp. 334–335, especially.

[5] John Lewis Gaddis, *Russia, the Soviet Union, and the United States: An Interpretive History* (New York: Knopf, 1978), pp. 27–56, for the origins of these concerns.

was at the time Gorbachev took power; but a more important test of the new regime's flexibility may come sooner than we think in Eastern Europe, which increasingly appears as one of the least stable areas in current world politics. Surely it is in our interests to see more enlightened Soviet policies, if a major crisis does develop there, than those of 1948, 1956, and 1968; although there can be no guarantees, that prospect seems more likely under Gorbachev than it would have under any of his predecessors.

Fourth, Moscow's acceptance of the need for democratization and decentralization represents a grudging but no less significant acknowledgment that the Leninist idea of reform through authoritarian rule has not worked. When combined with what has been going on in China and other Marxist countries, the implications—for the entire history of the twentieth century—are profound. This is probably not the time to be shooting off fireworks or holding parades to celebrate our "victory" over one of the most fundamental ideas of the Bolshevik Revolution. But it may be an appropriate moment to reflect that we ought to remember the decade of the 1980s as one that reinforced, much more than it called into question, our own faith in the basic soundness of our political and economic institutions.

Lest this essay seem to end on too euphoric a note, though, some words of caution are in order by way of conclusion. First, we should not lose sight of the fact that, even if Gorbachev's Russia should transform itself totally into a card-carrying liberal democracy tomorrow, that would not mean the end of direct Soviet-American rivalry, or of competition between Moscow and Washington for influence in the rest of the world. International conflict is a fact of life under the current and probably future system of near anarchy under which the relations of nations manage their affairs. These rivalries can be controlled; certainly as the history of the Cold War suggests, they need not all lead to war. But they will not disappear just because American and Soviet domestic institutions have moved somewhat closer to one another.

Our task must be to distinguish those aspects of Soviet-American rivalry that are inherent in the international system as it is now configured and that would be there regardless of ideological differences, on the one hand, from those dimensions of our relationship that grew out of a most unnatural disturbance of that system: the cumulative effects of World Wars I and II. We may now reasonably hope that Cold War tensions have, for the most part, abated; but we need to remember that not all causes of tension in Soviet-American relations will have been removed thereby.

That general caution, in turn, suggests two more specific ones:

1) Whatever our hopes, there can be no assurance that Gorbachev will retain power for very long, or that the reforms he has instituted will be perpetuated. Russian history is full of instances that saw reforms initiated to compensate for perceived military or economic weakness, only to have those reforms themselves fall apart with the passage of time.[6] We should be prepared for the removal of Gorbachev and the dismantling of *perestroika* at any point: our attitude, if that happens, should be one of neither panic nor despair, but rather of dignified regret, accompanied by a return to one of the traditional postulates of containment: that we hope for *eventual* change inside the Soviet Union, brought about by the Soviet people themselves, but that until that happens we will, so to speak, keep our powder dry.

2) We should also be aware that with the new Bush administration in Washington, we are at that most dangerous point at which urges become irresistible to re-invent wheels. New administrations tend, with remarkable regularity, to reject what their predecessors have done for no other reason than to be able to do something different. If not resisted, such an impulse could lead toward an uncritical search for accommodation with the Russians, as we saw in the early days of the Carter administration, when unilateral concessions accompanied an apparent willingness to negotiate on everything. Or it could lead to an abrupt toughening of policy and an apparent unwillingness to negotiate on anything. Neither extreme would, at this juncture, serve our interests. Serious students of Soviet-American relations, regardless of party affiliation, will have to acknowledge that during the second Reagan term—whether because of the president or in spite of him, whether because of Gorbachev or in spite of him—unprecedented progress was made toward moving Soviet-American relations onto a safer, more cooperative, and more open basis. That progress ought not now be lost just because the White House has new occupants: indeed, there is much to be said for encouraging the current custodians of our national fortunes—at least as far as Soviet-American relations are concerned—to place greater emphasis on continuity than on change.

---

[6] I am indebted to my colleague, Professor Steven M. Miner of the Ohio University Department of History, for sharing with me a most illuminating paper he has written on this subject.

The Russians, whether advocates of *perestroika* or not, do not like surprises in their dealings with the United States. Neither should we.

Much that is remarkable has happened in Soviet-American relations since the end of World War II, and especially since the advent of Mikhail Gorbachev in 1985. But there are always degrees of "remarkability." What Gorbachev is attempting to do is surely remarkable; it will be all the more so if he succeeds. But even that achievement would pale when set against a grander thing that we have accomplished, almost without noticing it: the fact that with all of our antagonisms, our ideological differences, our mutual suspicions, we managed somehow to get through four decades of pre-*perestroika* Cold War without ever resorting to—or even ever coming very close to resorting to—a real war between our two states. That is the truly remarkable achievement; certainly it is one that few if any in 1945 would have expected. Our chief priority, as we in the United States think about how we should respond to the remarkable Gorbachev "revolution," should be to do nothing that would compromise, or in any way threaten the future of, that even more remarkable accomplishment.

THE CHANGING SOVIET VIEW OF THE WORLD

Raymond L. Garthoff

As pragmatic realists, we Americans are inclined to discount political rhetoric and policy declarations—of others. The pronouncements of the leaders of a perceived adversary such as the Soviet Union are all viewed cautiously. While we may cautiously acknowledge statements that herald apparent changes for the better, our principal reaction is to say we want to see deeds, not mere words. Similarly, the constant injunction of the military to look to the capabilities, and not the intentions, of an adversary usually finds an acceptance that carries the advice far beyond its valid role in military contingency planning. As laconically expressed by an early American television figure, the unflappable police detective Sergeant Friday, "Just give us the facts, ma'am."

278 RAYMOND L. GARTHOFF

As serious students of criminology, history, and world politics know, just getting "the facts" is not easy. Nor is it even likely, if one looks only at deeds and capabilities and not also at a host of more elusive factors. Moreover, actions and words, and capabilities as related to contingent intentions, are constantly in flux.

Today it is clear to almost everyone that changes of potentially enormous significance are underway in the Soviet Union. One may question long-term purposes and aspirations, and also the sustainability and irreversibility of changes being implemented, but it is hard not to acknowledge that important changes of both rhetoric and deed are occurring.

It is natural and appropriate that we focus on specific key problems: Soviet positions in negotiations on arms reductions, Soviet behavior in the Third World, Soviet military programs, and the like. Together, they add up to the current expression of policy in action. Among "the facts" are Soviet acceptance of asymmetrical arms reductions in which they yield more implementation of verification involving intensive on-site inspection, withdrawal of Soviet forces from Afghanistan, enhanced Soviet support for the United Nations through payment of all back dues, and many others. But are these actions an amalgam of internal economic necessity and external dissimulation, or do they represent a more benign and cooperative Soviet policy?

In the long run, history will tell. But we cannot wait for the long run to make decisions that, moreover, can in turn help to shape the answer. But there is more to go on than may be recognized by adhering to too narrow a conception of "realism." Underlying Soviet policy is the way the Soviet leaders view the world, and perhaps the most momentous changes of all have been occurring in their perception and assessment of the world.

The changing Soviet view of the world is, in my judgment, the *most* important aspect of the revolutionary transformation underway in the Soviet Union. As the Soviet leaders and the Soviet "establishment" come to hold a different understanding of the contemporary world even basic ideological precepts are transmuted. There is, obviously, an active interconnection (a dialectical interrelation, in terms the Soviets recognize) between their view of the world and their ideological "world-view."

The Soviet leaders, while recognizing and declaring that they are applying a "new thinking," also assert that they are restoring rather than revising Marxism-Leninism. This is a debatable proposition, but what is of greatest interest to us is not whether the Soviet Union today is embarking on a path Lenin would have taken, but that the Soviet leaders today are taking it. The fact they claim, and probably believe, that a true "Leninist" path is less important than that they now define anew the ideology itself in terms that justify the new thinking. Rather than being put off by Soviet claims of continuity in their basic ideological doctrine, even as in fact it is being changed, or seeing some dark purpose or unaccountable "admission" that there is no real change, we should recognize that the Soviet leaders probably in their own minds and certainly in their utterances see a need to legitimize their new thinking by asserting its constancy with the historical source of legitimacy.

It is not too much to say that the "mellowing" of the Soviet world view foreseen as a possibility by George Kennan forty years ago is now occurring, and probably already exceeds his most ambitious hopes then.

Changes in the world, perceived despite contravening ideological expectations, are not unique to Gorbachev and the present leaders. Lenin soon discovered that the Bolshevik revolution was not going to touch off a world revolution, as he and his colleagues had anticipated in 1917. Stalin attempted to play the European balance of power game. Khrushchev realized that in the nuclear age war was not inevitable. But the too slow adaptation of the past decades has forced Gorbachev and his colleagues in the new era since 1985 to embrace a "new thinking" that goes much further than his predecessors in recognizing that the world is different from what they had believed. The present Soviet leadership still adheres to a Marxist-Leninist conception that poses "classes" as the ordinate political entities, and a competition between the systems or worlds of "socialism" and "capitalism" (or "imperialism," mature capitalism in the Leninist taxonomy, not a concept tied to colonial empires). Since the mid-1950s all Soviet leaders have understood that competition between these two systems *must* be waged and resolved only by peaceful means. But while advocating peaceful coexistence between states of the two systems, they also have advocated and practiced a continuation of the "class struggle" by means short of war. Détente of the 1970s was seen in this pattern.

Today, Gorbachev and his colleagues have recognized a new dimension of "coexistence:" along with the peaceful competition of the two worlds, there is another process at work—a growing global interdependence. The revolutionary new element in this view of the world is recognition that it is, in fact, *one world*. The common interest of humankind in preventing nuclear catastrophe has been a powerful contributor to this new thinking, but there is much more to it. Now it is recognized that there are interests of humanity that take precedence over those of *any* "class" (although, to be sure, peace is claimed as a constant goal of socialists). Today, a whole range of interests extending far beyond prevention of nuclear war are recognized.

Global economic, resource, and ecological interests are seen, calling for global collaboration. *Global interdependence* is now seen as a major and growing characteristic of the world.

At another level, the interests of each country are now given increased attention as well. Thus "class interests" (communist aims) in the world must compete and give way not only to a growing range of global interests of humanity, but also to national interests. Increasingly Soviet aims, interests, and actions are defined explicitly in terms of serving Soviet national interests. This has, of course, been true in practice throughout Soviet history; in effect Soviet leaders have held that "what is good for the Soviet Union, is good for the world revolution"—including pragmatic caution. But this predominance of national interests is now being more openly acknowledged.

Global, class, and national interests are, of course, said to be not only reconcilable, but non-contradictory and mutually reinforcing *if* they are properly identified. Thus peace, common security, economic prosperity of the world, ecological conservation, peaceful resolution of disputes between nations on the basis of mutual compromise based on recognition of the interests of all parties—as are seen to serve global, class, and national interests. While the inclusion of "class interests" is meaningless to us, in *this* context it is also benign (and, assuming we are correct, merely a superfluous categorization). That is new. And it is important.

The new view of the world includes revised Soviet assessments of the capabilities of world capitalism, socialism, and the Third World. The staying power, and even growing power, of the principal Western capitalist countries is now recognized. The economic problems of the Soviet Union, China and the socialist countries of Eastern Europe are recognized. The instabilities, political as well as economic, of the Third World, have long been evident, but no longer is an early transition to socialism expected, and no longer is it considered sufficient merely to blame these problems on a legacy of imperialism. An economic crisis generated by the growing problem of Third World debt would affect the Soviet economy too. And those Third World countries making the greatest advance include the "little tigers" of East Asia: South Korea, Taiwan, Hong Kong, and Singapore— as well as the more mature capitalist Japan, with a GNP now comparable to that of the Soviet Union itself.

It is not my purpose here to discuss any of these problems, only to flag the underlying changed assessments and more basically new view of the world brought into leadership deliberations and given the cachet of authority by Gorbachev. There are debated issues. While the concept of "common security," and the defense guideline of "reasonable sufficiency," for example, have been adopted, there remain differing views and judgments in Moscow on specific policy applications.

The new thinking on the world, and debated differences on particular issues, are important to Soviet-American relations and to American policy. We should make every effort, consistent with our security interests and potentially serving them, to engage the Soviet Union in areas such as arms reductions and political settlement of regional conflicts. We must show we are prepared to do our share in order to determine whether the Soviet Union is prepared to do its share. And in those instances where there may be divided Soviet views nothing would strengthen the hand of those seeking accommodation more than demonstration that an opportunity is there. What is called for is simply an affirmation of readiness in negotiation—in proposals and in responses to Soviet proposals; the American and Western position can and should be taken with prudence to assure (and to reassure skeptics) that our interests are protected, while encouraging developments under which our interests can be advanced. The greatest risk may be failing to take the opportunity. It would be ironic indeed if we failed to take advantage of the new Soviet view of the world because of an ossified *Western* view of the world posited on assuming an unalterable "communism."

SIGNIFICANCE OF THE CHANGES IN SOVIET POLICY

Who, five years ago, would have expected the Soviet Union to agree to asymmetrical reductions and elimination of intermediate and lesser range ballistic missiles? Or to accept far-reaching and intrinsic on-site inspection for verification? Or to withdraw its military forces from Afghanistan? Or to pay up in full its back dues and assessments to the United Nations and urge greater use of that international body in settling regional conflicts? Or to admit past errors and failures in their foreign policy?

Most importantly, what underlies these and other changes in both word and deed? There has been a significant change in Soviet outlook and objectives, grounded in new assessment of developments in the world, and indeed of the nature of world processes. Without rejecting Marxist-Leninist ideology, the Soviet leaders are reinterpreting its meaning for their own policy. It is not too much to say that the "mellowing" of the Soviet World view foreseen as a possibility by George Kennan some forty years ago is now occurring, and probably already exceeds his most ambitious hopes.

The implications for American policy and for the world, as well as for the Soviet Union itself, are enormous.

I should like to look back to some of the diplomatic arms control negotiations with the Soviet Union in the 1960s and 1970s to draw some observations that may be useful today.

The area of agreement in any negotiation is bounded basically by the interests and objectives of the parties, but also by the ability of the governments in framing negotiating positions and of the negotiators in attaining them. A broadness of vision is often required.

Take, for example, the nuclear test ban negotiations of 1958–1963. All parties (United States, UK and USSR) purported to seek a complete ban on nuclear testing, and I believe all, in fact, sought that aim. The main unresolved issue was verification, more specifically on-site inspection of suspicious events not susceptible to verification by existing seismic means. finally, in early 1963, Khrushchev believed that he had received a signal through certain comments of American negotiators that the United States was prepared to agree if the principle were met through a quota of only two or three on-site inspections. He rammed through such a decision over the objections of colleagues in the Soviet leadership and made such an offer. Kennedy had not, however, authorized any deal, and the United States negotiators thereupon began classical negotiating tactics—offering to reduce the American quota proposal from ten to seven. Some members of the administration, at least, expected an outcome of five (although the lowest authorized but never surfaced fallback was six). But Khrushchev believed he had been "burned," and refused to go above three. The negotiations stalemated, and were only resolved in mid-1963 by abandoning a comprehensive nuclear weapons test ban and settling on a ban on tests in the atmosphere, space, and underwater.

The limiting factor became not the basic objectives of the two sides, or even real requirements of verification, but beliefs about the negotiating tactics of the two sides. One can well imagine Gorbachev today meeting that situation by proposing five inspections or if necessary accepting seven. To be sure, it is not entirely clear in retrospect that Khrushchev could have accepted five or six, or if Kennedy could have accepted three, but it would clearly have been in the interests of both if either had had the acumen and the leeway to have taken such a step.

In the SALT I negotiations, throughout which I participated directly, a slightly different situation prevailed. Again, the real interests, and I believe objectives of both sides, included coupling real constraints on strategic offensive arms with an ABM Treaty. The United States could not, however, bring itself to accept the relevance of its forward-based nuclear delivery systems and the Soviet leadership could not set them totally aside. The great omission undercutting the SALT I Interim Agreement, the SALT II Treaty, and even the putative START Treaty—despite their virtues—was the failure to curb the growth of counterforce capabilities posing threats to the land-based ICBM forces of both sides through preventing (or, later, eliminating) MIRV systems. The United States, shortsightedly, owing to its five year advantage in developing and deploying MIRV, failed in 1969 to 1972 to make a real or viable MIRV ban proposal. And the Soviet Union, concerned over placing itself in the role of demandeur from a position of weakness, also did not then seriously press for an MIRV ban. One can well suppose that Gorbachev would have accepted the burden of proposing compensatory Soviet concessions in order to force the United States to seriously consider such a ban. And an American leadership more interested in arms limitations than the Nixon-Kissinger team—for example, the Johnson-Rusk-McNamara team of 1967—might have done so as well.

Today Gorbachev is trying to press both for maximal nuclear reductions, and for sharply restructuring and reducing theater general purpose forces. The problems involved in reaching agreement in those negotiations are complex and will not be easy to resolve. But the objectives of greater stability and lessened military threat and burden are in the interest of both sides. Today for the first time the Soviet Union is in the lead in seeking far-reaching agreements along these lines. We still need to test Soviet readiness to do what is necessary on their part, but we must also be prepared to do our part in order to make that test. It remains to be seen if the West will rise to the occasion.

PROSPECTS FOR THE GORBACHEV REFORMS

Townsend Hoopes

The Gorbachev domestic reforms raise three separate questions:

(1) Are the reformers serious, or are *glasnost* and *perestroika* really an elaborate ploy to seduce the West into "letting down its guard?"

(2) Assuming they are serious, can they succeed?

(3) Can they hope to succeed within the bounds of Marxist-Leninist socialism?

There is now an affirmative consensus on the first question. No one who has followed Soviet affairs since 1985, has read Gorbachev's remarkable book, observed the extraordinary relaxation in the political climate in Moscow, or talked with Soviet officials at almost any level can rationally deny that the reformers are seriously bent on reform. Except to those "strategic egocentrists" in the West who cling to the notion that the only purpose of the Soviet leadership is to lull America and Europe into a sense of false security, it is clear to informed observers that the Gorbachev reformers are motivated by an urgent sense of national self-interest. Indeed, they passionately assert there is no other choice—no rational alternative course for their country—if it is to emerge from its profound political and economic stagnation. The premise, implicit when Gorbachev came to power in 1985, but acknowledged now with increasing candor, is that the Soviet system has failed.

If the reformers are serious, can they succeed? Here the agents of reform are up against nearly 800 years of authoritarian inertia, including seventy years of Bolshevik micromanagement over every aspect of society. The Russian political-cultural tradition is one of rigid hierarchy with orders from the top. Persons in the middle ranges of this vertical structure are conditioned to taking and giving orders, but have little experience with, or instinct for, economic initiative, innovation or entrepreneurship. And whatever such instincts might exist have been stultified everywhere by total bureaucratic regulation.

This heritage has bred a distinctive set of economic attitudes. As an advisor to Gorbachev told me in Moscow in September of this year: "As we know, the American economic ethos is keeping up with the Joneses. What you must understand is that the Russian economic ethos is making sure the Joneses don't rise above you." He then gave me several examples of how this Russian mindset is frustrating Gorbachev's efforts to achieve a more decentralized, more market-oriented economy.

(A) The manager of a collective farm was ordered by Moscow to offer incentive contracts to individuals or small groups willing to work extra hours to increase production of fruits and vegetables. Several energetic people came forward, contracts were signed, and the contractors were soon outproducing the whole collective farm in both quantity and quality. One small group earned 800 rubles in one month under their contract. But the farm manager's salary was only 250 rubles. Here was the rub. His political and economic prestige, his standing in the community, were suddenly at stake, so he refused to honor the contract, trying to fob off the contractors with a few extra rubles instead of the 800 they had earned. They were left with the option of taking their case to court, a process fraught with long delay and great uncertainty. Incentive was squashed.

(B) There are hundreds of chauffeurs in Moscow whose only work consists of driving their bosses to the office in the morning and playing cards all day in the garage until it is time to drive their bosses home. Local political approval was obtained to use the cars as taxis during the day, and in one garage it was agreed that each driver would split his extra earnings fifty-fifty with the garage manager. One energetic driver earned 400 extra rubles the first month, but the garage manager then insisted on pocketing 80 percent of his take. He told the driver, "Fifty extra rubles are enough for you." So the driver is back to playing cards all day having concluded that harder work enriches only his bosses.

If we multiply these examples by several million, we obtain a sense of the scale of the psychological-philosophical problem facing the economic reformers. The good news is that they are now fully aware of this glue in the system. After four years in power, they have reached the basic conclusion that they must change the distribution of political power, through local elections, the creation of a new Congress of Deputies, and the dilution of Party influence at all levels, before they can make any real headway on economic reform. The bad news is that this is inherently a long, slow process with no quick payoff.

The whole movement toward decentralized economic decisions and improved product quality imposes new strains and great uncertainties on the work force. In the past, the workers used a cynical saying, "we pretend to work and they pretend to pay us." But now managers and workers must work harder and more efficiently, must forego traditional job security and accept sharper wage and salary differentials. Gorbachev has denounced "wage leveling" as a basic obstacle to economic revitalization. Meanwhile, the price of food and other basics, still heavily subsidized, must rise if the reforms are to succeed, yet there is no early prospect for a better selection of consumer goods in the stores. In short, the proposed reforms involve wrenching dislocations for millions of people and a period of economic austerity before significant improvements can be realized. And no one knows how long that period will last.

The third question is whether Gorbachev can achieve significant economic improvement without at least a *de facto* repudiation of Marxist-

Leninist socialism. Stated otherwise, can limited openness accompanied by limited reforms really provide sufficient incentives to modernize the Soviet economy to the point, for example, where the Soviet people can begin to enjoy quality products, or where Soviet products can begin to compete in world markets? Moreover, is a one-party state, even one run by an elite dedicated to reform, a sustainable political model in an environment of increasingly free expression? It is doubtful whether Gorbachev and his colleagues, or anyone else, can answer these questions with precision. Indeed such questions are rarely asked in the Soviet Union, for the asking places at risk the moral and intellectual foundations of the Soviet system, which is to say, the political legitimacy of the Communist Party, its right to hold and exercise power. If the Marxist theory is abandoned, then the Communist Party is no longer the ordained representative of the nation and the vanguard in the struggle for Socialism.

To paraphrase Churchill, Gorbachev was not called to power in the USSR to preside over the liquidation of the Bolshevik Revolution. Not surprisingly, therefore, he began by asserting that all solutions to his nation's malaise were to be found within the framework of socialism—although his model was "genuine Leninist socialism" as it existed before what he claims was its gross distortion by the Stalinist Terror and the catastrophic human and material losses of the Great Patriotic War against Hitler's invasion. Many of the reforms, however, sound much less like Lenin and much more like moves toward entrepreneurial capitalism—they embrace incentive compensation and the profit motive. But the remarkable development of recent months is that the reformers seem less and less concerned to conceal these basic discrepancies. Nikolai Shishlin, a major player in the reform movement and a deputy to Aleksandr Iakovlev (perhaps Gorbachev's closest associate in the Politburo and widely regarded as the most influential advocate of *perestroika*) said recently on American television: "we will do whatever is necessary to succeed."

To speed the process of economic reform—specifically to shorten and cushion the unavoidable period of austerity—the Soviet Union has now arranged lines of credit totaling more than $9 billion with Japanese, German, Italian, French, and British banks. Further extension of Western credit, including American, seems likely. The plan is to purchase and assimilate Western technology. Much of the initial money will be used to modernize 200 factories with the aim of improving both the quantity and quality of consumer goods. The arrangements include joint ventures where the Western partner holds a majority interest, and they appear to involve pervasive participation of western industrialists, consultants, engineers, and other technicians. Without question, the Gorbachev reformers, presumed socialists, are moving into uncharted territory.

The Soviet leadership is thus embarked on a fateful journey fraught with hope, uncertainty and potential peril. Full "success" for domestic reform is, by any definition, a matter for decades and perhaps generations, and will always remain an essentially elastic, subjective criterion. The immediate question is whether Gorbachev and his colleagues can produce tangible economic progress within "a reasonable time," and what will happen if they cannot.

The current conventional wisdom in the West is to assume that, if Gorbachev cannot produce within a certain finite timespan, then the Stalinists will reemerge from the shadows and the Iron Curtain will descend again. Such an outcome is conceivable, yet it seems doubtful for several reasons:

1. There is a broad and growing awareness throughout all leadership groups—including the military—that far-reaching political and economic reforms are absolutely imperative, if the USSR is to sustain a credible claim to superpower status, or is even to play a significant role in a world economy increasingly based on advanced computer technologies, and on more or less democratic methods of industrial organization.

2. The reform movement, at its core, is a movement of the Gorbachev generation—roughly the people now between forty and fifty-five. They lived through twenty years of repression, corrupt cronyism, and economic stagnation under Brezhnev and they seem determined to clear away the dry rot.

3. If they can put it to good use, time is on their side. Many upholders of the Old Regime are falling away by death or retirement (voluntary or otherwise). Moreover, the opposition has offered no alternative proposals for ending the widely recognized stagnation. Essentially they are fighting a rearguard action to preserve a status quo which benefits them personally even as the nation sinks around them. Already the process of *glasnost* has made it more difficult for any group to reimpose a rigid Stalinist orthodoxy enforced by repression. Not impossible, but more difficult. However, if by some turn of events the Old Guard should recapture political power, the outlook would be for some active resistance and for the larger-scale passive resistance of absenteeism, alcoholism, drug abuse, and crime—which is to

say, the manifestations of decline that gave rise to the reform movement in the first place. A belief that the Old Guard has nothing to offer has led the reformers to speak with a certain grim confidence. Nikolai Shishlin has said, "the path to the past is closed. No one will accept it."

4. The problem of passive resistance in the work force and in the middle levels of bureaucracy is probably the most intractable obstacle to economic reform. Yet here Gorbachev can use political power to replace recalcitrants with those who espouse reform. He can thereby buy time for Western credits and technical assistance to bring more and better consumer goods into the domestic marketplace, and to continue his broad efforts to educate the workforce (which is to say the whole population) to the benefits of a more open, more competitive society.

5. Within broad limits he can adjust the pace of reform to the success of his efforts to extend and deepen the political power of the reformers. They are effectively using the powerful instrument of television for this purpose.

To sum up, progress will be gradual, uneven, messy, and accompanied by much frustration and disappointment—even in the best of circumstances. Reality will fall short of expectation for both the leaders and the man in the street. Yet set against the present situation—and against the dreary history of suffocating bureaucratic regulation, chronic consumer shortages, shoddy goods, and endless queues—even modest progress can be presented as, and in fact will amount to, a success sufficient to maintain a politically skilled reform movement. This prospect will be strengthened if *glasnost* continues to release new energies and new creative ideas into the society.

The possibility of derailment will be ever-present. For example, an explosion in Eastern Europe that seemed to threaten Soviet security interests would add serious new tensions to the political situation in Moscow. On balance, the evidence is that the Gorbachev leadership would try very hard to restrain the hawks, and would succeed in the absence of an American attempt to exploit the situation militarily. But no one can be sure. However, if this kind of difficulty can be avoided through tightrope diplomacy and some luck, Gorbachev is unlikely to face any arbitrary deadline for the full realization of his domestic reforms.

Socialism will surely be altered, perhaps transformed beyond recognition into some uniquely Soviet mutation. But if the result is tangible economic improvement, the ideological backsliding is not likely to create a political opportunity for the return of hardline purists. Indeed we may be confident that the Gorbachev reformers will continue to adjust ideology to assure its ever-present alignment with the realities of the reforms. Whatever they do, they will call it socialism. Full realization of the reforms is an ideal. The key to success lies in maintaining a certain forward momentum.

GORBACHEV AND THE U.S.-SOVIET RELATIONSHIP

Stanley Hoffman

Gorbachev's attempt at drastic reform of the Soviet system constitutes undoubtedly the most innovative and exciting development on the Soviet scene in many years. It is remarkable, first of all because he appears to have understood that economic improvements require a transformation of the rigidly bureaucratic apparatus of the Soviet Union and greater participation from people outside the Party. Moreover, he is allowing, for the first time, a genuine intellectual debate, which often creates the appearance of confusion and cacophony but which has the enormous merit of challenging clichés and dogmas.

Inevitably, these reforms provoke strong opposition both from ideologues and from party members and bureaucrats whose authority, and perhaps even positions, appear in danger. Gorbachev, who appears to be a very skillful politician, has been sufficiently pragmatic to avoid siding with any fixed position. But this is, of course, no guarantee of survival, especially if, as happens so often, the loosening of the system provokes at first more economic turbulence than progress.

This situation creates major opportunities for the United States. Gorbachev currently needs a stable external environment for domestic reform, and the reallocation of resources in more productive directions that he wants cannot occur without a substantial reduction of the military burden. It might be argued that there is enough consensus in the whole "Gorbachev generation" for the search for a less militarist and contentious foreign policy to continue, even if Gorbachev himself should fall. Indeed, should this happen, one could argue that the hopes and aspirations for a better life which he has fanned without being able to satisfy them would continue to prod the leadership toward reform. However, it is clear that there might be a serious difference between Gorbachev and possible successors (such as Ligachev) in the realm of foreign policy. Recent remarks by Ligachev about the class basis of foreign policy are an indication. Both he and Gorbachev may want a less turbulent and conflictual international environment than that of the years 1973–1983, but in several respects Gorbachev has gone much beyond merely "cooling it." He has taken major initiatives towards nuclear arms reductions and at least begun a process that ought to lead to conventional force limitations. He has pressured client states into moving toward a peaceful resolution of the conflicts in which they have been embroiled. And he has proclaimed an entirely new attachment to the UN and international organizations. It is not at all certain that these features would persist if he should be overthrown.

It is often said that uncertainty about Gorbachev's future should incite the United States to considerable prudence and skepticism in dealing with him. I disagree with this approach. Should he fall, the United States is very well equipped, militarily, to deal with the "Soviet danger"; diplomatically, our alliances are strong and indeed usually more coherent when the Soviets are tough.

To be sure, there is little to be gained by unilateral concessions. Gorbachev himself has not made any significant ones. His policy of relative retrenchment has not led him to drop allies, it has only made him much more restrictive in the definition of the scope of Russia's commitments. If only in order not to weaken his domestic position, he is clearly unlikely to move boldly toward a Finlandization of Eastern Europe which could lead precisely to the turbulence he does not want and to more military interventions which he obviously would like to avoid.

So the choice for the United States is not one between unilateral concessions, in the hope that they will be reciprocated, and the cold war as usual. It is a choice between the latter and a policy which takes advantage of the new features of Soviet foreign policy in order to build a new relationship with the Soviets. It would differ from the détente of the early 1970s both by being less exclusively focused on arms and by not being based on the implicit assumption of the Nixon-Brezhnev era that the superpowers were somehow the masters of the whole world.

We ought to pursue as quickly as possible the possibility opened by Gorbachev of drastic reductions in offensive arms, even at the cost of giving up the pipe dream of SDI (as long as research is maintained, in accordance with the 1972 treaty). And we ought to put forward, with our allies, detailed proposals for a reduction of conventional forces in Europe. These should incorporate two guidelines: the balanced elimination of asymmetries, and visible changes in deployment that would give substance to the idea of a switch by both sides to defensive strategies. In the nuclear realm we ought to think of the stage after the reductions under current discussion, in order to focus on the qualitative aspects of the arms race. We should move, as I have often argued, toward elimination of weapons that are vulnerable and of weapons that are unverifiable. This might oblige both sides to reduce their lists of targets—a goal well worth pursuing!

One of the most interesting and least observed developments of the Gorbachev era is the increasing political cooperation between the U.S. and the Soviet Union toward the solution of regional conflicts. (This is of course the opposite of what the Reagan administration had announced it would do in the beginning.) This collaboration should be continued and expanded, in particular in order to help resolve the conflicts in Central America (the Arias plan does not deal with the superpowers' involvement directly) and in the Middle-East. There, the cautious rapprochement between the Soviet Union and Israel and Gorbachev's advice to Arafat concerning the recognition of Israel indicate a significant change in traditional Soviet positions. American positions, by comparison, remain unproductively frozen.

Finally, both the U.S. and the Soviet Union ought to make of the UN and other international organizations a much more important arena for their diplomacy, if only because neither one of the superpowers by itself can effectively lead international society as a whole, because an explicit U.S.-Soviet condominium would continue to be unwelcome to the American public and elite, and because even if it could be "sold" at home, much of the rest of the world would not obey its dictates.

Areas of contention will remain between the two top military powers and ideological contenders. The Soviets are unlikely to share the Western aspiration for a reunification of Europe on a pluralistic political basis, for instance. But both sides have now discovered that the Third World is a trap, not a prize. Both explicitly acknowledge the imperatives and constraints of nuclear survival and interdependence. Both have pressing domestic priorities. The great opportunity created by Gorbachev is the possibility of not merely reducing the intensity of the superpowers' competition, but expanding areas of cooperation that are in the long-term interest of mankind.

THE GORBACHEV ECONOMIC REFORMS: SUCCESS DEPENDS ON A NEW SOCIAL COMPACT FOR WORKERS

Donald M. Kendall

In the four years General Secretary Mikhail Gorbachev has been in power, unexpected reforms have been introduced into the Soviet Union which have had deep ramifications throughout Soviet society and the rest of the world. Gorbachev's reform program represents the most intensive and comprehensive effort to deal with Soviet economic problems in decades. Moreover, its emphasis on economic modernization is intended to change how capital and labor are used in the economy. These changes, if successful, will alter the path of growth of the economy for the rest of this century. But it is clear that the reallocation of limited resources from heavy industry to consumer goods is central to the success of the reform program.

The Soviet economy stagnated during the later Brezhnev years. Under the dominant Soviet policy of import substitution, the technological gap between East and West grew wider. Declining growth rates were exacerbated by the inefficient utilization of resources, both material and human, while an increasingly inadequate, inefficient transport and distribution infrastructure contributed to the near crisis economic situation. The social compact between the Soviet government and its people, a tacit understanding of compliance with the system and acceptance of low living standards in exchange for minimum levels of social security—such as basic food, housing, employment, health care, and pensions—engendered an increasing degree of complacency among the Soviet people. Present resistance to change in this notion of social compact should not be underestimated as a force against Gorbachev's reforms.

Glasnost has enabled the press and the public to play an increasingly shaping role in economic and social debates. For example, articles have appeared in the Soviet press discussing declining growth rates and the staggering statistics on absenteeism. This kind of public discussion highlights the critical state of the Soviet economy. Further, the press has emphasized the need for change by accenting the shortages of consumer goods and the cramped housing conditions in which most Soviet citizens must live. Sophisticated debates have emerged both in the government and in society at large over the nature and character of economic reform. But it is clear, that through the press, Gorbachev has sought to communicate the stark realities of the domestic situation in order to convince the population that reform is the necessary alternative. The press has been encouraged to prepare the population to accept the necessary reforms by publicizing the argument for new measures before they are introduced.

Faster economic growth resulting from reorganization of the economy will only be evident in the long term. In the short term, the effort to achieve greater output and higher quality from labor—initiated by Andropov and which foundered under Chernenko—has been revived in a new form. Gorbachev's anti-alcohol campaign scored an initial success, cutting alcohol consumption sharply, and reduced the number of days lost from drunkenness and absenteeism. These campaigns were credited as contributing factors in rise to labor productivity in 1986. But such disciplinary campaigns can only scratch the surface of the problems of deteriorating economic performance in the Soviet Union. "Dry Laws," which led to an improvement in worker productivity, also left Soviet workers with excessive purchasing power, little to buy, and some dissatisfaction and are now being eased.

Fundamental reform of the economy has been introduced from above. There is a shift away from a top-heavy, highly centralized economy—managed through administrative directives—to what might be described as a mixed economy, which contains elements of market mechanisms geared to balance supply and demand. The Law on State Enterprise (implemented from 1 January 1988 onwards) has introduced self-financing and self-management at the factory level. Managers who previously fulfilled instructions issued from above have now been given greater responsibility to run the plant, including the acquisition of raw material, and to distribute and sell the finished products. The Law on Individual Labor Activity indicates a major change in attitude toward private income. Instead of the former taboo on private enterprise, the Gorbachev leadership now stresses the significance of earned income, be it in a State factory or in a small privately owned enterprise.

In November 1986, the Soviet Government issued legislation to promote the establishment of joint ventures between the Soviet Union and the West as a way to enhance technological development and economic modernization. These proposals reflect changing Soviet attitudes toward the international division of labor and a recognition of increasing economic interdependence. The objectives of joint ventures are: (1) to provide the domestic market with adequate, high quality consumer goods and thus reduce the importation of these goods; (2) to learn how to produce higher quality goods; (3) to learn Western management techniques and methods of personnel training; (4) to acquire technology without spending foreign currency; (5) to achieve better use of raw materials; (6) to export and earn hard currency.

The Soviet work culture in the past was characterized by a lack of entrepreneurial spirit and in experience in management. Workers and managers were praised for toeing the line and doing as they were told. The Soviets recognize that for a long time there had been considerable waste in the utilization of labor and capital at every stage of the production process. It is recognized that, for industry, State-owned enterprises, or joint ventures to function sucessfully, Soviet citizens need to learn new working processes. In addition, managers must learn better how to apply and even where to acquire the necessary inputs. To facilitate this process, the shortcomings of the supply mechanism of raw materials must be solved.

While new management techniques must be learned for the success of the reform process, they cannot be acquired overnight. The shortages of trained managers is glaring, in fact, there are presently only fifty-six Soviet students studying these subjects in the United States in comparison with approximately 23,000 Chinese students. The need is well understood by the leadership. In a recent article by Vadim Medvedev, the new chief ideologist in the Soviet leadership, the need to borrow political and economic ideas from capitalism was outlined. He called for close study of Western social organization, industrial production and integration into the world economy.

The levels of production prescribed in the plan have created a disparity between supply and demand. Moreover, the work patterns of managers and workers are deeply entrenched in the Soviet Union and have been since the Stalinist period, and extend even further back into Tsarist times. There is a pattern of uneven work schedules, stormy efforts to meet the plan at the end of each month. This pattern is reminiscent of the traditional seasonal work patterns of the peasantry in which periods of extremely intense activity during harvesting alternated with periods of inertia. The production process must become more steady; this requires greater discipline by workers and more predictability in the supply system for inputs.

The quantitative orientation of the five-year plans was never seriously challenged in leadership circles until Gorbachev came to power. But it is clear that workers have found it difficult to accept the new Quality Control

Commissions introduced in 1986 as part of the attempt to redress the balance in the direction of better quality. The quality control program is disrupting production and the supply network for the present, as poor quality goods are being rejected for the first time.

Academician Tatiana Zaslavskaia, Director of the newly created Institute of Public Opinion, has shown that 90 percent of managers and 84 percent of workers believe they could work more effectively under different economic conditions. Workers and managers feel they would work harder if they had greater independence and scope for initiative, and if their income were directly dependent on the quality of their work. Accustomed to receiving orders from above, however, many managers and skilled workers have been reluctant to show initiative. Worker's earnings have not been increased by hard work or decreased by lack of industry. The problem, then, is that the system of economic and moral incentives does not yet inspire the worker's creative energy.

The old paternalistic social compact between the workers and the State must be replaced by a new compact. The Soviet worker cannot be expected to show greater initiative and work harder without compensation in the form of higher wages and adequate consumer goods. The success of Gorbachev's program will, in the end, depend on the performance of the Soviet work force. In recognition of this basic fact, a combination of measures is being implemented to strengthen discipline, improve labor utilization, enhance worker incentives and provide more skilled labor. The new wage system in Soviet industry, which was introduced on 1 January 1987, is designed to improve incentives to perform well and acquire advanced skills by reversing a long-standing trend toward wage-leveling. Under the new system, higher wage increases would go to those with skills vital to the modernization program. However, the introduction of wage differentials and incentive systems has raised deep-seated prejudices among workers against unequal incomes. The idea of encouraging the earning of a large income, more than one's co-worker, has deeply ingrained negative, ideological, and social connotations in the eyes of many Soviet citizens.

Many workers have, therefore, adopted a "wait and see" attitude to avoid any future recriminations from showing initiative. The lack of confidence in the possibility of successful change, coupled with a traditional preference for maintaining the status quo, has made workers unwilling to change. Moreover, any reform directed at overcoming inefficiency demands reassessment of the commitment to job security, thereby threatening a mainstay of the Soviet social compact—full employment.

In the past, shortages of both labor and supplies led to extensive hoarding—creating overproduction and underproduction at different times. The prevailing shortage of labor has given workers leverage over managers, who understandably fear losing their workers and subsequently not being able to meet the plan.

While a lack of benefits such as the availability of consumer goods plays a significant role in the low productivity level of the Soviet worker, more important is the widespread feeling among workers that they serve a now useful purpose in the system. The oft-repeated Soviet joke, "The State pretends to pay us and we pretend to work" reveals a deep truth about the relationship between the worker and the State. The overcentralized system and the impersonal, gigantic production plants have caused the individual to become so buried and lost in the system that he does not feel he has a worthwhile place. The woker's perception is intensified by the increasingly high education levels of the vast majority of Soviet workers in comparison with the average worker of Stalinist times.

A Soviet engineer recently told me, "There is the feeling that if we work two hours a day or ten hours a day it doesn't make any difference, so you might as well work two." The Soviet worker feels he has little control over production, fails to see the results of his work, and is well aware that much of his work is wasted in useless production. Many economists now acknowledge that the true meaning of "owning the means of production" has been lost. The Soviet worker is under no illusion that too high a proportion of his work ends up on the dust heap: many of the goods that are produced are too shoddy to use, and products are often assembled without all the right parts.

As the Gorbachev reform process develops, economists and managers must create a better relationship between the individual and the collective. Each worker must feel he has a vested interest in the system, that his work matters. Giving the worker a stake in the system is the most difficult challenge facing the Soviet government. Flooding the market with improved consumer goods or new consumer services are merely interim measures, and will fail in the end as the anti-alcohol/discipline campaign has already proved.

Making the "human factor" in the organization of the economy is the key to the economic reform process. The leadership's desire to arouse worker pride in his labor reflects the need to create a new awareness of individual and collective interests—a new social compact. The importance attached to this issue reflects the search for a balance between the logic and order of the planned economy and the motivation of the individual worker. In their analysis of the human factor, Soviet economists have sought ways of encouraging greater discipline, order and authority while at the same time stimulating greater freedoms of initiative, active participation, responsibility, and care for one's work.

For the first time, investment in the consumer sector has overtaken investment in heavy industry. Investment has also increased in housing, education, and healthcare. Unfortunately, as yet, there is no evidence that the supply of consumer goods and the provision of services has improved. Soviet economists acknowledge that time is needed to modernize light industry by equipping it with new machinery and providing better raw materials. While it is clear that greater variety of food and more appliances would make life easier, importing consumer goods only alleviates the problem in the short run. The best way to achieve lasting improvement is sustained and increased investment in the light industry sector.

If Gorbachev's economic program continues to be vigorously implemented, the result of adjusting to the new conditions will be a period of disruption that will lower economic growth over the next few years. The question of how long the workers will put up with short-term sacrifice in order to reap the benefits of reform in the long run is compounded by the high level expectations of the Soviet people who will not be willing to put up with continued food shortages and poor consumer goods in their presently dim mood of hope for the possibility of permanent change.

In sum, the Soviet leadership has a difficult task to make it through a very tough transition period. If the sacrifices the worker must make in the short-term to achieve long-term benefits and interests can be successfully sustained during the transition period, then there will be a great chance for the success of the reform measures.

ARE WE OVER THE HUMP IN U.S.-SOVIET RELATIONS?

Carl Marcy

Before answering the question posed above, permit me to recall several personal experiences that my wife Mildred and I have had with Soviet citizens over some years.

In 1946 I was assistant to Charles Fahy, then the Legal Adviser in the State Department, and later Judge Fahy of the U.S. Court of Appeals. Fahy was the U.S. Delegate on the Sixth (the legal) Committee at the meeting of the United Nations General Assembly, which at that time met at Lake Success before the UN headquarters in New York City had been built. The Soviet Delegate was Mr. Durdenevsky, a highly respected Russian international lawyer.

After a long day of wrangling over legal issues, Fahy invited the Soviet Delegate to ride with us to our hotel in New York City. I recall Mr. Fahy, a gentle and kindly man, posing a question to our guest rider. "Mr. Durdenevsky, why is it that we can't resolve our legal and political issues on the basis of rational discussion?" Mr. Durdenevsky's reply in the privacy of our limousine still sticks in my mind: "It's the regime."

Eighteen years later, in 1964, my wife and I were fortunate enough to spend a month in the Soviet Union on a joint fellowship of the Institute of Current World Affairs. By then I was Chief of Staff of the Senate Foreign Relations Committee and Mildred was an advisor in the U.S. Information Agency. In a July 1964 letter to the Director of the Institute entitled *Conversations on a Park Bench*, I recounted three personal conversations with Soviet citizens, abbreviated as follows:

> On a park bench in Kiev, a nondescript man in shabby clothes and a brimmed felt hat sat down next to me. Shortly he took off his hat to reveal a balding head, bushy red eyebrows, and penetrating blue eyes. Hesitantly he asked if I was a tourist. I acknowledged my role, admired the scenery in Kiev, and asked if he lived there. For only a few months, he replied, saying he had come from Asian Russia. He was a novelist, he said. From then on, in broken English, the conversation was a monologue, punctuated occasionally by my signs of understanding.
>
> "In this country," said the man, "there is no freedom. For forty years I have wanted to go to Moscow. The State, with its internal passports, will not permit it. I cannot go abroad, The State will not permit it. Here everything is organized. The State is everywhere—on the radio and in the press. It puts slogans in our parks. Children are told what to think. The individual means nothing. We cannot buy books or magazines from abroad. We don't know what goes on. The culture you think you see in our music and in our art is on the surface: It's for show; it doesn't run deep."
>
> The conversation recounted above led me to ask myself if I might have been reading my own thoughts and observations into what my companion was saying. I then recalled another conversation a few days earlier on a Black Sea beach at Sochi.
>
> There, absorbing the sun and George Kennan's *Russia and the West*, I was disturbed by the chatter of a boy and his father who sat down close by. When

I surrendered to the interruption, the man introduced himself as a vacationing machinist from Kharkov. He was anxious to practice his English. After the usual pleasantries and a few words with his son who was being taught English by the father, the machinist asked where I had bought the Kennan book and how much it cost. "Athens," I replied, "ninety-five cents." And "what was the book about?"

For half an hour we sat shoulder to shoulder scanning and discussing underlined passages—many of them critical of Soviet policies especially during the Stalin regime. My friend's remarks were "Yes, I understand"; "That's true"; "We can't buy books like that here." My main impression was that here was a man with an avid desire to know, to read political books, to learn what other peoples were doing and thinking.

The morning after the encounter in Kiev with my red-browed companion, I wandered back to the same park bench hoping to find him again. No luck. So, purchasing a copy of the *Moscow News*, a thrice-weekly English language reprint of the "best" of the Soviet press, I sought out an empty park bench. Shortly after laying aside the *Moscow News*, a man of twenty-five or thirty years of age sat beside me and asked to read the paper. "Go ahead if you read English," I replied. He did and five minutes later handed the paper back and in halting English said: "I don't know what you think of our press, but I think it's rubbish!"

This man was a student of naval architecture, and an avid reader of English novels. In the next half hour I found myself being quizzed on the meaning of such idiomatic expressions as "according to Hoyle," "carrying coals to Newcastle" (which is paralleled by the Russian saying "taking wood to the forest"), "a Gilbertsian situation," and "have you kissed the Blarney stone today?" I tried to steer the conversation back to politics, but aside from condolences at the death of President Kennedy—who this Russian believed was killed by a crazy man (contrary to the plot theory of most Russians)—I made no headway. As we parted, my new friend remarked: "Good voyage, good riddance," which gave me a chance to comment in good humor that an American would respond by saying he was being "fresh."

My method of observation in Russia became somewhat that of a birdwatcher. When I was learning the technique, I figuratively barged into the hills and forests in my sportsjacket and with dangling field glasses shouted: "Where are the birds?" They had flown. Later I learned to slip silently onto a park bench, dressed drably for the environment, and wait and watch and listen. Soon the inhabitants assumed, on casual inspection, that I was just another one of them. I could then make out their plumage, their worn shoes and shabby clothes. I saw these citizens traveled often in groups, red-kerchiefed "Young Pioneers" kindergarten groups. Even the older inhabitants were often grouped and led purposefully on their way to exhibitions of Soviet culture, stopping from time to time to read red-emblazoned slogans extolling work, comradeship, the cosmonauts, and the Motherland. I thought there must be a surplus of sign painters and red paint in the Soviet Union.

While I was engaged in my conversations on park benches, Mildred (on leave from the U.S. Information Agency) recorded for our sponsor (the Institute of Current World Affairs) her observations and conversations. Herewith an excerpt from one of her reports:

> Of the more than twenty countries we have visited so far this year, it was in the Soviet Union that, for the first time, we were unable to buy newspapers or magazines published any place but in the "peoples democracies" of the communist bloc. Newspapers and magazines published by the communist parties in the United States, Britain, France, and elsewhere in the West are the only examples of the Western press permitted to be sold in newsstand kiosks. Not just late, but absolutely unavailable, were the *New York Herald Tribune, Time, Newsweek, The Economist, Manchester Guardian,* or *Le Monde*.
>
> During an interview with a rather high-level Soviet official, I commented on the lack of news available in the USSR. His verbatim comment was: "Your publications don't serve our political purposes. They're too anti-Soviet. If you'll make them more favorable toward us, we'll be glad to let them in. Reading newspapers is, for Americans, merely a habit. Our people don't have the decadent habit you Americans have, of not being able to start the day without a shower, a shave, a morning cup of coffee, a first cigarette, and the morning newspaper. Newspapers aren't essential to maintain life. Our Brigades of Communist Labor are working too hard to spend much time reading uncomplimentary untruths about their country. And anyway we have a paper shortage. Besides, [and this was his clincher] by not letting your trash in, we protect our citizens from becoming confused."

I then observed that in every country we have visted this year, one overriding impression is the seemingly insatiable desire on the part of young people to know about other countries, other customs, other systems. "After all," I had said, (perhaps not exactly diplomatically) "the Soviet regime has been exhorting its people to overtake and surpass the Americans — whether in science, space, agriculture, industrialization or practically any other sphere. Isn't it to be expected then that your people (particularly your young people) are going to be curious about the Americans — who they are, what they stand for, and what their system has accomplished? How do you propose to satisfy this curiosity?" At that point the official did acknowledge that such curiosity existed and that a limited number of copies of major U.S. newspapers, magazines, and books do find their way into the government censorship office and, if cleared, into libraries and government offices where they are available on a "need to know" basis. Far from free access to information, but a crack in the curtain.

I doubt that American specialists in the area of U.S.-Soviet relations will discover surprises in the foregoing accounts by nonspecialists of their casual encounters and conversations extending back some forty years. The cynics might remark *"plus ça change, plus c'est la même chose."* However, what comes through to me as I review these conversations of so long ago, is that the seeds of *glasnost* were sprouting long before Gorbachev removed them from the cellar and put them in the greenhouse.

Reverting to the question posed in the title to these observations, "Are we over the hump in U.S.-Soviet Relations?" I note that it was twenty-five years ago that I concluded my nonspecialist observations with these words:

"In time the [Soviet] goal of creating a world in the communist image may be replaced by goals based on realization that a world of states recognizing the eminence of the individual rather than the State, hold for the international community and for all humanity the greatest hope for survival in happiness, prosperity, and peace. Another twenty-five years of peace might get the world over the hump." One more year to go!

THE BICYCLE IS AGAIN IN MOTION

Fred Warner Neal

With the Bush Administration, we have an American political climate more conducive to significant improvements in U.S.-Soviet relations than at any time since the end of World War II. There is no guarantee that the improvements will be achieved, but the framework for their achievement surely exists.

The only real improvement in U.S.-Soviet relations has come under right-wing Republican presidents—Nixon, on his own and Kissinger's initiatives, and Reagan, on Gorbachev's initiatives. Since to be accused of being "soft" on Communism or on the Soviet Union has always been the most dangerous risk facing American politicians, only Nixon and Reagan, who had both made careers out of hardline attitudes toward Moscow, could have done it. It is extremely unlikely that any Democrat could have accomplished either

Détente I or the improved relationship that marked Reagan's last year in office.

But Nixon's and Reagan's basic extreme ideological orientation also limited what they could—or would—do and made the improvements precarious and, as was the case with Détente I, short-lived. Today, for the first time, we have a more or less moderate Republican president, George Bush, starting his term in a period of developing détente rather than a Democrat, who would have inevitably felt more inhibited about policy toward the USSR. The already established warmer relationship between the Soviet Union and the United States thus has better prospects than ever for not only continuing but broadening.

Up until now, most of the improvements in U.S.-Soviet reactions in the last three years have reflected Gorbachev's new foreign policy orientation. His "new thinking" has involved a clearer recognition of the dangers of thermonuclear war, abandonment of Communist ideological commitments to conflict with capitalist countries, and unilateral moves such as an eighteen-month moratorium on nuclear testing, a commitment to a primarily defensive military policy, and some actual reductions of Soviet armaments.

Unquestionably, the most important development was Gorbachev's unexpected acceptance of the Reagan "zero option" plan for intermediate-range missiles. One reason "zero option" was proposed by the United States was because many Reagan Administration officials were convinced that Moscow would never accept it. Numerous commentators, including this one, more or less "proved" that the Soviet Union would reject "zero options" because it would leave the West with "superiority" in Europe-oriented nuclear weapons.

Gorbachev's surprising acceptance of "zero options" led to the INF Treaty, an apparent change in President Reagan's attitude toward the USSR and the resulting warming up of relations between the two countries—in short, what might be termed Détente II.

U.S.-Soviet relations invariably have been like a bicycle. When there is no forward motion, they tend to collapse. In the last two or three years many possibilities for new forward developments were proposed, but Moscow was showing increased unhappiness with the perception that the Reagan Administration was ill-disposed to make responses adequate to keep the process in motion.

There has been no indication that President Bush will rush to Moscow with open arms or abandon the Reagan slogan of "trust but verify"—with emphasis on verify. Nonetheless, the prospects for further progress in American-Soviet relations are good. The new administration is not encumbered with the ideological baggage—in terms of either ideas or personnel—of its predecessor. Further, in making new approaches to Moscow the Bush Administration can claim to be continuing a process initiated by Reagan.

Bush Administration appointees dealing with foreign policy lend credence to the likelihood that it will do so. Secretary of State Baker may not know much about the intricacies of foreign policy, but he is above all a pragmatist known for insistence on searching for solutions rather than conflict. He is backstopped by his chief deputy, Lawrence Eagleburger, also a pragmatist, who cut his foreign policy teeth under Henry Kissinger in the days of Détente I. Eagleburger not only knows the Russians well, but he is one of the most astute members of the American foreign policy establishment. General Scowcroft, the new National Security Adviser, reflects more of a traditional military view about the Soviet Union, but he is considered a moderate, at least comparatively.

Already Secretary Baker has pointed the way by indicating that he will focus on seeking a new START agreement without tying it to other issues. There is little question that this decision was warmly received in Moscow.

There are, of course, many possible pitfalls. There is a Romanian proverb to the effect that "it is difficult to predict, especially about the future."

Although the "Cold War" psychology so long prevalent in American society has clearly diminished, we really do not know how much inroad has been made in public opinion on the *idée fixe* that the Soviet Union poses a serious military threat. In the past, politicians have not been able to resist appeals to this bogey, and they have invariably been able to marshal public support for it. There is also a widespread belief that the Gorbachev "peace offensive" was the result of Reagan's hardline policies, and "Cold War types" argue they should therefore be continued.

Of course, much depends on the Soviet Union. While all visible signs in Moscow indicate not only the intention but the need to deepen the developing détente with the United States, opinion in the Kremlin is by no means unanimous. While it is extremely doubtful that the new openness of Soviet society—*glasnost*—can be altogether reversed, the overall reforms sought by Gorbachev, and consequently the position of the General Secretary, are by no means assured. Should Gorbachev's valiant efforts go down to defeat, the present Soviet foreign policy flexibility might well suffer. Even with Gorbachev, there are, of course, limits beyond which the Kremlin will not and cannot go.

What is called for, surely, are American initiatives that would help cement the businesslike, common-sense relationship that seems to be blossoming with the Soviet Union.

Ideally, first we should negotiate a mutual moratorium on nuclear testing. It makes no sense to talk about reducing nuclear weapons while undertaking to expand them. A test ban would do more than almost anything else to ensure progress in U.S.-Soviet relations.

Second, and simultaneously, we should redouble our efforts to reach an agreement for reducing ICBMs and conventional forces.

Third, as prerequisites for the second, we must maintain the ABM Treaty and hold up on SDI and deployment of cruise missiles.

Fourth, we should actively seek expansion of U.S.-Soviet trade, and, in this connection, abandon the Jackson-Vanik and Stevenson Amendments to the 1974 Trade Act.

Finally, we should work out a new Declaration of Principles of coexistence with the Soviet Union, similar to, but more precise than, the declaration signed in 1972.

In the fall of 1972, I wrote: "If the Declaration of Principles signed at the [Nixon-Brezhnev] Summit means what it says, the Cold War is over." Clearly, that Declaration of Principles did not mean what it said, neither to Washington nor to Moscow. Today we have another chance, under much more favorable conditions.

Thus the bicycle is again in motion. It is essential that we spare no opportunity to keep it moving forward.

CIVIL SOCIETY AND THE IMPEDIMENTS TO REFORM

Fred Starr

For thirty years after the death of Stalin in 1953 the USSR was ruled by men who had gained experience and promotion under the Georgian tyrant. Many of the gains made under the "thaw" proved ephemeral, the continuities with the previous era being far more striking. To be sure, the State's use of overt force against its citizens declined, millions of prisoners were released, controls on expression were relaxed, and in foreign policy the doctrine of peaceful coexistence replaced the notion of inevitable war with the capitalist powers. However, the political, institutional, and legal structure of the previous era continued almost unchanged, and leadership remained firmly in the hands of Stalin's heirs. Eventually, this proved a sure formula for stagnation.

Timor Timofeyev, Director of the Institute of International Labor Studies in Moscow, has noted that the present reforms were necessitated by changes in Soviet society from the 1960s to the present. These changes, which continued unabated during the "era of stagnation" under Brezhnev, affected four areas: first, urbanization, through which the balance of weight in Soviet society shifted decisively toward the cities; second, technological advancement, through which increasing numbers of industrial workers and managers were shifted into fields demanding high levels of competence and initiative; third, education, thanks to which the number of workers completing high school multiplied by five over a generation; and fourth, improved communications, through which horizontal links among citizens expanded, thus destroying the social atomization inflicted by Lenin and Stalin.

When Mr. Gorbachev came to power there existed neither a coherent ideology nor a program of reform. Initially, he underscored only the virtues of hard work and discipline. Campaigns against absenteeism and alcoholism reflected this focus, and had as their goal a general *uskorenie* or speed up of the economy. Gradually, however, the new leaders acknowledged that since such a quickening could not be purchased through additional inputs of labor, capital, or land, all of which were in short supply, they would have to be achieved through the more efficient use of existing resources. For such "intensification" to succeed, leaders had to devolve greater responsibility on local leaders, managers, and even ordinary workers.

From this realization arose the twin ideals of decentralization and self-government. The goal of decentralization was to strengthen on-site decision-making regarding the economy by freeing local decisionmakers from petty tutelage by the center. If such local decisionmaking is to enjoy the support of an increasingly sophisticated labor force, it must in turn be informed by public participation. From this arose notions of self-government through the elective *sovety* or councils, of worker participation in industrial management, and of a greater role in social life for voluntary associations as opposed to governmental organs.

Such measures directly reflect the changes that occured in Soviet society since Stalin's death and tap the energies released by those changes. This obvious congruence gave what began as a series of improvised reforms the character of a program, and transformed the separate ideas behind them into an ideology of reform. This ideology has been actualized through a number of specific measures, including the reduction of staffs in central planning agencies, the legitimation of private/co-operative production, the family contract plan for agriculture, increased worker participation in factory-level decisionmaking, and enhanced powers for local councils or *sovety*. Some degree of openness in communications is a necessary condition for the success of reforms. Serious differences exist among the Soviet elite over the degree of openness that should be permitted, but few deny that administrative decentralization requires more openness than does centralization, and that devolution calls for yet more.

As we read in the press of attacks on Mr. Gorbachev's policies from other Soviet officials we grow conscious of the existence of an anti-reform opposition in the USSR. Acknowledging this, it is important at the same time to appreciate the rapidity with which reforms have been introduced. Whereas all previous Soviet rulers except Lenin have taken up to five years to consolidate their power before taking dramatic actions, Gorbachev began instituting reforms after only a few months. Two conditions encouraged and justified such speed.

First, the economy of the USSR was growing weaker at the time Gorbachev assumed power and has continued since. Indebtedness has sextupled and now equals up to seven percent of GNP according to some estimates. In the United States, by contrast, the corresponding figure is 3.5 percent. Actual military expenditure has not declined, nor is it expected to before the beginning of the next five-year plan. Productivity has not grown. Given this, it is important for the State to enlist the economic initiative of society through the legalization of cooperative business and many other incentives involving both individuals and the labor forces of whole factories. By expanding local responsibility for the economy, the central government reduces pressure on itself.

Second, in many respects Soviet society has evolved far in advance of the governmental structures through which it is ruled. Thus, local managers have long since seized the initiative by manipulating the system— illegally if necessary—to assure their own and their factories' survival. Individual citizens have also long since developed independent and often illegal businesses. In both areas the policy of reform seeks to co-opt existing social energies and to bring them back into the legal mainstream in such a way that they might exert influence upon the system.

None of these changes can be considered real until it is embodied in law and until the legal system is reformed to the point that it can protect individuals and independent groups against the State. Hence, the most important indicator for the progress of reform as a whole is reform in the legal system.

The direction of both social evolution and recent legislation is toward the creation in the USSR of a "civil society," a society based on law in which individual citizens and voluntary associations enjoy extensive freedom of speech, assembly, and protection of property. In many respects the Lenin-Stalin system is the antithesis of a civil society, in that it atomizes individuals and rules them "from above." This, plus the authoritarian tradition in Russian political culture under the tsars, has caused many to doubt the viability of reform today. Yet imperial Russia between the mid-nineteenth century and 1914 evolved far in the direction of a "civil society," even to the point of establishing such basic freedoms as speech and assembly. These were confirmed by the February Revolution of 1917, but subsequently abrogated by the Bolsheviks. Even today, Soviet jurists (of which Gorbachev is one) are introduced to the works by imperial Russian authorities on civil societies based upon law.

Whatever vitality this old and long-neglected tradition may possess, the reform movement will be thwarted if a number of impediments to its progress are not removed. At least five such impediments to decentralization, devolution, and openness are widely recognized and discussed among Soviet leaders themselves.

1. The social evolution described above has been asymmetrical in that it has yet to extend its reach to all elements of the society. The peasantry has sharply decreased in number but many of those peasants who are still in the country remain outside the orbit of reform, as do many middle-level managers and workers in smokestack industries. Such people lack the psychology needed to make one sympathetic toward reforms of the type being proposed. The division between such people and those affected by recent social change dilutes and weakens the potential social base for reform.

2. The Communist Party as such is inherently hostile to democratic reform, which can only weaken its prerogatives. It is no surprise that most Party members profess support for their leader's program of renewal while actually preferring an authoritarian form of socialism that would preserve "top down" rule. Even if all Party members accepted the new ideology there would be problems, for no

nation has yet succeeded in creating a civil society or democratic system under one-party rule. At the very least, the 1921 rule outlawing factions within the Communist Party would have to be repealed.

3. The reform process has yet to embrace the federal system under which the various nationalities of the USSR are organized. True, various general statements have been issued on the need for increased autonomy in the economy, political system, and cultural matters, but these have yet to find expression in a coherent theory of federal reform.

    The basic dilemma that such a theory must address is the economic differentiation among regions that is bound to occur if greater powers are left to the republics and national groups. The fact that Russians would be on the losing end of such an arrangement makes the task of drafting federative constitutional reforms all the more difficult.

4. It appears unlikely that the reform program will benefit from rising national prosperity, at least in the near term, yet the leadership must somehow find money that can be turned over to the populace in the form of goods in order to strengthen public support for reform. No reduction in the military budget has yet been made, nor is this likely at least until the next five-year plan. It is still readily possible to borrow from abroad, but the regime is hesitant to do so. Unless Mr. Gorbachev is prepared either to increase borrowing or to sell oil or gold, he will have a difficult time rewarding adequately those workers who side with his program of change.

5. The unresolved issues remaining from the Stalin era are a strong brake on reforms tending toward a civil society. The individual who hesitates to speak out at a public meeting remembers that people died for speaking out in the past. The family farmer who refuses the government's offer for a private plot remembers that the same *kulaks* who took up Lenin's offer for private land in 1921 were shot or exiled in 1929–1931. The judge who hesitates to protect due process against the interference of local Party officials is probably also mindful of Stalin's purges of judges who failed to heed Party directives. Until the regime's past crimes are fully acknowledged and addressed, large parts of the Soviet populace will hold back from reform. A full airing of the "blank spots" in Soviet history is essential for the germination of the kind of political culture that will sustain a civil society.

All of these impediments to reform have been fully acknowledged by reformers within the USSR. Success or failure in addressing these issues will determine the extent of eventual reforms. Specifically, it will decide the question of whether the present era of change leaves the USSR under a reformed but still authoritarian socialism or under a more democratic civil society.

Acknowledging this, it is important in conclusion to stress the point made at the beginning of this essay, namely, that while Mr. Gorbachev's initiative is essential to the timing and precise content of the reform program, the basic impetus for change and its general direction arises not from Mr. Gorbachev but from the evolution of Soviet society itself over the past decades. Because of this, the long-term progress of reform may be less dependent on the fate of the top leader than on the pace of continuing social change. Whether or not Mr. Gorbachev succeeds in bringing the Soviet State fully into harmony with the direction of evolution in the society, he has already successfully begun the work of reducing the incongruence and has set down the general agenda for future efforts along the same line.

THE IMPORTANCE OF POLITICAL CULTURE

William Taubman

Of all the reforms that have been carried out in the USSR since the accession of Mikhail Gorbachev—economic, political, social, cultural, and in foreign policy—the most important change is the political culture. In the long run, none of the other reforms will last unless the country is able to move toward a more democratic political culture. And yet, although Gorbachev himself seems to recognize this need, and his most militant supporters are focusing their efforts precisely in this area, a host of obstacles stand in the way, leaving the outcome, at the very least, an open question.

Political culture is the way people think about politics—how they conceive of political activity, what they expect from it, and whether and how they are prepared to engage in it themselves. A democratic political culture requires a readiness to act politically, based partly on the expectation of positive results. It also demands a willingness to trust one's fellow citizens, that is, to observe majority rule, to respect minority rights, and to embark on constructive compromises in the name of the common good.

Alas, Russia has never had a democratic political culture—not before 1917 and not since. The pre-1917 Russian political tradition was authoritarian. For the Tsar and his court, autocracy was sacred. The kind of powerful middle class that was the carrier of democratic ideas in the West was conspicuous by its absence. Liberal democrats were few and far between even in the intelligentsia. As for the downtrodden peasants at the bottom, they alternated between passivity and fatalism on the one hand, and occasional outbreaks of anarchic violence on the other hand, both equally distant from the democratic norm. It speaks volumes about the obstacles to Gorbachev's *glasnost* that Harvard historian Edward Keenan describes the essence of the old Muscovite political tradition as *neglasnost*, or nonopenness.

The Bolshevik revolution was supposed to transform this authoritarian political culture. Instead, it strengthened it. Old-fashioned autocracy was replaced by Stalin's far fiercer totalitarian dictatorship. Those Bolsheviks like Nikolai Bukharin, who wanted to construct a more humane brand of communism, were wiped out. Stalin's terror pressured people to denounce each other, thus turning neighbor against neighbor, and even members of the same family against each other. Ironically, this deepened the mutual distrust among citizens that wars against democracy. The traditional Russian identification of freedom with license, and democracy with anarchy, was if anything strengthened by Stalinism, as was the traditional attachment to centralization and stability as overriding political virtues.

Gorbachev himself has recognized that democratization is the key to his reform. Along with "more socialism," the key slogan of *perestroika* has become "more democracy." To be sure, Gorbachev's attachment to democratization is largely instrumental; he sees it as a way to energize the economy and thus preserve Soviet superpower status, as a way to mobilize masses of people in support of his position and program and against those of his opponents. But for many of Gorbachev's supporters in the intelligentsia, broadening and deepening democracy has become an end in itself. Moreover, the logic of events has driven the Soviet leader to support more far-reaching reforms than he originally intended. At first, he and his colleagues tried to jump-start the stagnant economy with a crackdown on alcoholism and a demand for discipline. When that didn't work, they called for radical economic reforms. But so far those reforms haven't delivered the goods either, and they won't do so, Gorbachev now realizes, until the political system and the Communist Party's role in it have also been over-hauled.

The 19th Party Conference, held in Moscow in June 1988, took the biggest step yet in that overhaul. More important than the specific changes it endorsed (such as limiting the terms of Party leaders, instituting multicandi-date elections, and reducing the Party's role in the economy) was the nature of the conference itself—dramatic clashes in the hall, exchanges of charges and countercharges on prime-time television, the willingness of delegates to vote, "No!" for the first time in almost six decades. These events gal-vanized conference delegates and mesmerized the public. The medium was the message. Evidently, Gorbachev hoped the example of the conference, and of the struggle that preceded it to elect reform-minded delegates, would mobilize his supporters to fight for further democratization.

Democratization will need all the support it can get. Despite his valiant efforts and undoubted contribution, Gorbachev himself retains deep doubts about democracy. He has encouraged outspoken discussion of democratic institutions like the rule of the law, the separation of powers, and other guar-antees against tyranny. But his conception of these and other devices remains limited by his devotion to Leninist one-party rule. As long as the Commu-nist Party monopolizes power, democracy is drastically circumscribed. The single most important step the Party could take to democratize itself would be to rescind its 1921 ban on factions, yet Gorbachev shrinks from that as well.

Gorbachev's own doubts are in some ways the least of democracy's problems in the USSR. The exact shape and strength of high-level opposition to his reforms is uncertain. But clearly, such opposition exists. Gorbachev's own second-in-command, Egor Ligachev, is appalled by the flood of free speech that *glasnost* has released. Lesser conservatives, whether of the neo-Stalinist or Russophile persuasion, warn of the chaos and anarchy that the reforms can unleash. Most of these Cassandras are more concerned about losing their own power and privilege than about the fate of the nation, but the chilling effect on democratization is the same either way.

The very people who are theoretically the beneficiaries of democracy are themselves apparently uneasy with it. Enterprise managers hesitate to embrace new rights carrying with them responsibilities that cannot be ful-filled under the current economic system. Workers invited to elect new managers do so with equal hesitation, still skeptical that they are to be granted real power in what is officially called "the workers' state." Many ordinary citizens still look back with nostalgia on the Stalinist era when (they say) the leader's strong hand ensured that law and order prevailed.

Even Gorbachev's most fervent supporters, intellectuals and others who come closest to the Western image of true democrats, are as nervous about democracy as they are committed to it. Part of the problem is that they fear *perestroika* could still be reversed, leaving them to face retribution during a new period of reaction. But the deeper irony is that they fear success almost as much as failure. If democracy gives the people a voice, then whom will the people support? WIll they back the reforms, especially in the absence of concrete economic benefits that have yet to appear, or will they support a conservative backlash? The distrust between reformers and the people is dismayingly deep and mutual. Many common citizens view all the talk of democratization as yet another "campaign" to hoodwink and exploit them.

For all these reasons, the outcome is highly uncertain, less likely to be a result of the leader's intentions than resultant of the various forces at play in a complex and changing situation. Much depends on the capacity of the economy to deliver goods that reformers can cite as proof of *perestroika's* success. The explosive nationality question is also an unpredictable wild card. The restiveness in the Caucasus and the Baltic area is not the result of democratization, reformers say, but proof of the need for the same. Historically speaking, they are right, of course, but politically they will suffer if events in either area, or in equally restive Eastern Europe, get out of hand.

REDEFINING THE MARXIST FAITH

Olin Robison

The completion of Gorbachev's first four years as head of Soviet government seems a good time to comment on what he has tried to do and where he is trying to take the Soviet Union.

Even though he is now seen as the Great Reformer, some comparing him to Peter the Great, there is evidence to suggest that he did not think of himself that way when he assumed power. He was, in Soviet terms, a relatively young man who had made his way rapidly upward in a tough and unforgiving system. There is no reason to believe he was a closet liberal. There is more reason to believe that he intended to demonstrate that the system, Marxism-Leninism, could be made to work. It would now appear that he believes it cannot work and must be changed in radical and fundamental ways.

Gorbachev is such a superb publicist that it is difficult to sort out the significant from the superficial when looking at the recent changes in the Soviet Union. He does appear to believe that the system can be changed in major ways by virtue of his pronouncements and exhortations.

The phenomena of *glasnost* and *perestroika* are distinct yet interrelated. *Glasnost* is necessary in order to make *perestroika* possible. If the economy is to be reshaped, redirected and modernized then the climate in which it exists, Gorbachev appears to believe, must be radically different from that which has existed in the Soviet Union for the last seventy years. Gorbachev has found himself preaching the gospel of change to an entrenched and privileged Party, a skeptical military, an almost autonomous secret police establishment, and a lethargic and bloated bureaucracy. He faces the reticence of all these people who actually run the Soviet Union. In addition, change is made more difficult by virtue of a deeply conservative and cautious population.

Gorbachev's attempts to create a climate in which change is more likely has involved a number of initiatives that set him apart from all of his predecessors. The most creative of these seem to be the following:

First, Gorbachev, very early in his tenure, decided to create, direct, and use Soviet public opinion as a lever against the entrenched interests with which he must deal. In late February 1989, Gorbachev visited Kiev where he admonished citizens on the street to speak up on behalf of change. They replied that they were afraid. He then told them they must work from the bottom for change even as he works from the top. In a strange Soviet way he seems to be campaigning against the government he heads in ways not unlike the successful antigovernment presidential campaigns of Ronald Reagan.

For the last seventy years the Soviet leadership has consistently stifled the development of a coherent public opinion. The party knew best. People needed to be led. Gorbachev has clearly decided to change all that in the hope of forging a powerful alliance between himself and the populace. If it works, he wins big. If it does not work, he will have raised expectations which could be a part of his own undoing.

A second major effort on Gorbachev's part has been a successful attempt to co-opt the intelligentsia. While the intelligentsia is a relatively small proportion of the population, at least by Western standards, it is nonetheless extremely important to his efforts. They are the people who put words around ideas, they articulate the vision, and grant intellectual respectability to the reform movement.

His success in this effort is attributable to the fact that he is himself an attractive part of the intelligentsia, he is articulate and creative in his leadership, and he has loosened many of the restrictions under which the intellectuals have chafed. Also, most intellectuals in the Soviet Union believe that it is in their best interest that Gorbachev succeed. They believe that anyone who might replace him would likely be less progressive than he. Many of them therefore reason that, if they are to participate in the modernization of their country, Gorbachev is the last train leaving the station. Some quite literally believe that he is their last best hope.

A third important decision made by Gorbachev is to begin the process of confronting his country's dreadful history. It is a past in which death, war, carnage and obsession with control dominate every horizon and, to continue the metaphor, on every horizon looms the ghost of Iosif Stalin. Gorbachev and his colleagues now clearly acknowledge that the ghost of Stalin must be confronted and vanquished before their country and society can be at peace with themselves. This means rewriting history yet again. Perhaps, this time it will be permissible to have more than one version.

A fourth major effort on Gorbachev's part has to do with ideology. He is attempting to redefine the faith of Marxism; it is an attempt on Gorbachev's part to establish himself as the true prophet of the Leninist faith. All others since Lenin, says this new version of history, got it wrong.

There is currently no one in the Politburo with the ideological authority exercised by Mikhail Suslov during the Khrushchev and Brezhnev years. Suslov was the high priest of true Marxism. It is clear that Mr. Gorbachev's erstwhile rival, Egor Ligachev, had hoped to assume that mantle. In a deft move Gorbachev placed Ligachev in charge of agriculture and conferred the ideology portfolio on Vadim Medvedev. Not much is known about Mr. Medvedev's ideological views, but it seems probable that Mr. Medvedev knows who appointed him. It is unlikely that his interpretations of Marxism will differ very much from those held by Gorbachev.

Ideology counts a lot in the Soviet system. Without a firm ideological underpinning the rationale for so repressive a system does not exist. It is tempting to conclude that the traditional view of the Marxist vision is dead. Whatever comes next will indeed be called communism but it is unlikely to be anything Karl Marx would recognize.

Novelists often appear before American audiences to read passages from "works in progress." Gorbachev's Soviet Union is quite emphatically a work in progress. It is a good time to be a watcher of the Soviet Union.

APPENDIX I: SELECTED SOURCES FOR RESEARCH ON THE SOVIET UNION

by Claire Rosenson

In contrast to the commonly held Western view, debate and discussion of public policy have always existed in the Soviet press on some level. Traditionally, innovative ideas have been buried deep within lengthy quotes from Lenin or Marx, and expressed in subtle and sometimes obscure language. A key method of information gathering used by Sovietologists in the past has been to try to extract key phrases from the layers of screening language, and to trace the use of these phrases in different sources over time. The possibilities for misinterpretation were very great, and the means for confirming scholarly hypotheses were at best very limited.

Gorbachev's policy of *glasnost* has brightened this dismal picture in several respects. The most obvious change is that the latent process of debate has been brought to the surface. Soviet writers, whether they are scholars, government officials, or collective farmers, feel freer than in the past to express their opinions forthrightly, without recourse to linguistic camouflage. Also, the spectrum of publishable opinion has broadened to include the extremes of radical reformism and neo-Stalinism. The discussions of current affairs which used to take place between family members and friends around the dinner table are now making their way into the print media. More government officials are being identified and more statistical data are being published, which means that there is a wider range of factual information available as well.

All of these new inputs make the study of the Soviet Union richer and all the more fascinating, but certainly no easier than it has been up to this point. While certain information gaps are being filled, the volume of new information and opinions has created new pitfalls. Gorbachev's personal dynamism and the vitality of his programs have attracted many newcomers to the field of Soviet studies who may not be familiar with Soviet sources. Without an anchoring knowledge of the important sources, those who wish to know more about the Soviet Union will have no conception of what to expect from the various sources, and will therefore find it difficult to distinguish the ordinary from the innovative, the expected from the surprising.

This appendix is intended above all to serve as an introduction to important Soviet sources in the social sciences. The institutional affiliations of the various sources are noted and generalizations about their overall approach are made so that the researcher may choose the most appropriate sources on a particular topic. The secondary purpose of the appendix is to call attention to new trends in the press under Gorbachev. As the Soviets themselves recognize, certain publications are "the 'favorites' of *glasnost*," and this is noted where appropriate. The sources discussed here will serve as a solid basis for contemporary study of the Soviet Union, and will provide those who wish to probe more deeply with the means to find still more sources.

ANNOTATED BIBLIOGRAPHY OF SELECTED SOVIET PERIODICALS

The most widely read source for the official views of the Soviet leadership is *Pravda*, the official organ of the Central Committee of the Communist Party. *Pravda* is edited by Viktor Afanasev, who is also the head of the Journalists' Union. Equally important is *Izvestiia*, the organ of the Soviet government. Both are daily all-union newspapers, and both cover domestic and foreign affairs. Although there is, institutionally speaking, a Party/government dichotomy between the two papers, all important leadership activities are covered in both. *Pravda* is available in English translation through Associated Publishers, Inc., of St. Paul, Minnesota.

Pravda is more widely read by Western observers of Soviet affairs, but *Izvestiia* is no less authoritative. In fact, many of the more controversial discussions of General Secretary Gorbachev's reformist policies have taken place in the pages of *Izvestiia*. The freshness of the views expressed in *Izvestiia* is reflected in the recent increase in the number of its subscribers. *Izvestiia*'s circulation increased by 30.4 percent in 1988 over 1987, while *Pravda*'s circulation decreased by 3.6 percent as a result of a drop in subscriptions.

In addition to *Pravda*, two other important Central Committee publications are the journals *Kommunist* (Communist) and *Partiinaia zhizn* (Party Life). The "theoretical and political journal of the Central Committee," *Kommunist* contains information on high-level Party activities, including major speeches and discussions of current policies. Articles by Politburo members, prominent theoreticians, and foreign Communist leaders appear often. *Partiinaia zhizn* is similar in content to *Kommunist*, but is focused more on ideological-educational work and on the practical application of new policies.

Argumenty i fakty (Arguments and Facts) is the weekly newspaper of the *Znanie* Society, and is intended for use by "propagandists" and "agitators." Current events are summarized and analyzed with an eye toward familiarizing the reader with official views. *Argumenty i fakty* has gone farther than most other publications in shedding light on the Stalin era. A recent article on the adverse costs of collectivization, for example, gave a much higher estimate of the loss of life than had ever before appeared in the press.

Istoriia SSSR (History of the USSR), published by the History Institute of the Academy of Sciences, covers Russian/Soviet history and historiography from sociological and economic perspectives. Surprisingly little commentary on Gorbachev's call for a 'new look at history' has turned up here so far. In general, the editors of *Istoriia SSSR* seem less than enthusiastic about Gorbachev's policy of opening up Soviet history to new interpretations.

The daily newspaper *Komsomolskaia pravda* (Komsomol Truth) is the organ of the Communist Youth League, and serves the purpose of presenting official views to the youth of the Soviet Union. Another Komsomol publication is the monthly journal *Molodaia gvardiia* (Young Guard), a literary magazine for young people. *Molodaia gvardiia* has a decidedly conservative reputation, and is openly critical of many aspects of the new policy of *glasnost*. Articles have been published, for example, criticizing the rehabilitation of Bukharin, and the publication of Pasternak.

In contrast, some of the most vocal proreformist views find their expression in the weekly newspaper *Moskovskie novosti**† (Moscow News). This paper is available in several languages, including English, but the contents of the various editions do not always correspond. For example, an interview with Eltsin was recently published in the German version, but not in the English or Russian editions. Nevertheless, in any of its versions, *Moskovskie novosti* is an excellent source for examples of "new thinking" on current events.

Also in sharp contrast to *Molodaia gvardiia*, the weekly newsmagazine *Ogonek* (Little Flame) has been actively promoting Gorbachev's policies.

---

† An asterisk beside the name of a journal indicates that it is available in English translation.

Ogonek has always been popular for its features on sports, its movie star interviews, its crosswords, and the like. But now, under the editorship of the innovative Vitalii Korotich, the journal is stretching the limits of *glasnost*. Previously unpublished literature and memoirs of Soviet leaders such as Anastas Mikoian have appeared in its pages, as have reproductions of avant-garde artworks, interviews with prominent theoreticians such as Abel Aganbegian, and reports on the war in Afghanistan.

The daily newspaper *Sovetskaia Rossiia* (Soviet Russia), published jointly by the Party and government of the RSFSR, is similar to *Pravda* and *Izvestiia* in its broad coverage. Until the recent controversy over the antireformist 'manifesto' which appeared in its pages, *Sovetskaia Rossiia* was not thought to be particularly conservative. The full-page letter criticizing Gorbachev's policies was signed by Leningrad teacher Nina Andreeva, but many Western analysts speculated that Ligachev himself reworked the letter and was behind its publication. *Sovetskaia Rossiia*, however, should not be labeled as a forum for antireformist views on the basis of this one letter.

Another important national daily newspaper is *Trud* (Labor), the official organ of the central council of trade unions. *Trud* covers domestic and international news, with a focus on labor issues and the trade union movement.

The monthly *Voprosy Filosofii* (Problems of Philosophy) is published by the Philosophy Institute of the Academy of Sciences. The editor of *Pravda*, V. G. Afanasev, is also on the editorial board of this journal. *Voprosy Filosofii* covers all aspects of Marxist-Leninist philosophy, including ethics and theories of social development. Western philosophical thought is often discussed and critiqued within its pages. The current focus of this journal is on the philosophical underpinnings of the social and economic reforms that are underway. In general, the authors published in this journal tend to support the reforms.

The journal *Voprosy Istorii* (Problems of History) is issued monthly and is published jointly by the History Department of the Academy of Sciences and the Ministry of Higher and Secondary Specialized Education. Perhaps because of the connection to education, authors published here are particularly sensitive to Gorbachev's push for a "new look at history." Overall, they tend towards caution in this endeavor. Topics which are regularly treated in *Voprosy Istorii* are Soviet and bourgeois historiography and Russian/Soviet history from the Marxist point of view. Book reviews and conference reports are regular features.

Voprosy Istorii KPSS (Problems of the History of the CPSU) is the organ of the Central Committee's Marxism-Leninism Institute, and is devoted to the discussion of the history, theory, and practice of socialism. Current policies are analyzed and explained extensively. Authors from 'fraternal' Communist Parties often contribute, comparing the experience of their own countries with that of the Soviet Union.

Literary Periodicals

Druzhba narodov (Friendship of Nations), the monthly literary-political magazine of the Writers' Union of the USSR, publishes new literature from all of the republics. Political commentary in this journal often touches on nationalities issues, as the title implies. Several stories on the Stalin period have appeared here in recent months.

*Literaturnaia gazeta** (Literary Newspaper), the weekly newspaper of the Writers' Union, covers not only new literature and literary criticism, but also international affairs and social and economic policies. Fedor Burlatskii, Deputy Chairman of the Soviet Political Science Association and prominent social commentator, is a regular contributor. *Literaturnaia gazeta* has been issued in an English edition since in January 1989.

The monthly journal *Nash Sovremennik* (Our Contemporary) is the organ of the Writer's Union of the RSFSR, and publishes new literature and literary criticism by Russian authors. However, *Nash sovremennik* is best known for its political commentaries and its well-deserved conservative reputation. The journal has published criticisms of proposed economic reforms and some-times engages in polemics with *Literaturnaia gazeta* and *Sovetskaia kultura*. Dmitrii Vasilev, the leader of the Russian nationalist, neo-Stalinist 'Pamiat' organization, has endorsed *Nash Sovremennik* as his favorite publication.

Novyi mir (New World), the organ of the Writers' Union of the USSR, is the liberal counterpart to *Nash sovremennik* and is much more widely read. In keeping with the new openness, *Novyi mir* has published literature that was previously banned in the Soviet Union. *Dr. Zhivago* is currently being published serially and in full in this journal, under the editorial supervision of academician Dmitrii Likhachev. Sergei Zalygin, *Novyi mir*'s new chief editor, has taken strong stands in favor of the policy of interpreting Soviet history in a new light, and on environmental conservation issues.

Like *Nash sovremennik*, *Oktiabr* (October) is a publication of the Writers' Union of the RSFSR. This "literary-artistic and social-political monthly journal" also has a conservative reputation, but is thought to be less extreme than *Nash Sovremennik*. Mikhail Bulgakov's short story

"Adam and Eve" was recently published here for the first time in the Soviet Union.

The Central Committee's newspaper *Sovetskaia kultura* covers the arts, current events, social policies, and international cultural ties.

Economics

Ekonomika i organizatsiia promyshlennogo proizvodstva (EKO) (Economics and the Organization of Industrial Industry) is the published monthly by the Siberian branch of the Academy of Sciences. It is here, at the Siberian branch in Novosibirsk, that much of the innovative thinking on economic reform is taking place, and this is reflected in *EKO*'s editorial board: Abel Agenbegian is its chief editor, and Tatiana Zaslavskaia and Leonid Abalkin are among the other members of the editorial staff. The main focus of the journal is on the perfecting (and now the restructuring) of the economic mechanism of the Soviet Union, and on the social context for these changes. With its cartoon-like illustrations and its anecdotes, *EKO* appears to be aimed at a broad audience. These days, the butt of the jokes and cartoons is the stylized bureaucrat.

Ekonomicheskaia gazeta (Economic Newspaper) is the Central Committee's weekly newspaper on economic issues. All aspects and all levels of the Soviet economy are discussed, from questions of general policy to reports on individual collective farms and enterprises. Although *Ekonomicheskaia gazeta* is an excellent source of information and official views on the economy, it is only one good source among many. The current debate on economic policy has spilled over to literary journals, news magazines, youth magazines, and a variety of other sources.

Finansy SSSR (Finances of the USSR) is the monthly journal of the Soviet Ministry of Finance, and is devoted to the theory and practice of the Soviet financing system. It contains some political commentary on new economic policies, but for the most part deals with the more technical aspects of the system. Investment, credit, and insurance policy are discussed regularly.

The monthly journal of *Gosplan, Planovoe khoziaistvo* (Planned Economy), is similar to *EKO* in that it focuses on the Soviet economic mechanism as a whole and on the means of its improvement. *Planovoe khoziaisto* concentrates more on issues such as the assimilation of new technology, resource reserves, limiting waste—in short, on all aspects of plan fulfillment.

Sotsialisticheskaia industriia (Socialist Industry) is the Central Committee's daily paper covering economic news and current events.

Vestnik statistiki (Statistical Bulletin) is the monthly publication of State Committee on Statistics. Some political commentary on current policies is included, but the primary focus is on analysis of current statistics and on the methodology of analysis.

A good source for information on trends in Soviet foreign trade is *Vneshniaia torgovliia** (Foreign Trade). This glossy monthly journal is the organ of the Soviet Ministry of Foreign Trade, and is aimed at Western audiences.

The monthly *Voprosy Ekonomiki*, (Problems of Economics) published by the Economics Institute of the Academy of Sciences, covers various aspects of political economy. *Perestroika*, the acceleration of economic development, and labor issues are key topics. Abalkin is on the editorial board and is a regular contributor.

Social Policy/Nationalities

The newspaper *Meditsinskaia gazeta* (Medical Newspaper) is published jointly by the Ministry of Health, the Ministry of Medicine and Microbiology Industries, and the Medical Workers' Union. Its focus is primarily on developments in medical sciences, but articles on the healthcare system, conditions in the workplace, abortion policy, and alcoholism can also be found here.

Nauka i religiia (Science and Religion) is the monthly "scientific-popular atheistic journal" of the *Znanie* (Knowledge) society. Church history, religious culture, philosophy, and theology are discussed from the atheistic point of view. *Nauka i religiia* is not a forum for discussion of religious policy, but is aimed instead at believers themselves. The tone these days is relatively gentle, explanatory rather than abusive.

Obshchestvennye nauki* (Social Sciences) is issued six times a year by the Social Sciences section of the Academy of Sciences. Its editorial council includes, among other prominent members, Viktor Afanasev and the economist Oleg Bogomolov. This journal covers social and economic development, the economic system, political culture, and labor relations in light of new policies. It was in this journal that the term 'economic culture' was coined.

Russkii iazyk v natsional'noi shkole (Russian Language in the National School) is the monthly journal of the Academy of Pedagogical Sciences.

Language policy in the Soviet Union and the methodology of teaching Russian in non-Russian republics are the main themes. Statistics on language skills in the republics are often included.

Sotsiologicheskie issledovaniia (Sociological Studies), with Tatiana Zaslavskaia on its editorial board, is issued every two months by the Academy's Institute of Sociological Studies. This publication is similar to *Obshchestvennye nauki* and is an equally good source for articles by prominent theoreticians on a wide range of sociological topics. According to a recent agreement between the editorial board of *Sotsiologicheskie issledovaniia* and the State Committee on Statistics, the journal will now have access to more extensive data. As of December 1987, the Committee on Statistics will regularly publish new data in this journal.

The bimonthly *Sovetskaia etnografiia* (Soviet Ethnography), published by the Academy of Science's Ethnography Institute, covers issues of national identity, historical ethnography, and the problems of preserving national culture.

Issued monthly by the Academy of Science's Institute of State and Law, *Sovetskoe gosudarstvo i pravo* (Soviet Government and Law) deals with both domestic and international legal issues. This journal is the primary forum for the current Soviet discussion of legal reforms. In each issue, major articles are abstracted in (clumsy) English.

Uchitelskaia gazeta (Teachers' Newspaper) is the organ of the State Committee on National Education and the Union of Workers in Education. General issues of education policy are the primary focus of this newspaper, but Party-ideological work among Soviet youth is also discussed. Other frequent topics are cultural policy and the tools and methodology of teaching.

In addition to the periodicals mentioned here, republic and local newspapers are another good source for information on and discussion of nationalities policy in the Soviet Union. Each republic has at least one major Russian-language newspaper.

Foreign Policy

*Aziia i Afrika segodnia** (Asia and Africa Today) is one of the two important Soviet journals on Third World affairs, and is published jointly by the Oriental Institute and the Africa Institute of the Academy of Sciences, and the Committee for the Solidarity of the Countries of Asia and Africa. The chief editor of this journal is Georgii Kim, who has been influential in Soviet thinking on the Third World for almost three decades. *Aziia i Afrika* *segodniia* is conservative by reputation, and tends to interpret current events in the strict terms of class struggle.

Latinskaia Amerika (Latin America), the monthly journal of the Latin America Institute, provides commentary and background on current events in that region, as well as articles on its history, art, and culture.

Mirovaia ekonomika i mezhdunarodnye otnosheniia (MEMO) (World Economy and International Relations) is the monthly journal of the Academy's World Economy and International Relations Institute. On its highly distinguished editorial board are Vadim Zagladin, First Deputy Chief of the Central Committee's International Department; Vladimir Petrovskii, Deputy Foreign Minister; Evgenii Primakov, the head of the MEMO Institute; and the well-known political commentator, Valentin Falin. This journal is an outstanding source for official views on international affairs.

*Mezhdunarodnaia zhizn** (International Affairs), published jointly by the Ministry of Foreign Affairs and the *Znanie* Society, is another good source for viewpoints on foreign affairs. The focus of *Mezhdunarodnaia zhizn* is similar to *MEMO*'s, but is oriented toward the key issues of arms control and regional problems. Foreign scholars often contribute.

The bimonthly *Narody Azii i Afriki* (The Peoples of Asia and Africa) is thought of as the liberal, more innovative counterpart to *Aziia i Africa segodnia*, and is also jointly published by the Oriental Institute and the Africa Institute. The focus of this journal is on economic, political, and cultural developments in the Third World. Beginning with 1987, a selection of major articles from *Narody Azii i Afriki* will regularly be compiled in an English-language yearbook called *Soviet Oriental Studies*.

*Novoe vremia** (New Times) is a weekly news magazine on current domestic and foreign affairs (mostly the latter). The analysis is unsophisticated, and in general this publication is thought of as a propaganda instrument aimed at foreign audiences.

*Problemy daln'ego vostoka** (Far Eastern Affairs) is issued bimonthly by the Far East Institute of the Academy of Sciences, and covers both the Far East and Southeast Asia. The analysis focuses on the history of the regions covered and on political and economic trends. This is the best source for Soviet commentary on Chinese affairs.

The monthly journal of Communist and Workers' Parties, *Problemy mira i sotsializma**, is available in English as the *World Marxist Review*. This journal offers strict Marxist analyses of the world situation, concentrating on important events in the world communist movement. The contributors are mostly foreign, and often include members of the top leadership of allied socialist countries. The journal is not now considered to be a good source for innovative thinking on foreign affairs or inter-Party relations, but this may change in the near future. At a recent meeting held in Prague to discuss the work of the journal, both Anatolii Dobrynin and Vadim Zagladin called for its revitalization in keeping with the 'new thinking'. The journal is to be 'democratized' on the principle of equality between parties, which can be taken to mean that Moscow's control over the contents of the journal will be loosened.

Rabochii klass i sovremennyi mir (The Working Class and the Modern World) is another journal focusing on the international workers' movement, but is concerned mostly with labor relations and trade unions in the capitalist West and the Third World. Domestic labor issues are discussed occasionally. This bimonthly journal is issued by the Academy of Science's Institute of the International Workers' Movement.

The best sources for views on U.S.-Soviet relations and arms control and disarmament issues is *SShA: ekonomika, politika, ideologiia* (USA: Economics, Policy, Ideology). Also covered in this monthly journal of the Academy's USA and Canada Institute are American history, sociological issues, and current administration policy. Both Western and Soviet books are reviewed. Georgii Arbatov, the highly visible Director of the USA and Canada Institute, is a frequent contributor.

In August of 1987, the Ministry of Foreign Affairs began publishing the twice-monthly bulletin *Vestnik Ministerstva Inostrannykh Del* (Bulletin of the Ministry of Foreign Affairs). For Western observers of Soviet diplomatic activities, this is an invaluable aid. Major policy statements by Gorbachev and Shevardnadze are included without fail, as are official documents on foreign policy. Each issue contains a chronicle of the recent delegations, meetings, negotiations, and consultations of the Soviet diplomatic corps, and a section summarizing the briefings and press conferences which have taken place at the Ministry.

The Military

Kommunist vooruzhennykh sil (Communist of the Armed Forces), the "political-military" journal of the Soviet Army and Navy, is published twice monthly by the Main Political Administration. Included in this journal are commentaries on military-political education, ideological work, and the effects of policies such as 'new thinking' on military thought. There is also some analysis of foreign affairs, particularly East-West relations.

The daily newspaper *Krasnaia zvezda* (Red Star) covers current events in both the domestic and foreign spheres. As the central organ of the Ministry of Defense, it is one of the most important sources of information on the views held within the Soviet military apparatus.

Sovetskii voin (Soviet Soldier) is also issued twice per month by the Main Political Administration. Its focus is on the proper political upbringing of Soviet soldiers and, not surprisingly, is highly sensitive to the question of looking at Soviet history in a new light. In response to the recent reinterpretation of the twenties and thirties, defenses of Stalinism have appeared here. For example, in a recent interview appearing in *Sovetskii voin*, author Ivan Stadniuk defends Stalin's role as Supreme Commander during World War II, and warns that patriotism and love of the Fatherland can suffer from too much attention to the "bitter moments" of Soviet history.

The monthly *Sovetskoe voennoe obozrenie** (Soviet Military Review) is geared toward interpreting foreign affairs, arms control policy, and new domestic policies for the average soldier. Gennadii Gerasimov, the Foreign Ministry's spokesman, is a member of the editorial staff.

Voenno-istoricheskii zhurnal (Military-Historical Journal) is a Ministry of Defense publication, and is one of the best sources for commentary on current military policy. Also covered in this monthly journal are issues of military art and strategy, military-economic questions, military education, and the experience of other countries. More often than not, the context for discussion is the Soviet experience in World War II, but current questions are also dealt with.

Voennyi vestnik (Military Bulletin), like *Sovetskoe voennoe obozrenie*, is aimed at the young Soviet soldier. Articles on military discipline and friendship among nationalities within the armed forces are the usual fare. Simplified discussions of military theory and practice, and of new military technology and engineering, appear often. Trivia quizzes and articles on hunting, fishing, and chess are regular features. This may not be the forum for high-level debate on Soviet military policy, but it is an excellent source of information on how those policies are presented to the Soviet soldier.

INDEXES

Just as Western publications are indexed in *PAIS*, the Social Sciences Index, and elsewhere, Soviet publications are indexed thoroughly in analogous periodicals. Researching a specific topic in Soviet affairs does necessarily require leafing through years' worth of newspapers and journals. Using the Soviet system of bibliographies and indexes can save time for researchers and bring valuable resources to their attention.

Knizhnaia Letopis (Book Chronicle)

The weekly index *Knizhnaia letopis* covers virtually all books and pamphlets published in the Soviet Union, in all languages. Entries are divided by subject, with fifty major subject headings and considerably more subheadings. The list of subject headings begins with categories in the social sciences, including Marxism-Leninism, sociology, atheism and religion, history, economics, demography, and international relations. Subject heading number thirteen, military science and military affairs, seems to have been selected as the point of transition from social sciences to the hard sciences. After the hard sciences, the last ten subject headings are for sports, education, literature and the arts. The numerical system of subject headings is used uniformly in the book chronicle, in the chronicles for newspaper and journal articles, the chronicle of reviews, and the bibliography of Soviet bibliographies.

Knizhnaia letopis has two monthly supplements, or *dopolnitelnye vypuski*. The supplement *Avtoreferaty dissertatsii* (Abstracts of dissertations) covers dissertations in all fields. The other supplement, *Knigi i broshiury* (Books and Brochures), covers publications "not meant for mass distribution," that is, conferences, publications of various academic institutes, specialized bibliographies, and more. Because it is meant for a more scholarly reading public, this index can be very useful for in-depth research on specialized topics.

Both the basic issue *(osnovnoi vypusk)* of *Knizhnaia letopis* and the supplement *Knigi i broshiury* have quarterly indexes which are organized by subject, authors' names, and geographical area. Altogether, there are seven different publications under the general title of *Knizhnaia letopis*. Here is a hint for those (the majority of us) who find this confusing: on the back of every issue of *Knizhnaia letopis* is a chart that will help to determine whether the issue in your hand is the basic issue, one of the two supplements, or one of their four indexes.

Knizhnaia letopis is cumulated yearly in the *Ezhegodnik knigi* (Book Annual).

Letopis zhurnalnykh statei (Chronicle of Journal Articles)

This weekly index covers all of the major journals of the USSR, serial publications of academic institutes, and some of the popular journals. Each issue contains a list of the journals and collections from which the entries are taken.

Letopis gazetnykh statei (Chronicle of Newspaper Articles)

Also published weekly, this index covers *Pravda*, *Izvestiia*, and nineteen other all-union newspapers, as well as the main newspapers from each of the republics, two Moscow newspapers, and one Leningrad newspaper. Each issue contains name and geographical indexes.

Letopis periodicheskikh i prodolzhaiushchikhsia izdanii (Chronicle of Periodical and Continuing Publications)

The basic issue of *LPPI*, which is a listing of current Soviet periodicals, is published every five years in two parts. Part one lists journals published in all languages of the USSR and is arranged by subject. The second part of *LPPI* lists newspapers and is arranged primarily by republic.

LPPI has an annual supplement for irregular serials *(sborniki)* and a supplement for the bulletins *(biulleteni)* of various institutions which comes out every two years. Journals that are new, have been renamed, or have ceased publication are listed in an annual supplement.

Letopis retsenzii (Chronicle of Reviews)

This monthly index covers book reviews and artistic criticisms that have appeared in the periodical press. The contents are organized by subject and indexed by author/editor, book title, and reviewer. The indexes are cumulated yearly.

Bibliografiia sovetskoi bibliografii (Bibliography of Soviet Bibliographies)

This annual bibliography provides a shortcut to specialized Soviet sources, and is very useful for in-depth research. The types of bibliographies included are those published as monographs, bibliographical periodicals (such as the indexes described above), bibliographies from within scholarly books and articles, and bibliographies of State and Party publications. The entries in *Bibliografiia sovetskoi bibliografii* are arranged by subject.

INION bibliograficheskii ukazateli (INION Bibliographical indexes)

Two extremely useful series of bibliographies are published by the Academy of Science's Institute for Scientific Information on the Social Sciences (INION). The first is titled *New Soviet and Foreign Literature in the Social Sciences*. Under this general rubric, separate monthly bibliographies are devoted to new materials on the following countries and regions (translated from the Russian titles):

Czechoslovakia
The European Socialist Countries
The German Democratic Republic
The Hungarian People's Republic
The International Workers' Movement
The Near and Middle East, Africa
The Polish People's Republic
Problems of Slavic and Balkan Studies
The Socialist Federated Republic of Yugoslavia
The Socialist Republic of Romania
South and Southeast Asia, the Far East

In each separate serial, the foreign literature referred to is drawn from the press of the country to which the publication is devoted. For example, in the monthly publication *New Soviet and Foreign Literature on the Social Sciences: the Polish People's Republic*, the overwhelming majority of items included will be in Polish or Russian.

INION's other set of bibliographical serial publications is called *New Soviet Literature in the Social Sciences*, and includes the following titles:

The Countries of Asia and Africa
Economics
History, Archeology, Ethnography
Linguistics

Philosophical Sciences
Scientific Studies
Studies in Literature

In every INION bibliography, the subject headings in Russian are immediately followed by an English translation. The table of contents of every issue is also translated in English, but is not re-alphabetized.

The sources for all of the INION serials listed above are monographs, newspapers, journals, textbooks, brochures, collections, dissertation abstracts, reviews, et cetera. Both popular material and material meant for specialists are covered. In distinction from the chronicles described previously, many entries are annotated. Another advantage of INION bibliographies over the chronicles is that each INION series is devoted to a particular subject, rather than to a particular form of publication. For research on a clearly defined topic, the INION bibliographies can be much more convenient than the chronicles.

REFERENCES

Bolshaia Sovetskaia Entsiklopediia (The Great Soviet Encyclopedia)

'The Great Soviet Encyclopedia' (BSE) is an authoritative source on a broad range of subjects. The articles in it are not analytical, but they are informative and will give the reader a simplified summary of the Party line on a given subject. In each edition, one volume is devoted to the Soviet Union and contains important statistical information. However, the most recent edition of the BSE was completed in 1978, and in view of recent events much of the information in it is outdated.

Much more valuable than the BSE itself is the yearbook (Ezhegodnik) which supplements it. Part I of each yearbook contains basic information on the Soviet Union. If a Party Congress has taken place during the year covered, the first section will be devoted to a description of its activities and will list the membership of the Central Committee. The summary of the structure and functions of the government which otherwise opens the volume contains statistical data on the membership of the Supreme Soviet, and describes its activities and those of the Presidium for the past year. The functions of each branch of the government are briefly described and key personnel listed (Presidium members, ministers, chairmen of State committees, etc.). The Communist Party receives the same treatment, except that there is less information on personnel. Members of the Politburo and the Secretariat are listed, but personnel of the Central Committee departments are not. The same information for each of the Union Republics is repeated in separate sections.

Each yearbook provides a chronology of 'important events in the domestic life of the USSR' for the year covered and a similarly detailed chronology of major events in Soviet foreign policy. Following the chronologies are sections on the armed forces, the national economy, and the activities of the Academy of Sciences and other academies. Not surprisingly, the section on the military is the shortest and least informative.

Other sections of the yearbook cover foreign countries, international organizations, relations between communist parties, and science and technology in the Soviet Union.

The final section of the yearbook provides brief biographies of major actors in the Soviet government and Communist Party who have entered key positions during the year covered. For example, in the yearbook published in 1986, which covers the major events of 1985, the entry for Mikhail S. Gorbachev indicates that he was made General Secretary in that year. His educational and career history is summarized, beginning with his entrance into the Communist Party in 1952.

The 1978 edition of the *BSE* has been translated into English by Macmillan, Inc., but the yearbooks are not available in translation.

OTHER REFERENCES

Demograficheskii entsiklopedicheskii slovar (Demographic Encyclopedic Dictionary)

Issued for the first time in 1985, this encyclopedic dictionary contains the Marxist definitions of thousands of demographic terms. The *Demograficheskii entsiklopedicheskii slovar* is most valuable, however, for its maps, charts, and statistical tables. The well-known political economist Tatiana Zaslavskaia is on its editorial board.

Diplomaticheskii slovar (Diplomatic Dictionary)

The three-volume 'Diplomatic Dictionary' is produced under the aegis of the Ministry of Foreign Affairs and covers the history of the foreign policy and diplomacy of Russia and the USSR, as well as international law and economic relations. Major treaties between the Soviet Union and other countries are summarized, as are important multilateral agreements. Brief biographies are provided for Ministry of Foreign Affairs staffers from the rank of ambassador and above, including collegium members and department heads.

Volume three of the 'Diplomatic Dictionary' contains extensive thematic, country, name, and author indexes, as well as lists of Soviet ambassadors abroad and the ambassadors of other countries to the Soviet Union. Because of unfortunate timing, the value of the 'Diplomatic Dictionary' as a source of biographical information on personnel in the Ministry of Foreign Affairs is limited. Work on the fourth and latest edition was completed in November of 1985, just as the personnel turnover in the Ministry was shifting into high gear.

Ekonomicheskaia entsiklopediia: Politicheskaia ekonomiia (Economic Encyclopedia: Political Economy)

Published in four volumes between 1972 and 1980, this encyclopedia provides detailed definitions of economic concepts and terminology as they were understood in the Brezhnev era. Though the encyclopedia is out of date relative to the new program of economic reform, it presents an authoritative and comprehensive picture of pre-Gorbachev economic thought and serves as an excellent basis for comparison. Two economists who remain prominent under Gorbachev, L. I. Abalkin and O. T. Bogomolov, joined the editorial board of the encyclopedia in 1975 (with Volume Two).

Kratkii politicheskii slovar (Concise Political Dictionary)

According to its forword, the purpose of the 'Concise Political Dictionary' is to provide "an explanation of words, terms, and concepts of a social-political character often encountered in the periodical press and in radio and television broadcasts." Although it contains no statistics and very few hard facts, this dictionary can be as useful to the researcher as other reference books, because it explains how the current 'buzzwords' of the Soviet press are meant to be understood.

Voennyi entsiklopedicheskii slovar
(Military-Encyclopedic Dictionary)

Voennyi entsiklopedicheskii slovar (VES), covers Russian, Soviet, and foreign military history, technology, policy, and personnel. The latest edition was published in 1986. Important terms such as 'military doctrine,' 'military science,' and 'military strategy' are defined in detail. The *VES* contains numerous diagrams, portraits, political maps, and maps of military campaigns throughout history. Color illustrations of the military insignia, medals, and uniform of the Soviet Union and the Warsaw Pact are also included, as are the uniforms of certain Western armed forces. At the back of the *VES* is a chronology of "important events in the history of the Armed Forces of the USSR."

STATISTICAL SOURCES

The Census Bureau's Center for International Research publishes a *Bibliography of Soviet Statistical Handbooks*, a comprehensive compilation of Soviet and international sources useful for gathering data on the USSR.

Narodnoe khoziaistvo SSSR (The Economy of the USSR)

The annual of the Central Statistical Administration, *Narodnoe khoziaistvo SSSR*, is the most comprehensive source of Soviet statistics on all branches of the Soviet economy as well as on healthcare, education, demographics, living standards, and foreign trade. The most recent volume, published in 1987, is a jubilee issue in honor of the seventieth anniversary of the Soviet government. The information in this volume is more extensive than the regular yearly volumes, and a section of term definitions has been added. In addition, each union republic (and many oblasts) publishes its own *Narodnoe khoziaistvo*. The information available in these yearbooks is invaluable for researching regional variations in the economic and social development of the Soviet Union.

SSSR v tsifrakh (The USSR in Figures)

Basic statistics on the Soviet domestic economy are extracted from *Narodnoe khoziaistvo SSSR* and compiled in this annual, which is also published by the Central Statistical Administration. *SSSR v tsifrakh* lacks data on sub-branches of the domestic economy and foreign trade.

Statistics on Foreign Trade

The most comprehensive statistics on Soviet foreign trade are to be found in the annual *Vneshiaia torgovlia SSSR* (Foreign Trade of the USSR). The table of contents and the notes on methodology are given in English as well as in Russian.

The *Statisticheskii ezhegodnik stranchlenov SEV* (Statistical Yearbook of CMEA Member Countries) covers economic and social indicators for each of the CMEA countries, as well as their trade within and outside of the bloc.

GOVERNMENT AND PARTY DOCUMENTS

Vedomosti verkhovnogo soveta SSSR (Gazette of the Supreme Soviet of the USSR)

All laws and resolutions enacted by the Supreme Soviet and the edicts of the Presidium are listed weekly in this official bulletin. The first section of each issue contains the most substantive decrees of the Supreme Soviet or its Presidium, including treaty and protocol ratifications, new legislation or amendments to existing laws, and joint decrees with the Central Committee of the Communist Party and/or the Council of Ministers. Changes in the organization of government institutions, such as the formation or reorganization of ministries, are to be found here as well. The first section is a good source of information on elections, appointments, and firings within the government, including Supreme Soviet delegates and staffers, ministers, and ambassadors.

The second section covers the granting of rewards and medals to outstanding workers and, much more rarely, disenfranchisement for "activity not in accordance with Soviet citizenship" (i.e., emigration). In the third and final section, reports on the activities of Supreme Soviet members and committees are lumped together with information on the number of new 'hero-mothers' for the week.

The contents of the Vedomosti are indexed in the final issue of each year. The index is divided into two parts: a subject index and an index for honors and medals awarded.

Sobranie postanovlenii pravitel'stva SSSR
(Collection of Resolutions of the Government of the USSR)

This collection of official government acts is issued weekly in two parts. The first part lists resolutions on domestic issues, and the second part covers all international agreements. The last issue of each year contains cumulated indexes.

Spravochnik partiinogo rabotnika
(The Party Worker's Handbook)

The annual *Spravochnik* is the authoritative collection of documents on the activities of the Central Committee of the Communist Party and the Politburo. If there has been a Party Congress during the year covered, the new Program and Rules of the Party as well as a list of Central Committee and the Central Auditing Commission will be reprinted in the *Spravochnik*. Following the Congress documentation, reports on plenary sessions of the Central Committee, conferences on specific issues and Politburo meetings are printed with citations indicating the date of their original publication in *Pravda*. Documentation from major international events, such as summit meetings, Warsaw Pact and CMEA meetings, and government declarations can be found in the section on the international activity of the Communist Party.

In the remaining sections of the *Spravochnik*, key Party and government resolutions on issues such as economic strategy, social policy, and educational policy are divided by subject and listed chronologically with each section. The most important resolutions of the Council of Ministers and the Supreme Soviet are included, even if they are not ratified jointly with the Central Committee.

Stenograficheskie otchety (Stenographic Reports)

Stenographic reports are compiled following every Party Congress. The multivolume tomes contain the texts of all speeches given at the Congress, texts of the resolutions adopted, and the results of elections to the higher Party organs.

BIOGRAPHICAL INFORMATION

There are a number of excellent sources for tracking down biographical information on major Soviet political figures, both in English and in Russian. Some of the references just discussed, particularly 'The Great Soviet Encyclopedia' and its yearbook, and the military and diplomatic dictionaries, are very helpful in this 'kremlinological' pursuit. Their brief biographies of political actors on the Soviet scene give complete education and career histories, as well as information about Party membership.

Another good Soviet source of biographical information is the publication *Deputaty verkhovnogo soveta SSSR* (Deputies to the Supreme Soviet of the USSR), issued after every election of delegates to the Supreme Soviet. Here, among the hero-mothers and twenty-three-year-old lathe operators, you can find detailed biographies of key members of the *nomenklatura*. Among the deputies included in the latest *Deputaty* are Shevardnadze, Iakovlev, Iazov, and Gorbachev himself. Positions held in the Party, such as Politburo or Central Committee membership, are always noted.

The drawback of these sources is that they do not come out often, and so are not up-to-date. *Deputaty*, for instance, was last issued in 1984, after the last election to the Supreme Soviet. While the information on the careers of important leaders is valuable, the innumerable personnel changes under Gorbachev are not reflected in the latest issue. The next *Deputaty* is due out after elections to the 12th Supreme Soviet in 1989. The time lag for the diplomatic and military dictionaries can be just as great or greater.

The best bet for complete, up-to-date biographical information on key Soviet officials, as far as Soviet sources go, is the yearbook of 'The Great Soviet Encyclopedia.' However, as previously noted, the 'Biographical information' section of each yearbook has entries only for officials who have entered high positions in the year covered. Thus, Gorbachev's entry showing his promotion to General Secretary will be found only in the volume published in 1986, which covers the events of 1985, and not in later volumes.

If *changes* in personnel are more important for your research than the background of the officials in question, then there are shortcuts. The hirings and firings of State officials, including ministers, deputy minister, and ambassadors are published in the *Khronika* (Chronicle) section on *Pravda*'s and *Izvestiia*'s last page. *Khronika* appears only when such personnel changes are made, and therefore is not a regular feature. It does not give biographical information for the new appointees, but it is the fastest way to learn about new appointments within the government. The personnel changes which appear first in *Khronika* will be reprinted in the *Vedomosti Verkhovnogo Soveta* within a few weeks, and will eventually make their way into the yearbook of 'The Great Soviet Encyclopedia' with more background information.

Western sources of biographical information on the Soviet *nomenklatura* generally use the sources discussed above, but their advantage is that they compile the information. The most extensive compilation is done by the CIA, in its serial publication *Directory of Soviet Officials* (with various subtitles). Information is usually limited to the official's name, birthdate, and date of appointment to the latest position. All major positions in the Party and government apparati are covered, including Central Committee department heads, ministry and State committee staffs, and the judiciary, as well as professional organizations, academic institutions, religious groups, the media, among others.

The series *Directory of Soviet Officials* is broken down into subseries for national organizations, republic organizations, science and education, and for the Ministry of Foreign Affairs. The subseries for republic organization includes maps of administrative divisions of the Soviet Union. The *Directory of USSR Foreign Ministry Officials* differs from the others in that it provides information on positions held previously by top officials of the Ministry. While these publications are thorough, their drawback is that they are published irregularly, and are often out of date by the time they are available.

Another Soviet-watching publication of the CIA is *Appearances of Soviet Leaders,* which follows the activities of the members of the Politburo, the Secretariat, the Presidium of the Council of Ministers, the Minister and First Deputy Ministers of Defense, the Ministers of Foreign Affairs and Internal Affairs, and the chairman of the KGB. Appearances are listed alphabetically by the official's name, and chronologically.

Much more detailed biographies of Soviet officials are provided by the Radio Liberty publication *A Biographical Directory of 100 Leading Soviet Officials,* now in its third edition. The entries are selected according to perceived importance of position. First secretaries of major republican Party organizations are included. The biographical entries cover career and educational background, military experience and travel abroad, evident patrons, expertise, and major speeches.

A new Radio Liberty publication is the *Biographical Directory of Soviet Regional Party Leaders,* printed in its first edition in August 1987. Entries are listed alphabetically, and indexed by territory.

In addition to Radio Liberty's publications, another excellent and perhaps even more up-to-date source of biographical information is the SOVT database. SOVT is the creation of Michel Tatu, author of *Power in the Kremlin* and columnist for *Le Monde*. His database holds over 21,000 biographical notes on virtually all high-and mid-level Party and government officials, starting from 1917. SOVT also contains the texts of over 4,000 leadership statements. The Soviets themselves have taken notice of SOVT, giving it a very favorable writeup recently in *Literaturnaia gazeta*.

TRANSLATION AND ABSTRACTING SERVICES

FBIS/JPRS

The Central Intelligence Agency's Foreign Broadcast Information Service (FBIS) monitors Soviet television and radio broadcasts and the periodical press. FBIS publishes selected translations daily (Monday through Friday). Articles from the mass media of countries other than the Soviet Union which touch on Soviet-related issues are often included as well. Translations for the FBIS Daily Report are done by the Joint Publications Research Service (JPRS). Occasionally, articles will be summarized or abstracted rather than translated.

A wide range of topics are covered in the FBIS Daily Report, including arms control and disarmament, relations between communist parties, international affairs by region, and domestic affairs. FBIS has access to an extraordinary range of sources, and this is reflected in its translation selections.

JPRS publishes a number of series on the Soviet Union which delve more deeply into the available literature than the FBIS Daily Report. In addition to the general series on the Soviet Union, there are separate series of translations for agriculture, economic affairs, political and sociological affairs, and military affairs.

In addition to their Daily Reports and the translation series which are organized by general theme, FBIS regularly translates four of the major Soviet journals and issues them as separate series: *Kommunist*, *Problemy dalnego vostoka* (Problems of the Far East), *Sotsiologicheskie issledovanie* (Sociological Studies), and *SShA* (USA). Not all articles from each issue of these journals are translated in the FBIS series, but complete translated tables of contents are included.

A word of caution: Although the FBIS/JPRS publications are extremely useful to the researcher as time-saving devices, they should not be considered replacements for primary source research. While the range of materials that they cover is impressively broad, they do not meet the needs of all researchers on all topics.

The Current Digest of the Soviet Press

The Current Digest of the Soviet Press (CDSP) is similar to the FBIS Daily Report, except that it comes out weekly rather than daily. Here again, selections may be abstracted or incompletely translated. The distinguishing feature of CDSP is its extensive and detailed index, which is published quarterly and in an annual cumulation. The indexes list the publications from which articles have been selected for translation, (usually over 100 different periodicals), and are arranged in two parts, by subject and by name.

Summary of World Broadcasts (SWB)

This BBC publication is the British equivalent of the FBIS Daily Reports. The SWB series on the Soviet Union is published in two sections, the daily news reports and a weekly report on economic affairs.

ABSEES (Abstracts of Soviet and East European Series)

ABSEES, which comes out every four months, is a microfiche journal devoted to East Bloc economic affairs. Selections from the East bloc press are summarized in one or two sentences in the journal itself. Each summary gives a reference number for the much more detailed abstract, which is on microfiche and is sent together with the journal.

Glasnost

The unofficial publication Glasnost, edited by dissident Sergei Grigoriants, is available in translation through the Center for Democracy in the USSR in New York. Glasnost contains commentary on all aspects of current social policy in the Soviet Union and chronicles major events in the human rights movement and other protest movements.

ANALYSIS OF CURRENT EVENTS

Planecon Reports

Under the editorship of economist Jan Vanous, Planecon Incorporated publishes weekly analytical reports on current developments in the Soviet and
East European economies. The reports cover developments in individual
countries as well as intrabloc trade. *Planecon Reports* are an excellent source
for current economic statistics.

Radio Liberty

Radio Liberty's research department publishes its analyses of current events
in the Soviet Union in weekly Research Bulletins. The focus of Radio
Liberty's analysis is primarily on domestic affairs, including all aspects of
Gorbachev's reform program. Topics often covered are nationalities issues,
dissident activity, social, cultural, and economic reform, opposition to
reform, and personnel turnover with the Party and government. Articles
on foreign policy and the military appear more rarely. Special attention is
paid in the Research Bulletins to trends in the Soviet press.

A regular feature of Radio Liberty's Research Bulletins, in addition to
the analytical reports, is a continuing chronology of major events in the
Soviet Union. The section called 'The USSR This Week' contains one- or
two-paragraph reports on late-breaking news without analysis. Very often,
abstracts of articles which appear to have important policy implications or
are believed to reflect the point of view of a major faction will appear in
this section.

Radio Liberty publishes an annual index for its Research Bulletins, with
both subject and author indexes. Radio Liberty's associate organization,
Radio Free Europe, publishes Research Bulletins on Eastern Europe, and
also has a yearly index.

Soviet Analyst

The bimonthly newsletter *Soviet Analyst* contains commentaries on current
events in the Soviet domestic and foreign policy spheres. In each issue
there is a 'Survey' section that summarizes important news events relating
to the Soviet Union and Eastern Europe, but it is not as extensive as Radio

Liberty's 'The USSR This Week.' *Soviet Analyst*, unlike other Soviet-watching publications, reprints comics from the Soviet press. Robert Conquest is among the distinguished members of its editorial board.

Computer Conferencing: SOVSET

The Soviet Studies section of the Center for Strategic and International Studies founded the SOVSET computer network in 1984, with the aim of facilitating research and discussion among specialists on Soviet and East European affairs. Currently, over 340 leading specialists from the spheres of government, academia, and the media belong to SOVSET.

The computer conferencing service of SOVSET is divided by topic into thirty-two different sections, including domestic politics, foreign affairs, the military, nationalities, and Eastern Europe. The network also provides an electronic mail system which allows private, one-to-one communication between members. SOVSET's data library gives members access to a wide range of up-to-date materials including Radio Liberty and Radio Free Europe Daily Reports, which are intended for in-house use at the Radio and are not available elsewhere. Other items appearing regularly in the data library are *SOVSET News*, a computer journal containing special research reports, *The Tatu Column*, a monthly political analysis by Soviet expert Michel Tatu, and Kennan Institute meeting reports.

ADDITIONAL WESTERN SOURCES

Selected Journals

Current History: each year, one issue is devoted exclusively to the Soviet Union.
Foreign Affairs
Foreign Policy
International Affairs
Orbis
Problems of Communism
Russian Review
Slavic Review
Soviet Anthropology and Archaeology: translations of selected Soviet articles.

Soviet Economy
Soviet Geography: commentary and translations. Often covers such topics as population migration and labor resources.
Soviet Sociology: translations of selected Soviet articles.
Soviet Studies
Soviet Union/Union Sovietique
Studies in Comparative Communism

Other sources for scholarly analysis of Soviet affairs are the series published by universities and research organizations. Some of the organizations which publish newsletters or journals devoted to Soviet/East European affairs are Harvard's Russian Research Center, The Kennan Institute for Advanced Russian Studies (connected to the Smithsonian Institution), Indiana University's Russian and East European Institute, and the University of Pittsburgh's Center for Russian and East European Studies. Other institutions whose publications deal with Soviet affairs are the American Committee on U.S.-Soviet Relations *(occasional papers, conference reports, and Outlook)*, The Brookings Institution *(The Brookings Review)*, the Center for Strategic and International Studies *(The Washington Quarterly)*, Johns Hopkins' School for Advanced International Studies *(SAIS Review)*, The Harriman Institute for the study of the Soviet Union *(The Harriman Forum)*, the Woodrow Wilson International Center for Scholars *(The Wilson Quarterly)*, and the Rand Corporation *(Rand Reports)*. Many of these research organizations also publish occasional papers.

U.S. Government Publications

The analytical background reports that are prepared for congressional committees are a valuable resource for research on Soviet and East European affairs. Such reports are usually prepared by the Congressional Research Service of the Library of Congress, but papers are also commissioned from outside experts. Soviet economic and foreign policies are covered most extensively. Congressional reports are available to the public at government depositories in various libraries around the country and through the Government Printing Office. Inquiries can also be made directly to the appropriate committees (i.e., the Joint Economic Committee or the House Committee on Foreign Affairs). Besides the personnel listings mentioned above, the CIA publishes other useful information on the Soviet Union. The Agency's *Handbook of Soviet Economics Statistics* is one of the few sources for extensive data on the Soviet economy. Another widely used government publication is the annual *Soviet Military Power*, produced by the Department of Defense.

Writings on Gorbachev and His Policies

Gorbachev's own writings are widely available in the West. A collection of speeches from his first eight months in power were published under the title *A Time for Peace* (New York: Richardson and Steirman, 1985). The more recent *Perestroika: New Thinking for Our Country and the World* (New York: Harper & Row, 1987) is Gorbachev's explanation of his social, economic, and foreign policy strategies for Western audiences.

There are a number of well-documented biographies of Gorbachev to choose from, and new ones are appearing constantly. Among the biographies currently available are the following:

Zhores A. Medvedev, *Gorbachev* (New York: W. W. Norton, 1986). Medvedev, the well-known exiled Soviet scientist and historian, traces Gorbachev's rise and discusses his policies in power.

Thos. G. Butson, *Gorbachev: A Biography* (New York: Stein & Day, 1985, 1986).

Christian Schmidt-Hauer, *Gorbachev: The Path to Power* (London: I. B. Tauris, 1986). Schmidt-Hauer, the Moscow correspondent for *Die Zeit*, explains the politics and patronage involved in Gorbachev's rise. An appendix on "The Men Behind Gorbachev" contains background information on the men close to the General Secretary.

Time Magazine, *Mikhail Gorbachev: An Intimate Biography* (New York: Time Books, 1988).

A wide selection of books on Soviet politics, economics, and society under the new leadership have appeared since Gorbachev came to power three years ago.

Overviews and Collected Essays

Alexander Dallin and Condoleeza Rice, eds., *The Gorbachev Era* (Palo Alto, CA: Stanford Alumni Association, 1986). This edited volume contains chapters on various topics of Soviet domestic and foreign policy by leading scholars in the field. The chapters were originally prepared as lectures for Stanford University. Among the issues discussed are the nationalities question, dissent, and military policy.

Martin McCauley, ed., *The Soviet Union Under Gorbachev* (New York: St. Martin's Press, 1987). The chapters by Soviet experts in this edited volume cover various aspects of Soviet foreign and domestic policy, including legal reform, agriculture, labor productivity, and the military.

James Cracraft, *The Soviet Union Today: An Interpretive Guide* rev. and expanded ed. (Chicago: University of Chicago Press, 1988). A collection of thirty essays on a broad range of topics such as the cinema, environmental problems, and the KGB.

Seweryn Bialer, *The Soviet Paradox* (New York: Knoff, 1986). A thought-provoking analysis of the problems, both foreign and domestic, that Gorbachev confronted on becoming General Secretary.

Politics

Timothy J. Colton, *The Dilemma of Reform in the Soviet Union* rev. and expanded ed. (USA: Council on Foreign Relations, 1986). In his book, Colton analyzes the legacy of the Brezhnev leadership, the difficulties (chiefly economic) facing the current leadership, the politics of personnel policy, and the overall prospects for reform. A Soviet Leadership chronology for 1976 to 1986 is included as an appendix.

Martin Walker, *The Waking Giant: Gorbachev's Russia* (New York: Pantheon Books, 1986). The Moscow correspondent for *The Manchester Guardian* chronicles Gorbachev's career, sets the background and context for his reform program, and assesses the implications for the West.

Seweryn Bialer, ed., *Politics, Society and Nationality Inside Gorbachev's Russia* (Boulder, Colo.: Westview, 1989).

Gail Lapidus, *State and Society in the Soviet Union* (Boulder, Colo.: Westview, 1989).

Economics

Thomas H. Naylor, *The Gorbachev Strategy: Opening the Closed Society* (Lexington, MA: Lexington Books, 1988). Duke University's Thomas Naylor looks at the internal and foreign pressures that are driving the Soviet leadership to reform the system. The focus is on changes in the economy, but cultural reform and foreign policy issues are touched on as well.

Jerry Hough, *Opening Up The Soviet Economy* (Washington, D.C.: The Brookings Institution, 1988). Duke University's Jerry Hough examines the role of foreign trade in Gorbachev's economic reform strategy. The final chapter discusses the implications of these changes for American foreign policy.

Marshall Goldman, *Gorbachev's Challenge: Economic Reform in the Age of High Technology* (New York: W. W. Norton, 1987). Professor Goldman discusses the problems of technology transfer in the Soviet economic reform, drawing comparisons with the experiences of China and Hungary.

Abel Aganbegian, *The Economic Challenge of Perestroika* (Bloomington, IN: Indiana University Press, 1988). One of Gorbachev's top economic advisors outlines his views on the Soviet economy and the prospects for *perestroika*.

Edward Hewett, *Reforming the Soviet Economy* (Washington, D.C.: The Brookings Institution, 1988). Hewett, a senior fellow at The Brookings Institution, studies economic reform—past, present, and future—from the viewpoint of the conflicting goals of economic efficiency and social equality.

Joint Economic Committee, "Gorbachev's Economic Plans," (Joint Committee Print, 100th Congress, 1st Sess., Government Printing Office, 1987, 2 vol.). This two-volume collection features analytical essays by top American scholars in the field.

Alec Nove, *The Soviet Economic System* 3rd ed., (Boston: Allen and Unwin, 1986). The most recent edition of Nove's classic work is rich in material on Gorbachev's early reforms and a thorough analysis of issues in current Soviet economic theory.

American Committee on U.S.-Soviet Relations, *Forum on U.S.-Soviet Trade Relations* (Washington, D.C.: American Committee on U.S.-Soviet Relations, 1989). A compendium of views on U.S.-Soviet trade by leading figures in the business, government, and nonprofit sectors.

Social Policy

Moshe Lewin, *The Gorbachev Phenomenon: A Historical Interpretation* (Berkeley: University of California Press, 1988). Unlike most other analysts, Lewin approaches his subject from the sociological point of view, arguing that Gorbachev's policies cannot be understood outside the context of the long and varied history of Soviet society as a whole.

James R. Miller, ed., *Politics, Work & Daily Life in the USSR: A Survey of Former Soviet Citizens* (Cambridge, UK: Cambridge University Press, 1987). A collection of statistical surveys based on a series of interviews with the most recent wave of Soviet émigrés.

Horst Herlemann, ed., *Quality of Life in the Soviet Union* (Boulder, Colo.: Westview Press, 1987). Expert analysis on the living standards in the Soviet Union, the availability of State provided services, and the prospects for an increase in the standard of living through Gorbachev's reforms.

David Lane, ed., *Soviet Economy and Society* (New York: New York University Press, 1985). This book provides an overview of the interrelationship between the social structure and the economy in contemporary Soviet society.

Maurice Friedberg and Heyward Isham, eds., *Soviet Society Under Gorbachev: Current Trends and Prospects for Reform* (New York: M. E. Sharpe, 1987). The most prominent social developments under Gorbachev, such as the anti-alcohol campaign and *glasnost*, are examined by some of the fields leading specialists.

Foreign Policy

Raymond L. Garthoff, *Détente and Confrontation, American-Soviet Relations from Nixon to Reagan* (Washington, D.C.: The Brookings Institution, 1985). Raymond L. Garthoff, a senior fellow at The Brookings Institution, analyzes both American and Soviet policy in this look at the historical development of U.S.-Soviet relations from 1969 to 1984. He shows how differing perceptions of détente and foreign policy intentions led to the breakdown of superpower relations in the late 1970s.

Marshall D. Shulman, ed., *East-West Tensions in the Third World* (New York: W. W. Norton, 1986). This edited volume contains chapters on U.S.-Soviet competition in the Middle East, Latin America, Asia, and Africa. The military and economic dimensions of the rivalry are also examined.

Seweryn Bialer and Michael Mandelbaum, eds., *Gorbachev's Russia and American Foreign Policy* (Boulder, CO: Westview Press, 1988). Journalists and academics contribute to this work that addresses important issues and changes in the U.S.-Soviet relationship.

Jerry Hough, *The Struggle for the Third World* (Washington, D.C.: The Brookings Institution, 1986). Jerry Hough, Professor at Duke University, provides a comprehensive account of the scholarly debates in the Soviet Union over the conduct of foreign policy with developing countries.

Andrzej Korbonski and Francis Fukuyama, *The Soviet Union and the Third World* (Ithaca: Cornell University Press, 1987). This collection of twelve essays from the RAND/UCLA Center for the Study of Soviet International Behavior includes studies of general policy motivations guiding the Soviets and chapters on Soviet strategies in specific regions.

Arms Control

Michael MccGwire, *Military Objectives in Soviet Foreign Policy* (Washington, D.C.: The Brookings Institution, 1987). Michael MccGwire of The Brookings Institution examines the development of Soviet military doctrine since World War II and how it has shaped Soviet policy and force structure in that time.

Derek Leebaert, ed., *Soviet Military Thinking* (London: Allen and Unwin, 1981). This work addresses Soviet military doctrine in three parts: "The International Setting," "The Strategic Question," and "The Non-Strategic Dimension." It examines Soviet military doctrine and style of war, why the Soviets think the way they do, and what prospects their doctrine holds for arms control.

Jiri Valenta and William Potter, eds., *Soviet Decisionmaking for National Security* (London: Allen and Unwin, 1984).

David Holloway, *The Soviet Union and the Arms Race* (New Haven: Yale University Press, 1984).

Stephen Meyer, *Soviet Nuclear Forces, Parts 1 and 2*, Adelphi Papers nos. 187, 188 (London: IISS, 1983–84).

H. F. and W. F. Scott, *The Armed Forces of the Soviet Union*, 3rd ed. (Boulder, Colo.: Westview Press, 1986).

APPENDIX II: STRUCTURE OF THE GOVERNMENT OF THE USSR

Government of the Soviet Union

Under the 1977 Constitution (amended in 1988), the top organs of the USSR government are structured as follows:

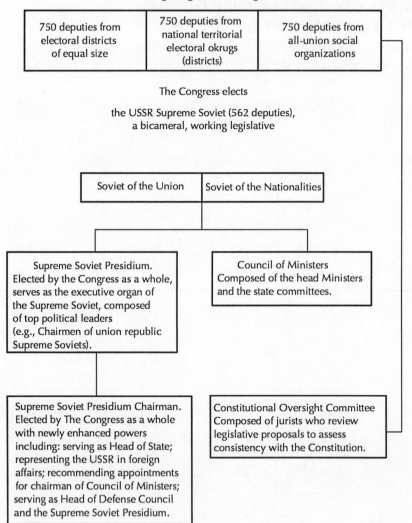

USSR Congress of People's Deputies (2250 deputies)
the highest government organ

750 deputies from electoral districts of equal size	750 deputies from national territorial electoral okrugs (districts)	750 deputies from all-union social organizations

The Congress elects

the USSR Supreme Soviet (562 deputies),
a bicameral, working legislative

Soviet of the Union	Soviet of the Nationalities

Supreme Soviet Presidium. Elected by the Congress as a whole, serves as the executive organ of the Supreme Soviet, composed of top political leaders (e.g., Chairmen of union republic Supreme Soviets).

Council of Ministers Composed of the head Ministers and the state committees.

Supreme Soviet Presidium Chairman. Elected by The Congress as a whole with newly enhanced powers including: serving as Head of State; representing the USSR in foreign affairs; recommending appointments for chairman of Council of Ministers; serving as Head of Defense Council and the Supreme Soviet Presidium.

Constitutional Oversight Committee Composed of jurists who review legislative proposals to assess consistency with the Constitution.

The Soviet, Council of Ministers and Presidium structures are replicated at the provincial and local levels.

Communist Party of the Soviet Union

According to its rules, the CPSU is structured as follows:

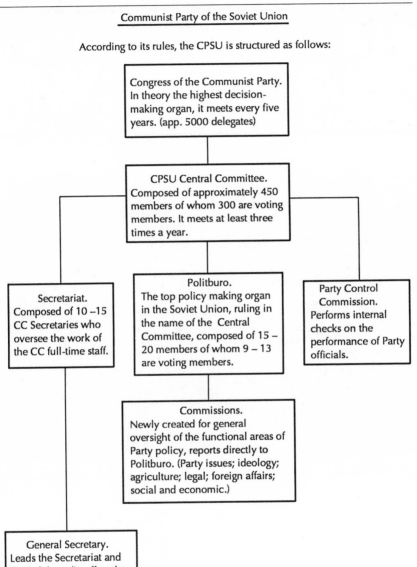

Congress of the Communist Party. In theory the highest decision-making organ, it meets every five years. (app. 5000 delegates)

CPSU Central Committee. Composed of approximately 450 members of whom 300 are voting members. It meets at least three times a year.

Secretariat. Composed of 10 –15 CC Secretaries who oversee the work of the CC full-time staff.

Politburo. The top policy making organ in the Soviet Union, ruling in the name of the Central Committee, composed of 15 – 20 members of whom 9 – 13 are voting members.

Party Control Commission. Performs internal checks on the performance of Party officials.

Commissions. Newly created for general oversight of the functional areas of Party policy, reports directly to Politburo. (Party issues; ideology; agriculture; legal; foreign affairs; social and economic.)

General Secretary. Leads the Secretariat and the Politburo (in effect the USSR's top political leader.)

Between Congresses, the Central Committee may also convene an all-union Conference, which has the power to decide issues of Party Policy. This structure is replicated at the provincial and local levels.

ABOUT THE CONTRIBUTORS

George Ball served as Under Secretary of State and as the U.S. permanent representative to the UN during the Kennedy and Johnson administrations. In 1983, he published his memoirs, *The Past Has Another Pattern.*

Linton H. Bishop received an A.B. in Government from Centre College of Kentucky in 1976 and an M.A. in Political Science from Columbia University in 1984. He is currently a Doctoral Candidate in Political Science at Columbia University. He has worked at the American Committee on U.S.-Soviet Relations since 1987, after having served as an Intelligence Analyst at Naval Intelligence Command.

William Brazier received a B.A. in Political Science from Boston College and an M.I.A. in International Affairs from Columbia University. He was awarded a Certificate from the W. Averell Harriman Institute for Advanced Study of the Soviet Union at Columbia University in 1986, having completed there his thesis on the Soviet Union's interests in the 1975 Helsinki Conference on Security and Cooperation in Europe (CSCE). He has served as a Soviet Analyst at the American Committee on U.S.-Soviet Relations for two years, and continues to research issues in his main area of interest, Soviet foreign policy.

William Colby was director of the CIA. His experiences in government are recounted in *Honorable Men: My Life in the CIA.* He is currently an attorney practicing in Washington, D.C.

Arthur Macy Cox is Secretary of the American Committee on U.S.-Soviet Relations. He has specialized in Soviet affairs since World War II, having served in the State Department, the Marshall Plan, the Psychological Strategy Board, and the Clandestine Services of the CIA. He has written extensively on U.S.-Soviet Relations.

Gerald M. Easter received an M.A. in Political Science (1983) and a Masters of Philosophy in Political Science (1986) from Columbia University. He is a Doctoral Candidate in the Political Science Department at Columbia University, and he has been a Soviet Analyst at the American Committee on U.S.-Soviet Relations since 1987.

John Gaddis is Distinguished Professor of History at Ohio University. His most recent books include *Containing the Soviet Union* and *The Long Peace*.

John Kenneth Galbraith, distinguished economist and former U.S. Ambassador to India, is a Co-Chairman of the American Committee on U.S.-Soviet Relations and a Professor Emeritus of Economics at Harvard University. His most recent book on U.S.-Soviet relations is *Capitalism, Communism, and Coexistence*.

Raymond Garthoff, a Senior Fellow at the Brookings Institute, has had a long and distinguished career in government. He was a member of the SALT I and SALT II delegations and worked on arms control issues throughout the 1960s and 1970s. He was ambassador to Bulgaria during the Carter administration.

Eric Green received a B.A. in Political Science and Russian from Grinnell College in 1985 and an M.A. in International Relations from Yale University in 1988. He has also studied at the Pushkin Institute in Moscow. He has worked at the American Committee since 1988, concentrating on economic and environmental issues.

Anne M. Gruber graduated from the University of Michigan in May 1985 with a B.A. in Russian and East European Studies. She worked at the American Committee on U.S.-Soviet Relations as a Research Associate from 1985 to 1988, and is currently a Master's candidate in Political Science at The London School of Economics and Political Science.

Stanley Hoffman is currently the Chairman for the Center for European Studies at Harvard University and the Douglas Dillon Professor of the Civilization of France. His recent books include *Primacy or World Order?*, *Dead Ends*, and *Janus and Minerva*.

Townsend Hoopes, a member of the Board of Directors of the American Committee on U.S.-Soviet Relations, has served as Under Secretary of the Air Force and as President of the Association of American Publishers. Author of *The Limits of Intervention*, he is now at work on a biography of Secretary of Defense Forrestal.

Donald Kendall, the Chairman of the American Committee on U.S.-Soviet Relations, is the Chairman of PepsiCo, Inc. and the President of the U.S. Chamber of Commerce. He was formerly the Co-Chairman of the U.S.-USSR Trade and Economic Council.

Carl Marcy, attorney and member of the Board of Directors of the American Committee on U.S.-Soviet Relations, served for over twenty years as staff director and on the staff of the Senate Foreign Relations Committee.

William Green Miller is President of the American Committee on U.S.-Soviet Relations. He served in the Department of State, was Staff Director of three Senate committees, and was sent by President Carter as an emissary to Iran in an effort to free the hostages held in Tehran. He was also Associate Dean and Professor of International Politics at the Fletcher School of Law and Diplomacy. He is a board member of the International Foundation for the Survival and Development of Humanity.

Janet E. Mitchell graduated from Reed College in 1983 with a degree in History. She has worked at the American Committee on U.S.-Soviet Relations since the Fall of 1986 as a Research Associate specializing in cultural affairs.

Fred Warner Neal is a founding member of the American Committee on U.S.-Soviet Relations and former Chairman of the International Relations Faculty at Claremont Graduate School.

Olin Robison is currently the President of Middlebury College. He served in the Department of State and has long been active in promoting educational and cultural exchanges between the United States and the Soviet Union.

Claire Rosenson received her B.A. in Russian Language and Literature from the University of North Carolina at Chapel Hill. In December 1987, she received her M.A. in Russian Area Studies from Georgetown University.

Timothy J. Smith graduated from Union College with a B.A. in Comparative Communist Studies in 1984 and received a M.I.A. in International Affairs from Columbia University in 1987. He was also awarded a Certificate from the W. Averell Harriman Institute for Advanced Russian Study of the Soviet Union at Columbia University. Mr. Smith worked as a Soviet Analyst at the American Committee from January 1987 to May 1988, and was an Exhibit Guide for the U.S. Information Agency in the Soviet Union. He currently works for the U.S. Information Agency in the Moscow Bureau.

Frederick Starr is the President of Oberlin College and a scholar of history and Slavic studies. He has served as the Secretary of Kennan Institute for

Advanced Russian Studies and the Vice President for Academic Affairs at Tulane University. His most recent book is *Red and Hot: The Fate of Jazz in the Soviet Union*.

William Taubman is the Bertrand Snell Professor of Political Science at Amherst College. He is the author of *Stalin's American Policy* and *Moscow Spring*.

INDEX